THE FINEST HOTEL IN KABUL

Lyse Doucet

THE FINEST HOTEL IN KABUL

A People's History of Afghanistan

HUTCHINSON
HEINEMANN

HUTCHINSON HEINEMANN

UK | USA | Canada | Ireland | Australia
India | New Zealand | South Africa

Hutchinson Heinemann is part of the Penguin Random House group of companies
whose addresses can be found at global.penguinrandomhouse.com

Penguin Random House UK,
One Embassy Gardens, 8 Viaduct Gardens, London SW11 7BW

penguin.co.uk

Penguin
Random House
UK

First published 2025

002

Set in 12.8/16pt Dante MT Pro
Typeset by Six Red Marbles UK, Thetford, Norfolk

Printed and bound in India by Manipal Technologies Limited

The authorised representative in the EEA is Penguin Random House Ireland,
Morrison Chambers, 32 Nassau Street, Dublin D02 YH68

A CIP catalogue record for this book is available from the British Library

ISBN: 978–1–529–15102–2 (hardback)
ISBN: 978–1–529–15103–9 (trade paperback)

Penguin Random House is committed to a sustainable future
for our business, our readers and our planet. This book is made
from Forest Stewardship Council® certified paper.

To the many Afghans who welcomed me into their hearts and homes, who trusted me with their stories, who still dare to dream big – for themselves, their families, their country.

Contents

Preface

'How long will you be staying?' asked the man behind the black marble counter. I didn't know the answer. It was Christmas 1988, the day after my thirtieth birthday, and the gloam of the Inter-Continental Kabul was an unlikely place to be celebrating. The cavernous lobby, chilly and dark, stretched into forbidding corners, brightened solely by a shiny blue-and-white banner promoting the Soviet airline Aeroflot. Most of the chandeliers, their dangling crystals hushed by dust, were dark; only one glinted stoically above the reception desk. But the wooden grid of pigeonholes behind the front counter, packed with chunky metal keys, left little doubt. Almost no one else was staying here.

Would it be six days or six weeks? I wrestled with all the forces that might keep me in this ghostly place and all the ones that might not. An awkward pause pressed down upon me and the Afghan receptionist, his brown suit as gloomy as the lobby. He raised a quizzical eyebrow. And then he smiled, his welcome illuminating the room.

I had just landed in Kabul for the first time. The spiralling descent into one of the world's highest capitals stuns its visitors into an awed silence. Sharp undulating ridges of rock puckered in folds of black, grey and a rusty red had given way to the sharp, snowy-white peaks of the Hindu Kush. Far below, the latticed landscape of miniature mud houses was dotted with flat-roofed factories and domed palaces and mosques that loomed ever larger. It was no ordinary arrival. The aircraft had banked sharply in a breathtaking corkscrew manoeuvre, flares bursting outwards with white-hot fire – a way to divert any heat-seeking missiles blasting from mountain bunkers, the foxholes of the Western-funded rebel fighters known as the *mujahideen* who were locked in battle with the Soviet-backed government in Kabul.

That winter, the harshest in more than a decade, Kabul was in the crosshairs of a Cold War conflict that was decades old. Afghanistan's unravelling had begun in 1973, four years after the Inter-Continental Kabul's grand opening, when its mild-mannered King Zahir Shah had been toppled by his cousin. The putsch soon tipped Afghanistan into a blood-soaked spiral: another coup, three leaders assassinated one after the other, then the Soviet invasion over the Christmas of 1979, which sparked what would become the most grievous war in the world.

I had travelled to the Afghan capital to report on the Red Army's pull-out, following a disastrous decade-long occupation. As I departed from neighbouring Pakistan, where I had spent the past few months, one *mujahideen* commander cheerily told me he would soon see me in Kabul, since their victory was now in sight. Another warned that I would certainly be killed there.

I had been nudged out of Pakistan by a competitive colleague who had made it clear that I should find a different patch. The kindness of strangers and friends had helped to secure me an escape route: a rare Afghan visa. The advice had been that there were really only two places to stay. The older, more conveniently located Kabul Hotel – smack in the centre, but with dubious communications and cuisine, and an even murkier history. And the Inter-Continental – high on a hill on the edge of the city, but with better telephone and telex links and food worth eating, as well as a certain faded splendour. As the clapped-out yellow taxi chugged out of the airport in a fug of diesel fuel, I made a split-second decision. We headed for the hill.

I soon discovered that hospitality is hard-wired in Afghans. At the front desk, Sharif, with his sunbeam smile, and Salem, his dour sidekick, were a delightful double act, offering assistance with a wink, as spooks of the Soviet-backed ruling party lurked. Amanullah, at room service, scribbled caricatures of journalists on food bills to bring some cheer to the bleak bedrooms – a very Afghan vision of 'service with a smile'. Nasir, the telephone operator, offered Dari-language lessons during anxious waits for a telephone line in that once-upon-a-time before the ease of the internet and mobile phones. His impromptu class started with learning the phrase *dostad daram*. I soon found out it means 'I love you'. As so often among Afghans, the gift was laughter.

I ended up staying nearly a year. The hotel became my Afghan home. The masking tape criss-crossing my windows offered scant protection from rocket fire, but looked the part. Carpets from merchants who always lent their wares before demanding a purchase – a tactic honed through history, to all but ensure a sale – provided a personal touch. As the Soviet troop withdrawal on 15 February 1989 approached, the Inter-Continental started bursting with journalists who came and went, until the hotel echoed with emptiness again.

Over the decades, when returning to Kabul to report on momentous times, I have often stayed in the place that everyone called simply 'the Inter-Con'. And, over time, I came to realise it was more than just a hotel. As Afghanistan lurched through decades of trial and terror, laced with bright but brief beginnings, the Inter-Con was an unbreakable constant. A white box of cement and steel, it stands on a hill watching over the city, a front-row seat to history. On its roof, its kicking letter K still proclaims its pedigree – even though its connection to the global

Inter-Continental chain was severed soon after Soviet tanks rumbled into the capital in 1979. Afghans stubbornly held on to the name, in the hope of restoring its early glory and membership in that coveted club. It never gave in, never gave up; the Inter-Con is a very Afghan hotel.

Its brutalist exterior lacks the graceful arches and elegant domes of the city's historical royal palaces. But what was born in 1969 as the finest hotel in Kabul became its most storied building. History – good, bad and bloody – was made within its walls. It became home to fashion shows and beauty pageants, bikinis by the pool, vodka-soaked Soviet receptions, warlord rockets, a guest named Osama Bin Laden, American election observers, Afghan female MPs and Taliban suicide bombers. Its doors stayed open through every kind of political system: a peaceable kingdom, Soviet-backed communism, warlordism, Islamism and a would-be democracy bankrolled by the West. Politics, like hotel guests, checked in and out. Whoever rules Afghanistan sets the rules at the Inter-Con. Today it is run by the Taliban, again.

In a listing of the world's finest hotels, some sparkle for the elegance of their architecture, their exquisite cuisine, the standards of their service. The Hotel Inter-Continental Kabul, Afghanistan's first five-star luxury hotel, earned a distinction of its own. It survived. At times guests cursed it as the 'worst hotel in the world' – a place without running water, reliable heating or even bread that could pass a taste test. Bedrooms became bunkers. Chandeliers shattered. Floors were ravaged, renovated, ravaged and renovated again. In a land where most Afghans worried whether they would see their next meal or their next day, the Inter-Con was a constant. Through moments of heart-rending uncertainty and suffering its receptionists kept smiling, waiters kept serving, cooks kept pots on the boil, cleaners snapped sheets across beds, bellboys kept lugging luggage up and down the stairs when the lifts were broken or the electricity was cut. The hotel became their *misl-e khana* – like their own home.

History always moves in a multitude of singular stories that carry far bigger truths. Afghanistan's story tells us that war is more than the blast of bombs, the whistle of bullets. It's a mother's anxious eyes, the song of a soldier, a soul-soothing camaraderie, the pause before going out the door. It plays out on the frontlines of everyday life, in dashed dreams, wrecked weddings and the courage of people who hold each other close and do what they can to carry on.

This book is a history of Afghanistan told through the story of this landmark hotel, and through the lives of the staff who kept it going. Most Afghans, when asked for old photographs or videos, reply apologetically that they lost almost all their physical keepsakes during one upheaval or another. But I have always marvelled at their memory. Perhaps when so much is snatched away by forces beyond their control, remembering becomes a weapon to hold fast to the past. But memories can blur, take a new shape in each telling. This book is based on recollections of the many Afghans and foreigners who have gone in and out of the Inter-Con. I have listened carefully to their accounts, checked translations, and backed up their stories, as far as possible, by historical records. Every effort has been made to tell their story faithfully, as they told it to me. At moments in this book you will also read my own stories too.

It is written with enormous gratitude for the many Afghans, over many years, who have made me feel at home. For all that's been lost, Afghans' deeply ingrained sense of hospitality still remains. Of all the country's many proverbs, one has always been my favourite: 'It doesn't matter how big your home is, what matters is how big your heart is.'

Introduction

The Year of Reckoning

Summer 2021

It was no way for a young man to spend a Saturday night in Kabul. Sadeq had been quietly considering his options. He could have joined his friends at their favourite hangout, the Nokhbagan snooker club, home to the best tables in the city. His friends kept calling him, pleading, 'Come on! Sadeq *jaan*, you work too hard.' Or he could have hung on in the hotel after his shift ended, to get his head around more English grammar. He needed it for the language tests that could speed up his long-awaited exit to study in the United States. Perhaps he should have gone home. He could hear his father's caution ringing in his ears: 'Don't stay out late, my son. It's too dangerous these days.' But as the lengthening shadows began to dance with the shine of the chandeliers, the hotel's human-resources manager burst into Sadeq's cubbyhole office and threw a sheet of paper on his desk. 'Sign here. You're in charge.'

Sadeq's decision was made for him. There was no one else to look after the Inter-Con tonight. Only the sharp dresser with the megawatt smile. He had risen to the role of acting front-office manager less than two years previously, at twenty years old, just under a fortnight into the job. It was, Sadeq believed, down to his sheer force of personality and prodigious effort. True, his big brother Hasib had put in a good word. But he did the rest.

He looked down the list that was staring up at him. There was the wedding getting under way down by the pool: about 240 guests. Some of them would certainly linger, dine, dance into the early hours. Then there was another wedding in the ballroom in the morning. Both were in the safe hands of banquet manager Sadozai. He'd been around this hotel for more than thirty years; he knew what to do. There was a sprinkling of guests across the hotel's five floors, some of them now browsing the buffet in the Bukhara Restaurant. And if he tugged open the curtain of his snug glass-fronted office he was certain to see two of his colleagues, also twenty-something strivers, sitting calmly behind the reception desk, probably scrolling on their mobile phones under the gold-rimmed clocks that marked the time in Dubai, London, New York, Paris and Kabul. He could do this.

His only worry was security. His role demanded a laser focus on the Inter-Con's three rings of steel. Afghan media was burning with reports that the Taliban were advancing towards Kabul at lightning speed. The US president, Joe Biden, was still vowing to bring every American soldier home by the date seared in everyone's memory: 11 September. Every other NATO army was packing up after twenty long years, if they hadn't left already. But the stories from the frontlines were mind-bending. That Afghan soldiers were running out of bullets, even running out of bread. That entire units were cursing their commanders, fleeing for their lives. In some places Taliban fighters were said to be simply walking in, taking over.

But a Taliban conquest of Kabul? *Impossible*, Sadeq told himself again, as he tucked his hotel checklist into the pocket of his best blue suit. Not when this capital was defended like a citadel. Not when the powerful Afghan army, still backed by US and British troops for a few more weeks, was standing strong. And not when the fortress-like Western embassies still hadn't pulled up their drawbridges. He saw the formidable security at the US compound every time he went to check on the status of the visa applications for himself, his father and three sisters to join their mother and brothers, who were already in America. Not even a pigeon could fly in undetected.

Sadeq leaned back in his chair, just short of the point of completely tipping over. Mood music from the '3 Hours Best Romantic Relaxing Music' playlist was wafting under his door. Sometimes he asked why God had decided to make him an Afghan. So much kept getting in his way. He was at the stage of life when a young man should be well on his way to his future. By the time he was twenty-seven, when so many responsibilities and maybe even marriage kicked in, his chance to make his dreams come true would be over. Only five years to go. And here he was, stuck in the starting blocks.

He pushed away from his desk, stepping into the luminous lobby and out of the revolving front door; the balmy August night was washed by the magic of a half-moon. As Sadeq took the steps down to the lower terrace he walked into a nocturnal fairyland. A sweeping canopy of twinkling lights was mirrored in the glimmering pool. Sequins winked on women's dresses as they shimmied to the wedding band, the flashes of phone cameras and cascades of laughter adding even more sparkle. On the rim of the oblong pool, a singer with a mop of slicked-back hair was belting out the lyrics of Ahmad Zahir, the 'Elvis of Afghanistan':

'Although my spring has turned to autumn because of your
absence, why should I fear?
Oh flower! May you always possess the spring of youth,
may no autumn befall you.'

Sadeq half-listened as he looked around, noticing that only a small number of guests still dawdled around the titanic buffet table on the far side of the terrace. Ahmad Zahir's laments were bringing the event trickling to a close: *From above, the rain came. My beloved entered the hallway. I asked for a kiss . . . O woe, her eyes filled with tears.*

Ahmad Zahir's songs weren't Sadeq's favourites. But how Afghans still loved, still missed, their great star. He had performed and partied around this very pool five decades previously. He had been killed – most Afghans believed assassinated – in 1979. But his music and his memory would never die.

Sadeq tripped back up the stairs. The outer rim of the watchtowers, nestled in dense thickets of evergreens, hugged the hillside, the highest lookout straddling the rocky knoll that faced the front entrance. Another cordon of razor wire shadowed the wall around the hotel. The third stretched from the bottom of the hill to the top on the main lane. Along the way it passed three striped barricades; three boxy guard cabins; two electronic scanners; two possible pat-downs; and a heavy steel slab of a gate on the crest of the hill stretching across the entry to the forecourt. And there was a fourth, of a sort: the thick arboreal fence formed of tall pines, elegant Persian and Russian willows and flowering fruit trees, lining both sides of the path.

This hotel had been the domain of the trees long before the arrival of all this metal, the pines rising high and straight like watchtowers. The elegant spherical shrubs called *Pasha Khana*, 'mosquitoes' houses', were there to catch insects. And on the fringes of the forecourt and down by the pool, the graceful acacias rustling with the faintest of breezes. The gardeners who lovingly tended them by day Afghanised their name to *akst*, 'photograph'. They saw everything, just like the multiple banks of security cameras across the hotel.

Sadeq circled around the splashing fountain, festooned like a Christmas tree with garlands of tiny bright lanterns. On the far side of the forecourt, inside the ballroom's golden double doors, trusted Sadozai and his waiters were putting the finishing touches to another wedding layout. '*Shab Bakhair*,' Sadeq called out. 'A good night to you.' All was in order. Of course. Round tables were covered in white tablecloths embossed with tiny white flowers. Straight-backed chairs were dressed up in folds of red fabric pinched into a bow at the back. And, at the far end of the ballroom, the regal thrones of the bride and groom were draped in white sashes.

Sadeq admired honest, hard-working staff like Sadozai. They were the real cement and steel of the Inter-Con. But he could not stomach the thought that he too would be here in thirty years, still riding a bicycle back and forth to work. Still, this was a good job, he reminded himself, as he slipped back into his office and shut the door with a reassuring click. And it made good sense for someone studying for a business degree, down at the American University of Afghanistan. Some day he would run his own company.

His eyes wandered to his walls. When he looked straight ahead, he faced an impressive Afghan snow leopard, the rare big cat that was able to cross the largest of rivers, swim the coldest of waters. Behind him were painted silhouettes of the *Chapandaz*, mighty Afghan horsemen galloping across the steppe in a frenzied game of *buzkashi*, a rough-and-tumble Afghan version of polo. This, too, was what it meant to be an Afghan.

And at his feet, on the floor beside his desk, were his new finds. The spiralling horns of a Marco Polo sheep, a trophy dating back to the days of the last king, Zahir Shah, who had loved to hunt, but tried to protect these precious animals. Next to it, a finely engraved round plaque with a K dancing at its centre, wreathed by the words 'Inter-Continental Hotels'. Hotel heirlooms – Sadeq had dug them out of the dusty jumble in one of the outhouses behind the ballroom, in his efforts to unearth this hotel's history and put it on show for everyone to admire. The flaring horns would be mounted above the entrance to the coffee shop.

He leaned back in his chair. The past week had been stress-ful. The hotel's new managers had fired 160 people – about half of the hotel's staff, including some of its longest-serving, most loyal employees. It had been a painful week. But the office of the president of Afghanistan had been categorical: 'This hotel isn't even making enough money to pay its electricity bills!'

So much of Sadeq's time was spent trying to bring in more business. In the spring he had escorted security teams from embassies and aid agencies around the hotel, so that they could inspect the reinforced defences – his attempt to reassure them it was safe to stay. His old general manager, who had also just been sacked, had even revealed to Sadeq that he was rekindling the hope to rejoin the global luxury hotel group, after all these decades. The Inter-Continental's head office in Britain hadn't even answered his emails, but the manager wasn't sure if he had the right address.

The hotel had been a no-go for most foreigners since the bloody Taliban assault of 2018. Entire floors had been shredded. Forty guests had been shot dead or blown up, fourteen of them foreigners. The Taliban were warning Afghans to stay away from dens frequented by infidels and enemies, like this one. But it was Afghans who kept coming. And there were many here tonight.

It was a little past 3 a.m. Within hours all the well-rehearsed steps of another day at the Inter-Con would begin again. Sadeq made one last stop to chat with his fellow twenty-somethings behind the front desk and exchange final greetings. *Khoda Hafiz.* 'May God protect you.' *Manda na bashi.* 'May you not be tired.' He picked up one of the brand-new electronic keys to access the lifts. He had reached the end of his list, the end of his energy. All the gates were checked, all the main doors locked. The last of the wedding guests had vroomed down the hill, their voices carried in the quiet of the dark. Only the distant rumble of US military aircraft powering in and out of Kabul's international airport broke the silence. That and the staccato barks of stray dogs, the kings of the night, reclaiming their streets.

Sadeq fell into bed in a third-floor room, out like a light, safe on the other side of its heavy door. Every door of the Inter-Con was bulletproof.

'Don't watch the news!' Abida's doctor told her, over and over again. 'The news is making you sick.'

That was the hardest prescription to follow. Abida obediently took the doctor's pills for high blood pressure, diabetes, tummy ache and more. She swallowed a rainbow of colours for her assortment of aches. But she had to watch the news. She couldn't fall sleep until she saw the late-evening bulletin. And, even then, she was still sometimes jolted wide awake in the middle of the night. At fifty-five, Abida lived her life in a haze of worry. Fear for the future of her eight children. Grief for her lost husband, killed by a rocket decades earlier. And now, since exactly one week ago, anxiety over her own fate after she had lost her job as a sous-chef at the Inter-Continental.

Abida shoved all these thoughts to the back of her mind as she reclined on her red-and-gold *toshak* mattress, a mug of steaming green tea in her hands.

'*Salaam*. Welcome to the News at Ten.' The TOLOnews anchor Waheed Ahmadi was in Abida's mud-and-timber home again. The deep-set eyes on her TV screen were so dark and intense that he seemed to be staring directly at her. *Pay attention!* 'Our top headline, some important news.' Abida leaned in; Ahmadi's bushy black moustache curled at its tips as he spoke: 'President Ashraf Ghani is consulting Afghan and international partners to prevent further instability in the country.'

Ghani was her president. She had voted for him in 2014, and again in 2019. Her whole family had. She told them to. And she was sure they heeded their mother's word. Abida wriggled into a more comfortable position, listening attentively. The screen cut to her president, addressing the entire nation: 'I know you are worried about your present and your future,' he said. 'As the president, I assure you that my focus is to prevent further instability, violence and displacement of my people.'

Abida sank into the soft, squishy cushions; she had embroidered them herself. All her worries somersaulted in her mind. Her future, and that of her family, hung in the balance. The Inter-Con's, too. A team of her fellow hotel workers, the oldest and wisest men, had been meeting the president's legal advisors today to argue their case of unfair dismissal and to demand compensation: 160 of them had been let go, in one fell swoop. Hotel managers had apologised. 'These are the president's orders,' they told her. *My president has done this?* she asked herself. They kept repeating the same refrain: 'We are so sorry, but there is no money.' They said they had done it according to the rules.

But Abida had only found out last Saturday, as she trudged up the hill to the hotel. An angry knot of her colleagues, including four women from housekeeping and laundry, had been halted at the second security gate. 'Let us through. We work here!' they shouted. The guard waved a long list of names in their long faces. 'Look! You no longer work here.'

Abida held onto the hope that she could get her job back. But now the Taliban were said to be at the gates of Kabul, back at the door of her life. And here was her president on TV, dressed in a dark blazer, crisp white turban and a Covid mask, walking solemnly down the long red carpet outside the presidential palace as if there was nothing to worry about.

The news report switched to him looking straight into the camera reassuringly, his turban now removed. 'Security forces will be consolidated and serious measures will be taken.' Abida kept watching, now breathing a little easier. At least their security was in safe hands.

Her tea was now lukewarm. She sipped the last dregs. The next report was all the way from New York and the leader of the United Nations, the secretary-general, Mr António Guterres. 'Afghanistan is spinning out of control and facing an unbeliev-able catastrophe,' he declared.

Abida gasped, her heart tightening in her chest, exactly the way her doctor had warned her. She couldn't bear to watch. When the Taliban had taken power in 1996, she had been forced to leave her first job as a cook in the Kabul Hotel in the city centre. Afghan women were told they couldn't work outside their homes; their place was in the house. It had been one of the worst days of her life. Then, five years later, came one of her best days. She had pressed her radio set to her ear, so as not to miss a single word on Kabul Radio from her new leader, Hamid Karzai, who had taken over from the Taliban. 'We respect Afghan women, who are half of our country's popu-lation,' he said, the applause that was erupting from the radio competing with its crackle. 'And we give rights to them under the country's law.'

Abida Nazeri – chef, seamstress, widow, mother of eight children – had been the first woman to sign up for a job at one of the government-owned hotels. She had dazzled the Inter-Con's new foreign managers with her mouth-watering Afghan dumplings. They had never tasted *mantu* and *ashak* before; had never even heard of them. They gushed over the plump pockets of pasta stuffed with oniony Afghan leeks and finely chopped meat and onions, smothered in a velvety garlicky yogurt sauce. She was hired on the spot.

Last week, the day she was sacked, had been another of her darkest days. Abida had never imagined it would happen to her. Not in a hotel where they respectfully called her *Madar jaan*, 'dear mother'.

She admitted that her aches and pains told her loudly every day that she had worked too long, too hard, for too many years. Her doe-eyes were now ringed with dark circles, crinkled at their corners. But when she applied a touch of pink lipstick, perfectly matching her favourite headscarf, she still shone a fine-looking smile. And how she could cook! Only months ago she had received the hotel's 'Star Performer for the Month. In recognition of her Valuable Contribution.' They gave her a certificate in a gilded frame. A golden star-pin she fixed to her chef's whites. Even a week's extra salary.

But last week one of the managers had belittled her with his dark eyes. 'Dear mother, isn't it time for you to go home and spend time with your children, and grandchildren?' The hotel she had loved for so long no longer loved her in return. How could she pay the fees for her son, studying dentistry at a private university? Who would pay the medical bills for her daughter, Mariam, who had studied journalism, but had suffered for years with tumours in her ovary? This had been Abida's life's real work: an illiterate mother educating all her children. She had come so far. And now it felt as if her past was in hot pursuit. The Taliban could be coming back to take it all away.

Abida cradled her empty teacup. Her hands looked older, too, calloused from years of cooking and sewing. The Taliban were promising they had changed. Their leaders kept telling journalists they would govern differently this time. She had to believe this was true. Otherwise she was sure she'd be struck down by a stroke.

The last TOLOnews bulletin of the night was almost over. The final story was about the United States providing 500 million doses of the coronavirus vaccine to poorer countries. It was good to end with good news. The camera cut to a wide view of TOLO's grand studio, with its vivid red desk and pulsing blue backdrop. Waheed Ahmadi sat in the distance, his eyes no longer in close focus, as he signed off.

'Thank you for joining us for this hour's news. Good night.'

The morning of 15 August began with the dawn call to prayer bouncing from one hill to the next, the first light filtering through the beige smog sitting stubbornly on top of the city. Mohammad Aqa made his way to work in a dust-caked commuter minibus in the tangle of morning traffic and the racket of the streets: the blaring horns of luxury bulletproof 4x4s, the revving roar of motorcycles, the tinny tinkling of bicycle bells, the hapless shouts of the traffic cops with their outsized peaked caps.

His shift began at 7 a.m. He hopped off at his usual stop at the bottom of the hill to make his way up the slope, through the gauntlet of bollards and barriers and through the roll call of obligatory courtesies. *Salaam Salaam . . . Sobh Bakhair*, 'Good morning . . . How are you? How is your health? May you not be tired.' By the time he reached his staff locker in the basement, he was a bit tired in fact. He swiftly changed into his black trousers, slipped into his white shirt, tightly knotted his black tie and pulled on his black jacket. The manager of the Bukhara Restaurant was ready to work.

Mohammad Aqa stood behind the waiter's cabinet at the entrance. He hadn't expected much footfall; so few guests were checking into the Inter-Con these days. But today no one at all had shown up for breakfast. The thunderous silence was jarring. He kept his eyes peeled for the Afghan family who had been staying at the hotel for so long they were no longer allowed to eat there, such was the thumping bill they had run up.

His eyes roamed across the modern forest-green chairs that covered the marble floor. The young waiters, dressed in brightly bordered black waistcoats, sprang from table to table – setting cutlery in straight lines, dropping tissue boxes with golden Inter-Continental branding with a soft thud. Everyone knew what they had to do. A warm summer's sun seeped through the curtains cloaking the floor-to-ceiling windows.

He let out a wistful sigh. How he missed the balcony. It had been removed when the hotel was renovated a decade ago, after the last suicide bombings, to make space for more guests. With it had gone a slice of his hotel, his favourite spot since he started work here as a teenage busboy decades ago. On unsettling days like this he could have slipped outside, inhaled deep gulps of fresh air, smiled at the swallows, gazed at the teeming city below and the sharp white peaks of the Hindu Kush beyond. Instead he stayed rooted in place like a potted plant, behind the scuffed waiter's cabinet – the restaurant's last keepsake from the king's days when this hotel had first opened. And, to Mohammad Aqa's great relief, he was still holding onto the most important thing of all: his job. Not all his old colleagues had been so lucky.

At 9 a.m. waiters unlocked the golden double doors of the grand Kandahar Ballroom at the end of the long corridor that ran perpendicular to the restaurant. The first to arrive was the DJ, Nabila, dressed in a bright-turquoise tunic and trendy black jeans that matched her black headscarf. Her nine-year-old son tagged along in his own skinny jeans. They threaded around the white-cloaked tables, heading straight to the far corner next to the stage where her equipment sat. Sadozai, the banquet manager, was moving through the hall too, standing tall in his hotel uniform, his badge of authority. Back on the job after his late night, his run-of-show was in hand: *150 guests confirmed; 180 could show up*. A mixed wedding. Men and women would celebrate together. Most Afghan weddings separated them into adjacent rooms, even separate buildings. But marriages were becoming more modern these days. Just like Afghanistan itself.

Sadozai ran through the details of the wedding lunch. Special Afghan dumplings, three salads, sheep stew, *degi* kebabs, lamb *karahi*. Of course *qabuli pulao*, the national dish of rice and meat speckled with sweet raisins and thin slivers of almonds and carrots. A *chalow* rice, special *ferni* rice pudding, one bottle of water and one Fanta soft drink per person and, of course, green tea and black. And flat rounds of steaming Afghan bread. Every meal had to have bread.

A small wedding, by Afghan standards. But small didn't mean cheap, especially at this hotel. Kabul was awash with money these days, at least for the lucky. Such were the spoils of two decades of Western armies and embassies, aid agencies with big budgets, fat salaries, eye-watering contracts, hard work and ingenuity – as well as, it had to be said, corruption. No expense was spared on weddings. And no venue matched the prestige of this historic hotel. Not even the glittering wedding halls that kept popping up across the city, bathed in blinking lights and with names like Dubai City, Star Palace and Kabul Star. Sadozai took one last look around his golden hall, decorated with ruched red curtains and faux opera boxes. Not his style, but the guests seemed to like it.

By 10 a.m. they started trickling in. Women in figure-hugging dresses swaying on stiletto heels, others in patterned shawls. Men in dark suits jazzed up with colourful ties. Little boys with black bow ties and girls in frilly pink, skipping excitedly around the tables. Everyone clutching presents wrapped in shiny foil, and an assortment of bags bulging with more modest scarves and shoes to change into when they left this wedding bubble.

The clack of heels and murmur of voices filled the lobby, too. Mohammad Aqa poked his head around the door with a smile. Everyone loved a wedding. He knew that, from his own days in charge of the ballroom. The last major renovation had transformed the main banquet hall into a fussy pastiche of a theatre, dripping in chandeliers. The Kandahar Ballroom. This had always been its name, to honour Afghanistan's storied second city to the south, its eighteenth-century capital. It had a different ring now, though. Kandahar's modern claim to fame was as the spiritual heartland of the Taliban.

Lunch hours loomed. It was time to bring in the bowls of salads and plates of sweets to prepare the buffet spread. But not a single diner had set foot inside the restaurant. Mohammad Aqa nodded to his waiters who were nervously hanging about, obsessively checking their mobile phones for the latest news and messages. He pulled his own phone from his suit pocket and was met by a waterfall of detail. The Taliban had been spotted in Wardak, the apple-growing province to the west, just beyond the gates of Kabul; and in Charasiab, several miles to the south. There were even sightings in Kampani; and that was even closer.

He stared blankly into the middle distance. Most Afghans were dumbfounded. 'How could the Taliban return to power?' they kept exclaiming. 'It's unimaginable!' Mohammad Aqa could imagine it. It didn't weigh quite so heavily on his mind. He had worked with them in the 1990s when they were last in power, when they ran this hotel and everything else. But now he had three precious daughters, in high school and university. 'Will the Taliban allow us to be educated?' they kept asking him. 'That's what they're promising,' he kept reassuring them, as best he could.

He played idly with a napkin, his fingers smoothing and folding the cloth. This first waiter's skill was one he still knew by heart: *Lay the white square of fabric on the table. Fold it to form a rectangle. Hold the short side and fold it again to make a pleat. Press down firmly to make a sharp crease. Keep folding to create an accordion of pleats.* Today it felt like folding his worries away into the fabric.

Down the corridor the wedding was beginning. The hall had filled with the bouncy beat of the wedding march, *Ahesta Bero*: 'Walk slowly, my light of night, go slowly . . . ' The bride and groom made their entrance. She was glowing in her Gande dress, elaborately embroidered in seven brilliant colours. He walked beside her in his traditional waistcoat, tunic and billowing trousers. Family members held the holy Quran above their heads while guests ushered the couple forward with showers of kisses, rose petals and clapping.

Sadozai watched with a knowing smile. It was always a relief when a wedding got going. He checked his run-of-show again: *150 guests confirmed; 180 could show up.* He looked at his watch. It was late morning, not too long until lunch. But hardly anyone was in the hall. Perhaps about sixty people so far, at most.

The wedding show had to go on. Nabila spun her disks, playing *Qataghani* music of longing and love. The familiar tunes tugged couples onto the dance floor, some rushing up to the DJ to request their favourites. Soon the honeyed voice of Aryana Sayeed, Afghan pop star and women's activist, was ramping up the vibe: *'In your pure heart I see a clean light, in your gaze I see a world of modesty, I see you as the best of God's creations, I am so happy that you are always only mine . . .'*

Onstage the henna ceremony – the 'blessings on the skin' – was beginning. Rich red dye was painted on the bride's hands, the intricate hatching gradually morphing into swirls of flowers and vines. Tradition said that the darker the stain, the deeper the love.

The bride and groom stared into each other's eyes. But their love couldn't stop their gaze from occasionally darting across their wedding party and all the empty tables. And most guests weren't looking back at them. They were looking at their phones, at each other, frantically trying to reach loved ones at work, children at school.

Sadozai took a deep breath and straightened his shoulders. He moved in to eavesdrop on the tables, which were ablaze with worry. 'The Taliban are in Wardak and Kampani . . . No, no, they're already in Kabul, in the district next to the hotel . . . The rest of my family aren't coming to the wedding, they're too afraid to leave the house . . . What should we do?'

Sadozai swallowed. He summoned the full force of his authority, the weight of three decades of wedding service. 'Nothing will happen,' he insisted in his warm, grandfatherly voice. 'This is a wedding! You are all safe . . . Even if the Taliban come, they won't hurt you. We are all Muslims.'

From the corner of his eye, through the open doors, he spotted a clutch of men in the corridor in taupe *perahan o tunban*, traditional clothing, with chequered scarves partially hiding their faces. He froze. *Were the Taliban here?* Relief washed over him. It was only the hotel's own security guards. But they had changed out of their uniforms. That was worrying, in its own way.

He looked towards the stage. The bride had now changed into her emerald dress and veil: green to symbolise purity and happiness, the second of three wedding dresses that brides wear on their special day. But even thick layers of beige and pink powder couldn't hide her trepidation. She was trembling on her wedding throne.

A family elder appeared at his elbow. 'You should serve the food now,' he insisted. Sadozai checked his watch. It was only 11.30. And the ballroom wasn't full. Only about eighty guests. 'Serve it now,' the elder hissed. 'No one else will come.'

In the kitchen, situated between the ballroom and the Bukhara Restaurant, there was a sudden clatter of pots and pans. Mohammad Aqa heard it. Everyone did. He went to check on the commotion. 'We need to serve the wedding lunch,' banquet waiters shouted. 'Now!' Preparations lurched into fast-forward. Staff scurried about, pulling salad bowls from fridges, slamming serving plates on steel counters. Chefs in white toques plunged their biggest spoons into huge cauldrons of steaming rice. This had never happened before. But there wasn't the time to discuss it.

Mohammad Aqa returned to his refuge in the restaurant. His waiters roved around the room, straightening knives and forks for the umpteenth time, tweaking the tips of folded napkins, but most of all checking their phones. Mohammad Aqa instructed them to start preparing the oil burners to heat the serving pans for lunch. He paced the floor.

Down the hall, the mood in the ballroom was now veering

wildly between optimism and alarm. 'Look at this message on Twitter from the presidential palace,' one person shouted. 'It says there have been sporadic shootings in Kabul, but the situation is under control.' There was a Taliban statement, too, ordering its fighters to 'Stay at the city's gates. Don't enter Kabul.' Phones vibrated with stories from the streets. 'My cousin spotted some Taliban outside his house – they're hearing gunfire.' In the corner the DJ was on edge, too, balancing her phone in one hand and mixing music with the other. Her husband had been trying to call, but the phone signal was weak, the lines clogged. 'I'm coming to get you,' he finally told her. But he warned her that the streets were gridlocked. 'It may take a while.'

Sadozai kept checking the stage. The bride was sobbing. 'The Taliban are going to come and kill us,' she wailed. Sadozai, banquet manager turned consoler-in-chief, hastened to her side, his own eyes beginning to moisten. 'The Taliban are Muslim and you're Muslim, too,' he whispered. 'They would never harm you in your wedding dress.' He invoked an Afghan tradition from centuries past, handed down by the modernising King Amanullah and his wife Queen Soraya. 'On your wedding day, you are the Queen, and your husband is King,' he reminded her. He stole a glance at the groom, whose face was drained of colour. 'Comfort your bride!' Sadozai chided him. 'If you don't show courage today, you will always disappoint her.' And so the groom did.

The parade of plates was now in full swing. The scent of steaming rice and meat, the clink of cutlery on crockery, the service as smooth as a marble floor helped restore Sadozai's sense of self. But it didn't last long. A scream drowned out the soundtrack of lunch. 'There's a Taliban pickup on this hill. Their white flag is on the roof!' The music juddered to a stop. 'It's not true!' came a rival cry. But it was too late; the room was in havoc. The DJ rushed to the nearest table, begging for someone to share something long and loose for her to cover up. Women yanked voluminous shawls out of carryalls. Men shouted into their phones trying to find out what was happening.

Sadozai's heart pounded so hard he feared his shirt would rip. What if a guest had a heart attack? What if *he* did? At the main entrance to the ballroom, next to the double doors, Zahir the cleaner, in a purple tunic, held fast to his broom. 'There are no Taliban in the hotel,' he kept repeating, over and over again, to anyone who would listen. 'And if there are, the Taliban are Afghan, too.' But no one had time to hear. Everyone was grabbing their bags and their children, pelting from the ballroom, tumbling into their cars, speeding down the hill.

The groom leapt from the stage, his inconsolable bride in her glittering green dress in tow. They swept past tables covered in plates of untouched food, clumps of rice and shiny drink cans strewn across the floor, and bolted out of the door. The last outfit of her special day, her pure-white wedding dress gleaming with dreams, still hung on its hanger in her bridal changing room.

Sadozai stood dutifully at the double door, a rictus grin on his face, until the very last guest had left. He stood as tall and straight as he could.

It wasn't even 1 p.m. His shift didn't end until three. He scuttled to the lobby, which was buzzing with a congregation of managers and receptionists, waiters, busboys and bellboys, cleaners and cooks. Everyone was asking about the latest, demanding their salary, no one knowing what the next day – or even the next hour – would bring. Even the security guards were now inside. He spotted Hashmat, who had been here as long as he had, starting out as a teenage bellboy, anxiously pacing the lobby. Young Sadeq was darting to and fro, gathering all the female staff to help them get home.

Mohammad Aqa stood silently at the entrance to the restaurant, sheltering in the quiet on the edge of this din. No one had eaten lunch in the Bukhara. Not a single person had turned up. The feast was going cold under metal lids and coverings of clingfilm. And then there was the wedding that wasn't. All that wonderful food going to waste. The story reached them that the bride had fled in tears, that she hadn't even worn her white dress. He shook his head in sorrow.

His eyes roved the restaurant again. He was relieved that Malalai, with her bright-yellow headscarf and sunshine smile, wasn't on shift today. The other waiters' eyes and ears were stuck to their phones.

Kabul is surrounded – that's what everyone was saying. It was the last domino. One after another the biggest cities had all fallen. It had only taken ten days. He could hear a crackle of gunfire rising from somewhere on the streets.

Hazrat sat at home, waiting. He had summoned his children who were in Kabul to sit with him. Four of his sons, his three daughters and their children encircled the seventy-year-old patriarch. Other family members were calling in from Germany.

He had just slipped back inside the safety of their compact brick home, still unfinished. He carried news from their neighbourhood mosque, where he had conferred with other elders; their world seemed to be shifting beneath their feet. Shops on their street were shuttered. Rifles popped not far away. Taliban fighters were said to be close by.

Hazrat was stunned. His day had begun so happily. He had risen with the sun for morning prayers, bracing green tea, warm fresh bread, *watani* eggs with tomatoes, and the scrumptious taste of victory. 'We won!' he had announced to his family yesterday afternoon when he bounced through the door after his meetings at the government offices. His delegation, representing all the employees fired from the Inter-Continental, had argued the case for compensation. They were owed six months' salary, not the paltry three months offered by the hotel, which no one was convinced they would ever see. The light of the blue sky had been in his eyes.

His greatest worry had been how he would keep supporting the education of his youngest son, Samir, particularly in the sports he loved so much – exactly as Hazrat had done in his youth, in a Kabul boxing club, so long ago. As day broke, the summer's sun streaming through his windows, he had felt a tingling sense of celebration. A heavy weight had been lifted from his shoulders.

His reverie had been punctured by a commotion on the main street that ran past their door, not long after daybreak. From their first-floor windows they could see a large crowd forming at the roundabout they called Pharmacy Square. The family could feel the gathering disquiet. Hazrat sent his sons out to investigate. They returned with startling news: the Taliban had freed all the prisoners. Some were now running amok. One of the escapees had made a beeline to the house of a soldier nearby and had shot him dead in cold blood. The word on the street was that the victim might have been a prison guard who had mistreated him.

Hazrat quietly absorbed this dramatic turn. He drew his loved ones close. All of this had been compartmentalised at the back of his mind while he tried to remain focused on his hotel. But the past always came surging back. This time he had tried to keep it at bay, lest it sap his spirit. Now all the questions were rushing at him. Would the Taliban share power with the government they had been meeting in peace talks? Would there be another bloodbath? Who would now sort their hotel compensation? It was a moment of a thousand questions with no answers.

He knew he would get through it, though. 'Whoever is the donkey, we are his dress' was the proverb Hazrat had always lived by. He had worked with everyone who took charge, took over the reins of the Inter-Continental – royals, communists, warlords, Taliban, wannabe democrats. His job was always to serve.

A glimmer of hope stirred within him, too. If the Taliban returned to the hotel, they might ask him to return, too. They would need him. They must know that. Possibilities started taking shape. For a moment it helped ease his seething anger. Not only had his life's work been ripped away from him last week. His honour had been too, stamped on by the fine leather shoes of government officials with graduate degrees from foreign countries. People who thought they knew everything, but knew nothing about him and his work. They kept saying it was the decision of the president, Ashraf Ghani, who knew all about finance and planning. *Was it really his decision or that of those new hotel managers?* Hazrat wondered.

A half-century of service. This hotel had been like his own home. *Agha Sahib*, the 'honourable master' – that's what they had called him on the hill.

Even as the Taliban closed in on the city, the greatest assault on Hazrat came from his own memories. He had been trained by the experts when the Inter-Continental Kabul had been one of the finest hotels in the world. He knew everything there was to know about running a hotel. He had all his papers to prove it. His Certificate of Special Merit in 1978 from the head office of the global chain, praising his 'outstanding entry on what makes a great hotel'. The commendation of the communists who took over the hotel and had promoted him 'to advance the high goals of the victorious Saur Revolution'. Even a note from the current order, the Republic, which had hailed him for 'competence, aptitude, and integrity in the performance of your duties'. Even after so much had been lost, as war pushed them from house to house, one frontline to the next, he did everything he could to keep all his certificates safe.

Hazrat read the room. His eyes, hooded with age, took in the anxious murmur of his grown children, the giggles of his grandchildren, the clatter of cooking in the kitchen. Four of his sons were around him – the guard, the nurse, the clerk, the high-school student; the other two now working in Germany. His three daughters, including his eldest, Sahida, who lived in Germany but happened to be visiting with her family, were with him too. Her presence warmed his heart. Clever Sahida, his first child to live after three babies born before her had died, one after the other, even before they had reached the age when they could toddle into his arms. His beloved wife, Laila, wasn't to blame. God tested them. Then, one after another, nine healthy children had blessed their lives.

They took care of him and Laila. They had recently moved out of their rented mud home into this two-storey brick house, another floor still to be built (money permitting) by one of his sons, who sent money home from Germany. Hazrat had always spent whatever he earned on his family, thinking only of today, not saving for tomorrow. And of course there were the months when he had kept working even when the hotel said there wasn't enough money to pay him.

When he had started at the Inter-Continental the king, Zahir Shah, was trying to take Afghanistan forwards. Today Hazrat struggled to comprehend why his country, his hotel, kept going backwards. In the hotel they were now relying on the 'Masters', the young Afghans with university degrees and no experience, no knowledge of hotels. Young Sadeq on the front desk was smart, but he was not as smart as Hazrat.

Last week they had pitched a big tent by the security post at the bottom of the hill. Everyone who had been unceremoniously sacked, from the oldest to the youngest, had joined the protest. Some managers came down to see them, bringing nice words, but nothing more. Even engineer Amanullah – who was now known as Dr Faqiri, a university dean of engineering – who used to keep this hotel going, came by to shake his head with worry and shake their hands. Their bosses didn't budge. One of their colleagues, who knew all about these legal matters, prepared their documents, their ammunition in this fight. A fight they had won yesterday.

They should have known Hazrat was a fighter. It was true that he no longer had the muscular build he had once honed in the boxing ring. But he knew his own mind, and he spoke it. His children knew that, too. Until the sudden disruption, he had planned to go up the hill today. He resolved that tomorrow he would head straight there. If the old managers were still in charge, he would set them straight about their compensation. If it was the Taliban, he would tell them, too. *Agha Sahib* was ready to return to work.

Hours earlier he had kept calling his co-workers at the hotel who were still on the job. Sometimes they answered, to reassure him they were still there. But now he couldn't reach anyone. Phone signals were weak, lines congested. The word from the streets was that they were chock-a-block with beat-up yellow taxis, clapped-out white Corollas, swish SUVs. A wave of panic was crashing over the capital, beeping, shouting, shrieking. The pavements were packed with pedestrians, everyone rushing somewhere, nowhere. The summer's sun began to cast long shadows across Hazrat's floor, the last light of dusk slipping away like the certainties of his old life.

At six o'clock, after the family kneeled in evening prayer, they huddled round the TV set to watch the nightly TOLOnews bulletin. It started with its pacy music and cameras sweeping over stunning vistas of Afghanistan. 'Many parts of the country have fallen into the hands of the Taliban,' said the newsreader. Everyone knew that already. 'The Taliban announce they will prevent war in Kabul.' Some of Hazrat's children sighed audibly.

Then came comments from the streets. 'We ordinary people are suffering,' exclaimed one man. 'All those who had money fled.' Poor Kabulis were venting their anger. Hazrat's heart went out to the man; he felt what they felt.

The newsreader announced 'a possible meeting between politicians and the Taliban in Doha', cueing images of Afghan security chiefs in mottled-green camouflage uniforms standing in a straight line, shoulder-to-shoulder. The army chief announced to a nervous nation that they were 'going to go to Doha tomorrow and will discuss the issue of Afghanistan and reach an agreement'. Hazrat locked onto this thought as he shifted on their communal carpet. So there was still a chance. Then, suddenly, the camera cut back to a wide-angle shot of the bright-blue TV studio.

The news anchor, Waheed Ahmadi, was back in close focus. His face spoke more loudly than his words. He paused, looking down at a piece of paper, furrowing his bushy black eyebrows with even greater intensity. 'First, pay attention to the news that has just reached us,' he said.

Hazrat leaned in. They all did.

'Two sources tell TOLOnews that President Ashraf Ghani has fled the country.'

PART I

The Golden Years

CHAPTER I

Hazrat's Hotel

Summer 1971

It was the towels.

It wasn't just that they were white, fluffy, soft. It was the way the guests, so smartly dressed in shirts and skirts, slung them ever so nonchalantly over their shoulders as they slid across the gleaming ground floor to the swimming pool below. It was the smooth, effortless poise of the privileged.

Twenty-year-old Hazrat observed this scene as discreetly as he could. But he stood out a bit. At more than six feet tall, he towered above almost everyone else in the hotel's waiting staff. And he stood even taller in his busboy's uniform, a yellow tunic edged with a darker stripe. A top from the West, with an Afghan trim. It fitted well. Hours spent punching a rock-hard boxing bag and lifting weights in a Kabul gym had not been for nothing. As he strode purposefully through the lobby's soaring colonnade, his chiselled chin jutting out a bit, his Inter-Continental shoes clicking quietly across the marble floor, Hazrat savoured the aura. *Pur*, he thought – 'quality'. *Arami* – 'peaceful'.

The Hotel Inter-Continental Kabul felt like a different country. In a land where most Afghans, including his own family, lived hardscrabble lives, it was a place apart. But Hazrat had found his place here from the day he started. Since the first time he strode up the gentle slope, inhaling exhilarating gulps of pine-scented air, he had found the Inter-Continental unlike anywhere he had ever known. His journey here had not been easy. Hazrat's father, an employee of the Royal Ministry of Transportation, had breathed his last when Hazrat was just a teenager, killed by electric shock when a heater fell from the wall during his ablutions before morning prayer. As the eldest son, Hazrat had stepped up to care for his mother, three sisters and six brothers. He had done it without question or complaint. These were the rules of life, unspoken and understood by all. He had quit secondary school and enrolled in Kabul's Hotel Management School to become someone with a skill. They moved him back a grade, telling him he required more study in some subjects. He pressed ahead, studying by day, working by night, sleeping little.

His part-time jobbing had taken him into the old hotels and restaurants that dotted the city centre. The mustard-yellow blocks of the old Soviet-style Hotel Kabul, which had gone up in 1945, its words usually inverted to become the Kabul Hotel. The sharp green multi-storey Spinzar, a relic from the Cotton Company of the same name, built decades previously. Eventually he completed hotel school, with a certificate from the Department of Vocational Education at the Royal Ministry of Education, and was introduced – by someone who knew someone – to a manager at Kabul's first and only five-star hotel.

Hazrat's previous employers had offered train-as-you-go, do-what-you-can jobs. But not the Hotel Inter-Continental Kabul. It was not that kind of place. This was a job you were proud to tell your family and friends about. A place that kicked you into gear. After receiving exacting training about what to do and what not to do, he had been given two uniforms branded with the iconic letter I. One to wear, one to circle in and out of the hotel laundry. His personal grooming kit included an Inter-Continental toothbrush and a tube of toothpaste, nail clippers and shoe polish. Each day, before he even set foot in front of any guests, he was to shower in their staff locker room downstairs. Then his uniform collar was checked, his hair inspected, his thick fringe nudged into place, to ensure that all was as it should be.

It was made abundantly clear that the Inter-Continental was a very international hotel. But it was also very Afghan, in its way. On the very top storey the swanky Pamir Supper Club and Cocktail Lounge took their name from Afghanistan's northernmost Pamir mountains, known as the 'roof of the world'. Its sweeping windows offered a spectacular view of the no-less-breathtaking Hindu Kush. On the ground floor the Nuristan Cocktail Lounge was decked out in distinctive wood carvings of aromatic cedar and walnut, taken from the remote eastern region of that name. On the day the hotel opened, not much longer than a year ago, Nuristani master craftsmen were still sculpting the last of the filigree. And, at the far end of the foyer, stood the Bamiyan Brasserie – on its wall a frieze depicting the stunning limestone cliffs of the Bamiyan valley in the central highlands, including a miniature replica of one of two sixth-century giant standing buddhas. The Buddhas of Bamiyan were the crown jewels of Afghanistan, prominently displayed on the front cover of the hotel's publicity brochure and on the tourism banner in the lobby.

The Bamiyan was Hazrat's entry into the world of the Inter-Continental. A busboy, his job was to clear tables, carry crockery and scrape plates. He was dazzled by the more senior waiters with their knowing air, dressed in jet-black suits and crisp white shirts, gliding around tables draped in pristine white cloths and perfectly folded white napkins. Young men like Najib and Sher Babarkel were so sure-footed. 'Garçon!' he would watch the diners shout, bringing a waiter sailing to their side with a nod and a smile, a serviette folded over his forearm, to take orders for the very finest food. Afghan kebabs and tender Texas steaks. Fragrant rice and creamy European mash. And the desserts – from juicy Afghan melons and grapes to luscious cakes and jellies iced with swirls of sugar and cream. The hotel called it 'casual dining', unlike the otherworldly 'fine dining' at the Pamir upstairs. Even American guests there were heard to gush, 'I've never eaten *escargots* back home . . . or even aubergines.' It was all very posh.

The sweetest treat was the view. The Bamiyan Brasserie opened onto a wide balcony with a zigzagged cement railing. Umbrellaed tables looked out upon the city's golden sunrises or magical nights of twinkling lights. On the horizon, cradling the Kabul valley, loomed the rough-hewn rock of the Hindu Kush, ribboned with white snow. Eyes were drawn downwards, too, to the rolling vineyards and the exquisite palace of Bagh-e Bala, the 'High Garden'. Built at the end of the last century, its dazzling blue domes, scalloped white walls and arched windows stood in sharp contrast to the hotel's stark straight lines. The palace had long ago fallen into disrepair, but had recently been renovated into a restaurant and wedding hall, its rooms ornamented with mirrored tiles. The two venues shared the hill, competing for customers among the moneyed elite. But the Hotel Inter-Continental Kabul was the shiny new thing.

From the balcony Hazrat could sometimes steal a glimpse of the guests on the terrace below. He liked to stand and listen to what was happening beyond the evergreen trees and the flowering yellow acacias – the *thwack-thwack* from the tennis courts, the *splash-splash* from the swimming pool. He could spot the tidy stacks of towels, symbols of a life of ease. And he could see the waiters, in turquoise tunics the same dreamy blue as the water, weaving around the metal poolside tables. They held plates of sandwiches, crispy grilled tuna or crunchy cucumber, and drinks, with or without alcohol, emblazoned with the Inter-Continental insignia and poked by straws and swizzle sticks. Hazrat observed their bearing as they served their guests, rehearsing the motions in his head. A slight bow, a bent elbow, a full tray balanced on a flat outstretched hand – precisely what they had all been taught at hotel school and in this hotel.

Young women, mostly foreign but some Afghan, lolled around the pool. Some wore only small, bright strips of cloth, which he had heard called bikinis. Men socialised with them or in their own noisy gaggle, most of them of fine physique. It shocked most Afghan staff at first sight, but Hazrat's eyes didn't linger. 'Don't stare at the guests,' they were told during training. Hazrat didn't have to be told; it was so obvious.

The Hotel Inter-Continental Kabul was for those with a fortune, or fortunate in life: the royals; the privileged; high-ranking officials; foreign residents, envoys and entrepreneurs; wealthy tourists on holiday from their lives in far-away lands. Even the pitched roofs of the poolside cabanas were status symbols. One of them rising to a point shaped like the nib of a pen, the other sculptured into an open book, they spoke to the learning of guests in a country where only one in ten people went to school.

The whole place was an iridescent bubble floating above the city's cares. And the world was here. Lebanese and Swiss managers, a German chef, a Palestinian engineer, a Filipino accountant, a British personal assistant, and more. All of

Afghanistan worked here, too. Most staff, including Hazrat, were too focused on their own tasks to know much about their colleagues. But they exchanged *Salaams* as they hastened in and out of the staff cafeteria to tuck into the best of Afghan food: the heaped mounds of rice scooped from the colossal kitchen pot, the lamb, beef, chicken, slaughtered in the Islamic halal manner. Sometimes the Afghan chef even slipped them some of the Western guests' food: a basket of soft, glistening butter rolls that melted in the mouth, a treat different from their own incomparable flatbread.

Over the food, staff – from managers to cleaners – rubbed shoulders without hierarchy. There was little Naser Ali who couldn't read or write. He had started as a labourer, sweating under loads of bricks and wood, to help build the hotel. He was taken on in the kitchen to shell nuts and pit cherries and dates, alongside the German chef. There was teenage Qudus, with his twinkly eyes and cheeky grin, who had stitched the hotel's uniforms long before it opened. He walked through the doors on the very first day to work as a tailor in the sewing room downstairs. And there was Masum, the young boy who poured green tea with great ceremony from the lobby's elegant samovar. He enrolled in both the English and French classes offered by the hotel and was slowly working his way up to become front-desk cashier. Hazrat would have signed up for classes, too, if he wasn't working such long hours. Still, he felt his fluency in French from his school years at the Lycée Esteqlal stood him in good stead. Some guests even told him he 'looked French', with his grey-blue eyes. The staff all put their faith in the hotel's power to elevate their own lives as smoothly as the lobby's shimmering gold lifts.

But this was not a hotel staffed solely by the disadvantaged. Anything but. Some employees had royal ancestry – like Zia, the urbane front-desk manager who was also tall and handsome. Others had the loftiest educations – like Afzal, who held a political-science degree from a distinguished university in India and had become assistant manager for guest relations. Jamal, the night auditor, had been studying at Kabul University. He and others had come up the hill looking for work when the university was temporarily shut down by the government in 1969 to stop the raging protests over everything from exam grading to arguments between Marxists and Islamists.

There were also Afghan women in almost every department. They didn't wait on tables; that wasn't seen as respectable. But they worked behind the front desk, in uniforms as deep blue as the best lapis lazuli stone. And they also worked alongside foreign women in the management suites on the lower ground floor. Some, like Fauzia, the sales manager, had come home to Kabul from university in America. Others had studied at Kabul University after it opened its doors to female students in 1950, or simply came looking for work straight after high school. They moved through the lobby with that confident Kabul stride, some sporting short bobs or bouncing ponytails, Western-style dresses or, occasionally, jaunty miniskirts cut above the knee.

Staff from all of Afghanistan's many tribes and ethnic groups came together to serve their esteemed guests. The entitled royals, who had their own regular tables. And the well-to-do families who were comfortable letting their young daughters spend time here for afternoon tea – unlike the stricter rules they set for other establishments in the city. Their presence reflected the changing social mores in this very small corner of this very conservative country. Hazrat agreed with His Majesty, King Zahir Shah. Afghanistan had to move forward. It should open up to the world. But it had to move slowly, respecting Afghan traditions.

Hazrat had never caught sight of his king in the hotel, had never even heard whispers that he was there. But his presence was forever fixed in the gleaming plaque right next to the revolving front door: *This hotel was opened on the ninth day of September 1969 in the reign of His Majesty Zahir Shah for Mailmah Pall Saham Sherkat designed by Taylor Woodrow International Limited London England.*

The memory of that first night lingered in the hotel. Sometimes a staff member who was there would remember some detail and feel suddenly compelled to share it. Sometimes a dog-eared copy of the English-language *Kabul Times* of 10 September 1969 surfaced in a drawer or on some shelf: the Inter-Continental splashed on the front page with the words 'Biggest Hotel in Kabul Opened'. Even those who couldn't read English – and most staff didn't – could linger over the photograph of the prime minister, Noor Ahmad Etemadi, snipping a shiny ribbon in a blaze of lights, surrounded by Afghan and foreign bigshots.

Sometimes, on long overnight shifts or during breaks in the staff cafeteria, someone – a waiter, a receptionist, a cleaner, a guard – would regale them all with their tales of this special night. They spoke of the bewitching moment when the golden light of an autumn day dipped beneath the hills, and a murmur of Muslim prayer rose from the Bagh-e Bala hill on the city's western verge. And of the rhythmic beat of Afghanistan's national instruments: the plucking of the *rubab*, the patter of *zerbaghali* drums. Of the shimmering Afghan tricolour – black, red and green – being hoisted slowly, steadily, everyone's eyes rising with it.

They spoke of the hotel hosting *le tout* Kabul: Afghan princes, bejewelled princesses and the privileged elite; foreign envoys from East and West in silk ties, satin saris, Arab *keffiyeh* headdresses, all seated on straight-backed chairs in straight long rows in the forecourt under the slim crescent moon. And of the prime minister – impeccably dressed, as always, in a finely tailored suit accented by a silk pocket-square – clasping the symbolic key handed to him with great aplomb. Some mentioned the new hotel soaring behind him, a rectangular white box of glass and steel, its façade of room balconies like 200 eyes watching over their city. And they spoke of the first time they saw its apex: a bold letter K in the most beautiful blue. It seemed to dance.

On that opening night the staff had peered around doors, through windows and over the front desk as the first guests streamed into the gleaming lobby, oohing and aahing. Every one of more than 500 seats in the chandeliered Kandahar Ballroom, a banquet hall draped in gold and black, had been taken for the grand feast. A travel editor from an American weekly, who had crossed an ocean for the occasion, would later write that it was like 'Massachusetts Avenue in the Hindu Kush'. Even Eastern Bloc diplomats seemed impressed. Kabul was one of the world's only capitals where Cold War enemies socialised – always looking over their shoulders – at everywhere from basketball tournaments to amateur theatre clubs. There had been a recent staging of the musical *Kiss Me, Kate* where the male lead was played by the Soviet cultural attaché and the female by an American Peace Corps volunteer.

At the grand opening, the man of the hour had undoubtedly been Peers Carter, Her Majesty's ambassador to Afghanistan. After all, it was a British company whose name was on that plaque next to the front door. Taylor Woodrow had built Afghanistan's first luxury hotel, ahead of time and against all the odds. The endeavour included an arduous five-week truck and trailer journey across ten countries, carrying the best of British building materials and fittings, to the foothills of the Hindu Kush. Tonight nobody dwelled on the doubts and difficulties that had almost scuppered this project. No one knew about them, except for the handful in the know; the account in the *Kabul Times*, covering almost half the front page, only hinted at a minor disagreement. The president of the Afghan Air Authority, Sultan Mahmoud Ghazi, a *sardar* or prince himself, was quoted expressing 'the hope that a more favourable loan will be received for the repayment'.

The truth was that Britain hadn't only built the hotel. It had bankrolled it with a loan of 2.5 million British pounds, a whopping 500 million afghanis. But the Afghan government had soon found itself unable to repay the money – it spent years trying, unsuccessfully, to renegotiate the terms. From his fine desk in Britain's magnificent white stucco compound down the road, Ambassador Carter wrote and received messages about an escalating row. 'Nearly every minister I see nags me about this, from [Prime Minister] Etemadi downwards,' he lamented in one cable sent back to Whitehall. It became known in certain circles as 'the hotel problem'. In the minds of some, the Hotel Inter-Continental Kabul was just too expensive, too luxurious, for a country where too many Afghans lived with too little.

For others, it wasn't simply a matter of bricks and mortar. Having built the hotel, they argued that the British shouldn't squander the Afghan goodwill and prestige it had secured them. 'Her Majesty's Government must be off their heads,' was how one civil servant, Winstanley Briggs, candidly put it. 'With this splendid building dominating the Kabul skyline we could collect more kudos . . . and we were throwing it all away for the sake of precedent and financial considerations.' The head of the Diplomatic Service's South Asia department, in its own graceful high-ceilinged offices on King Charles Street in London, had chimed in, too. 'The present government with all its defects is as friendly as we have seen for a very long time,' he wrote. 'It would hardly fit our policy of preserving Afghanistan independence [from Moscow] if we were to show so little concern for her government's difficulties.' The missives went back and forth, some ferried fortnightly by couriers through mighty mountain passes to neighbouring Pakistan, others painstakingly typed in secret telegrams.

Both sides understood what was at stake. In the late 1960s the rivalry between East and West had been hotting up; the Inter-Continental was in the game. Britain could ill afford to argue over an occasional late repayment when the trajectory of the Cold War was in play. And some argued that Britain needed the hotel as much as the hotel needed Britain. This project alone had halved Britain's trade deficit with Afghanistan. Moreover, it was the modernising project of a modernising king – one whom the British would do well to keep onside. Zahir Shah, mild-mannered and Paris-educated, was trying to nudge his nation forward. Thrust onto the throne at only nineteen years of age when his father was assassinated by a vengeful high-school student, the king was now cautiously advancing what became known as the 'democratic experiment'. A new constitution had been forged in 1964 and a new parliament elected five years later, just in time for the opening of the hotel.

With Afghanistan's fragile modernisation in mind, Peers Carter emphasised the importance of keeping the king happy. He knew a thing or two about diplomatic derring-do. He had traversed the Sahara Desert with Free French forces in the Second World War. He had once parachuted into Yugoslavia to liaise with President Tito's partisans. Now his job was to keep Afghanistan out of the hands of the Russians. An *eau de spook* lingered everywhere in Kabul – and there was no guarantee that the king's men would favour the West indefinitely. But beneath the monarch's mellow demeanour was the hard-wired strategy of *bi-tarafi* – neutrality – a refusal to take sides in the Cold War. It was built into the geography of this country. Most roads running north and south were the work of Soviet engineers; east–west highways were courtesy of the Americans. Moscow built Kabul's international airport; Washington constructed another, in a stunning Art Deco design, in Kandahar to the south. *Bi-tarafi* delivered. By the early 1960s Afghanistan was receiving one of the highest levels of aid per capita of any country in the world. And Ambassador Carter felt that Britain needed to keep that generosity coming. He had cultivated a wide range of contacts, including the king's eldest daughter, Bilqis; she had gifted him an elegant Afghan hound from the royal kennels, *Chipak* or Little Sparrow, who became his constant companion.

In the end Ambassador Carter's lobbying paid off. In the flurry of diplomatic cables, the Diplomatic Service had emphasised to Her Majesty's Treasury the risks of being too harsh on Afghanistan's fledgling democracy. The king's ministers were 'deeply and genuinely nervous' about how Parliament would react if they couldn't pay. 'Those deputies in the Lower House of Parliament who are not sufficiently sophisticated to realise the economic value of the country's tourist trade . . . have consistently argued that the money should be devoted to other development projects,' one cautioned. If the Afghan government defaulted, it could collapse altogether.

Of course the calm and collected Ambassador Carter was too diplomatic to mention any of this on the opening night. He just sat back in his elegant black-and-white evening wear and listened to Afghan officials waxing lyrical about the coming era: an age of fast communication and easy transport that made this hotel even more urgent, given Afghanistan's 'scenic beauty and historical significance for attracting domestic and foreign tourists'. Kabul had long catered to the low-budget travellers and hippies, high on weed and low on cash, who lived as cheap as chips in hostels in the city centre. Ambassador Carter and his consular officials occasionally had to rescue them from drugs, destitution or disease, sometimes even on their deathbed. Now, the Afghan officials enthused, this fine hotel would welcome an altogether more well-to-do class of foreign visitor. Ones with more money to spend.

Kabul had joined a global club – the forty-eighth link in the fast-growing Inter-Continental chain, which had signed a twenty-year lease to manage the property. The company's visionary American founder, Juan Trippe, who also launched Pan American Airways, was pioneering a new era in luxury travel: connecting the world's capitals and helping to spread American culture and clout in this Cold War bout. Kabul, known in rarefied circles as the 'Paris of Central Asia', was a jewel in his crown. A few dozen foreign staff and more than 300 Afghans – including Hazrat – were now putting their shoulders to the wheel. All trained to the highest Inter-Continental standards, and naturals in Afghanistan's rich traditions of hospitality.

Once a day Valerie skipped up the stairs for lunch in the Bamiyan Brasserie. It was a perk of her post, even if it was restricted to the cheaper choices on the menu. She didn't mind that too much. What mattered was the chance to get out from behind her desk and soak up the atmosphere of the lobby. It was all so very glamorous.

Like a princess castle out of a storybook on a far-away hill. That's what Valerie thought when she first walked through the door the year after the Hotel Inter-Continental Kabul opened. Blonde-haired and blue-eyed, she was described by some as 'a typical

English rose'. She had left London on the wings of a Foreign Office assignment, a twenty-one-year-old in search of something different. She had soon fallen in love with Afghanistan, as well as with an Afghan, left her posting at the British embassy and landed one here on the hill. In her office downstairs, in the well-appointed executive suites, the fairytale was made up of detailed spreadsheets, packed diaries and tasks ranging from pouring coffee to pitching ideas.

A year later she was still discovering something different every lunchtime. Some days it was the gorgeous carpets adorning the marble floor. They had been specially knotted in traditional geometric patterns, all medallions and floral motifs, except not in the familiar Afghan reds and blues, but in golden yellows and black. They blended seamlessly with the hotel's modern's aesthetic. Emboldened, she had ordered her own rug in grey and black. On other days she would pause to window-shop at the glass-fronted pocket stores lining the lobby. One was piled high with fine handmade Afghan carpets and kilims. Another, run by the German wife of the mayor of Kabul, was filled with chunky gemstone-studded jewellery, brightly embroidered leather bags, the bluest of glass and the best of engraved wooden boxes.

Another still was the boutique of Afghan designer Safia Tarzi, pioneer of an avant-garde style that blended Western and Afghan styles, menswear and womenswear. She was known for adding female touches to traditional turbans and waistcoats, and for her own version of the embroidered Afghan sheepskin coats, the *pustinchas*, that were fast becoming a fashion craze in the West. One of Tarzi's claims to fame included being the first Afghan woman to model in *Vogue* magazine – staring down the lens in a turban made of twists of brightly coloured fabric, the shortest of miniskirts and the highest of leather boots.

Valerie admired the ambition of this hotel. But sometimes

it left her breathless. 'Very brave.' That's how she described her boss, the suave Swiss general manager, Pierre Martinet. 'We want to do things which had never been seen before in Kabul,' he would often tell her. It was, he would sometimes confess, a highly ambitious undertaking. It was hard at the start to tempt even Afghans and foreigners with deep pockets to take the time to travel all the way to this distant corner of Kabul, to a grass-land of rolling vineyards and grand mulberry trees and very few houses. But it was worth it, because the hotel was special. 'Very special,' Pierre would say. The Afghans they trained were so dedicated, displayed such seriousness. And he had a real eye for spotting talent. Valerie was impressed when he signed up, on the spot, the smart and polished Fauzia for his top sales position – and at a time when Afghan women were only beginning to take on senior roles in society. She stepped into the shoes of the Afghan man who had just left and flawlessly fitted the role, at ease in both Afghan and foreign worlds.

Valerie discreetly observed her boss from behind her tidy desk as she kept track of all his many ideas. It was clear that the Inter-Continental Kabul had stolen his heart. When Pierre was asked to cross the border to manage an Inter-Continental hotel in Pakistan he insisted that he would only do so temporarily, and on the condition he could come back to Kabul. His Iranian wife was smitten with this city, too. And Pierre also spoke perfect Persian.

But he was very much a European hotelier, with a flair for flamboyance. There was a certain French note, a *je ne sais quoi*. You could hear the musical lilt of the language; could even smell its style wafting through the lobby. Women paraded past with bulbous bouffants sprayed into place with perfume so powerful it could transport you to Paris. Pierre had convinced his friend, the Parisian stylist Jean d'Estrées, to open a salon on the lower ground floor. Every few months the celebrity coiffeur blew in from France, his arrival causing a stir among the Kabul elite – including his star customers, the king's two daughters Bilqis and Maryam, and even Queen Humaira Begum herself. He also coiffed brides, brought by the families who were able to scrape together the considerable sum required for a ceremony in Kabul's most prestigious banquet hall. Weddings at the Inter-Con were modern and 'mixed', men and women celebrating together, and a Parisian hairdo and make-up were part of the package.

But there were also many uncomfortably long days when nobody came by at all. A lonely Jean d'Estrées, his salon facing Valerie's open door, would call out across the corridor to invite her to test a new shade of eye shadow or to have a coffee. It was hard to say which was more luxurious: coffee was a treat in Kabul, almost impossible to find in a city of tea drinkers.

Pierre's most audacious idea of all was launched in the spring of 1971. The hotel made another splash in the *Kabul Times*, which reported on 'The first well known Paris designer to appear in person in Kabul, and . . . the first time the Paris collection will be shown to the Kabul audience'. The 'world famous couturier' Pierre Balmain had descended on the Inter-Con – as everyone increasingly called it – with his glamorous French 'mannequins' to model his Spring/Summer Collection. The hotel's Pierre had personally persuaded his friend to bring his catwalk to Kabul, 'the Paris of Central Asia', before taking his collection to the Phoenicia Inter-Continental in Beirut, 'the Paris of the Middle East'.

A fashion show in Kabul wasn't really a first. The Kabul Hotel had staged a few of its own, including an 'East meets West' event where Afghan models strutted down a makeshift runway in calf-length embroidered Afghan coats, swinging miniskirts, satin gowns with silky black gloves and luxurious furs with matching pillbox hats. One model ambled in more traditional attire, accessorised with a raised headdress and an antique British rifle.

But the Balmain show at the Inter-Con was haute couture – and much more. Even Valerie gasped. The leggy French models sunning themselves by the hotel swimming pool were wearing black see-through chiffon georgette blouses, not bothering with bras. And they swept through the lobby in long, even strides, shoulders straight, arms swinging slightly, as if they owned the space. In those moments they did. The staff, Afghans and foreigners alike, couldn't help but break the rules and stare.

The show itself called for all hands on deck – at least for the women. In the ballroom-cum-pop-up Parisian atelier, Valerie lent a hand with the final fittings. So did Afghan seamstresses, many of them designers in their own right. The dapper couturier with his signature monocle put the finishing touches, inspecting the last stitches and seams. Three 'fabulous shows' had been advertised in Kabul newspapers – including a luxurious lunch, afternoon high tea and a gala dinner, serving prime rib of Texas beef. Valerie was backstage helping the models swiftly change from costume to costume as they revealed Balmain's sunny new collection: a two-toned yellow chemisier dress with a wide-brimmed white hat; a chic sailor-style cropped jacket and pencil skirt in navy blue and white; a long-sleeved evening dress with a black satin belt. Such expensive frocks would never be 'in season' in Kabul. Very few could afford them. Still, it was a sight to behold; that was the point. And the general manager did purchase a very beautiful Balmain dress for his wife.

The show was Pierre's most successful 'first' yet. It galvanised him to organise even more. And his marketing savvy told him it was time to showcase Afghan excellence, too.

The high-ceilinged ballroom was brimming with appreciative applause and admiring eyes when the Afghan designer Najiba, known for top-notch tailoring, put her collection on show: a celebration of Afghan embroidery, swirling dresses with beautifully patterned bodices, as well as chic Western wear. Modelled by Afghan women, accompanied by traditional Afghan music, its sophistication struck a note entirely different from the Parisian show. Sales were brisk; Valerie bought her favourites, too, adding to a wardrobe filled with London fashions that she found at the Marks and Spencer store downtown. Every time its latest styles arrived on flights into Kabul, it sparked excitement in a certain crowd.

Valerie cheered on her female colleagues. Even for the privileged, life still had its daily battles. The twenty-somethings she worked with in the hotel were old enough to remember that historic summer's day in 1959 when the prime minister, Daoud Khan, had boldly signalled it was time to change some of the rules. It was the annual *Jeshn* celebrations, marking forty years of independence and celebrated by a day of high-stepping royal horses, hulking army tanks, and marching brass bands. Zamina Begum, the wife of the prime minister, appeared in the royal box unveiled. So too did the queen and her eldest daughter. Gasps shot through the crowds. Daoud Khan, the king's ambitious cousin and son-in-law, had then challenged critical conservative clerics to show him proof in Islamic scripture that the all-enveloping *chadri*, often called a burka, was obligatory. They never did. He didn't ban it. But he announced that royal women were no longer required to wear veils. Others took their cue.

What women wore, what they did, how they lived, was still a lightning rod in some circles. When some of Pierre's most spectacular shows ended, the staff quietly breathed sighs of relief that they had unfolded without incident. Conservative newspapers, publishing in Dari and Pashto, had begun spear-heading campaigns against women's rising hemlines. One young MP had stood up in the newly elected assembly to disparage 'the rising nudity in fashion and dresses'. On the poplar-lined campus of Kabul University, and in the city centre, there were cases of young religious zealots hurling acid into women's faces.

Rabble-rousers of every ilk had a megaphone these days. Islamists, socialists, nationalists and liberals were all maximising the small political openings that had emerged through the cautious reforms of the king. But the hotel on the hill still managed to remain above it all, untouched by the stirrings in the city below.

It was the bottles. Hazrat eyed the rainbow of colours neatly lined up in the bar, glinting in the backlight. There was liquor from foreign lands – whiskies, vodkas, gin, rum. And Afghanistan's own potions, too: brandy and red and white wine, much of it produced in the Afghan-Clemd distillery on the eastern edge of Kabul. Hazrat often drove there, about twenty minutes away, to pick up the bottles. Not for the Inter-Con, where he worked by day. For the New Marco Polo in the city centre, where he mixed drinks in the discotheque by night. And he served drinks without alcohol, too – such as fresh Afghan juices and the new distinctive bottles of real American Coca-Cola, not the pretend pop from Pakistan.

This wasn't the first Marco Polo in Kabul. Its owner, Sultan Malikyar, had enjoyed such success with his first venture that he had opened another in the up-and-coming neighbourhood of Shahr-e Nau, the 'New City'. An Afghan of royal ancestry, Malikyar had returned home after studying in America and dutifully became a civil servant like his siblings. But he soon left to pursue his dream of building a hospitality empire. It now encompassed restaurants, a travel company, the very first flower shop and all manner of entertainment. There were *thés dansants*, chaperoned afternoon dances for the young and affluent and monthly piano recitals, by his Vienna Conservatory-trained cousin Najib, for the cultural cognoscenti. His wife Rahella, when she wasn't translating articles from glossy American or French magazines, organised poetry readings and teatime discussion groups for Kabuli women and men.

For Hazrat, the second job was born of the need to support his family. But his forays also fed his curiosity about his fast-changing city. These days his life in Kabul felt like he was standing on a fast-moving bus, holding onto a strap as you were thrown from side to side, savouring the sense of going somewhere. Shahr-e Nau, the most Westernised quarter in the capital, was a billboard for the city's changing times. There were still poultry sellers with squawking birds at the end of the fabled 'Chicken Street', and buckets of blooms on the adjacent 'Flower Street'. But the area also boasted a French perfumery and a Lebanese boutique with the latest European fashions. And it had morphed into a magnet for the growing influx of long-haired Western hippies in bell-bottom jeans and flowing dresses who stayed in its cheap and charming hostels, drank strong Afghan tea and smoked even stronger *charsi* weed. Juice stands produced heavenly nectars for the equivalent of five cents. And the shops were a treasure chest of traditional delights, not least the popular embroidered *pustincha* vests that some Westerners were now taking home to sell. Even The Beatles were wearing them.

As Hazrat ambled by, he noted how free the hippies seemed. He would watch them strolling the streets or sprawled on the grass in Shahr-e Nau Park into the early hours, smoking weed, strumming guitars, singing softly. He secretly marvelled at their happy-go-lucky lifestyle. Some Afghans were affronted by their loose ways. Hazrat, like many others, was indifferent. *Live and let live*, he thought. Besides, he rarely saw them for long. The hippies could not afford to stay at the Inter-Con or even get through the door of the New Marco Polo. These places barely catered for the travellers on slightly bigger budgets, the 'over-landers' taking journeys in buses and minivans across Europe, usually through Iran, then Afghanistan and Pakistan and on to India. Some occasionally made it past the Inter-Con's ever-vigilant doorman, in his cherry-red coat with gold buttons, to savour the calm, a rare cup of coffee, perhaps even pinch some toilet paper. But not very often.

Like the Inter-Con, the New Marco Polo was oozing with oomph. It prided itself on serving a plate for every palate. On the top floor, a lavish restaurant offered European fare created by a chef whom Malikyar had persuaded to join from the Inter-Continental in Delhi. A Chinese chef poached from an eatery across the border in Pakistan also served up proper Asian food. Outside, a hamburger grill did good business. And in the back garden there was a finer version of the kerbside kebab stalls that elsewhere appealed to people with much shallower pockets. For an emerging Afghan middle class, without the wherewithal to travel, these were their first tingling tastes of other worlds.

The most exotic nook in the New Marco Polo, where Hazrat spent his hours, was the Paizar, the basement discotheque trans-formed into a grotto. 'Drink and dance in a cave' was its catch-phrase. 'Once you are in the Paizar you will live the real life.' Beneath the bar's blazing spotlights, Hazrat got a grip on the drinks menu. Afghan booze laid claim to noble names: Nerone, 'the brandy of the emperors'; Clemd, a grappa announcing itself in bold red script; Castellino and Turin wines decorated with antique Italian scrolls and the ramparts of Afghan castles. All produced and bottled in Kabul, the initiative of an enterprising

Italian student, Tonino De Feo, who had roared into Kabul in 1965 in a dusty Buick sedan and vowed to become 'the Italian Vintner of Kabul'.

Hazrat wanted to make his own mark as an Afghan cocktail mixer. A parade of ingredients – lemon juice, tomato juice, pepper, salt and more – stared at him alongside the backlit liquor. *A shot of Scotch whisky in the metal cocktail shaker. A shot of Italian liqueur. A lot of ice cubes. Stir. Strain into an old-fashioned glass over more cubes of ice. Pop an Afghan cherry and a slice of a Nangarhar orange on top.*

There was a lot to keep juggling in his head. The recipes had to be followed. The rules, too. Serving alcohol was still a controversial business in a conservative Muslim country. In its early months the Paizar was billed as 'now only open to members'. And there was an offer to the 'diplomatic community and high society' to hold private parties and 'bring your own drinks, pay corkage'. In 1968, the year after the Afghan-Clemd factory opened, the king's government had ruled that alcoholic drinks could only be sold to non-Muslim expatriates. That meant most of the distillery's bottles had to be exported, travelling east to Pakistan, westwards to Iran under the rule of the Shah or north to the Soviet Union. But enterprising smugglers ensured that the bottles circled back across the border. And alcohol from embassies found its way to the back lanes of the bazaars, with exorbitant price tags.

Hazrat kept many secrets in his head, too. A prominent patron with royal connections sometimes engaged his services as personal protection, impressed by his muscular physique and observant eye; Hazrat would accompany him to illegal gambling dens in a nearby neighbourhood. Kabul nightlife was popping, for some. On the same street as the Paizar, the Twenty-Five Hour Club prided itself on being Kabul's first discotheque, the brainchild of another larger-than-life character who styled himself as the 'King of Nightlife'. Prince Ali Seraj, who traced his royal lineage through nine generations, came back from America in 1969 and kept lamenting loudly that Kabul 'ceased to exist after 8 p.m.'. He complained to anyone who would listen that the only options for a night out were watching scratched copies of spaghetti westerns in cinemas or listening to Indian music on Japanese tape-decks in the old-fashioned Khyber restaurant in the city centre. With bushy sideburns and a trendy goatee, the playboy prince had become a familiar face at the Inter-Con, particularly in the top-floor Pamir Supper Club, where he was known for charming his guests and boogying the night away. He had launched the Twenty-Five Hour Club less than a year after the Inter-Con opened. By 1972 the Fodor's guide to Central Asia was listing the Hotel Inter-Continental Kabul and the Twenty-Five Hour Club as the most popular places to visit in Afghanistan.

Hazrat didn't mind a drink or two himself. Not on his shift, of course. He bounced from one foot to the other as he shook tipples for Afghan and foreign customers. *A shot of vodka, 4 ounces of tomato juice. A bit of lemon juice. Pour into a jug of ice. Dashes of hot sauce and Worcestershire sauce. Pinches of salt and pepper. Stir. Strain. Pour into a highball glass, over ice. Add a celery stick, if there is celery. And a Nangarhar lemon slice.*

He people-watched as he mixed. Some Paizar regulars just whiled away the hours at the bar, tapping their fingers to the music, downing their drinks. Others hardly left the dance floor, especially when new live bands were belting out popular tunes. Music was taking off in Kabul, too. When the Inter-Con opened in 1969 there wasn't much in the way of bands for hire: only the Blue Sharks, four male Filipino songsters in the city, with electric guitars and shiny silk tunics, who played every Thursday night at the elite International Club. But before long another Afghan band – the Four Brothers – was performing at the Paizar and the Kabul Hotel with a style and sound that some Afghans regarded as their own Beatles, a 'Fab Four'. The Inter-Con had to go one better. The hotel's German food-and-beverage manager asked a former Sri Lankan army sergeant, Claude Selvaradna, a rock-music aficionado who happened to be in Kabul, to create the hotel's own house band. Musicians came from Colombo to form the Esquire Set. They produced a whole new vibe, pumping out raucous rock tunes such as Led Zeppelin's 'Whole Lotta Love' that always brought party-goers to their feet.

Hazrat had got into the spirit of loud foot-tapping music working in the discotheque. But, by day, he preferred the gentler strains of the Afghan musicians who provided an ambient soundtrack to the Inter-Con lobby, sitting cross-legged on woven *takht* benches playing their *rubabs* and *tabla* drums. He didn't recognise any of the foreign music that often played in the Kandahar Ballroom and the Pamir Supper Club; most staff didn't. There were The Merrymakers, described as 'world-famous entertainers', with dancers twisting in feathers and bikinis; the Eddie Keane Show, 'imported directly from London'; a performer called Danny, 'one of the greatest Limbo dancers'; not to mention belly dancers, Spanish flamenco, Indian *sitar* maestros. They all came and went at the Inter-Con.

The greatest draw, beyond any doubt, was Afghanistan's star of stars, Ahmad Zahir. He often burst into the hotel cocooned by his buddies, shadowed by hotel staff, so that he wasn't mobbed by fans who had spotted his signature sideburns and flamboyant dress. Sometimes he would lounge by the pool, with friends, in his swimming trunks. Or huddle, in a smart suit, in a cosy corner of the Nuristan Cocktail Lounge or the Pamir Supper Club. He even appeared, at least once, at the same time as his father, Abdul Zahir, one of the king's many former prime ministers. He turned heads in the Paizar, too, where he performed in the back garden. Some nights he bought drinks for everyone at the bar. Hazrat never forgot how merry the mood was, how jaw-dropping the bills.

On 21 March 1972 – *Nowruz*, the new-year celebration in the Persian solar calendar – Ahmad Zahir performed a sold-out concert in the Inter-Con ballroom. The edgy wail of the saxophones, the sharp blast of trumpets and the warm notes of the harmonium could be heard well beyond the banquet hall. He had crooned on the Inter-Con stage in his classy black suit and loosened striped tie: *'One is heartbroken, one is sincere, and one is burdened with a hundred problems . . . One is trapped in water and clay, while the other is enchanted by the skies.'*

The 'Elvis of Afghanistan'. That's what people called him. It was the talk of the hotel for months.

CHAPTER 2

The Prince's Order

Summer 1973

The bartender tried to look like he wasn't listening, but it was impossible not to eavesdrop. Even the wooden sculptures behind the bar seemed to lean from their frames to hear.

As the last of the afternoon light waned from the windows and the glow of red table lamps took over the tables, the Inter-Con's Nuristan Cocktail Lounge was simmering with speculation. 'Who was behind this morning's security sweep? Was it a conservative crackdown? Was the king's new prime minister flexing his muscles?' The questions hung in the air, mixing with the ringlets of cigarette smoke rising above the tables and the tinkle of piano keys from the corner.

Musa Shafiq, the young prime minister with a movie-star moustache and a head of grey-flecked hair, had been in power for a mere seven months. He was a man of East and West: the son of a *mullah* from the eastern province of Nangarhar, with one law degree from Columbia University in New York and another from the centre of Islamic learning at Al-Azhar University in Cairo.

The question was whether he was looking east or west now.

In the early hours of Saturday morning, when the streets of Shahr-e Nau were just waking up, there had been a sudden jarring shout: 'Open the door!' Special police, their noses nearly touching the doors, were at the entrance of the Paizar, the Twenty-Five Hour Club and more. They were on a mission to confiscate every drop of alcohol, to shutter each and every premise, until further notice. One after another the clubs and bars went dark. Royal orders yielded to no one.

The news travelled through the city as fast as a *buzkashi* horse. But on its distant hilltop the hotel kept its cool. Nothing untoward interrupted an Inter-Con day. In the Nuristan Cocktail Lounge and the Pamir Supper Club liquor glasses kept being polished; the usual preparations for the usual patrons – possibly a prince or two – who would be arriving later. In the Bamiyan Brasserie copper pots and serving pans clattered as chefs in towering white hats prepared the day's special offer. It was only in the executive offices on the lower ground that the day's events were met with concern. Surely, the managers reassured themselves, it would be business as usual; this was, after all, a government-owned hotel. It was starting to bring in much-needed revenue to help the hotel pay its bills and to develop the tourism sector with all its untapped potential. Still, a few senior staff made haste to the grey-marbled Foreign Ministry in Shahr-e Nau – just in case.

The truth was that there had been disquiet in the city for a while. Western diplomats, in hushed conversations and confidential cables and telegrams, had concluded that Musa Shafiq was essentially pro-Western; in his short time in office, the king's sixth prime minister since the dawn of his 'democratic experiment' had broadened Afghanistan's ties with the West and finally injected some life into his limping reform programme. However, the shrewdest observers suspected that things were not as stable as they seemed. British diplomatic cables had cautioned that some Afghans found the new prime minister conceited and corrupt. And the mood in the country was grim. The recently departed British ambassador Peers Carter, who admired the monarch's liberal tendencies, had despaired of the 'political and economic stagnation; even for the still relatively small urban population the new order has meant little change and for the tribespeople and peasant none at all'. Just months before his post ended, in 1971, he warned that if nothing changed, 'as external influences of all kinds are raising the temperature . . . sooner or later, autocracy will return'.

The king was not in Kabul now. He had left suddenly, a little more than a week previously. A volleyball was said to have smacked him in the eye. The grapevine was buzzing about this, too. The king had seen his Afghan physician and had been examined by the American director at the respected Noor Eye Clinic, established years earlier by Christian missionaries. The injury, it seemed, was not serious. But the king, with his penchant for foreign travel, set off for London to see an ophthalmologist there anyway. And now he was taking a regal rest at a seaside spa in Italy.

The next few evenings in Kabul felt strangely quiet. In the dead of night, the streets of Shahr-e Nau – used to being disrupted by the ruckus of patrons spilling out of restaurants and clubs in the early hours – were all but deserted. It felt as if some quarters in the capital had taken a deep breath.

Early mornings in Kabul were like a symphony orchestra warming up: the rooster's crow; the tinkling of bicycle bells; the rattle of fruit and vegetable crates; the chatter of school-kids clutching books. But on 17 July 1973, three days after the crackdown, morning brought nothing but a discordant silence. As the full moon gave way to a summer's day, signalling the start of everyday rituals, nothing happened. School buses didn't show up. Corner bakeries stayed shut. Families fortunate enough to have telephones plugged into the walls of their homes picked up their handsets to discover the lines were dead. Normal programming at Kabul Radio stopped.

Even the Inter-Con staff shuttle, so reliable you could set your clock by its arrival, never appeared. Employees who had their own cars drove to work. Others walked, or bicycled, or hitched rides to be on time for their 7 a.m. start.

As they strode up the hill, past the evergreens and the fading pink-and-white apricot blooms, they spotted other staff – mainly the foreigners – bunched around the entrance, peppering every new arrival with questions about what they had seen or heard. Staff who lived close to the presidential palace had been jolted awake in the dead of night by bursts of small-arms fire and the rat-a-tat-tat of machine guns. Tanks growled through the streets. Not long after 6 a.m. one of the hotel managers had spotted a gold-coloured sedan speeding away from the Bagh-e Bala palace next door, with one of the king's uncles crouching in the front seat along with his driver, and three soldiers in the back. Two military jeeps, packed with gunmen, sped past.

Word had it that soldiers had taken control of the telephone exchange, the radio station, the international airport. Kabul was cut off from the world. Every person's story added another piece to this new jigsaw. But the biggest chunks were still missing.

A shout went up from the huddled staff: 'Sardar Daoud will address the nation at 7 a.m.!' The hotel's guests and employees sped to the lobby to cluster close to the radio fixed high on a wall. It had been crackling on and off with martial music and nationalist anthems. Was this all Sardar Mohammad

Daoud's doing? Prince Daoud, the king's cousin and son-in-law; Lieutenant-General Daoud, loyal army officer?

The radio suddenly thundered with Daoud's unmistakable voice. 'I have always pursued a goal for my people – for the people of Afghanistan,' he explained, invective spiking his speech. The king's rule, he said, had been 'corrupt and effete . . . a pseudo-democracy'. Today marked the start of 'a genuine democracy', based on Islam, backed by the military, aligned with neither East nor West and ready to rescue the country from ruin. The 1964 constitution, the parliament, the judiciary, were suspended. Prince Daoud was now President Daoud of the Republic of Afghanistan.

Daoud's words washed over the country. Afghans stood by their stoves, stopped on the street, slowed their cars, huddled around beaten transistor sets in teahouses. The speech echoed across a country into villages ravaged by three consecutive years of drought; some were too poor, too cut off, even to have radios. The monarchy was no more. Martial law was in force.

The Inter-Continental staff were stunned into silence, daring only to raise their eyebrows or shake their heads. Nobody said much. Now, more than ever, nobody could be sure who was on which side. They simply went back to work, immersing themselves in their well-rehearsed routines. Accountants focused on piles of paperwork on ground-floor desks. On the top floor German and Swiss chefs perused new menus after their recent success with a Scandinavian buffet, billed as 'a Viking's meal'. Pamir Supper Club waiters in crimson blazers busied themselves pleating white linen napkins into standing fans.

Only later did the magnitude of the day's events sink in. As staff shuttle buses wended through the city before dusk, their passengers saw menacing tanks positioned at key intersections.

They heard military jets streaking across the sky. And in the safety of their homes, with the volume on their radio sets carefully dialled down, Afghans filled in the details from foreign stations, most of all the BBC World Service. The king's family, including Queen Humaira Begum and their children, were under house-arrest in the palace. Prime Minister Shafiq and his Cabinet ministers had been rounded up before dawn; by daybreak the prisons were said to be nearly full. The king's son-in-law General Abdul Wali had put up a fight until a tank blasted a hole in his wall and he turned himself in. Almost the only casualties had been several police officers who confronted mutinous troops at their station, and a tank crew who perished when their armoured vehicle swerved off the road and into the Kabul river to avoid colliding with a bus.

It had been a near-perfect palace coup by little more than a dozen officers and a few hundred troops: executed with remarkable efficiency and secrecy, and nearly bloodless. Moscow was first to recognise the new order, sparking much discussion about whether it had been involved in the coup, or at least knew it was coming. It was followed by Delhi shortly afterwards. Western capitals quickly fell into line, without much discussion of the rights and wrongs of this putsch. The Japanese ambassador relayed his admiration to Tokyo that the former British ambassador Peers Carter had predicted exactly this outcome.

The waiting staff waited. They waited for guests. They waited to see what would happen next.

Hazrat sat on a royal-blue cushion on one of the restaurant's wooden chairs, next to the earthen mural of the Bamiyan Cliffs. He stared into the distance, through the floor-to-ceiling windows that framed the Kabul sky. There was a comforting continuity in the view, but the hotel itself was eerily silent. The tasselled umbrellas on the terrace had only the company of red geraniums and yellow marigolds spilling playfully from planters. Even the swimming pool had lost its splashes, despite the baking temperature. Afghans and foreigners were still staying away – only for a while, the staff were told, until the situation settled down.

The hotel kept up appearances. On his occasional and brief forays into the lobby Hazrat absorbed the enduring sense of calm. In the immediate aftermath of the coup the few foreign guests who checked in had loudly and excitedly recounted how their planes had sat on the tarmac surrounded by soldiers, how their bags were thoroughly searched in the terminal. But the excitement soon gave way to a sense of foreboding. Reports started swirling that President Daoud's men were on the prowl in the city, harassing people, taking some in for questioning, throwing some into prison.

The Inter-Con was not exempt. Word went round, sotto voce, that a few senior Afghan staff with royal blood had left the hotel in a hurry after being summoned to the Interior Ministry. They had been grilled for hours. Conspiratorial questions. 'Why do you work for an American hotel? Do you work for the CIA?' And sillier ones, too. 'Why do the women wear short skirts? Do you take American aspirin when you don't feel well?' In an international hotel where the staff, especially Afghans, rarely raised sensitive issues, everyone became even more cautious, cupping their mouths and lowering their heads to avoid being heard.

Hazrat's eyes lingered for a moment on the wooden pigeonholes packed with clunky keys behind the front desk. Something was missing. The king's image. All his portraits in the hotel – behind the front desk, in management offices, in rooms here and there – had been swiftly taken down. On postage stamps stored in drawers, the king's head was rubbed out. Only the weathered inauguration plaque bearing his name remained stuck to the wall outside.

Their king was gone. Everyone now understood that the only leader they had ever known, and whom many had loved, wasn't coming back. Hazrat pondered Zahir Shah's fate. He had been good and kind, a monarch with modern ideas. Perhaps he had been too cautious. But past Afghan kings had paid a price for trying to move faster. On 24 August, no doubt by *force majeure*, he had formally abdicated. The letter was gracious: he respected 'the will of my compatriots' and recognised that the people of Afghanistan 'with absolute majority welcomed a republican regime'. His wife, Queen Humaira, his two daughters and four sons – more than a dozen royals in all – had joined him in Rome after being freed from palace arrest. President Daoud, their renegade relative, had allowed them to fly out of Kabul on a private jet. One of the king's sleek limousines, from his beloved collection of classic cars, was sent to him too. Then, for all his criticism of royal excesses, President Daoud moved himself and his own family into the presidential palace, the imposing Arg citadel encircled by high walls.

Now it was the face of the 'leader of the revolution' that stared down at the staff in the hotel, and in multiplying places in public spaces. Hazrat had clocked them when he wandered round his old haunts in Shahr-e Nau. He had seen President Daoud's bald, dark-browed face, sometimes replete with his trademark dark glasses, tacked to the front of his old gym, glued on shop windows, nailed into teahouse timbers. Carpet weavers started knotting the new leader's face into their rugs. Artists were painting him on towering banners to be placed in government ministries and, when the massive portrait was complete, in the main Ghazi stadium.

For the most part, the rhythms of the city continued uninterrupted. Down in the city, shoppers with more money to spend than Hazrat paid greater attention to the season's best produce from the provinces arrayed on rickety wooden carts dotting the streets: the first white and black mulberries; sweet cherries and apricots; even plump strawberries dripping with juice. Hawkers shouted their best prices, higher here than in more humble neighbourhoods, sprinkling water on the ground around their stalls to calm the dust. But stories were being traded, too, in whispers and asides, as horse- and donkey-drawn carts clopped by, along with the occasional yellow taxi and small gaggles of sheep and goats. *Akbar-e sar-e chowk*, 'the news from the roundabout', is what Afghans still called it: a phrase harking back to a time when Kabul only had one roundabout, the place where kings had dispatched trusted courtiers to listen in on what their people were saying. Now, in the bazaars of kingless Kabul, one story was told and retold. The time a decade earlier when General Daoud, then the king's prime minister, had inspected an army base. The soldiers' loudest lament was the poor quality of their bread, the staple of Afghan life. General Daoud immediately ordered the baker to do better. When he returned a few months later, the soldiers' complaint was the same. There still wasn't bread they could stomach. So, the story went, General Daoud ordered the baker executed. Nobody seemed quite sure whether or not that was true. But it felt real, becoming for some the tale of a tyrant; for others the story of a strongman the country needed.

Hazrat paid little attention to this kind of *gupshup*. He sometimes picked up more reliable information anyway. You could learn a lot about the new leader just by keeping your ears peeled in the Inter-Con, or by tuning into foreign radio channels. Bald-headed, hard-headed Daoud. When he was the king's prime minister for a decade until 1963 he had single-mindedly pursued his modernising projects. The roads, dams, electricity pylons, greater rights for women – they were all seen as his work, with the king's blessing. But he was also seen to favour the Soviets in awarding contracts, and infuriated neighbouring Pakistan with his impassioned support for fellow tribesmen, the Pashtuns, across the border. It provoked a diplomatic crisis that sealed the border and strangled the economy.

Vengeful Daoud. He'd spent the last decade, since the king eased him out in 1963, appearing to be a man-at-ease, entertaining visitors in his graceful residence. But his late-night rendez-vous, fuelled by cups of green tea or tumblers of harder stuff, were steeped in intrigue. He was said to have conspired in this coup with one faction: the *Parcham*, the 'Flag', of the only semi-legal communist party, the People's Democratic Party of Afghanistan (PDPA). Foreign radios weighed up whether Daoud was a communist or a nationalist. Most decided he was the latter.

Not much had really changed in Hazrat's life. When he ventured into the city, he merely circled around the armoured vehicles still positioned at key junctions. They seemed more like martial decorations now, their preening gun turrets no longer so threatening. He sometimes peeked nostalgically into the main office of Afghantour in Shahr-e Nau, just around the corner from the Paizar. The government tourist agency also had a small glass-fronted office in the hotel lobby.

Hazrat riffled through the colourful tourist brochures printed on shiny paper. There was always a big ad for the Hotel Inter-Continental Kabul, with a picture of the large blue swimming pool with happy people all around it. 'All the modern facilities one can possibly think of' was its boast. A few years earlier the hotel had asked Hazrat to accompany some of the foreign tour groups. With his athletic strength, and some fluency in French, he had guided jet-setters on their excursions. Sometimes they journeyed to places so remote – even to the far foothills of the Pamir mountains – that a cook would come with them, along with portable stoves and canvas tents to sleep in. This re-inforced his belief that Afghan hospitality was always five-star, no matter the circumstances. In many places off the beaten track, the absence of electricity and running water earned the only rooms no official hospitality stars at all. But the welcome in mud-brick family homes was always bright and warm. One dollar a night would get you a breakfast of hot bread straight out of the tandoor, and fresh cream from the cow. For another dollar, the son would give visitors a tour. It was said that out in the provinces the coup had changed nothing; a changing of the guard meant little to villagers who lived simple lives so many miles away.

But Hazrat's days as a tour guide seemed distant now. In fact there were hushed questions about whether the new leader even thought tourism was particularly important. Since the coup, adventurous tourists and organised tour groups had started showing up again. In the main Afghantour office in Shahr-e Nau visitors were still trickling in, especially the hippies who kept dropping by to check for mail, and maps; to take a look at the great message board hanging on the wall, always packed with paper notes, tacked on top of one another; to ask for advice, or for rides here and there, desperately seeking someone or something. A palace coup was of little consequence in their world, too. But there was chatter that the new presi-dent would soon put an end to the hippy trail. These travel-lers were no longer merely seen as harmless weed-smoking adventure seekers. Global drugs gangs were spreading their tentacles, now luring Afghans in as smugglers, and smokers. President Daoud, it was rumoured, was planning a crackdown.

By the end of 1973 Kabul nightlife was back with a bang. The Inter-Continental urged high society to 'usher in the '74 with a swing at the ballroom' at a black-tie New Year's Eve ball. One of Kabul's new Afghan bands, The Stars, would bring in the new year with its popular cover versions of American disco hits which had reached Kabul. Not to be outdone, the Paizar discotheque also promised a live band with tickets priced at 200 afghanis, less than half the Inter-Con's 500 afghanis per person. It was pricey even for government ministers, whose official salaries were somewhere between 10,000 and 20,000 afghanis a month. Most Afghans were getting by on fewer than fifty afghanis.

Hazrat was back at work among the glinting bottles of the Paizar's underground bar. The clubs and bars had been allowed to open again; customers started trickling back in, some returning to their regular seats at the far end of the bar as if nothing had happened. There was hushed speculation that, three days before the coup, when these premises had been briefly shut down, it was to ensure that no one was out on the streets when the coup's tanks and troops rolled out of the barracks. Hazrat revelled in returning to expertly flipping bottles with a flick of his wrist, pouring pints, shaking and stirring cocktails. He was reminded again that he wasn't just serving drinks, he was part of everyone's escape from their everyday cares. Including his own. At the end of his shifts, as he hastened home to his family's humble mud-and-timber house, he would smile tiredly to see the long-haired Western hippies still hanging out in the park.

Not every bar restored its old vibe. The popular Twenty-Five Hour Club next to the Paizar stayed dark; Prince Ali himself had brought in the wrecking ball. He had fumed over his bar's precipitous closure. But his troubles had started much sooner than the security sweep. Months before, some of his best patrons, including Western diplomats and spooks, had suddenly stopped running up hefty tabs at the bar. A fuller story slowly emerged. Prince Ali's dashing manager, a former French perfumier with the air of a film star, was caught red-handed trafficking in illicit drugs. It turned out he also had a side-hustle in intelligence-gathering. And the German engineer with Coke-bottle glasses who kindly offered to design the ingenious glass dance floor with blinking lights had a bigger plan. He had also installed listening devices; he was an East German spy.

With his self-styled status as the 'King of Nightlife' to defend, Prince Ali had soon set his sights on a new venture: a Chinese supper club. Within a few months the Golden Lotus opened its glinting doors to a pagoda-style restaurant with a splashing indoor waterfall and a sunken hexagonal bar. It was only streets from Shahr-e Nau in the upscale neighbourhood of Wazir Akbar Khan. Revenge was sweet – it was just around the corner from President Daoud's house.

These days Hazrat was less interested in the latest developments in Kabul's nightlife. He was increasingly preoccupied by his military service. He would soon start a second stint in the army. His first posting, before he had started work at the hotel, had been spent at an uneventful checkpost in Qargha, at a dam and reservoir of stunning beauty about five miles from the city centre. It had been an easy watch. When President Daoud was prime minister he had developed the area into a retreat for harried city-dwellers, with pink plastic swan-boats ferrying hand-holding lovers, Afghan families picnicking under wide-boughed trees, even a nine-hole golf course that became popular with diplomats.

Hazrat suspected his next stint would not be so idyllic. He was to guard a jagged mountain in Kabul, Koh-e Asamai, named after the Hindu goddess of hope. It was the site of an ancient fort besieged by British forces in the Second Anglo-Afghan War of 1879. And its namesake Hindu temple, nestled in its foothills, was one of the oldest in the capital.

The past, and politics, was far from his mind. At twenty-three, Hazrat was living from one day to the next, focused on supporting his family, catching up on courses to complete his high-school education, and now his military service for his country. He had neither the time, nor the money, for anything else. Not even marriage. God would provide that blessing when it was time.

CHAPTER 3

The Bloody Fall

Spring 1978

The soothing strains of European classical music wafted through the room. Alone in a guest suite, Hazrat had turned on the music system built into the bedside tables. The silky voice of the violins interlaced with the light seeping around the edges of the curtains.

He went about his work with a studied gaze, able to summon up his Inter-Continental training despite his absence from the hotel for the past several years. Coming back to this hill felt like a homecoming. Better, it was a promotion. He had risen from his job on the ground floor to join housekeeping on the storeys above. His new uniform was in a mustard-yellow trimmed with red collar and cuffs – a step up from the room boys in his department, who swept the floors and carried the rubbish away in their dark-blue tunics. He respected his co-workers, whatever their work. But he knew he was slowly but certainly making his way up the hospitality ladder. Only employees who earned the managers' trust were allowed to work in the guest rooms.

Hazrat pulled open the balcony door to let in the cool spring air. He knew exactly what to do. Cast a clean white sheet across the bed, tuck it tightly into corners, fluff the smooth white pillows, drape the fresh white towels over the bathroom rails – Inter-Continental insignia facing forward, naturally.

Before he took a last look around the room, he slipped onto the balcony to let the spring wash over him: the sprigs of green and first tight bunches of tiny flowers poking from the rolling vineyard; the chirping of swallows in the thickets of pines. *How simple*, he thought, *the happiness of birds*.

He was pleased that his rough interlude in the soldiers' world was over. His second military service hadn't been hard, in the end. There had been an easeful camaraderie in his unit. He and a fellow conscript even took turns taking care of each other's guns and of the lookout, while the other wielded a sledgehammer to smash stones on the mountainside. They sold them on for a little extra money; maximising every opportunity was Afghans' superpower.

But this five-star hotel was where he could, and would, excel. He knew that he knew about hotels. And he knew that his bosses knew it, too. When the Inter-Continental had organised a worldwide competition for its staff through its Six Continents Club, Hazrat had entered his own ideas on 'what makes a great hotel'. He had focused on blankets. He had absolute clarity on this matter, as he did on so many others. How they should be cleaned, how often, when they should be discarded: washed every week; changed every six months. Not long afterwards, his know-how was rewarded. He had received a Certificate of Special Merit for his 'outstanding entry', signed by the Club's president with all the names of the Board of Judges listed, a who's-who of the top brass running the show on all six continents.

For weeks it had put a bounce in his stride as he trundled his housekeeping trolley of lotions and linens down the hallway.

Hazrat awaited his prize with blissful anticipation: a plane ticket to fly around the world and visit other Inter-Continental hotels.

But the ticket didn't arrive. He had never boarded a Pan American Airways plane. Hazrat had wrestled with this issue. Could he have misunderstood? He never got a clear answer. He was told to forget about it. His new Afghan housekeeping manager, Mrs Trina, told him in no uncertain terms, 'Get on with your work.' She was a strict, efficient, no-nonsense boss, related to the former king through her own family, through marriage.

But it ate away at Hazrat. And the more he thought about it, the more he suspected that someone else, someone well connected, had snatched his prize. That hurt. He had stopped turning up for work – staying away to let Mrs Trina know that he had his honour, his dignity, to defend. She had kept calling him to come in.

Eventually he had relented. He gave in to her pleas when she asked him to help at a dinner that she hosted for high-up politicians in her high-society home. Hazrat knew she rated him and his work. She scolded him to try harder, do more to improve his English. 'You could go so much further,' she would say. And, in her matter-of-fact way, she would point to other employees, sometimes standing right next to him, who were doing exactly that. Hazrat understood its value. But he also knew what he had to do in his world; he didn't have to be told.

He vowed that some day he would fly away somewhere, just for a visit. His only travel so far had been across his own beautiful country as a tour guide. Now that the winter snows had all but melted, and temperatures were warming, the tourists would start coming again. These days they were often people, including foreigners living in neighbouring countries like Pakistan, India and Iran, who came to Kabul for the weekend, especially in the summer months. They were here to enjoy the city's high mountain air, as well as the lively nightlife and bazaars chock-a-block with treasures unavailable in their own cities. Business bosses from foreign capitals would start turning up, too. And the Rotary Club would keep holding its confabs and charity balls.

The next few days would be busy. A major international conference was about to kick off in Kabul. From the room's balcony Hazrat could see stretches of the road leading to this hill. Along this route, houses and fences had just been given fresh coats of white paint. Trees were neatly trimmed. President Daoud had ordered the clean-up to impress delegates who would fly into Kabul from all over the world and drive straight from the international airport to this international hotel. There was a new look to the president's policies, too. After the communists had helped him seize power in 1973, he had eased them out, one by one, and inched back to the former king's *bi-tarafi* neutrality. Daoud wanted friends in Washington as well as Moscow, including America's allies who were in power in neighbouring countries.

The president's own road had not been smooth, though. In the past ten days the city had churned with grief and rage. Thousands of protestors, brandishing banners and flags, had thronged the streets to condemn the death of Akbar Khaibar, a prominent ideologue in the communist PDPA. He had been murdered in his own home by two men who had roared up to his door on motorcycles. Left-wing intellectuals, who had been mostly moving in the shadows, were now out in the open – crying by Khaibar's graveside and cursing the government, yelling, 'Down with American imperialism! Down with the CIA!' as they marched past the US embassy. So many rumours swirled over who was to blame.

Eventually the clamour subsided and Kabul's regular rhythms

returned: the vendors' occasional hollers, the lilting *hoop-hoop-hoop* of the hoopoe birds. Besides, politics never got in the way of the partying. Last night the Inter-Continental ballroom had flowered with a 'Springtime Dance', a celebration of carousing and conspiring that drew the well-heeled. In the city Soviet diplomats had converged on the American Cultural Centre's library, smelling of new and old books, in what was billed as a Soviet–American Friendship night. The Russians had already fed and watered their American counterparts with large lashings of vodka at their own cultural centre in Kabul. But there was still an uneasy air in the city.

Hazrat looked down onto the terrace. Last night a storm had broken over Kabul. Cleaners were sweeping away puddles, twigs and leaves around the hotel pool and tennis courts, which were open again after their winter snooze. An Inter-Continental ad in the *Kabul Times* had urged readers to sign up for these members-only privileges. The hotel's in-house volleyball team was also in action in Kabul gyms, part of a so-called friendly tournament that had been set up by American diplomats who fielded a team of men and women called 'The Fighting Kachaloos'. Hazrat smiled to hear players called *kachaloos* – it meant 'potatoes' in Dari. Even sport couldn't escape the Cold War rivalries dividing Kabul. It had become a highly competitive, male-dominated league. Eastern Bloc squads wrangled over every point in every game. The Inter-Con's Afghan team displayed its own wiliness by secretly recruiting players from Afghanistan's top-flight national team – a strategy that had taken them all the way to a tense final between the United Nations and the Inter-Con.

As he moved from room to room, Hazrat found himself lingering in the quiet spaces on his floor. They were hard to find on days like this when the hotel was almost full, but he relished his rare moments of silence. Last night's evening news on Kabul Radio had been troubling. Prominent communists had been arrested on charges of treason and conspiracy to overthrow the government. They included names like Babrak Karmal, a founding member of the communist party whose resting face looked like a death-stare. And Nur Muhammad Taraki, the party's secretary-general, with his silver swept-back hair and a dark moustache tracing his upper lip. They were known to head rival factions that were often at each other's throats. But now they were accused of joining hands against the president. People suspected the mailed glove of the Soviet KGB.

This morning the Cabinet was meeting in the Dilkusha, the 'Heart's Delight' palace, inside the crenellated Arg citadel, to consider their sentence. The punishment for treason was often death. And in a country increasingly under one-man rule, President Daoud was certain to have already made up his mind.

A sudden sharp blast disrupted Hazrat from his musings, but it was only the noon gun. A rusting British cannon at the summit of Tap-e Top, Cannon Mountain, had been marking this hour ever since Afghanistan won its independence from British control in 1919. Its signal thundered across the city, spewing wispy trails of smoke into the city.

Hazrat, like so many others, set his clock by it. Twelve o'clock already. Time was flying by; there were rooms to ready. He picked up his pace. Yet he was soon stopped in his tracks again. Shouts ricocheted down the corridor. The metal door to the staff stairs kept banging sharply, opening and shutting. Young room boys hurried breathlessly from door to door, trembling like leaves in the wind. 'The tanks are shooting!'

With the boom of the noon gun, something had started. Tanks recently put in place to protect the presidential palace against possible plotters suddenly swung their turrets round and sent shells ripping into it. On the edge of the city a column of armoured vehicles snaked out of the military base shadowing the airport, slithering into the city to block key intersections and surrounding the Afghanistan Radio compound close to the US embassy. The hotel's telephones were ringing off the hook. Within minutes, hearsay and I-saw-it-myself accounts were coursing down the wires – warning of the clanking of tank tracks, the whistle of bullets, the stomach-churning sight of soldiers' bodies splayed on the streets, rivulets of red blood staining the grey cement.

Many of the hotel staff seemed lost. Some froze on the spot. Some discreetly turned the dial on radio sets sitting on desks. Others ran frantically to the lobby, looking for a source of reliable information. Hazrat watched his colleagues tripping down the stairs or zipping to the ground floor in the lifts, to look up at the radio. It stared back. It had gone silent. The telephone lines were dead, too.

But the skies soon spoke. Hazrat legged it to his favourite watch-post, the lobby's wraparound windows, to listen and look. Others crowded in, open-mouthed. Soviet MiG fighter jets, piloted by the Afghan air force, screamed across the city, streaking white trails across the blue. You could hear the distant thump of tank fire and the rolls of rattling machine guns drifting towards the hill. Soon a rhythm started to emerge. A few minutes of shellfire, then silence. A few minutes more, then more silence. The silences were worse, filled only by horrors conjured by the imagination. No one had ever heard or seen anything like it. Even the swallows scattered.

Employees on the afternoon shift were still tumbling into the lobby with stories of what they had heard and seen. The sounds in the centre, around the presidential palace, were deafening.

74

Armoured vehicles were grinding slowly down the city streets, clearly searching for people. Tank shells were punching through walls, striking strategic ministries such as Defence and Interior, hitting the radio complex, sailing over the US embassy. But many were missing their mark, slamming into gardens, crashing through windows, shrapnel killing people in their yards and homes. The Ariana Hotel next to the Arg was on fire. The most ferocious firefight of all was inside the palace; Daoud's troops were fighting back.

By mid-afternoon a different darkness fell across Kabul. Storm clouds had closed in. Rain pounded the streets, wind whipped through the trees. Thunderclaps scratched the skies, grounding the warplanes. The radio was now quivering intermittently with staticky martial music and appeals for calm, from voices vowing to root out 'anti-revolutionary elements'. Managers urged staff to get on with their work. They wanted to create a business-as-usual bubble for the guests huddled in anxious bunches in the bar or on the balconies. That wasn't easy, though. When the skies turned blue again, low-flying planes surged overhead, bombs dropping from their bellies into the palace.

That night Kabul Radio sputtered back into life with a chilling announcement: 'The power of the family has been put to an end. Now, for the first time, power has come into the hands of the people.' There was a sharp intake of breath. It must be the communists. Lieutenant-General Abdul Qader, commander of a new 'revolutionary council', soon appeared on the airwaves to convey that the new order would remain 'democratic, Islamic, reformist and non-aligned'. He reassured the outside world they would honour 'international commitments and will respect [their] neighbours and the honourable and respectful religion of Islam'. And to the Afghan people he promised the 'protection of the people's honour . . . The National Revolutionary Council is looking after your rights.' A 10 p.m. curfew was in force; battles still raged in the streets.

The next day dawned with even darker news. Kabul Radio announced that Daoud was 'gone completely and for ever'. Few details were given, but the gist was clear. No one in the hotel could find out more. They were trapped. Two tanks had clanked into position at the bottom of the hill – one blocking the road to the Inter-Continental, the other to the Bagh-e Bala restaurant. No one was allowed to leave or enter.

Thursday rolled into Friday and then Saturday. Stuck in the hotel, staff took refuge in the routine of daily chores. Reception-ists comforted guests. Accountants buried their worries in trying to balance the books, fuelled by coffee and fear. Chefs whipped up special dishes, turning tender steaks and scrumptious cakes into weapons of distraction. Hazrat and the little army of house-keepers kept freshening up rooms, trying to air them of anxiety. And all the while, the sounds of a city's unspooling blew up to the hotel on the spring winds.

For two nights and three days, for seventy-two hours, the Inter-Continental staff and guests were pinned down in the hotel. When they were eventually let out, they spilled into streets where they could still taste the smoke, still smell the gunpowder. Streets where everyone had a story. Hundreds were dead, more likely thousands.

President Daoud had gone down with his gun. Surrounded by family who refused to leave his side, he had drawn his pistol on the mutinous soldiers who came demanding his surrender. The first family had been killed, one after another, eighteen in all, including children and grandchildren – some just toddlers, one not even a year old. Their bodies had been tossed into trucks, taken away in the dark, corpses and crimes covered in the dirt of unmarked graves.

The Republic of Afghanistan was now the Democratic Republic of Afghanistan, born in the *Saur* Revolution, the April Revolution. The new leaders took pains to say they weren't communists, that this wasn't a Soviet-backed coup. Not many believed them, but reports soon circulated that the Russians had also first heard about it on the radio.

Whoever they were, the new rulers weren't done with the Inter-Con. They came for the files first. A few days after the coup, soldiers in olive uniforms marched in, demanding, 'Where are the documents?' They stomped across the lobby and down the stairs to the management offices, trying to find out what the hotel had been up to. They wanted to see everything: the tourist brochures, the reels from the government's Afghan Film agency, anything the hotel had used to advertise itself, to promote Afghanistan; all the images of a country that once upon a time had a smiling king welcoming presidents and prime ministers from East and West, waving to excited crowds on Independence Day or at a spirited *buzkashi* match. Snapshots of a president with a shiny bald head and a hint of a smile greeting dignitaries. Hotel flyers for German and Scandinavian buffets, American Thanksgiving, Parisian fashion shows, Rotary Club charity balls. Photographs of happy hotel teams on marketing missions to Bangkok, Bahrain, Dhahran and Dubai to bring more guests to Kabul. Heavy boots trudged from floor to floor, invading the suites where some managers lived, rough hands rifling through cupboards and cabinets. Books and clothes were hurled from balconies into the forecourt.

Then they came for the staff. Anyone with royal connections – who had links with what the radio had called 'the power of the family' – was a suspect. One of the first to go was a manager married to one of the former king's relatives. A man in a blue suit who didn't give his name showed up after breakfast one day and took him for a little walk. The manager returned for his bags, and his wife. Staff working that day formed a tearful line to bid him goodbye, not knowing where he was going, but suspecting the worst.

It wasn't only the hotel where this happened. For months, soldiers went from house to house taking people away. They came for hotel staff like Fauzia and Zia, for top soldiers, senior officials, civil servants, teachers, students, religious leaders, business people. The Pul-e Charkhi prison built by President Daoud on the eastern edge of Kabul was full to bursting, heavily guarded. Stories emerged of people crammed into dirt-floored cells, living on little more than watery soup and the thick-crusted black loaves from the Soviet-built Silo bakery just down the street from the hotel. At night they had one thin grey blanket to sleep on, another to sleep under. Guards took the mattresses away. When some prisoners protested, they were told with a sneer, 'This isn't the Inter-Continental.'

In time, some detainees were let out. But many disappeared into the black hole of the prison. Everyone inside could hear the sounds. The cries of detainees tortured to extract confessions. The commotion in the dead of night as people were dragged away. When darkness fell, prisoners in top-floor cells could watch the headlights of vehicles moving along the main road – some convoys turning towards the cell blocks, others heading to the execution grounds. The crack of a pistol often kept piercing the night.

Some, tipped off that they were on the blacklist, fled to avoid arrest. Prince Ali, a fixture around the hotel from the first days, was among them. Sultan Malikyar, Hazrat's former boss at the Paizar, was on a business trip at the time and didn't come home.

They shut their businesses, restaurants and clubs, locked their villas, leaving almost everything behind and slipping away. Some left in disguise, hiding under all-enveloping *chadris*, or dressed as hippies on the Pakistan bus service to the border. Others squeezed inside the secret compartments of oil tankers or in the elaborately painted jingle trucks that ferried goods back and forth every day. Many of the hotel's most familiar faces, staff and guests, disappeared overnight.

In their stead came new workers and bosses, many of them card-carrying members of the PDPA. More spooks loitered in the lobby. The new leader's eyes and ears were everywhere. Staff felt that Nur Muhammad Taraki, president of the Democratic Republic and general secretary of the Revolutionary Council, was looking right at them. And he was – a framed portrait of their greying leader, with his bushy eyebrows and a black brush of a moustache, stared out from behind the front desk and from the walls of the management offices. In some images his smile was so wide you could see the gleam of his back teeth capped in gold.

Everything had changed, but nothing had changed. The Soviet-built tanks, which had helped push President Taraki into power, were pulled back from the streets. The gaping holes they punched in the high wall encircling the presidential palace were filled in; now it was known as the 'People's House'. And the Inter-Continental Kabul was still the city's finest and only international hotel. It simply kept carrying on as a five-star hotel should, from one season to the next.

When autumn gave way to winter, Swiss and Afghan chefs kept their heads down as they laid out a warming buffet every Friday. A *Frühschoppen* brunch in the Austrian and German style. The hotel's *Nowruz* new-year celebration in the spring equinox of 1979 still tried to bring a buzz, urging Kabul residents to 'swing the night away'. The Esquire Set drew in affluent foreigners as well as Afghans who still felt safe enough to stay in their city. Yet even in the bright sun of summer there was no escaping the dark pall that hung over this city. Some of the happy-go-lucky fizz of the Inter-Con's early years was gone. The hotel hadn't lost its allure. But it had a new aura.

CHAPTER 4

Red Christmas

Winter 1979

A guest stood at the front desk. The counter was so polished the clerk saw the visitor's face looking at him from two directions. There had been little else to do but polish. It was 30 December 1979. The dawn of a new decade on the calendar that most of the world followed. No one checking out; no one checking in. Until the arrival of this young man with a tousled mop of blond hair and outsized black-rimmed glasses.

The visitor flashed a schoolboy smile and said his name. 'Mr François Lochon. From France.' The sombre-suited reception-ist wrote it, slowly and carefully, on a stiff white registration card, with Mr Lochon's instructions. L-o-c-h-o-n. A photographer. Working for an agency called Gamma. He was in a rush. *Non*, he didn't need his key. *Non*, he didn't need to see his room. *Merci!* 'Thank you!' He yanked his bulging camera bag across his thick winter coat and headed straight back out the door.

The hands of the clocks had moved only inches when another blast of December's breath blew through the doors, announcing a second visitor. 'Mr Robert from America. Robert Reid.' Easier to pronounce. Easier to spell. 'Mr Bob' would be fine, he informed them, as he handed over his credit card, a requirement of every guest to ensure they wouldn't do a runner. The hotel needed every American dollar it could get these days.

Brown-haired Mr Bob said he was a writer. The poker-faced clerk faithfully wrote that on his card. The American had flown in on the same overnight flight from Frankfurt as Mr Lochon. It was an Ariana Afghan Airlines flight, the first civilian carrier to taxi down the tarmac in days. Only about a dozen passengers had been on it.

Mr Bob joked, in his chatty American way, that he'd been told even the pilots were scared to fly. The receptionist smiled politely. A real Afghan would never admit to being frightened. But 'the guest is always right'. That was Inter-Continental training. Mr Bob, on his first trip to Afghanistan, had been told the Inter-Con was the place to stay. He asked about phones. Only house-phones worked at the moment. All landlines, connecting to anywhere outside this hotel, were dead. A rectangular metal slab of a room key was carefully lifted from a little hook. All the other pigeonholes were full, resembling birds perching in their nests.

The American made his way to the lift as the eager young bellboy, just a hint of facial hair above his lip, clutched his luggage. With a ding and a swish, the elevator took them to his floor. In no time at all, with another ping, Mr Bob was back in the lobby, heading out. 'To explore the city,' he informed them. The receptionist offered another half-smile, raising a quizzical eyebrow once the honoured guest was out of sight.

The cleaner appeared with his bucket and broom to wipe away the puddles of slush and dirt left by winter boots, before retreating to his chair in a far corner. Only the hands of the clock moved, a metronome of this monotony. In the back offices, staff added up numbers or doodled. One clerk stood guard at the reception desk, occasionally glancing at the door. Word had reached the hotel that another Ariana Afghan Airlines flight, this time from Delhi, had landed; a rare sight among the Soviet military transporters and MiG fighter jets touching down and taking off.

But when the revolving door swished around again, it was only Mr Bob. He lingered in the lobby for a little while, wearing his easy smile, then ordered a taxi to go back out again. 'To explore.' Yet before his clapped-out yellow cab had wheezed up to the entrance, the front door juddered with another blast of freezing air. A burly Afghan immigration official barged in, trailed by a posse of police bearing rifles and clad in pillbox hats. 'I got you!' he bellowed with a menacing laugh. He pointed at Mr Bob, sending his security detail closing in on the American. 'Why did you lie to me at the airport? You're a journalist!' the official said.

'I'm a writer!' Mr Bob protested. 'I said I was a writer.'

The apparatchik's chest heaved with fury in his olive-green coat. 'You're a journalist. Come with us. We have special procedures for journalists.'

The receptionists lowered their gaze as Mr Bob was given a moment to collect his belongings from his room. Then he was back to hand over his bulky key and retrieve an unused credit slip. The bellboy, feeling a pang of pity, held fast to his guest's luggage. No one said anything as the vice-squad and their victim squeezed through the revolving door, bellboy in tow. The receptionists exchanged furtive glances. One, a party loyalist unable to hide his smirk, tore Mr Bob's registration card into small pieces. Another, a little sad about the lost guest, tucked the key back into its pigeonhole. He took out a cloth to give the counter another little polish.

The lobby went silent once more. The more time passed, the

louder the tick-tock of the clocks. Until, as the last light slipped from the sky, the receptionists heard a crunch of tyres on the snowy crust of the forecourt. The bright-yellow high beams of a bus lit up the evergreens, playing with the festive lights festooning their branches. Moments later there came an unhappy mumble from outside.

A clutch of glum journalists was piling into the lobby. Until a few hours ago they had been telling themselves, and each other, how lucky they were: the first hacks who had managed to bag a seat on one of the most coveted flights on Fleet Street, and in newsrooms the world over. The first journalists to make it to Kabul for 'the biggest story in the world!' – the Soviet invasion of Afghanistan.

The year of 1979 had been one like no other, even for a city that had lived through two coups in six years. In just over half a decade Afghanistan had gone from being a monarchy to a republic to a democratic republic, its Soviet leanings only barely disguised. Enthusiastic tour groups from Western cities had stopped showing up in large numbers. Western business executives had started staying away. And this year everything had escalated even further.

It had started on 14 February, with the murder of the American ambassador in a room in the Kabul Hotel. Shortly before 9 a.m. the popular diplomat Adolph Dubs, nicknamed 'Spike', had been on his way to the embassy when his bulletproof Oldsmobile was stopped at gunpoint by armed Afghan men posing as police. They hustled him into the hotel, into Room 117. By early afternoon Ambassador Dubs was dead. Afghan police had stormed the chamber in a hail of gunfire, ostensibly to rescue him, tailed by a phalanx of Soviets, including the Kabul chief of Moscow's KGB security agency. Nobody could say who had fired the bullet that killed Ambassador Dubs. Was it the shadowy group of kidnappers demanding the release of a political prisoner? Or was it the KGB?

The envoy's assassination was cloaked in suspicion and sorrow, like so much in Kabul these days. And it wasn't just Kabul. A nervousness had begun to colour the entire region. On that same blood-stained Valentine's Day, militants in next-door Iran attacked the American embassy in Tehran. Tensions had been deepening since Iran's revolutionary leader Aya-tollah Khomeini had returned from exile two weeks previously; now, Islamists took a US marine hostage and briefly occupied the mission. Then, in April 1979, another crisis flared to the east. Pakistan's charismatic prime minister, Zulfikar Ali Bhutto, was overthrown and hanged in a military coup by one of his generals, Zia-ul-Haq. The new military strongman was proving to be a staunch American ally, willing to back the growing revolt against Afghanistan's left-wing leaders and their Soviet friends.

In Kabul, month on month, Soviet advisors were slipping into government offices, into military bases, hiding in plain sight. Russian commandos were reinforcing Afghan forces who had been struggling to stem the uprising of men calling themselves *mujahideen*, warriors of *jihad*, against the infidels. The unrest was starting to spread through farmers' fields and villages across Afghanistan, causing a wave of army defections and desertions. Politicians in the capital were fighting a battle of another kind, as rival factions in the ruling party vied for supremacy.

Suddenly it was all change again. In September every portrait of the president in the Inter-Con was quickly pulled down. The big framed one in the lobby behind the front desk, the smaller ones behind glass in the management offices, the little paper ones tacked here and there. Even the multicoloured postage stamps stored in drawers showing President Taraki and a tank were ripped to shreds.

The president was dead. Kabul Radio solemnly announced that 'ill health and nervous weakness' had taken the life of the man once hailed as the 'Great Leader' and 'Great Teacher'. But the city's scuttlebutt carried a far different account. It had been death-by-pillows. The sixty-two-year-old leader was smothered in his bed.

There were reports of a bloody shootout in the presidential palace between Taraki's supporters and those of his deputy, Hafizullah Amin, his clever protégé who had created the president's flowery sobriquets. Amin had called himself Taraki's 'Faithful Student'. Clever, and cunning. Many suspected he had really been in charge for a while: the henchman behind the purges in which the PDPA's *Parcham* faction had been sent abroad as ambassadors, or to death in prison. It was said that Amin had ordered his dear comrade snuffed out.

New portraits went up. Amin in a tailored suit and tie, clean-shaven and even more dark-browed than the last president. Amin, the former teacher who went to study at Columbia University in New York, was drawn into radical student politics and came home a Marxist. It was said he kept a framed portrait of the Soviet leader Joseph Stalin on his desk. Others suspected he was a CIA spy. Truth was as hard to find as flowers blooming in an Afghan winter. Only the hardiest pushed through the thick snow.

There was unrest across the western border, just as there had been in February. In November 1979 Iranian students, foot soldiers of the Islamic revolution, took over the US embassy for a second time, in a significant escalation, taking dozens of American diplomats and citizens hostage. There was nothing brief about it this time round; they would hold the hostages for months. A few borders away, in the Saudi kingdom, the sacred Grand Mosque of Mecca was besieged by Islamists calling for the end of the House of Saud and a stop to the country's modernisation. The region trembled. The world shook.

But the hotel's American Thanksgiving went ahead – a 'typical Thanksgiving luncheon' at the Bamiyan Brasserie and, at the Pamir Supper Club, 'a dinner buffet in the traditional western atmosphere' – whatever the streets outside had to say. White-toqued European chefs hid any nervousness under their hats as they stuffed imported turkeys and mashed Afghan spuds with an abundance of butter. And if desserts could hug, their cakes did it. On flagpoles across the city, and in the hotel forecourt, the new national flag fluttered – blazing red with two bright-gold stalks of wheat and a star in its top-left corner. It was emblazoned with the word *Khalq*, 'the People', and a ribbon banner that hailed the communist coup of the previous year.

Red was also the colour of the Inter-Continental in December. These were the last lingering weeks of the pomegranate season, its tart ruby juice served in tall glasses. It was the season of Santa Claus lookalikes, with wild white beards and rounded bellies squashed into scarlet tunics and trousers. On Christmas Eve what was left of *le tout* Kabul's expatriate community, including Western diplomats, CIA spooks, aid officials and a small sprinkling of well-to-do Afghans, slipped into the shimmering lifts to ascend to the roof of the city. Entertainment options in Kabul, for a certain kind of clientele, had dwindled. The Americans, the Germans, the United Nations – all had their own clubs in which to drink and dine. But the Pamir Supper Club was packed: a place to rise above daily crises and cares and to drink in the view. With a curfew still in force, that also meant taking up the hotel's special offers to spend the night.

They descended on the Pamir, a favourite haunt resplendent

in red-clothed tables, each topped with chimneyed oil lamps and brass goblets brimming with drink. The kitchen's swinging doors flapped back and forth as waiters in smart crimson dinner jackets and pressed white shirts wove through the tables – expertly balancing a tray with one hand, emptying ashtrays with another.

In the din of the Inter-Con dance floor, spies and envoys, expatriates and Afghans, let their hair and their guard down, the sound of the city drowned out by the music. The Esquire Set belted out their favourites, as well as the requests shouted out by guests. Someone always cried, 'Play "Hotel California"!' and they always obliged. No evening was complete without it, nor a rousing rendition of 'Kung Fu Fighting'. The nimbler merry-makers had a go at the limbo, inching their bodies under the long pole before collapsing in a heap of laughter. Beyond the icy windows Kabul twinkled, its tapestry of light stitched from the glowing apartment-block windows, hurricane lamps in mud homes, wood fires on freezing streets and a sky full of stars.

In the witching hours past midnight, a low buzz began to fill the night. Husky grey planes, red stars on their fuselages, rumbled over Kabul. One after another, just minutes apart, bombers and transporters taxied down the ice-ridged tarmac. It was Christmas Day. The Soviet invasion had begun.

Well before dawn on Christmas morning, two-way security radios in Inter-Con rooms hissed into life. 'Have you seen what's happening in Kabul?' The devices, carried by expatriates, from UN workers to spies, had been placed on bedside tables when their owners fell into their room's silken pillows and sheets.

As the sun rose over a flat grey winter's day, the Soviet airlift continued. Bulky transporters ferrying soldiers and supplies kept coming in, day and night. Troops and tanks were also clattering into Afghanistan across the northern Soviet border. Russians in yellow-brown jackets started staking out strategic junctions; Afghan soldiers' serge uniforms disappeared. Sporadic gunfire pocked the cold.

Kabul Radio avoided mentioning the invasion. The news, as always, came from foreign stations, mainly the BBC. Night after night experts from East and West weighed in on why the Soviets had intervened. Some said they had moved reluctantly, weary of the PDPA backstabbing that was tearing the government apart. Others pointed to anxiety about the impact of Afghanistan's growing Islamist uprising on Muslims in the Soviet Union. Still others insisted it was a signal of Moscow's imperial ambitions.

Whatever their reasons, the Soviets were making their presence felt. Two nights after Christmas an Inter-Continental banquet room thrummed with chit-chat and the clink of glasses and forks. The Soviet minister of communication, Nikolai Vladimirovich Talyzin, was hosting a get-together for a select group of senior Afghan officials. Rumour had it that he had flown into Kabul to oversee the accelerating invasion. Shots of vodka, neat and strong, were knocked back along with the food. Waiters in black jackets and white gloves threaded through the crush of drunken dark suits.

Elsewhere in Kabul, Soviet military advisors were entertaining some of their brothers-in-arms in the Afghan forces. It was jolly there, too, Afghan officers disguising whether they were relieved, or uneasy about Moscow's move. As both events wound down, the mood suddenly switched. All the guests were taken away by their Soviet hosts, nobody knew where. Hotel staff could only watch as they went into the night. No one dared ask any questions. Even questions had consequences.

The next day, Kabul Radio started to bring the answers that Afghans had been waiting for.

'At last, after terrible sufferings and tribulations, the day has come of freedom and rebirth of all the fraternal peoples of Afghanistan,' a familiar-sounding voice announced on state radio. 'Today is the breaking of the machine of torture of Amin and his henchmen, wild butchers, usurpers and murderers of tens of thousands of our countrymen, fathers, mothers, brothers, sisters, sons and daughters, children and old people.'

Rumours had been circulating about a bloodbath in Tajbeg Palace, the stately mansion on a gentle knoll in the south-west of Kabul. President Amin, increasingly anxious about possible Afghan–Soviet plots, had been persuaded to move from his city-centre citadel to a more remote royal residence. Accounts on the BBC had spoken of a massive night-time assault on Tajbeg, in which hundreds of Afghan guards and soldiers were reported to have been slaughtered by the Soviets. Two of Amin's sons, aged nine and eleven, were killed. Now Kabul Radio confirmed some of the details. The president was dead; it informed the nation that he 'had been sentenced to death at a revolutionary trial for crimes against the state and that sentence has been carried out'.

Questions whirled. Was it all lies? Was their leader's life really ended by a trial or in a random burst of gunfire, or even a targeted assassination? Some said that earlier that day a Soviet KGB agent posing as a cook had tried to poison the president. The carbonation in his Coca-Cola seemed to have saved him; it diluted the poison, meaning it only left him ill and groggy. Not that it made any difference in the end anyway.

The Inter-Continental staff got their hammers and nails out again. Portraits came down; new ones went up. Now it was President Babrak Karmal, with his prominent nose and pointy hairline, keeping a watchful eye behind the front desk and in the management offices. A former student rabble rouser who had spent time in prison, Karmal was a co-founder of the PDPA and a member of the less extreme, more Soviet-leaning faction of *Parcham*, the 'Flag'.

It was Karmal's voice that had announced Amin's death on the radio. But Karmal had not been in Kabul when he said it. After falling out with his PDPA rivals in 1978, he had been sent away to Prague as an ambassador, then went into hiding under Soviet protection. The day after his speech, as 1979 somersaulted to an end, the Soviets flew him into Kabul. Afghans reeled from the third murder of their president in less than two years.

By the night of 30 December the Inter-Continental was filled with journalists, a lot of them unhappy. They had managed to arrive on one of the first Ariana Afghan Airlines flights to land since Soviet troops took over the airfield. They had made it out of the terminal, into the icy streets of the world's most prized dateline, but they had been chased down, one by one, by beady-eyed spies and dutiful police. Tense standoffs had drawn curious crowds. 'We're not leaving! We have a right to be here!' the journalists had shouted. But Western reporters and their questions were not welcome at this moment. Time was not on the appa-ratchiks' side; the last civilian flight of the day had already flown into the gloom. As the sun slipped behind the Kabul skyline, the journalists were bundled into a government bus and escorted under armed guard to the hotel, told not to leave the premises until the next flight out the following day.

Mr Bob, 'the writer' from the Associated Press, was among them; there had been no flight left for him to board, either. He was in no rush this second time around as he faithfully wrote his details on a stiff white registration card: 'Robert Reid. American. Associated Press. Journalist. One night.' As he handed over his credit card again, the party loyalist at reception didn't bother to hide his disappointment to see him return.

They were now under house-arrest. Hotel-arrest – the Inter-Continental their luxury prison. They couldn't file a word, couldn't even alert editors and families to their plight. There were no international telephone lines. No telexes. No satellites. So they spent the evening in the Nuristan Cocktail Lounge, downing cold beers, ears pricking up with every stammer of gunfire from the streets below and every screech of a warplane from the skies above. Nobody could suppress the pang that they were missing a story.

Everyone except François Lochon, of the French photo agency Gamma, who had been the first to check in that morning. He paid for his room and never came back, grabbing one of many empty seats on the last flight out of Kabul, his precious film rolls hidden in his boots. He had managed to whip around the city, snapping everything. The tented Soviet encampment at the airport, bristling with armoured vehicles, smoke from wood fires drifting in the winter's air. The steel stockade of military trucks at the presidential palace. One photo captured ruddy-faced Russian troops poking out of a tank, stirring memories of past invasions when Moscow's men had rolled into Budapest in 1956 and Prague in 1968.

As Lochon flew out, savouring his scoop, snowflakes started tumbling gently to the ground. By morning a thick white blanket covered Kabul, including the airfield. No commercial planes would be flying in or out. The Inter-Continental's special guests would spend another day here, at least.

They were advised to head to the top floor for the best breakfast the hotel could offer. The Pamir Supper Club, its wooden chairs upholstered in inviting red weave, offered a splendid view of an Afghan winter wonderland. Waiters in traditional waistcoats produced outsized menus with a flourish, each emblazoned with the familiar Inter-Continental insignia.

'An omelette please,' one journalist said. 'Sorry, we are out of eggs,' the waiter replied apologetically. 'Sausages for me, please,' chimed in another. The waiter paused, shifting onto his other foot uncomfortably. 'Sorry, we don't have any this morning.' The diners skimmed the menu for something else edible. 'Cheese?' The waiter shook his head, as nonplussed as his guests. Nothing had reached their kitchens so far this morning. Even bakers and butchers were lying low after the sudden entrance of the Soviets, and now all this snow. 'So what do you have?' the journalist asked. The answer came with a cheeky grin: 'Beer!'

So beer it was. By the time a US diplomat journeyed up the hill to check on the journalists – and to offer to send messages on their behalf from the embassy to let editors and families know they were safe – some in the press pack were a bit tipsy. Mr Bob tried, unsuccessfully, to embed a bit of news in his missive in code.

A long day stretched ahead for the frustrated guests, and the bored spooks lurking in the lobby. Journalists broke the monotony by hunkering down with diplomats who came bearing insights into Moscow's moves. Friendly snowball fights in the forecourt also helped pass the time. Afghan staff watched through windows framed in snow, grinning enviously. A sympathetic guard keeping watch from the portico even furtively confided to one guest, 'We don't like foreigners taking over our country.' But that was as much as he dared to say.

When the last hours of 1979 could be counted on one hand, the hill was transformed again. A procession of snow-dusted sedans ferried women in fancy frocks and men in well-cut suits up to the New Year's celebrations at the Inter-Continental. The hotel touted a 'superb set menu' to welcome in 1980, 'on the top of Kabul'. Black tie was requested. Hotel staff had scoured the bazaars all day to secure the ingredients for a suitably sumptuous meal.

And the music hadn't died. The Esquire Set was in fine form, warming up the packed Pamir Supper Club with Bee Gees hits. 'Tragedy' had become a favourite of late. They dialled up the mood with disco beats. A rousing version of 'Night Fever' and Gloria Gaynor's uplifting 'I Will Survive' brought party-goers to their feet, in a tangle of polished dress shoes and strappy high heels. Skirts swirled. Jackets flew open.

The journalists joined the revelry. So too did some of the diplomats who only hours earlier had been briefing them in sombre, sober tones. Two-way field radio sets were tucked into purses or set on tables, just in case.

Mr Bob felt an odd sense of déjà vu. He'd spent the previous New Year's Eve at the Inter-Continental in Tehran. He was in that wave of reporters who had flooded into Iran to cover protests against the ruling Shah. A night-time curfew had kept them indoors there, too. In Tehran in 1978 they had welcomed in the new year in a tenth-floor suite with a well-stocked bar, solely for journalists. They had enjoyed a functioning telephone switchboard as well. No such luck in Kabul.

But there was not time to dwell on that. The countdown had begun, drunken shouts bouncing off the Pamir's roof. As 1979 ticked into a new decade, a rowdy crowd thrown together in a political earthquake came together over cherished rituals. Nothing else seemed certain now.

PART II

The Red Years

CHAPTER 5

Amanullah's Ambition

Winter 1981

It was, without question, the best place to be. At least for now. In one direction, at the top of the hill, the Inter-Continental Kabul; in the other direction, at the bottom, the Soviet-built Polytechnic University. A place between the capital's most luxurious building, where one day he'd like to work, and its best engineering school, where one day he'd like to study. For now, nineteen-year-old Amanullah was standing guard in his dull green-grey police uniform, his Russian AK-47 automatic rifle at the ready. He was performing his personal duty: carrying out his military service defending Kabul's finest hotel.

Things could have been worse. Much worse. He could have been sent to a far-flung checkpost in the provinces, where the armed uprising against Russia's presence was steadily building. He could have been sent to an even more distant rim of Kabul, where the fighters calling themselves *mujahideen* were lying in wait: long-bearded Islamic warriors, nineteenth-century British rifles slung over their shoulders or held close under traditional wraparound shawls, waiting to pounce. Amanullah heard about it on Kabul Radio and Radio Moskva – where voices denounced the 'bandits' backed by 'American imperialists and their Pakistani and Iranian puppets'. If he was at home he would huddle around the staticky radio set with his family, cross-legged on carpets, listening to reports on foreign stations. The BBC World Service was now broadcasting in Pashto as well as Persian, and the Voice of America (VOA) had started a service in Dari; a Pashto service was coming. Even listening was dangerous these days, regarded as suspicious, even treacherous.

His place, for now, was as good as it gets. 'You're educated!' his commander had exclaimed when he saw Amanullah's graduation certificate from Naderia High School, embossed with its impressive red stamp. The officer beamed from behind his jumble of a desk, piled with teetering files. So few who showed up in front of him could boast a qualification. He also took to Amanullah's easy smile, the gentle hint of humour that tugged at his cheeks and lifted the thin beginnings of a moustache. 'We're sending you to the Inter-Con,' he announced. 'You'll know how to behave with guests going in and out. You'll know how to work with hotel managers.' A good boy; that's what Amanullah was.

And a lucky boy, too. *Lotf Khoda*, by God's grace. As the son of a farmer from the neighbouring district of Paghman, his father had died of cancer when Amanullah was just five years old. He was the last in a family of ten – five sons, five daughters. His eldest brother dutifully supported the family with his modest earnings from teaching in the Lycée Khushal Khan Khattak, a west-Kabul boarding school that trained students from rural areas to become teachers in their villages. His mother, whose education went no further than the Quranic verses she could recite from memory, wanted more for her last-born. Most Afghan parents, at least those who understood the importance of education – and many did – wanted their sons to become doctors or engineers; some even wished this good fortune for their daughters, too. Amanullah was determined to do her proud. He would become a learned man.

From his guard post he caught glimpses of the students, young men and women, going to and from the Polytechnic down the road, textbooks under their arms, sometimes an easy gait, sometimes a hurried jog. Some day that would be him: not a gun-slinging policeman, but a student with an open mind and an armful of engineering books. He'd have to learn Russian to study at the Polytechnic. He'd master that, too.

For now, his horizons were much narrower. They stretched across three different lookouts. On some shifts, Amanullah was posted in the hotel forecourt, outside the ballroom that lay perpendicular to the hotel's principal building. On others, he stood watch from the opposite side of the forecourt, on top of the gentle incline paved over for parking. And sometimes he was posted on the side of the hotel facing the city, on the lower terrace dotted with the oblong pool, the rectangular tennis courts and the pointed cabanas. All three guardhouses were quite spartan. But they were luxurious compared to the countryside. In summer they were cooled with electric fans, in winter warmed by electric heaters. No need to rub his hands over the fires whose woody smoke suffused the chilly streets of Kabul.

As he looked over the hotel and the city, Amanullah could glimpse another life – being inside the building looking out, rather than outside looking in. The ballroom position was the best for imagining that. From here, he could see the moustachioed doorman pacing back and forth between the sky-blue pillars of the portico in his impressive knee-length coat, his barrel chest decorated with an ever-expanding galaxy of lapel badges gifted to him by guests. His name was Shahabuddin, 'king of the stars'. Every so often Shahabuddin's forecourt would come alive, echoing with the clunk of car doors and snatches of chit-chat drifting across the concrete. Sometimes the doorman would even natter with the guests – his traditional turban, wrapped loosely around his head, jiggling as he laughed, his walrus moustache looking even larger. With other visitors he was more formal, even reverential.

Amanullah's job was very different. He wasn't welcoming guests; he was sizing them up. He wasn't meant to exude warmth; he was meant to ooze authority. There was a way to stand, a way to work. He didn't expect the *dushman*, the enemy, to suddenly leap out of the almond and apricot trees, or to peer menacingly through the conifers' foliage. But he was on alert. They all were. Soviet helicopters circled in the skies, tank tracks rattled on the streets below. In daylight hours it was mostly Afghan soldiers poking their heads out of those metal hatches, many of them just as young as him. But some were unmistakably Russian: pink faces and tufts of light hair escaping from their green metal helmets or grey hats adorned with a Soviet red star and a hammer and sickle. Amanullah usually spied them on his night-shifts, when the Red Army men moved from their tented encampments outside Kabul to come into the streets to enforce the curfew.

Salaam Alaikum, Amanullah would call out to Shahabuddin at the start of his shift. *Walaikum Assalaam*, the doorman would reply. The traditional courtesies shot back and forth like a tennis match. *Chetor asted? Sa'at shoma khub? Familie-e shoma khub ast?* 'How are you? How is your health? Your family is fine?' These first replies were always short and sweet, whether one's near and dear were well or unwell. That was the tradition, strictly respected.

Then they got on with their work. Black sedans, some with flapping flags from East or West, would come to a halt not far from Amanullah's boots, their bonnets so shiny he could discreetly check if his police cap was correctly placed. Ambassadors or other bigwigs in back seats staring straight ahead from behind car windows, the curtains only slightly parted to give away as little as possible. Drivers and bodyguards, some smiley, others officious or obnoxious, insisting on immediate right of way. The buses of visitors from brotherly communist countries, whose passengers showed up shaking revolutionary fists from behind steamed-up windows. Not to mention the journalists – almost always Western – who pulled up in beat-up yellow taxis or high-security state-provided minivans.

In such moments Amanullah felt the distance between his world and the hotel's. That feeling was most pronounced when their food arrived. Three times a day grimy green trucks trundled up the hill, snarling and snorting and dripping diesel, ferrying hot steel cauldrons of food for the guards. *Biya Polis!* 'Police, come here!' the drivers would bellow, before idling in the forecourt, sometimes for more than an hour, spewing blasts of black smoke as they doled out their grub. Their presence burst the five-star bubble. Amanullah felt the stares burning into his uniform, the finely dressed wedding guests and restaurant-goers wondering – sometimes worrying – about what the trucks were doing here.

Most of the time Amanullah didn't have much time to think about it. But sometimes he found it weighing upon him. Until one day, in a moment of silence between the chatter of magpies and the warplanes' screech, he concocted a plan. When he saw his chance, he seized it.

He caught sight of the hotel manager alighting from his car by the ballroom and made his move. First, the facts – delivered respectfully. '*Rais sahib*, honourable leader, it's an honour to serve here at this five-star hotel, Kabul's most beautiful hotel, an international hotel. You have so many important guests – ministers from foreign countries, ambassadors, our leaders.'

The besuited Afghan manager stopped in his tracks, head cocked to one side, hearing out this self-assured teenager.

Amanullah kept going, gesturing at the ballroom behind them. 'You have so many wedding guests going in and out of those doors. They hear the soldiers shouting, "Come get your food!" They see us going to those dirty trucks to be fed.'

He paused, before tossing out his real question with a white puff of winter's breath.

'And what if the guards see all your guests' nice food? What if the guards ask, "What about me?"' Amanullah set out his stall. 'There are only eighteen guards around your hotel, around the clock, keeping you safe. Why don't we eat the hotel's food, with your staff? Why don't you tell our office to stop sending those dirty trucks? It would be good for us; it would be good for you.'

Nineteen-year-old Amanullah, dutiful conscript, wannabe hotel worker, engineer-to-be, lowered his eyes, bowed his head, touched his right hand to his heart and smiled inside.

The hotel saw everything. No longer simply the breathtaking mountain vistas and the sprawling cityscape below. Now it also had the best view in the house for the Soviet sound-and-light show. The first-floor terrace looking over the city, the room balconies, the rooftop restaurant – all were front-row seats to history.

Day after day Soviet helicopter gunships thumped through the sky, tracer fire flashing trails of green light. Warplanes swooped over the serrated edges of the Hindu Kush, bombs whistling towards suspected insurgent hideouts concealed in the massif's cliffs and crannies. To the north-east, at the snow-swaddled international airport, Russia's mammoth grey transporters taxied in and out, interspersed with the commercial planes still brave enough to fly here. To the south-east, on a distant lip of the city, an immense Red Army camp was also taking shape around the ancient Bala Hissar, the 'High Fort', once a theatre of nineteenth-century Anglo-Afghan wars. Today it was teeming with Soviet weaponry of war – tanks, artillery, rocket launchers and more.

When the night wrapped its velvet curtains around Kabul and the curfew forced residents indoors, the sky was transformed into an even more sinister stage. The pyrotechnics of Moscow's killing machines sparked awe as well as dread. And they kindled courage. From flat earthen roofs in barely lit neighbourhoods, the chants of *Allahu Akbar* – 'God is Greatest' – rose in unison, each a brave act of resistance against the infidel *Shuravi*, the Soviets, who had taken over the city. The cries carried through the hush of night up to the hotel on the hill, along with the occasional rat-a-tat-tat of gunfire and the haunting ululations of Afghan women. The dark kept many secrets.

This million-strong capital had been thrust into the eyes of the world. By early 1980 the Soviets reported having 60,000 troops on the ground. By the Americans' count, it was 85,000 or more, and still coming, despite Moscow's mantra of a 'very limited military contingent'. After the not-so-secret blizzard of flights into Afghanistan at the end of December 1979, thousands more troops and tanks were still crossing the northern border, over the mighty Amu Darya river, on a rickety pontoon bridge surreptitiously constructed over several months. Their passage south to the capital was smoothed by the long stretch of highway built by the Soviets in the 1960s as an enduring symbol of neighbourly friendship.

Western diplomats, whose numbers in Kabul fell as the ranks of Soviets climbed, often headed to the hotel watch-post. It was, ostensibly, still merely a jaunt for shots of strong coffee, or cocktails with fancy umbrella swizzle sticks, depending on the hour. But now the real draw was the spectacle. It was where they got the colour to add to the confidential cables they sent zipping back to their capitals, now more frequently than ever. Easeful moments were more necessary than ever, too. The hotel's famed steaks with cracked peppercorns still did the trick.

The Inter-Continental Kabul still kept up appearances even as the world outside its doors unravelled. It was still the finest hotel in Kabul; it still radiated its aura of refined luxury. But it was starting to unstitch. The first sign had been the departure of the dapper Austrian general manager. A few months previously Gerd Koidl had tearfully appeared in the lobby along with his ebullient Scottish wife and their gurgling baby to say goodbye. They had begun to feel like hostages in a hotel they had loved like their own home. Apparatchiks in the ruling party had wanted more control of what was, after all, a government-owned hotel. They wanted to be in charge of everything: the fine plates and polished glasses embossed with the Inter-Continental I; the tempting bottles of liquor lined up in the bar; the special provisions stored in the pantries. Even worse had been Mr Koidl's anguish over his team – the senior employees who had fled or been taken away, party faithful put in some of their places, stoking unease among his most loyal and long-standing staff.

And there had been upset among his guests, too. In recent weeks they had mainly been Western journalists. Koidl hadn't minded that little frisson from helping them out: giving someone access to the telex machine that he kept behind his locked office door, or even typing a message to an anxious editor on a reporter's behalf.

But the tension had kept building. On one occasion Afghan security turned up and singled out the eighteen American journalists staying in the hotel. The officers demanded their passports so that they could all be expelled 'for continuous interference in the internal affairs of Afghanistan and continued biased reporting'. The journalists revolted, shoving cameras and microphones in front of the officers' faces, forcing them to take cover in a locked room behind the front desk. It became a diplomatic incident.

None of this had been part of Koidl's job description when he became general manager. His role began to feel like something from a Cold War thriller, fascinating and frightening in equal measure. He wanted out. But even that had proved an ordeal. The officials wouldn't let him leave. He had to send a surreptitious SOS to the US embassy in Kabul: 'Help. Can you get us out of here?' The Americans obliged, advising the Inter-Continental's regional head office in Athens to invite its Kabul general manager to an urgent meeting. And so Koidl's dear Afghan staff waved him and his little family goodbye, saying, *Safar khosh*, 'May your journey be happy', even though they knew it wasn't a happy journey at all.

Koidl wasn't the only one. One day Santos, the chief accountant from the Philippines, casually told a colleague he was 'going out to get some fresh air'. He dumped some files on the desk and headed to the airport, never to return. The in-house band, the Esquire Set, announced they were 'just taking a little holiday' and flew back to Sri Lanka. They never performed at the Inter-Continental Kabul again. The days of catwalks and French stylists were a distant memory; Valerie, the British executive assistant in the office downstairs, had long since moved on to another job in the American Peace Corps, while the Parisian stylist Jean d'Estrées had gone home for good.

In the months after Koidl's departure there was a back and forth between many capitals over the fate of the hotel. Even Pierre Martinet, one of the first general managers who had long since moved on to even loftier roles in the Inter-Continental group, pitched in to try to keep the connection. The new Afghan bosses knew the value of having an international brand in Kabul. But they also believed it was high time that this national guest house, the biggest and best in Afghanistan, was run by them rather than a Western capitalist corporation. Some party members even refused to visit it, turning up their noses at its bourgeois excesses. Others had discreetly enjoyed its luxuries for many years.

Both sides eventually agreed that it was time to part ways. The government would run the hotel. But the Inter-Continental way would carry on, in the Afghan staff who had been so meticulously trained. They weren't going anywhere, at least not yet. They were far too committed. Qudus, who had started out as a teenage tailor, was by now a polished thirty-year-old waiter. Naser, the illiterate village labourer who had somehow landed a job shelling nuts and pitting cherries for the German pastry chef, was now a fine baker himself; even the Russians kept asking for his cakes. And Jamal, who had shown up for a job interview when Kabul University closed over political protests, was now a fine trusted accountant. Like many others, he worried that the Inter-Con, now deprived of its international elan, would become just another ordinary hotel.

Hazrat was more stunned than anyone. He spent the weeks after the Inter-Continental divorce staring absently into the city from the third-floor balconies. What would this mean for his hotel, his job, his future? But happier thoughts also cartwheeled in his head. He had fallen in love. Hazrat had spotted Laila strolling down the street; her family, as modest as his, was also renting a house in their neighbourhood. His uncle stood in for his late father and went to Laila's cob home to ask for her family's permission. On his engagement day, Hazrat had been so overwhelmed that he tipped over on his bicycle as he raced home with the sweets to celebrate their union, getting his brand-new wedding clothes covered in dirt. But his heart was pure.

Once again, everything had changed and nothing had changed. The iconic letter K still stood proudly on the roof. But another national flag was hoisted up the flagpole in the forecourt, the sixth design since the hotel had opened in 1969. President Karmal had brought back the traditional tricolour: black for the dark past, red for blood shed for independence, and green for the Islamic faith. A new seal in its top left-hand corner symbolised the new order: the sun of *Khorasan*, the land of the rising sun; a pulpit for the holy Quran; a book for communist texts; a cogwheel of industry; a red star of communism.

In the lobby the president's portrait graced the wall behind the reception desk. Dog-eared brochures from Afghantour still sat at the end of the counter, advertising 'the friendliest country', even if thick strokes of ink blacked out any references to an Afghan Republic, or Afghan royalty, from days gone by. The little signs for Western credit cards were still stuck to the wall; no one was sure why.

A new advert to promote the hotel was placed in the main English-language newspaper, now called the *New Kabul Times*. The ad still took pride of place on the back page, marked by the kicking letter K. But the Inter-Continental name was gone. It was no longer the Pamir Supper Club but the Pamir Restaurant, albeit still offering 'delicious food and dance' to the music of Shine, Kabul's still-popular Afghan band. In days gone by, the notice would have competed for attention with adjacent ads for the New Marco Polo's Paizar Discotheque, the Twenty-Five Hour Club, the Khyber Restaurant and a hotchpotch of tiny posts for cheaper hotels for hippies and overlanders. Now it was beside a mid-sized announcement from Baihaqi bookstores informing readers of its newest arrivals: Karl Marx's *Capital*, volumes one to three, and the latest literature on dialectical materialism.

Afghanistan's door opened again to Western journalists, but only by a crack. A small number began showing up in the lobby of the Inter-Con – as it was still called – straight from the airport. Television crews carting stacks of heavy metal boxes. Photographers with caramel-coloured Billingham camera bags draped over shoulders. Newspaper correspondents landed from Moscow, Delhi and Frankfurt clutching weathered suitcases, coil notebooks protruding from their pockets. Government officials shadowed them conspicuously.

They were the lucky ones who managed to secure visas – from Afghan diplomats who defiantly handed them out before they defected, or from PDPA loyalists hailing their country's new progressive course. Sometimes the officials keeping watch at Kabul airport directed the media to this government-owned hotel. Sometimes the taxi drivers helpfully suggested it. There were other good-enough hotels in the city, but some Western journalists instinctively made a beeline for an Inter-Continental, confident that it could deliver the *sine qua non* of the trade: dependable telephone and telex links, predictable food and drink. 'If it takes an invasion to get some guests, we can live with that,' Shahabuddin was heard to quip, hopping from one foot to the other in his scuffed Inter-Continental shoes.

That is what they were there for, after all. Kabul had pulled the media's gaze away from other world stories; history was happening here in the Inter-Con. The staff could taste it. There was something in the bearing of the pressmen – and they were mostly men – that projected urgency, intensity. They treated the most ordinary of upsets in the most ordinary of lives as worth magnifying, or even exaggerating, to tell a much bigger story. Their ubiquitous notebooks always seemed primed for a quote. Sometimes their questions were too loud, too direct, too dangerous. Even staff who spoke little English found a lingua franca to signal caution. A flicker of a glance at the agents lolling in the lobby. A subtle arching of eyebrows. A nervous little laugh. Over time, staff who felt sure-footed disclosed select details, wry observations – but very discreetly, and with very few. They all knew the wisest Afghan proverb: 'Walls have mice, and mice have ears.'

And they came to understand the odd vernacular of the journalists. They always greeted each other with the same questions, over and over again, like an LP record trapped in its groove. 'You made it!' 'When did you get here?' 'How long are you staying?' It was like the roll call of expected Afghan courtesies, but different. Their collegial questions, the more observant staff noted, disguised a certain competitiveness, even a hidden penchant for backstabbing. Afghans knew that trait all too well; a decade of coups had left their mark. Yet there was in the journalistic tribe also a sharing of information, a checking on each other's whereabouts, a telling and retelling of rumours simply too good to fact-check – if there were facts to find.

Sometimes they hunted in packs. The staff still mostly addressed them by first name. Mr Gavin of the BBC and Mr Robert of *The Times* of London often sallied out together, piling into a Peugeot taxi early in the morning, its front windows fringed with purple plastic flowers. Mr Robert Fisk, that is, who kept reminding them he was Irish, not a Britisher from Englestan; not to be confused with Mr Robert of Reuters; or Mr Bob of Associated Press, who had got to Kabul long before them.

There was also a Mr James from London, and a Mr James from Washington. And a Mr Martyn of ITN, who checked in before Mr Gavin of the BBC. That who-got-here-first business seemed to matter, a lot. One of the journalists, another Irishman called Mr Conor, joked that this little media invasion was a Great Game of its own – a 1980s version of the nineteenth-century struggle between imperial Britain and Russia for control of Afghanistan. That was a joke that everyone, on both sides of the front desk, understood.

On occasion the hotel itself had the best stories. Diplomats had a way of showing up to hold court. Indian envoys, whose sympathies lay with the Soviets, kept warning of the dangers posed by Afghan *mujahideen* colluding with powerful Islamist forces in Pakistan and stirring sentiments among Soviet Muslims. There was an East European, who said he was a journalist, who often stopped by to argue that the Soviets had no wider ambitions beyond Kabul. One American predicted almost daily that all of Afghanistan was about to rise up and the Russians would soon cut and run. The Soviets themselves were rarely seen in the hotel. They knew that western journalists had made up their mind before they even got here.

Serendipitous encounters could turn out to be the most prized of all. Mr Bob of Reuters, Robert Evans, secured a scoop when he happened upon the Libyan ambassador in the sauna in the bowels of the hotel. A towel loosely wrapped around his waist, the diplomat was disrobed of discretion, too, gossiping about the infighting within the Soviet-installed Afghan leadership.

When the night-time curfew took hold, the press corps would venture to the Cocktail Lounges, the liquor loosening their tongues. One lament loomed larger than the rest: that they were cut off from the world. Day after day the journalists marched to the front desk to check, yet again, whether international telephone circuits had been restored, or would be sometime soon. And when would that sorry excuse for a teletype machine, sitting silently in a glass cubicle at the far end of the lobby, ever be fired up, so they could send off their stories? Some journalists expressed their discontent while slyly searching receptionists' faces for hints that secret deals could be cut – the government censors be damned. After all, it seemed that some journalists were finding a way to get their stories out.

The satellite facilities at the state-run broadcasting compound, which as of last year included television as well as radio, were also off-limits, occupied by Russian forces. The only connection available was at the PTT: the main post, telegraph and telephone office on Pashtunistan Square. Censors skulked behind desks and laid down the law, offering preferential access – and on some days the only access – to Eastern Bloc reporters. Many Western journalists traipsed back and forth to Kabul airport, on the lookout for passengers or crew willing to carry bulky envelopes with typed copy, TV cassettes or film rolls to any other capital where their material could be handed over to colleagues or friends. Some even entrusted their precious cargo to couriers taking the buses bumping along the perilous road slicing through the Kabul Gorge all the way to Peshawar in Pakistan. There, in another Inter-Continental hotel, telex and telephone operators were happy co-conspirators, for a modest price.

One of the few dependable tools was a shortwave radio set. Many journalists' days began and ended by turning the dial on their portable transistor to hear the latest news from Kabul and beyond on the airwaves of the BBC and VOA. If there were unconfirmed reports of fighting somewhere in Kabul, they could step out onto their balconies to check.

And sometimes the war came to them. One winter's day

a loud clatter enveloped the entire hotel. A Soviet helicopter gunship was hovering ominously above, while a clutch of bearded men on a nearby hill defiantly shook their fists and old British rifles at it. Journalists, always the first to rush towards a racket of any kind, leaned over the rails of their balconies. Afghan hotel staff weren't far behind, spilling into the forecourt, fixating on the gunship with bated breath. The chopper paused. Then it swooped, sending the fist shakers diving for cover. The helicopter held its fire, tilting sideways, turning back towards the city. A round of applause rose from the Inter-Con's ringside balcony seats. The men with guns on the next hill dusted themselves off. The hotel staff went back to work.

Amanullah was in; all eighteen guards were. The hotel manager put a stop to the smelly food trucks in the forecourt. Instead, in groups of six on rotating shifts, the guards made their way down the gravelly slope around the back of the ballroom, down the tiled steps to a plain door – the staff entrance.

It was Amanullah's first glimpse of the labyrinthine inner workings of the hotel, the 'back of the house' in the basement. The laundry spitting hot steam and a bite of bleach. The housekeepers' room bristling with buckets and mops. Engineering, which stored sharper tools. Staff lockers and spaces for prayer.

And the staff cafeteria on the ground floor, tucked behind the kitchen. Amanullah found himself in a canteen humming with a pleasing murmur punctuated by laughter and clinking dishes. It was utterly different from the food trucks, and he relished it. He savoured the comforting hug of the hotel's central heating and camaraderie, the heady aromas wafting from their compact kitchen at the end of the narrow dining room. It felt clean and orderly. It felt good. And he felt respected. The baccalaureate soldier – that's how they saw him.

At these communal tables it didn't matter where you came from, what you did. Everyone in this cafeteria would have been happy to push away the benches and chairs and sit around a *dastarkhwan*, a traditional tablecloth laid across the floor, as they would at home, not bothering with cutlery, expertly scooping food with their fingers or chunks of bread. It tasted so much better that way. But at the Inter-Continental they took their seats at the table and tucked into steaming mounds of rice and meat, clasping bits of bread like a fork.

Afghan food: that's what they all wanted. Not the foreign stuff that sometimes tempted them. Amanullah listened, all ears, as they remembered the days when the hotel first opened, and they sometimes ate the same special food as the guests, provided they were sure the meat had been slaughtered in the correct halal way. Hotel workers ribbed each other about the times they had stuffed their faces in the kitchen once their supervisors left, even taking some of it home so that their families could try it, too. But it was never as delicious as their own fare, with its mingling of taste and memory. Sometimes the chef joined their repartee. They teased him, beseeched him, to make their favourite *Ash* soup, the thick soul-warming broth full of fat noodles, chunky beans and ground beef, with lashings of sour yogurt.

There was no politics on this menu. No one discussed what they had heard that morning or the night before on foreign radios. No one would even admit they listened. No one wanted to be reported to someone upstairs. And when someone suddenly didn't show up in their regular spot, no one said much. Some knew why, but they didn't say. Others wondered whether they had been hauled away for some indiscretion, perhaps randomly stopped by Afghan or Russian troops at some checkpoint. Or maybe they had fled with their families, crossing the border to Pakistan in the east or Iran in the west, like so many others were doing. For most, though, the deep soil of their lives kept them rooted in place.

The windows misted up with the warm breath of things said and unsaid. Stories from the head, from the heart, from hearsay. Sometimes, when it was safe, they would swap comments about the guests. But the biggest news about them was that there were hardly any, yet again. Amanullah could tell from the way waiters and chefs dawdled at the staff tables; there weren't many other people to serve. The big-spender tourists from Europe and America had stopped coming. The Soviet invasion and the Iranian revolution next door had put a stop to the hippy trail, although they had never made it up the hill anyway. The overland route hadn't been blocked – not yet – but buses didn't want to risk it. The hotel instead welcomed government visitors, comrades from friendly countries and the journalists, when they were allowed in.

When there were journalists in Kabul, the foreign radio stations – even the state-run and Soviet ones – crackled with more information. There were more eyewitness accounts of what was happening, or not, on the streets of Kabul below. And staff occasionally caught some of their guests on state TV asking pointed questions to top officials, which mostly raised them in their estimation. But some of the names they remembered were now 'reporting from inside Afghanistan', from the restive countryside, where they were travelling with the *mujahideen*. Amanullah had never really met a journalist, just caught glimpses of them as they drove through his checkpoint – some wearing a friendly smile, others a preoccupied stare. But he came to know some of their chatty taxi drivers.

His own job kept getting better. Now he wasn't merely another guard. He was training other guards. How to stand by their post. How to check vehicles and visitors. What to say. How to say it. He put all the new recruits through their paces on the elevated terrace, on the other side of the parking space, close to the *ziyarat*, the shrine of Pir-I Baland, a prominent Sufi saint. Kabul was sprinkled with revered shrines set in hillsides, tucked into neighbourhoods. No one was sure if *baland* – 'on high' – referred to the hill or to the Pir's elevated status. Some even speculated that the grave belonged to the British soldier Peter-the-Blond, who was killed in an Anglo-Afghan war. Either way, the shrine commanded authority even though it was receding into the thick shrubbery on the outer edge of the hotel. Women wrapped in *chadris*, children tagging along, often made pilgrimages to the site to offer prayers, pay their respects, ask for blessings to ease hardship and heartache. Amanullah and his men kept a respectful distance as they went about their work.

They needed the Pir's graces, too. Securing this hotel was a serious business. And it was becoming more so by the month. It wasn't that they felt particularly threatened out here on the western rim of the capital. But by late 1981 resistance to Russian rule was swelling in villages, spilling into valleys. The *mujahideen* now held sway across large swathes of land.

Even Kabul, the most heavily defended of all, was not immune. The biggest jolt to the city had come in February 1980 with the *Qeyem-e 3 Hut*, the '3 Hut uprising', named for the last month in the Afghan calendar before *Nowruz*. It began just eight weeks after the Soviet invasion. First there were the *shabnama* – the night letters by anti-communist activists calling on Afghans to rise up – secretively slipped under doors, thrown over fences, taped onto walls. Then came the cries rising from roofs on moonlit nights, echoing across the city with a ferocity never heard before. *Allahu Akbar, Allahu Akbar*. Then Kabul streets and bumpy dirt roads were thronged with protestors. Green flags of Islam were waved. Anti-Soviet slogans were shouted. Shops shuttered early. Security forces ordered crowds to disperse, shooting into the air, to no avail. Then they fired into the crowds. Hundreds were killed in six days of unrest, many thrown into prison, never seen again.

Staff at the Inter-Con watched from afar as other hotels were wrenched in. The Kabul Hotel, just steps from the presidential palace, was encircled by angry crowds. Inside, Soviet citizens, about twenty in all, huddled on the second floor – some of them journalists from *Pravda*, *Tass*, *Izvestiya*, *Literaturnaya Gazeta*; others diplomats, senior party officials, pilots on secret missions. Another hotel across the way was already on fire. Blackened carcasses of overturned buses smouldered in the middle of the road. Thick black smoke leached into the Kabul Hotel. A bonfire of anger burned outside. *Shuravi – marg, marg, marg.* 'Death death death to the Soviets!' Only at the eleventh hour, within an inch of their lives, were they all rescued; Soviet para-troopers descended on the hotel in a blaze of gunfire, pelting up the fuggy stairs and down the smoke-filled floor, pushing their fellow citizens towards armoured vehicles at the ready outside; the crowds held, barely, at bay.

Since that week there had been more house-to-house searches, more reports of assassinations of party loyalists, more attacks by *mujahideen* infiltrators inside the city, and firing barrages from outside. All the while a beleaguered President Karmal kept trying to bolster his standing in the eyes of Afghans and the world. He signed the UN convention eliminating all forms of discrimination against women. He pushed through sweeping land reforms. But stories from the countryside spoke of sparks flying when party delegates wearing suits were dis-patched to explain the principles of communism. Village elders were up in arms, and some even took up arms, when told that their daughters and wives had to come out of their homes to be educated. Landowners were taken aback when told that their holdings would now be divided up among the poor farmers who tilled their soil. *Zar, Zan, u Zameen* – 'gold, women and land': that's why men went to war. That, and for God.

The president made heavily publicised visits to Eastern Bloc capitals, most of all Moscow, where he was welcomed with boisterous applause and hearty back-slapping. But he needed to prove Kabul was safe and sound for his well-wishers to visit him in turn. A date was set for a foreign visit: late November 1981. Red-and-gold banners were strung along the main boulevards and above the hotel's front entrance, to warmly welcome comrades from the Afro-Asian People's Solidarity Organisation.

Security was especially tight. Amanullah wasn't on shift, but his fellow guards patrolled the grounds. The *mujahideen* sent their message in the morning: a salvo of rockets slammed into the hill, crashing into the hard ground, shards of shrapnel spraying into naked fruit trees easing into winter slumber. Windows cracked with the force of the blast. The hotel went dark. Staff crouched.

No one was hurt. The distinguished delegates hadn't checked in yet. But the hotel shuddered. It was the first knock to its sense of sanctuary, its prestige – a place away from the fray; its belief that it could bear witness and not be wounded itself.

CHAPTER 6

Room Service and Reconciliation

Summer 1986

His clean blue shirt felt good. Amanullah slipped into its sleeves and gently pulled it over his shoulders, carefully doing up each button and then each cuff. He tugged each sleeve sharply, and then the collar. He knotted his black tie, a narrow sliver, exactly the way his older brother had shown him, expertly nudging it into precise alignment with the buttons. He looked in the little mirror inside his staff locker. His jet-black head of hair was neat, his dark moustache nicely trimmed. *Still handsome*, he thought.

Then he made for the stairs, hoping his new shoes didn't pinch. There would be a lot of walking inside the hotel. 'If you want to work, come and work with us,' the Afghan general manager had told him. 'We have good memories of you.'

His four years and four months of military service were over. He had done his duty: protecting his country and praying five times a day, all while trying to maximise every opportunity that came his way. 'Trust in Allah, but tie your camel,' as the prophet Mohammad told them, peace be upon him.

Amanullah had dreamed big. Not too big, but big enough

for a high-school graduate whose starting gate had been the guard-post of Kabul's best hotel. From 8 a.m. until nearly 2 p.m. he now studied, in Russian, at the Polytechnic at the bottom of the hill. From 2 p.m. until nearly 10 p.m. he worked in the hotel at the top of the hill as a room-service cashier, practising his English as he took orders from guests, when there were guests. 'What would you like to order, sir?' 'Will that be all, sir? It will be with you in twenty minutes.' His inner compass looked both east and west. His engineering instructor from Moscow once asked him, in Russian, 'Did you finish your homework?' 'Yes!' came Amanullah's immediate reply, in English. The professor corrected him, in Russian. 'You mean *Da*?' 'Yes,' Amanullah repeated with a cheeky grin. '*Da!*'

His new office, so to speak, was a step up from his squat security hut. Now he was in a windowless nook next to the service lift, facing the kitchen. On the other side of the flip-flap doors, cooks rustled up orders in a mist of tantalising smells. In his own tidy cubbyhole in quiet hours Amanullah would take out his hefty engineering textbooks, stealing time to study. At the end of his shift he relished stepping out into the night, inhaling gulps of fresh air, taking in the skyful of stars. It was the gift of a city often plunged into darkness; the *mujahideen* stalking the capital kept cutting the electricity pylons, sending the hotel lurching onto its generator. At this hour the forecourt was eerily empty, the final stragglers lingering around the ballroom doors, relishing the last moments and swapping the last jokes before rushing home ahead of the 10 p.m. curfew. Sizzling tips of cigarettes dotted the dark, augmented by the occasional flash of government artillery, a Soviet searchlight scanning the skies.

With every month, the war seemed to inch a bit closer. You could hear it in the sounds drifting up the hill. The staccato crackle of rifles, the thump of rockets, the whistle of an incoming round. For now, they mostly targeted the other side of Kabul, aiming for the airport. Sometimes as many as thirty missiles struck the city in a single night, some landing not so far from this hill. Ominous thuds somewhere in the black sent the imagination spinning. There were more checkposts now on the slope of the hill, and on the road below.

Amanullah always looked up at the white-and-blue hotel as he left. Some now called it by its official name of *Mailmah Pall*, the 'Guest House'. For most people it remained the Inter-Con; it would always be the Inter-Con. A student of civil engineering could see that its sturdy old bones were still strong. The pillars under the portico, along the front and in the lobby were still solid; the floors of the best Afghan stone still gleamed; the golden lifts still thrilled. Whenever Afghans came through the door for the first time they still looked around, wide-eyed, taking in every detail so that they could faithfully share them later with family and friends.

But the shine was fading a bit, it had to be said. Some chandeliers had been stolen of their glitter, to save on electricity bills. The front desk sometimes cut a lonely figure. One day a newly arrived guest was even found wandering helplessly through the lobby looking for someone to check him in. Amanullah still hadn't seen, or felt, that energising hustle and bustle he'd heard about in the staff canteen.

In its most lacklustre moments the hotel could even feel like a musty old museum pining for visitors. The blue-and-white *We accept American Express* sign was still perched on the front desk, even if it wasn't true. Inside the mirrored lift a curvaceous blonde in a snug dress still smiled at guests and offered tennis and other diversions: a cardboard cutout that felt like a ghost of times past. So too did a glossy banner in the lobby: *After a busy day at work or an exhausting game of tennis, what would be better than relaxing in the sauna?* Except the sauna was now shut. So was the swimming pool. So was the Pan Am Airways office at the other end of the lobby, its counters only collecting dust, its travel posters curling at the edges.

Some of the gems in the hotel's five-star crown were tarnished. A Mr Tom – Tom Heneghan of Reuters – had turned up one day, enquiring about the wonderful local Italian-Afghan wine that he had so enjoyed a decade earlier. A waiter proudly produced a bottle of the fabled Vino Castellino with its distinctive label, uncorking it with a loud pop and a satisfied grin. Mr Tom eagerly took a sip. His face twisted into an ugly grimace. 'It tastes like turpentine!' It had gone sour. The hotel's wine cellar needed the care of a connoisseur. But none of the waiters – all observant Muslims – would permit a drop of alcohol to pass their lips. Meanwhile the wine factory, born in 1967 of an Italian student's dream, had been nationalised, although it was still doing brisk business, selling thousands of bottles of wine a day and copious quantities of vodka.

The tennis courts were open, though. And you could get shoes shined and laundry done overnight. All this for $77.50 for a single room, plus an extra ten dollars for a television. Most importantly, the best of the staff still flashed their widest hotel smiles, bidding guests good day and goodbye in English and an assortment of other languages.

There was a new language now, too. Month after month, everyone was learning the vocabulary of war. 'Scorched earth.' The Soviets were now said to be razing entire villages to the ground, punishing families accused of protecting the men with guns, forcing them to take refuge across the border in Pakistan. 'The evil empire.' The US president Ronald Reagan was vowing to give the *mujahideen* everything they needed, and more, to defeat the USSR. In the wintry hills around Kabul the *mujahideen* now had warm jackets and winter boots instead of sandals and shawls. Their old single-shot British Lee-Enfields were replaced by automatic rifles. Heavy machine guns were also added to an arsenal groaning with goods from their friends in America, Britain, Saudi Arabia, China and elsewhere, most of it smuggled in through Pakistan. Above all, there was a game-changing weapon: the Stinger, a powerful US anti-aircraft missile fired from the shoulder, sending Soviet and Afghan aircraft falling from the skies, and a chill down their enemies' spine.

The Russians didn't show up at the hotel very often. Some Eastern Bloc diplomats occasionally dropped in for coffee and cake, and to browse and buy in the well-stocked bookshop, the best in Kabul, that had opened in the lobby. But there was a certain Mr Viktor – Viktor Polyanichko, the new advisor to the ruling PDPA. When he came through the doors, everyone nearby knew it. His presence filled the spaces between the pillars. A big man with a big voice and an even bigger mission: to sort this Soviet–Afghan mess. On Moscow radio he was lauded. On Western radio stations he was painted as 'the butcher of Afghanistan'. There was a sense the Soviet strategy was shifting.

In his cubbyhole, lit by bars of white fluorescent light, Amanullah focused on memorising the room-service menu and mastering engineering formulas. This unrelenting war was destroying roads, buildings, homes; his classes were about designing and building them. But for now his job was to ensure that the guests were fed, and happy. 'What would you like to order, sir?' 'Will that be all, sir? It will be with you in twenty minutes.'

The hotel's engineering department brought its battered wooden toolbox with hammers and nails to the front desk. The clerks knew what to do. The scowling President Babrak Karmal was taken down from the wall. He had been removed from the Revolutionary Council and sent to Moscow, where he was given a comfortable state-owned apartment in the capital and a nice *dacha* in the countryside.

The staff quickly put up the new pictures: behind the front desk, in management offices, in security cabins, in rooms here and there. Moscow's new man, Najibullah, stared down at them now, smiling. He was nicknamed 'The Ox' for his bull-necked bearing. He had been known as Najib, but an Islamic suffix (-*ullah*, 'of God') had recently been added. Or as Dr Najib, for his medical degree, although he never got to practise. He had been living in the minds of Afghans because of his job heading the feared intelligence agency *Khadamat-e Aetla'at-e Dawlati* (KhAD), the Afghan version of the KGB. Whispers had it that he tortured people to death with his bare hands. Whether or not it was true, it struck fear and fury into many hearts.

There was a new leader in Moscow, too: Mikhail Gorbachev, the general secretary of the Communist Party of the Soviet Union, the balding leader with a distinctive deep-red birthmark on top of his head. He was using a new vocabulary as well; one that made Afghans crouch closer to their television set, if they had one, or turn the knobs this way and that on their radios in search of the clearest signal. On 26 February 1986, at the opening of the party's 27th Congress in Moscow, General Secretary Gorbachev had spoken for five and a half hours about everything from nuclear arms to a new economic blueprint for his nation. For Afghans, a few phrases leapt out. 'A bleeding wound': that was how he described Afghanistan. 'In the nearest future': that was when he said they would like 'to withdraw the Soviet troops stationed in Afghanistan'. Only 'at the request of its government', he carefully noted.

And he spoke about 'national reconciliation'. No one seemed

to agree, even in Moscow and Kabul, what that meant. For some, it involved widening the base of the ruling PDPA party. For others, it meant bringing in the *mujahideen*, even if they showed no signs of wanting to join, especially when Soviet boots were still on the ground, Soviet warplanes still in the air, and their allies – particularly the US – firmly against it. Gorbachev was using other words, too, that excited some young communists in Kabul. Russian words like *glasnost*, 'openness', and *perestroika*, 'reform and restructuring'. Words that inspired Afghan comrades who had long been calling for the same.

A new sign went up in the window of the lobby's lone gift shop, accompanying a fetching display of fine carpets and stone-studded silver jewellery: *To welcome our national reconciliation*, it read, *we present a special discount*. When guests cautiously put one foot in the door, the shopkeeper explained that he was lowering his prices by as much as 10 per cent to honour the search for peace. Of course in the best traditions of Afghan haggling, it was never clear what the true prices were. It brought a knowing half-smile from hotel staff, who steered clear of both prices and politics.

Still, some journalists couldn't resist the thrill of a potential bargain. They were now descending on the hotel in far larger numbers. The Afghan and Soviet governments were offering opportunities to the media to come and see the situation for themselves. In late 1986 the country was to witness the first pull-out of 8,000 Soviet troops, a token number compared to the estimated 115,000 in Moscow's 'very limited military contingent'. But it still sent a signal. And a Soviet-sponsored visit flew in dozens of Western journalists based in Moscow to observe what President Najibullah officially announced as the start of an Afghan six-month ceasefire, even if the fighting never stopped.

The spectacular descent into Kabul, across the undulating

ridges of its stunning mountains, was a story in itself. Soviet helicopter gunships, and even civilian carriers, had started dropping
bright flares to trick the heat-seeking missiles fired by the *mujahideen* that would otherwise strike aircraft, including passen-
ger planes. In the middle of the descent the journalists would
suddenly find themselves spiralling downwards in a breathtaking corkscrew manoeuvre – another tactic to evade enemy fire –
before taxiing down a runway flanked by Soviet aircraft and
artillery. In the terminal the media were greeted by posters of a
beaming US President Reagan kitted out like a cowboy, next to
boxes of American ammunition and an Afghan child left legless
by the war. They were escorted through a Kabul swelling with
the influx of families fleeing the more ferocious fighting in the
countryside. Its population had ballooned to two million people,
more than twice the number who had lived in the capital when
the Soviets came in.

The journalists often became the news themselves, filmed
and photographed by state media as they toured streets festooned with bold banners proclaiming: *We Want Peace all over the
World*. Colourful hoardings honoured the revolution's heroes,
and mocked *mujahideen* leaders with bloodied daggers between
their teeth and tattooed with dollar signs. The media were
taken to schools run by educated Afghan women to emphasise
the government's commitment to their rights, and to women-
led charities. One such organisation, launched soon after the
invasion, proudly sent Afghan children to the Soviet Union to
be educated in 'Marxist-Leninist thinking and the greatness of
the Soviet state and the evils of imperialism'.

The journalists brought some bustle back to the Inter-
Con. Crispy croissants and fresh fruit juices were served with
warmth, and sometimes a wink, as Soviet helicopters whooshed
past the windows. The teenage conscripts doing their military

service – most of them speaking neither Russian nor English – manned a new checkpost halfway down the hill to ensure that no one tried to head out on their own. And just before one junket ended, housekeeping staff were instructed to place official gifts in guest rooms: smooth prayer rugs; multicoloured marble boxes; coffee-table books. Most Western journalists, mindful of their employers' rules about not accepting official gifts, left them behind, although some were of the view that taking one little thing wasn't such a big deal. There were rich pickings for the cleaners and room boys who happened to be on-shift.

On 30 November 1987, shortly before 10 a.m., in the quiet pause after the end of breakfast and before the start of lunch, there was a loud bang. Everyone looked up, from their tables, their stoves, their brooms. A rocket had slammed into an open field nearby. Its target appeared to be the hall in the Polytechnic University next door, where President Najibullah was speaking. He was only halfway through the seventh page of his twenty-nine-page text. Three more missiles soon whistled in. He kept reading. His audience remained in their seats.

The event was the *Loya Jirga*, a centuries-old tradition when a leader summons tribal elders and other notables to make decisions of national importance – or to rubber-stamp ones already made. Delegates from thirty provinces, from the ruling party, the army, the labour unions and more, were assembled in the room. The *mujahideen* had flatly dismissed an invitation to attend, declaring that a *Loya Jirga* under foreign occupation was illegal. Their delegation came in the form of the rockets launched from hills to the west of Kabul, the lush garden town of Paghman, a former royal retreat.

Inside the auditorium, brows lifted and knowing looks were exchanged. But the *Loya Jirga* simply carried on. Rocket fire was now part of the city's soundtrack, punctuating the birdsong, the beeping horns, the hubbub of heaving bazaars. God would decide if, and when, a rocket had your name on it.

So, one by one, every decision was dealt with. President Najibullah was confirmed in his post for seven more years. 'The sacred religion of Islam' was confirmed as the country's official faith. And it was all change – at least for the terminology. 'Democratic' was lifted from the Democratic Republic because it made Afghanistan sound like a communist country, something the party had always denied. The dreaded KhAD became WAD, the Ministry of State Security. The ruling PDPA – the People's Democratic Party of Afghanistan – became the *Watan*, the 'Homeland Party'.

Foreign radios wondered if it was all just words. And they also assessed what it meant for the *mujahideen*. Some names were mentioned more than others. One was Ahmad Shah Massoud, a former engineering student at the Polytechnic who never completed his studies and was remembered by classmates for chiding them to observe their religious duties. His supporters now called him the 'Lion of the Panjshir' because he commanded forces based in his birthplace north of Kabul, Panjshir, the 'Valley of the Five Lions'. Another was his rival Gulbuddin Hekmatyar, who had also studied engineering at Kabul University before being sent to prison, accused of murdering a fellow student who was said to be a Maoist. Rumours swirled that he had been known to hurl acid in women's faces. He always denied all such claims. They both worried many Kabul residents, especially educated women who prized their work outside their homes and preferred to wear Western-style clothes.

Amanullah was not drawn to politics of any kind. They often came knocking on his door, asking him to join one group or another. But he never joined any of them, never took sides. He was a proud Afghan and a pious Muslim. That's what mattered. Besides, this war didn't map neatly into some simple Cold War divide. Many of the Western-backed *mujahideen* were deeply conservative Islamists, fiercely opposed to Western ways. And Afghans living under Soviet sway also bristled against foreign interference. On both sides there was a vicious battle for power.

All Amanullah could do was carry on with his own life, as most people did. By the end of 1987 even President Najibullah admitted that '80 per cent of the countryside and 40 per cent of the towns are outside the government'. The word in well-informed circles was that Mikhail Gorbachev had given his military chiefs a year to crush the insurgency, to do whatever it took. Then he would turn to talks. No matter what happened, next year Moscow would start bringing home all of its troops.

CHAPTER 7

Russia Checks Out

Winter 1989

The room-service telephone rang off the hook. Opposite Aman-ullah's cubicle, waiters dashed in and out of the kitchen, past raging pots and pans, doors flapping with a whoosh of steam. Unflappable servers, beads of sweat glistening, rushed past with food trays piled high. Journalists were calling to order something to eat or drink at all hours, wolfing it down where they worked. All the way down the hall, stacks of dirty plates sat ready for room service to collect outside the doors – smeared with oily spinach, bits of bread, cold French fries. Many ordered exactly the same thing, night after night. Amanullah kept his cool, keeping it all in his head. Who liked what, in which room. The names. The orders. The personalities. 'Let me repeat your order . . .'

The journalists were here for the story; they were here for history. In a matter of weeks, by 15 February 1989, every Soviet soldier would be gone. Moscow had promised. Their catastrophic decade-long stay was finally coming to an end.

It had sparked a media invasion. Most journalists made a beeline for the Inter-Con on the western edge of the city as soon as they landed at Kabul airport, not put off by what were likely to be maddening queues for the telex and telephone lines. Others headed to the Kabul Hotel, whose telex could send reports, but not receive replies, and which had a menu of little more than Afghan bread and 'chicken rice', but was smack in the city centre. The Afghan Foreign Ministry was inundated with visa requests from the media. By early January it shut the door, insisting it didn't have enough interpreters and vehicles to assist any more journalists. There weren't enough minders to keep an eye on everyone, in other words. The Soviets might be opening up in a way they hadn't done in years, but they didn't want too much *glasnost*. In case something went wrong.

The Inter-Con was buzzing. Crazily busy, but a good kind of crazy. Conversations thrummed in English and Italian, Japanese and German, French and Finnish and many more languages never heard before within these walls. And the hubbub brought with it hope. Maybe, just maybe, the staff dared to think, this was the start of a better time.

But in the swell of history there was a riptide. The tension sometimes slipped through when someone rang room service and joked, but didn't really joke, 'I'm still here! Not sure how long . . . ' Staff earwigged the nervous conversations between journalists, by the lifts, in the lobby, in the restaurants. 'How long are you staying?' 'Do you think it will be safe?' No one wanted to leave unless almost everyone else was leaving too, especially their competitors. The only casualty so far was the correspondent for the French weekly *L'Express*; he was hit in his right buttock when a bullet shot by a Soviet soldier sliced through the door of his taxi.

Some journalists who had turned up weeks earlier had resolved to stay put. One BBC journalist was overheard recounting that a UN official had pulled her aside and warned her,

The Inter-Continental, still under construction, glistens against the Kabul skyline in 1968.

THIS HOTEL WAS OPENED
ON THE NINTH DAY OF SEPTEMBER
1969
IN THE REIGN OF
HIS MAJESTY
MOHAMMAD ZAHIR SHAH
FOR THE
MAILMAH PALL SAHAMI SHERKAT
DESIGNED BY
TAYLOR WOODROW INTERNATIONAL
LIMITED · LONDON · ENGLAND
CONSTRUCTED BY
TAYLOR WOODROW OF AFGHANISTAN
LIMITED
AND
AFGHAN CONSTRUCTION UNIT KABUL
JOINT VENTURE
CONSULTING ARCHITECTS PATON PITT
AND ASSOCIATES
CONSTRUCTION COMMENCED
8TH APRIL 1967

An early 1970s postcard captures sunbathers sipping cocktails by the Inter-Con pool.

A plaque by the front entrance commemorates the grand opening and the international origins of the hotel.

A chef in the Bamiyan Brasserie serves up some 'casual-dining' fare, 1971.

A relaxed evening in the Nuristan Cocktail Lounge, 1977.

Service with a smile at the Pamir Supper Club, 1977.

Ariana Afghan Airlines offers intrepid travellers the chance to follow in the footsteps of Marco Polo, 1977.

The Esquire Set, the Inter-Con's first in-house band, entertain guests with their thunderous rock tunes, 1971.

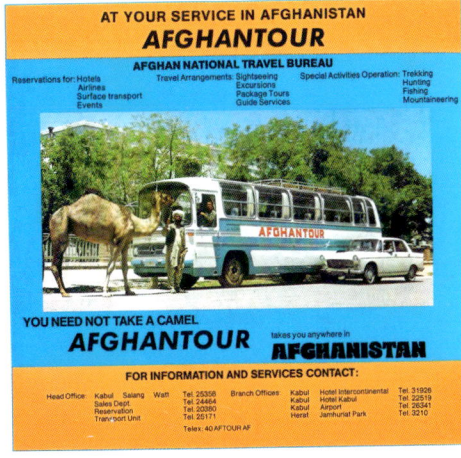

'You need not take a camel': words of reassurance from an AfghanTour advert, 1977.

Chadris and miniskirts on the streets of Kabul, 1972.

A newly arrived LyseDoucet and soon-to-be Engineer Amanullah in the Inter-Con, 1989.

An Afghan soldier plays a flute at his guard post just beyond the Inter-Con gates, 1989.

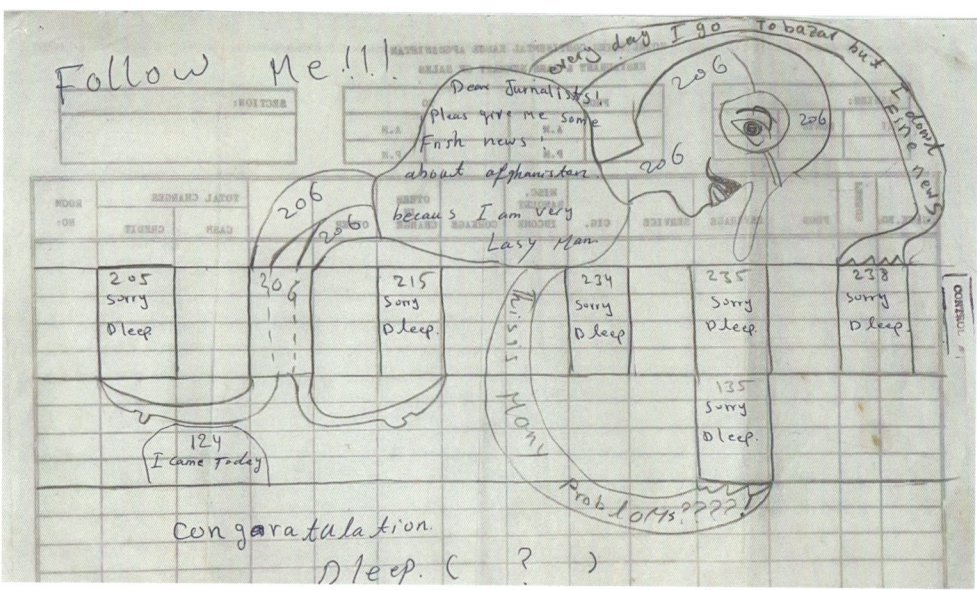

Amanullah's take on the visiting journalists' need for 'frish news', as sketched on the back of a late-1980s ledger.

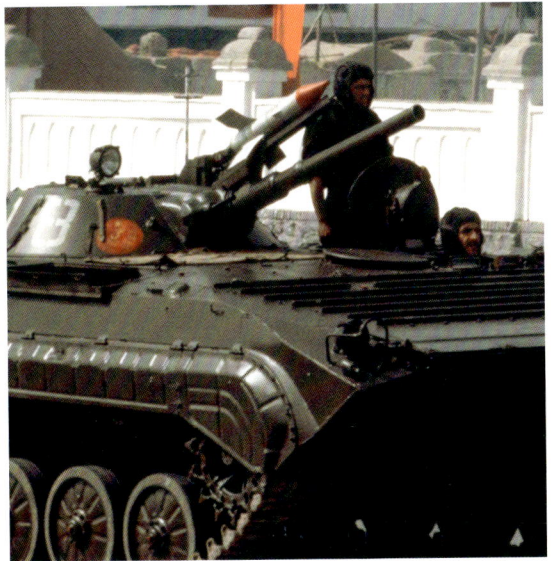

One of François Lochon's rare photos of the Soviet invasion of Kabul, developed from a film smuggled out in his boot in late 1979.

British Embassy,
Kabul.

Tel: 30511

I must advise you that you should leave Afghanistan without delay while normal flights are still available.

It is entirely your responsibility to decide whether or not to act on this advice, but I must make it clear that this is a final warning and that there is no question of any subsequent evacuation being arranged by the British Government. If the Embassy is obliged to close there will be no British Consular protection once the Embassy staff have left the country. If you should decide to stay, please inform the Embassy immediately.

C Meath Baker

W J C Meath Baker
Chargé d'Affaires

KABUL 19th January, 1989

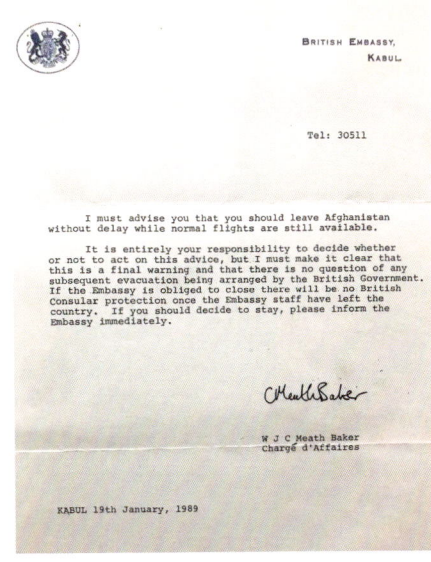

The British Embassy urges its citizens to 'leave Afghanistan without delay' in January 1989 amidst the Soviet withdrawal.

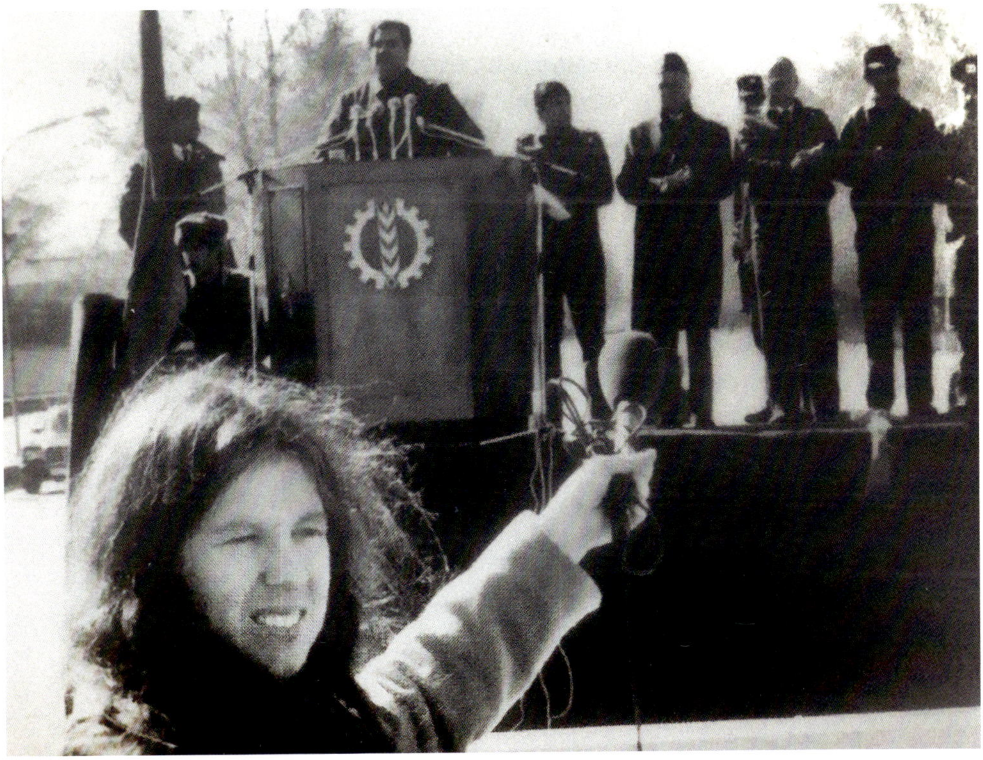

President Najibullah delivers a speech covered by various journalists – including the junior BBC reporter LyseDoucet – in early 1989.

General Boris Gromov is the last Soviet soldier to leave Afghanistan, meeting his fourteen-year-old son, Maksim, on the Friendship Bridge into the USSR, February 1989.

A group of *mujahideen* ride into Kabul on the back of a jeep, April 1992, following more than a decade of warfare.

Rounds of tracer-fire light up the Kabul skyline as the civil war escalates in spring 1992.

A skirmish between the forces of warlords Abdul Rashid Dostum and Gulbuddin Hekmatyar on the streets of Kabul at the peak of the civil war, April 1994.

A family displaced by the civil war clings onto their belongings.

After being told only men could travel with the Haqqani fighters in the *mujahideen*, LyseDoucet dresses like one in 1991 to report from a major frontline.

The Taliban arrive in Kabul, September 1996.

Engineer Amanullah sporting his new beard and turban shortly after the arrival of the Taliban.

Cooking by gaslight in the Inter-Con kitchen, early 2001.

'Leave! Now!' He implied that, if she stayed, she would be raped by the rebel fighters whose entry into Kabul was now all but certain. The staff called her LyseDoucet – always one word – as they had heard it on the BBC's translated Dari and Pashto bulletins.

As the days counted down to 15 February, anxiety levels kept inching up. On 19 January LyseDoucet's face went pale when she was handed an envelope at the front desk, delivered by the British embassy. Its single sheet of fine stationery carried a stark message: *You should leave Afghanistan without delay while normal flights are still available.* She was so lost in thought, pacing Room 132, that she entirely forgot to attend a diplomatic dinner at the French chargé d'affaires' residence. The telephone operator on the night-shift put through the call of the furious French envoy, a diplomat of Asian ancestry who taught karate in Kabul in his spare time. She had ruined his table setting and blown her chance to sit next to a most interesting Eastern Bloc ambassador.

On the second-to-last day of January, with snow whipping through the pines and swirling past the windows, journalists piled into taxis to speed to the US embassy as fast as the icy roads allowed. Chargé d'affaires Jon Glassman stood tall next to the memorial stone to Ambassador Dubs, killed in Room 117 in the Kabul Hotel almost a decade ago to the day. A clutch of marines, snowflakes melting into their caps, solemnly lowered the Stars and Stripes. The bugle rang out, duelling with the bitter wind. 'So, as we say goodbye to Kabul, we honour the memory of Ambassador Dubs and say, "God Bless the United States of America, we're going home",' announced America's envoy, his emotion visible. The embassy was shutting, with a promise to return once Kabul fell to the *mujahideen* – an outcome that Washington was now predicting as often and as loudly as it could. The howling blizzard swallowing the city grounded the last of the Americans a little longer, including about ten missionaries and a handful of reporters. Two car bombs exploded in the city shortly after the ceremony.

The British were next. At the beginning of February a bunch of British journalists tumbled into the hotel in high spirits, within a whisker of the curfew, having just helped to empty the wine cellar at the last supper at their embassy, the magnificent white stucco compound built in 1927 to ensure Britain's envoy lived in 'one of the finest residences in Asia'. Shortly before the chargé d'affaires, Ian Mackley, shut off the lights at the start of February, he proclaimed it had to be done, 'because the future looked so bleak as to make it not worth having an embassy here'. He also put the Afghan leader on notice: 'The simplest solution for Afghanistan would be for Dr Najibullah to be on the last Soviet plane out of Kabul.' In the months before almost all Western diplomats pulled out, their dining rooms had turned into gambling tables, everyone placing bets on how long the Afghan leader would last. An American put his money on a date in January. An Asian envoy boldly predicted Najibullah would never fall.

Bets were being placed in the Inter-Con, too. In one fizzy huddle in the Nuristan Cocktail Bar a French journalist eyed his digital watch and mused that 'the guerrillas should be coming to Kabul soon.' They took note of every whoosh and crump carried up to the hill, holding forth on whether it was outgoing or incoming. But now that the powers-that-be had called off the censors, the newspaper hacks mostly spent their time queuing around the clacking telexes in the lobby. Some stood chain-smoking, some chatting, others focusing on the latest gadget they were clutching – the first portable computer, a beige Tandy about the size of a large book. All groaned loudly when the power went out, the lobby went dark and the bulky telex machines wheezed into silence.

On good days there were two working machines. One was offline. It allowed journalists to bang away on the sticky keys, punching reams of ticker tape that fell in long folds on the floor, which they then fed it into the other telex to be transmitted to London, Paris, Washington and more, slowly bouncing between satellite links to reach their offices. Sometimes journalists simply hammered out their copy on the online telex, which whirred like a monstrous electric typewriter. Then they would repeatedly stab the bell key – *DING! DING! DING! . . . rcvd??* – trying to attract attention at a far-away desk and praying their precious turn at the telex would not be wasted. Sometimes it was. Hours later the machine would belch into life – *GA GA*, their editors typing the *go ahead* signal – by which time their 'man in Kabul', or woman, was nowhere to be seen. The cubicle was a rollercoaster of emotions triggered by the terror of deadlines. The Japanese journalists seemed to cause the most consternation. Their files took so long to type. And no one else knew what they were typing.

When all else failed, a gangly technician with a roguish grin would show up from the PTT downtown, a burning cigarette dangling from his lip and a faded brown briefcase hanging by his side. Everyone knew Momin; Momin knew everyone. It was widely suspected that he carried a mickey of whisky inside that battered case. He was usually in a buoyant mood, occasionally a little bit tipsy. But he was a magician on the machines. A sympathetic soul. Sometimes, he did expect a little something in return for sorting these do-or-die issues.

The telephone situation was no less stressful. There were only a few international telephone lines out of the country, most of them passing through Moscow. In normal times, each call was limited to three minutes. Five minutes maximum. But the city's merchants were now waiting days, even weeks, for their turn. International journalists were the priority at this moment – the government didn't want Western media reporting that Kabul couldn't even run its best hotel. Even the duration of each slot was stretched. And a more powerful generator was brought to the hill to cope with the power cuts. In an effort to explain to Nasir, the night-shift telephone operator, how much a line mattered, LyseDoucet said that for a journalist in Kabul a telephone connection now mattered more than a marriage. It was only half in jest. Curiously, one telephone line went through the Glasgow exchange. The Scottish operators soon started calling her themselves at a fixed time each day; they understood how much she needed a line. They even put calls through to her from journalists outside Kabul desperately trying to get in.

Most Afghans would not miss the nightly news and commentary on foreign radio stations, especially the BBC. It was even said that guns fell silent on frontlines so that warring sides could listen in and find out who was winning. Radio bulletins hissed and crackled with ever-greater intensity. 'President Najibullah's rule will end in a matter of days,' Western capitals were breathlessly predicting. 'The Afghan army will collapse once the Soviets are gone.' Even some Soviet observers quoted on foreign radios didn't mask their worry. But the drumbeat pounding on Kabul and Moscow radios was confident, bellicose, even mocking. The closure of Western embassies was mere 'psychological propaganda, to frighten or spread fear'. The president and his supporters kept confidently claiming he wasn't going anywhere.

The foreigners must know the real story, Amanullah thought in his room-service nook. So did Nasir at the basement switchboard, Hazrat cleaning the rooms above, Salem, Sharif, Najib and others manning the front desk, serving in the restaurants, sitting in the back rooms. Nerves were jangling. In quiet corners, when the coast was clear, they summoned courage to whisper to their guests, 'What will happen next? Do you think it will get better?'

The spooks had the same questions. Agents of the dreaded intelligence agency, which Afghans still called KhAD rather than its new name of WAD, not only lurked by day. They stayed the night. Front-desk staff suspected that listening devices were being installed in guest rooms. Spooks ordered room boys to bring the bins from journalists' rooms so that they could lift anything and everything of value: discarded documents, torn photographs, scribbled notes, typed stories. They dropped by the telephone switchboard in its dim cave downstairs to ask what the journalists were saying. The savviest operators begged off, insisting their English wasn't good enough to be exactly sure. Besides, they had too much of their own work to do, fielding the incessant requests to reserve one of the few international lines with the PTT downtown. The bravest pointed out that they worked for the hotel, not the spy agency.

Besides, they might not be in power for long. Rumour had it that tens of thousands of *mujahideen* were simply biding their time beyond the sharp white snowy peaks cradling the city. As winter tightened its grip, their rockets magnified the chill. Some days Kabul international airport, the gateway to the city, was shrouded in black smoke. Afghan and Soviet pilots took to the grey skies, striking targets across the border in Pakistan where the main rebel groups were based, smashing mud villages and valleys along the main road out for the Russians. The United Nations had managed to broker the Geneva Accords, which included a timetable for the Soviet troop pull-out. But the United

States reneged on its pledge to stop arming the *mujahideen*; the Soviets wouldn't agree to stop aiding its own allies.

The war showed no sign of stopping, and every indication of escalating. Kabul held its breath.

And almost every night, at a guard-post just below the hotel, a young Afghan soldier in a chocolate-brown uniform played haunting tunes on his flute.

The boyish Soviet commander was in the news again. About a year earlier, in the spring of 1988, Lieutenant-General Boris Vsevolodovich Gromov had first made headlines in the Inter-Con at a rare press conference – the first time a senior Soviet military commander in Afghanistan had appeared before Western journalists since Moscow sent in its tanks in the winter of 1979.

Brown-haired and blue-eyed, the general first appeared on the ballroom stage the previous May, the day before the Russians started bringing their soldiers home. The banquet hall had been humming. More than 200 journalists had flown in to cover the story. The general had been ready to make his case in person, under the vigilant gaze of a spokesman for the Soviet Communist Party's Central Committee in Moscow. He kept fielding questions suggesting that the Russians' mission had failed. 'The troop withdrawal is not a defeat,' he declared. The journalists kept grilling him on what would happen when rebel forces carried out their threat to attack the departing troops. 'Certainly the retribution will be quick and severe,' Gromov stressed. The queries kept coming until eventually the soldier in his green camouflage gave up on disguising his impatience. When asked another question on whether he really had enough firepower to fight back, he just shrugged and smiled as if to say the answer was obvious. He also tried to stamp out any suggestion that

Afghan forces would collapse once they left. 'We have a high opinion about the combat efficiency of the Afghan army' was his line.

Now Gromov's face was back on the screen, his story in the headlines, as the last of the Red Army troops clattered across the Friendship Bridge connecting the northern Afghan town of Hairatan with Termez in the Uzbek Soviet Socialist Republic. They were heading home, exactly as they had said they would. At 11.55 a.m. on 15 February 1989 General Gromov was the last to cross the Amu Darya river. When the officer, bundled up in a fur-collared military peacoat, reached the middle of the bridge he hopped out of his armoured carrier's hatch. His fourteen-year-old son, Maksim, walked towards him clutching a fistful of red carnations. Smiling, arm-in-arm, father and son strode across the border towards a waiting Soviet television crew. The last commander didn't look back. The Afghan TV broadcast ended. An occupation lasting nine years and fifty days was over.

At the Inter-Con the staff turned off the TVs, or at least lowered the volume, and went back to work. But the moment weighed on their minds as they went about their everyday tasks. Waiters readied tables for the lunch rush. Cleaners eyed journalists with muddy boots tramping back and forth in the lobby. In the basement more fresh towels were lifted from the giant dryers, sending up hot clouds of steam. At the bottom of the hill Faiz, the taxi driver, played one of his favourite Michael Jackson songs at full tilt in his car's beat-up cassette player, grinning – his own private celebration.

No major disasters had marred the historic exit. Soviet officials had repeatedly insisted there would be none of the frenzied scenes of the Americans' last days in Vietnam, when they had scrambled into helicopters from their embassy roof in Saigon. The relatively smooth exit had been secured partly through a secret truce with the pragmatic *mujahideen* commander Ahmed Shah Massoud, whose fighters were dug in along the main road out. Yet the Red Army left behind a grim legacy. They took pains to point out that they had built irrigation systems, cultural institutions, hospitals and schools. But they had also lost at least 15,000 of their own, and had spent billions of roubles. And nobody knew for sure how many Afghans had been killed in this cruel Cold War contest: the estimates started at 1.5 million and went up to twice that number, not to mention the more than five million more who had fled their ravaged homeland.

Kabul was now on its own. Mikhail Gorbachev was even reported to have fumed, in a private conversation, that he couldn't care less if Afghans installed an emperor in Kabul. But he assured his allies that food, fuel and funds would keep coming in the cavernous Soviet transporters. In this harshest winter in more than a decade, Kabul was wrapped in a prickly coat of ice and snow, suspicion and uncertainty. The city's mayor swore that he had a three-month stockpile of food and fuel – enough to make it through any rebel blockades, any stoppages caused by blankets of snow blocking the Salang mountain pass on the main northern highway. In this merciless war, weather was an enemy, too.

But queues of vehicles, their engines idling, were already stretching down the sub-zero streets of Kabul, along with shivering ragamuffin kids clutching jerrycans and jugs, all waiting to buy fuel. The lines were just as long and fretful outside pocket bakeries tucked into street corners. Even before the Soviets pulled out, the United Nations had been sounding the alarm. Without emergency supplies in this capital of two million people, half of them displaced by war, the most vulnerable would starve.

The *shabnama* night-letters surfaced again. *Mujahideen* sympathisers hurled them over walls and shoved them under doors, warning residents to leave the city to escape the hellfire of rockets. But on 15 February, the capital remained eerily quiet. Only Kabul's thin paper kites bobbed in the skies. The day before, five children had been killed in a salvo of rockets. Nobody really knew what the next day would bring.

Amanullah gingerly tore one blank page from the hotel ledger. The long rectangular pad was marked: *Hotel Inter-Continental Kabul Afghanistan. Restaurants & Bars Summary of Sales*. It was a page from the past. The hotel was still using the same stationery from the days when it was a proper Inter-Continental. On one side of the thin greyish paper there were neat grids traced in black lines to record the daily tallies: 'food', 'beverage', 'service', 'cig', 'misc', 'banquet income', and so on. The other side was blank.

Months earlier, in the fridge of winter, all the numbers in all the boxes had been big because so many journalists had checked in. But most had soon checked out, taking their cameras and portable computers to another war, long before the fruit trees edging the Inter-Con had exploded into their pretty pastel blossom.

Now, in the oven of the summer of 1989, as red geraniums tilted towards the sun, there were only a few guests. There was LyseDoucet of the BBC, now in Room 135, where she had placed a blue Baluch carpet on the floor; she had to move rooms because some of the spooks had moved into hers when she left for a short break. There was tall, bearded Mr John in 124: John Burns of *The New York Times*, who only took notes by pencil, so always carried a sharpener – something that caused questions at security checks. His pencils were always lined up, perfectly straight, next to his notebooks on his desk. There was Mr Dilip in 206, with his dark moustache and black-rimmed spectacles:

Dilip Ganguly from Delhi, with Associated Press. And a few other journalists scattered along the second and third floors.

President Najibullah was still in Kabul, too. His army had survived its first major test. The *mujahideen*'s audacious spring assault on the eastern city of Jalalabad, 100 miles east of Kabul, won them quick gains, but eventually failed. By early July the Afghan army had broken the siege and recaptured a key garrison that had once been a Soviet base. This prize was vital to the government's survival. And to Kabul's. Jalalabad, with its citrus groves and verdant fields, fed the capital with fruit and vegetables as well as electricity. The victory was totemic, too. President Najibullah poured even greater scorn on all the prophets of doom. 'Those Western media that yesterday were chanting our defeat today are forced to admit that the armed opposition cannot achieve any success and that they have no future.'

But Kabul was still being squeezed by rising prices and supply shortages. Amanullah still did his best to take care of his guests. When the food-and-beverage manager announced that chicken would be taken off the menu, Amanullah had protested fiercely. And he sent a reassuring message, on the back of a room-service bill, to the guest who often ordered it in 135: *I talked to management and told them if you don't buy chicken from bazaar – I don't work in their room service. They say today we will buy chicken for LyseDoucet.*

On the blank side of the ledger he had drawn a cartoon. It brightened his mood. *Service with a smile*, Amanullah thought, chuckling to himself. He could make the journalists smile, too, even when they were so busy and often seemed so stressed. He had started down this path in February when he first sent a cartoon to Mr Arthur: Arthur Kent, a Canadian with an American news network, who often showed up at the hotel. The picture showed Gorbachev and newly elected US president

George H. W. Bush lassoing Afghanistan as they tussled to control it. Amanullah knew Mr Arthur needed a smile. The government had been doing its best to kick him out; Mr Arthur and his team had been doing their best to stay, piling their heavy luggage against their room door to stop WAD agents – everyone still called them KhAD – from breaking in. Foreign Ministry officials accused them of getting up to no good. 'We want that guy out of this country!' Mr Arthur's direct appeals to Soviet diplomats in Kabul stalled – but didn't stop – their expulsion. He left dejectedly, with his TV cases, and his cartoon, too.

Amanullah drew long lines across the paper with the blue ink of his room-service pen and the black lead of his stubby pencil. The sheet was the perfect rectangular shape to sketch a diagram of the rooms along the corridors of the first and second floors. And to poke fun at the journalists' never-ending pursuit of news. One of his principal targets was Mr Dilip. The journalist's jolly demeanour barely disguised the intense pressure of a wire service with an insatiable appetite for stories. Amanullah pondered. He traced his pencil right across the sheet, stretching the Indian journalist's hands and legs into every room and scribbling above them: *Dear Journalists! Please give me some Frish news about Afghanistan . . . every day I go to bazar but I don't find news.* Then he penned, in blue ink, in every box identified by a room number: *Sorry Dleep.* Except for Room 124, which said, *I came today.*

He tore another sheet from the ledger, his black moustache lifting with his merriment. On this one Amanullah drew the elongated arms of Mr John – taller than everyone else and wearing a many-pocketed jacket – brandishing a piece of paper with *Yes! Frish news* written across it. Then he added more figures. *My hands are too short!* exclaimed a cartoon figure in 234 with outstretched hands. *I can't!* protested 215 and 238. Lyse-Doucet raised her arms too: *Frish news belongs to me!* Amanullah sprinkled the odd *yes!* and *no!* into the composition. Then he put down his pen and picked up an official hotel stamp. He smacked the four corners of his cartoon with *Control* in purplish-blue ink to give it even more authority.

He slipped his cartoons and scrawled notes under the room-service orders of the journalists he knew best, the ones he knew wouldn't take offence. They always called him immediately. Sharing laughter, they forgot about the war. At least for a moment.

Sadly, there was all too much fresh news. Rockets were now raining down on Kabul, often as many as 100 missiles a day, smashing into fruit stalls in heaving markets, into dolls and desks in a daycare centre, striking the grounds of government buildings, killing people as they walked down the street. In July alone, projectiles fired blindly into the city by rebels entrenched in outposts outside ended the lives of at least 200 Kabulis. Afghans simply went about their day, knowing their destiny was drawn by God's hand and there was little they could do about it. They kept going to work to feed their families, to their mosques to pray for peace. There were still snarling dogfights with frenzied crowds on Friday, kite-flying and kite-fighting and the stirring sight of *kaftar bazi*, the 'play of the pigeons', the birds flying in tight flocks above their owners' flat-roofed houses.

Inside the hotel the lobby was full of silence, occasionally punctured by the ambulances' wail and the dialogue of war nearby. It was mostly staff footfall as summer's short shadows made their daily passage across the marble floor. At night a chorus of canines' high-pitched barks and mournful howls drifted up the hill. In the dark hours the hotel was mainly a students' world. University learners like Amanullah, along with high-school hires, were juggling work and study to care for their families. A young man's world. In the daytime some women worked in the Inter-Con, too, often in the laundry or the house-keeping departments. But not at night.

Nasir, the night-shift operator in the telephone exchange, had upped sticks for Canada, not wanting to wait and see what happened next. A quiet young man named Sharif slipped into his seat. He came to be known as Little Sharif, to avoid confusion with Big Sharif at the front desk. Little Sharif had been scrubbing floors in the hotel since his secondary-school days. And Nasir had already shown him the ropes on the antiquated Siemens switchboard, so that he could take any calls during Nasir's breaks. Some card-carrying staff grumbled that this new operator was 'not one of us'. But they couldn't say no to Little Sharif; he was already trained, and was ready and eager to work. Now at university studying Arabic literature, he needed this promotion to support his six siblings. The spies occasionally dropped by the booth in the basement, just to check.

In the dead of night, telephone operators could also chat more easefully with the clerks at the PTT downtown, forming friendships that could help secure the lines. Every so often they were even invited to come up the hill and have lunch at the Inter-Con as a treat. The hotel still hadn't lost its charm, especially for those who never had the earnings or opportunities to come through its doors.

Young students worried about their future. Many Afghans did. Even the president was worried. In early August 1989 the Soviet foreign minister Eduard Shevardnadze flew into Kabul in a surprise visit to reassure the Afghan leader that Moscow would keep supplying essentials such as food and fuel. The top Soviet diplomat conveyed that message to Afghan security and intelligence chiefs, too. He landed on the third day of blistering salvoes by his American-backed enemies. For three hours that afternoon shellfire pounded the north-west of the city, crashing into barren hillsides, buildings and busy streets, including the neighbourhood of Kart-e Parwan below the hotel, mainly home to the city's Sikh and Hindu merchants.

The shellfire hit the hotel, too, smashing into rooms on the first floor. It happened to be the week when the few journalists still staying there for months on end, including LyseDoucet and Mr John, had left for a few days. They had travelled to the other side of the war, crossing the Pakistan border with the *mujahideen* to see for themselves who really controlled the hills of Jalalabad.

PART III

The Dark Years

CHAPTER 8

Mohammad and the *Mujahideen*

Winter 1991

It was a time when so much was ending, but Mohammad Aqa felt like his life was just starting.

At nineteen, he had entered a waiters' club, his sunny yellow uniform edged by an electric-blue collar and a sharp stripe down his trouser leg. He even wore a tie. His captain's outfit was more impressive still: a black butterfly bow tie and matching black suit, worn proudly as he stood, all-knowing, behind the wooden waiter's station at the entrance to the restaurant. The cabinet, slightly scuffed, had graced the front of this brasserie since the king's day. The older waiters sometimes gave it a reverential nod, even the odd pat. Mohammad Aqa was told to position himself a bit further inside the restaurant, closer to the kitchen door, where he could sometimes catch a glimpse of the ragged white peaks of the Hindu Kush.

Whenever he moved closer to the wraparound windows, sometimes even slipping onto the balcony, he got the chance to inhale the eye-popping view. In the distance aircraft spewed blazing flares to repel rebel fire as they approached the airport.

The older waiters explained that there were now far fewer of these hulking Soviet transporters than there once were. A deal had been struck months earlier between Moscow and Washington to stop sending military support to their respective allies, in an effort to finish this war. Many in Kabul feared Moscow's vital air-bridge of lifesaving food and fuel would be next. A halt to the kerosene needed to fire up their storm lamps, which was all most Afghans had to light the night. A halt to the flour they needed to feed their families, which made up so much of what most had to eat.

It was 25 December 1991. That didn't mean much to Mohammad Aqa. But older staff reminisced that it had been one of the most sparkling days in the Inter-Continental calendar: a day of cheery music, big-bellied Santa Clauses, and German cakes chock-a-block with dried fruit and nuts that Naser Ali, the pastry chef, prided himself on still being able to produce. And then there was that unforgettable Christmas of 1979 when the loudest music was the growl of Soviet warplanes rumbling into Kabul.

There was something in the air this Christmas, too. Mohammad Aqa slipped into the lobby, where the night-staff crowded around a time-worn TV set. Shoulder-to-shoulder, no one uttering a word, they were listening to Mikhail Gorbachev. Seated in front of a red Soviet flag, far away in Moscow, he wore a black suit and tie and a white shirt. Someone couldn't resist joking that he was dressed as if he worked at the Inter-Continental Kabul.

But this was deadly serious. 'Dear compatriots! Fellow citizens! Due to the situation that has taken shape as a result of the formation of the Commonwealth of Independent States, I am ceasing my activity in the post of President of the USSR,' Gorbachev was announcing. 'I am leaving my post with a feeling of anxiety. But also with hope and with faith in you, in your wisdom and strength of spirit . . . I wish all of you the very best.'

The Soviet Union was over. The hammer and sickle over the Kremlin would soon be lowered for the last time; the Russian Federation's white, blue and red tricolour hoisted in its stead, its bright stripes rippling from the illuminated flagpole. Gorbachev's ten-minute speech had ended seventy years of history.

The weight of his proclamation pressed down on the restaurant staff, pushing out thoughts of anything else. No one could yet grasp what it would mean for them, for their families, for Afghanistan. Questions tumbled around their heads; how much of life as they knew it in Kabul was going, or gone?

Of course there had been omens. Months earlier there'd been a coup attempt in Moscow – a plot by hardliners in the Communist Party who rejected Gorbachev's reforming *perestroika* and *glasnost*. Gorbachev survived that putsch. But the USSR had been crumbling state by state since 1989, just months after the last of its troops finally said farewell to Afghanistan. A wave of revolutions had swept across Eastern Europe. The wall dividing East and West Germany had been brought down by the people, stone by stone. Boris Yeltsin, head of a newborn Russian Federation, was now in charge. And he was no friend of Afghanistan's rulers.

As Mohammad Aqa slipped out of the hotel's staff entrance at the end of his shift, shortly before the 10 p.m. curfew, he paused briefly in his stride to observe the surroundings of his hotel: on one side, the kerosene lamps glowing in mud-brick homes that clung higgledy-piggledy to the slopes of the low-lying Koh-e 'Aliabad, the mountain of Aliabad. During the day you could see kids in tatty coats scrambling up and down its rocky incline, lugging plastic buckets brimming with water or jerrycans of fuel. They came from families who had never known the ease of flicking a switch for electricity, twisting a water tap in their home. A paper kite or two always danced in the sky, children's giggles cascading like their playthings. Some believed it was their country that had invented these toys.

Mohammad Aqa also knew what lay on the other side of the hotel, over the roofs of the Polytechnic. He had never seen the *mujahideen* up close, not even during his time as a soldier, but he knew about them – how they launched rockets from behind the hills outside Kabul, dug in behind earthen walls and along craggy ridgelines. He had just completed two years of military service to the south-west of Kabul, in Maidan Shahr, the poor-farmers capital of Wardak province. It was two years spent clutching his Kalashnikov rifle, squinting into the distance on the lookout for the glint of an enemy gun, a glimpse of a turbaned head. A rocket occasionally screamed in, often smashing into a barren no-man's-land inhabited only by ghosts from skirmishes past.

As he pedalled home furiously, Mohammad Aqa reflected on his blessings. His life as a soldier had started the day Afghan squaddies found him hanging around the Foroshgah-e-Bozorg, the 'Big Store', in the centre of Kabul. It was the first shopping mall in all of Afghanistan and a magical place for a poor Afghan teenager. Chunky chocolates wrapped in twists of shiny foil. Smooth cotton shirts on hangers. Plastic white-faced dolls and mini-trucks arranged along tidy shelves. The young soldiers, not much older than Mohammad Aqa, were suspicious. They grabbed him from behind, bundling him into their truck, taking him to their base. His fate was sealed when they hitched up his trouser legs. 'You have hair!' On his legs. That was the test. If he was old enough to have dark fuzz growing on his legs, then he was old enough to do his military service. They made him sign up, on the spot.

But the most loyal of Afghan personal-protection services came to Mohammad Aqa's rescue – his family. A cousin in the army, much older than him, quickly took charge of Mohammad Aqa's military paperwork: took him to his base in Maidan Shahr, about an hour and a half's drive away and one of the better places to be posted. And so ended Mohammad Aqa's school days, in seventh grade, and began another education. He didn't know how to hold or fire a gun, but he learned fast. And he puffed up his chest in his new military uniform. It was dangerous, but everyone knew that if you did your duty further south these days, in provinces closer to the Pakistan border, then there wasn't much chance you'd come home alive.

From his checkpost in Maidan Shahr, Mohammad Aqa heard the worst of war stories from the travellers and traders who lived to tell them. From nomadic *kuchis*, their womenfolk in vivid clothing shepherding flocks of sheep and goats; from caravaneers keeping pace with their camels' rocking two-toed gait; from freewheeling smugglers with their stashes of illicit goods. All carried haunting images of a scarred land. They spoke of mile after mile of humble adobe houses charred and gutted, only timber protruding like rotten teeth. Entire villages levelled by merciless Soviet carpet-bombing. Entire villages looted, down to the door handles, by rampaging rebel forces. Farmers' land transformed into weed-tangled fields of landmines that ripped off the limbs of unknowing children. There were also occasional tales of places where *mujahideen*, more respectful of customs and beliefs than the communists, had established a more mindful local governance.

The rebels were said to be inching ever closer to provincial capitals, and to Kabul itself. Some people that Mohammad

Aqa knew secretly idolised the *mujahideen*. Others cursed them. As he cycled through the icy streets he wondered what would happen now that Gorbachev was gone.

There had been a new, nervous undercurrent in the hotel for a while. It had been ignited in the spring of 1990, just months before Gorbachev resigned from the presidency and Mohammad Aqa joined the Inter-Con. He was told about what happened as if it had occurred yesterday. Moments like this never have a full stop; they continue in the telling and retelling. Mohammad Aqa's fellow waiters remembered every detail.

It had been a still spring day. Only the high-pitched chatter of the myna birds and the chirping of tree sparrows had drifted through the open windows. Pretty pastel blooms had lined the approach to the hotel and circled the forecourt. Butterflies had danced. But Inter-Con staff knew that the flowers of the fruit trees – almonds, apricots, cherries and more – were as fragile and fleeting as life itself these days. For too many years spring had also heralded the start of another kind of season – the fighting season – when snows melted on mountain passes and the *mujahideen* took up their rifles and rocket launchers after a winter's break in Pakistan or Iran, and Afghan soldiers readied their big guns.

That morning had been quiet. Until there was a menacing whistle and a very loud thud, setting the windows rattling and the birds scattering in all directions. Najib was on the front desk that day. He came through the revolving door, turning left, tripping up the cracked cement steps to the parking lot. A shell had torn into the pavement, landing short of the almond trees, skimming the tips of the pines. Najib, calm in every crisis, looked down to inspect the ruptured concrete. He looked up to the hills of Paghman to the west. A security guard and a hotel driver stood by him, checking the damage too.

Minutes later there was another whoosh, another crash, another crater . This time the hotel shook; some windows shattered. Staff ran pell-mell to the basement, holding their breath, waiting in silence for the next blow. Then an anguished cry pierced the quiet in the lobby. 'Najib!' Panic flooded the forecourt. Najib, always impeccably turned out in his pressed black suit and spotless white shirt, lay sprawled in a spreading pool of blood. He was dead. All three men were.

Something precious died with him. Najib had been part of this hotel since its very beginning in September 1969, twenty-one years in all. He had lived its history when the morning soundscape had been the gurgle of drip coffee machines, the chit-chat of foreign tourists and glamorous models; when the nights roared with laughter in its cocktail lounges and restaurants. He was as much a part of the Inter-Con as the kicking K on the roof.

The white-bearded doorman, known as *Baba*, 'father', welcomed the team of journalists who drove up to the entrance an hour later with grief and anger. 'Rockets. Rockets. Rockets,' he moaned. 'And now, you see, they come right to our front door.' Even hard-bitten journalists couldn't hold back the tears. They all knew Najib. And they all knew it could have been them, too, had they pulled in a bit earlier. A week later Salem from the front desk would take the Canadian Mr Arthur to the spot, still stained by dark blood. 'This is where it happened. Our friend was killed here. There was nothing we could do.'

It seemed there was nothing anyone could do. For so long Najib had threaded the painful needles of this war. Cooperating, up to a point, with the secret police when they prowled in his corner. Gathering the journalists at short notice when the president's office summoned them for an interview. Collaborating with them fearlessly in their everyday emergencies: driving a hotel car post-curfew until trigger-happy soldiers shouted *Dresh!*, 'Stop!', and demanded the day's password; miraculously making the telex burst into life and telephone lines appear; sometimes a source of news, at other times quietly sharing his own stories. Afghan patriot, loyal hotelier, devoted husband and father. Whatever happened – and so much did – Najib had held onto hope, and his smile.

And the rockets still kept coming. US officials acknowledged helping to supply them as part of a whopping $700 million package of arms, ammunition and financial aid to the rebels they called 'freedom fighters'. They even spoke of *another fighting season*, or two, before they were certain to bring down Najibullah's government.

In Kabul there was no sign of surrender, or defeat. The Afghan army had a formidable arsenal of its own, including Soviet-made Scud missiles, still pulverising valleys and villages. Slaying civilians, too. Now it was Afghans killing Afghans, each with the firepower of their friends.

When death stalks every door, the only antidote is to live. Najib's story shot sadness and fear into every heart. But everyone simply picked themselves up and kept going. Within days of their deaths, the ballroom with boarded-up windows was bouncing again with lively wedding tunes. And within weeks it was playing host to an even more audacious celebration. 'Miss Afghanistan' was returning to the Inter-Continental.

The first time had been in 1972, when eighteen-year-old Zohra Daoud had been crowned Miss Afghanistan in a glittering ceremony in the Kandahar Ballroom, attended by Princess Bilqis and senior government officials and ambassadors.

Speaking confidently, bare-headed in her bare-shouldered floor-length evening gown, the daughter of the surgeon-general had described the competition as a forum for 'appreciating the talents of women and their claims to equality with men in this basically masculine society'. But that had been a different world, decades before words like 'scorched earth' and *'glasnost'* and *'mujahideen'* had become part of everyday conversation. In 1990 even the left-wing magazine *Sabawoon* pondered how 'many questions were raised in the press, in people's dinner parties, and even in the parliament, over whether choosing the girl of the year was at the right moment?' Besides, the paper said, it should have been made clear that this was not the kind of beauty contest staged in the West; the criteria in Afghanistan were different.

It went ahead anyway. Thirty-five young women, out of nearly 200 who applied from universities and high schools, vied for the title of *Dokhtare Shayesteh Saal*, 'Talented Girl of the Year'. The audience clapped in time as the women strutted down the runway to the rhythmic beat of electric guitars and harmoniums. The female host, sporting a high blonde ponytail and bold red lipstick, listed the talents of each contestant as they paraded past in frilly gowns, one even carrying two doves of peace. The winner was nineteen-year-old Qudsia: a home-economics student at Kabul University who skipped across the stage with flowers in her hair, swinging a basket by her side. 'A very good chef who speaks foreign languages', Qudsia had just started work as a flight attendant with Ariana Afghan Airlines. Her victory was a rebuke to the rockets fired by Islamists, some of whom wanted to keep women at home, curtail their education, force them to wear veils – although certain rebel groups were known to be more progressive.

Mohammad Aqa listened to all these stories, the sorrowful and the enthralling. And he studied his new hotel. Even as Kabul was showing its cracks, it still mostly kept its veneer of a fine hotel, even an international one. And for a young waiter who had never stepped inside a hotel, much less a five-star one, it felt special. He spotted the insignia of the global Inter-Continental chain everywhere – on glasses, plates, tissue boxes, carpets, even shoe brushes, and of course on the pocket of his uniform. He had been told, from the very start, that it wasn't really an Inter-Continental now. Not a proper one. It should be called *Mailmah Pall*, the 'Guest House'. But, after his first day at the hotel, he never heard anyone call it that. It was still the Inter-Continental, or simply the Inter-Con. He had never seen such beautiful knives and forks. The plates looked as if they came from a palace. Some of the senior waiters sometimes muttered, to themselves, but loud enough so others could hear, that standards were dropping, that the meat was so tough, the vegetables so oily.

Mohammad Aqa still felt proud just to be here. And relieved. As so many had feared, the Soviet Union's collapse had stopped the vital airlifts of food, fuel and funds to Kabul. Wheat shipments from Russia had slowed to a trickle. Money was running out for the monthly food coupons for government employees who had been dutifully going to work, not for their meagre salary, but for their rations of flour, sugar and tea. Naan bread, the staple of life, cost five times more than it did a year ago. The most vulnerable Afghans were starving. There were only a few places where bread still seemed to be in ample supply: at the grimy yellow Silo, the Soviet-built industrial granary, where mammoth trucks were still grinding in and out, loaded with loaves to keep the security forces loyal. And in the Inter-Continental, too, where there was still food to serve, fuel to heat. When it went dark during one of the constant power cuts, a massive generator would kick in with a thunderous snort.

In the restaurant the waiters kept picking up scraps of

information and intrigue along with the smeared cutlery and crockery. Members of powerful militias sometimes swaggered in, gobbling up hillocks of rice, even emptying liquor bottles loudly. These gunmen, many from far-flung northern provinces, were now the backbone of President Najibullah's rule; many among his regular forces had deserted, or defected. Now they were grumbling, too, complaining of not being paid. Even agents of the ubiquitous secret service seemed to be conspiring in corners these days.

And the ebullient UN envoy Benon Sevan occasionally held court in the lobby bar with journalists who seemed to hang on his every word, laugh at his every joke. The silver-haired envoy from Cyprus was said often to be meeting President Najibullah late into the night. There was talk of a UN peace plan. But they seemed to have been talking about talks for a very long time. Then, on 18 March 1992, the president dropped his own bombshell. In his booming voice he announced on state media that he would resign as soon as an interim government, including the *mujahideen*, was forged under a UN scheme. Afghanistan's leader seemed to have recognised that his time was up.

As the snow melted and spring knocked on the door, Afghans went about their days shivering in the last snaps of winter's cold, shuddering to think what the milder air of the next fighting season would bring.

They're here. Mohammad Aqa watched goggle-eyed from the restaurant door. The *mujahideen* were coming into the hotel. Or at least trying to. They were stuck in the revolving door. A dozen or more had somehow squeezed into its narrow sections, their protruding rifles and rocket launchers pressing against the glass. Hooting and laughing, they attacked the glass, battling against this strange kind of door they had never encountered before. Hotel staff and a handful of journalists cautiously inched closer, watching in disbelief. Before long, the fighters prevailed. The revolving door was smashed open to cries of *Allahu Akbar!*, 'God is the Greatest!'

Their victory was great indeed. The day before, 25 April 1992, the *mujahideen* had seized power in Kabul. The old order had collapsed, falling victim to backstabbing within the PDPA and back-room deals between party top brass and the *mujahideen*. It was over – almost fourteen years to the day since the first communist coup had plunged Afghanistan into a decade and a half of bloodshed. The world's last – and bloodiest – battle of the Cold War had ended.

Armed men kept streaming into the lobby through the yawning hole in the door. Front-desk staff and waiters, busboys and bellboys shrank into their workstations: courteous, as expected by the rules of the hotel, and of Afghan hospitality. Right hands touching hearts; some hesitant, others unable to disguise their delight.

Young Mohammad Aqa was dumbstruck: *The* mujahideen *are here.* He had never seen one up close. And since the day the Inter-Continental first flung open its doors, it had never been a place for this traditional attire – the baggy *perahan o tunban* tunic and trousers that hotel staff only wore at home, in their other lives. Not here; it had not been allowed. It had only appeared, sequined and embroidered, when local musicians performed. Now it was everywhere, caked with dirt and wrinkled by war. Long-haired, long-bearded fighters ambled around everywhere: some wearing their signature soft rolled-up *pakol* caps, others in swirling turbans. And there were guns everywhere, too.

Yesterday Mohammad Aqa had wavered about returning to work. Gunfire had crackled in the streets around his home just steps from the main road; staccato ripples of machine-gun fire wafted from the military base nearby. Peering through a window, hidden from sight, he watched as this new page turned. Fighters brandishing assault rifles, quivers of warheads sticking out of their backpacks, were dragging cement blocks and heavy rocks across the road to set up checkpoints. Stopping every car that lurched into view on the slush-covered roads. Mohammad Aqa could see the fear on the faces of Afghans pulled from cars, hands clumsily tied with the cloth of rebel turbans, and taken away. The men on this street were said to be the fighters of Gulbuddin Hekmatyar, one of the most powerful and radical of the *mujahideen* leaders.

The next day, when the jabber of weapons waned, Mohammad Aqa warily ventured out and bumped into his neighbour, a colleague from the front desk. He said that a new general manager for the Inter-Con had already been appointed – an employee who, all along, had been secretly linked to the other famed commander, Ahmad Shah Massoud, the 'Lion of the Panjshir'. The new regime was formed of different *mujahideen* factions who had tentatively come together to form their own interim government; Massoud, the main rival to Hekmatyar, had now been named as Afghanistan's interim defence minister. Hekmatyar refused to sign their accord.

Mohammad Aqa cycled cautiously to work. Fighters from different groups, long entrenched in the hills, were pouring into Kabul – on foot, in trucks, in commandeered taxis and buses, in Afghan army helicopters. The word on the street was that rival groups were racing to the presidential palace, the police stations, government ministries, army garrisons and armouries, meeting almost no resistance from the army. Rumours spread of security forces shucking their uniforms and speeding home to seek cover, or ripping off their insignia and pledging allegiance to the men they had battled for years. Insurgents giddy with victory rode tanks with flowers poking from grey-green gun turrets, flinging rose petals and purple wild flowers on passers-by and hailing the dawn of peace and a truly Islamic government. Educated women who dared to go out hid their hair and Western dress under long wraparound shawls or an all-enveloping *chadri*. Men who once donned Western suits only left home in traditional tunics.

In the hotel the revolving door wasn't the only wonder. Village men who had never set foot in multi-storey buildings, never been to a second floor except to a mud roof via a rickety wooden ladder, were thunderstruck as the shimmering doors of the lobby lifts magically swished shut, only to open on a different floor. Crammed into the mirrored cavity, wide-eyed and giggling, they whooshed up and down, punching all the lift's buttons. Those who opted for the stairs instead also confronted urban obstacles: backpacks bulging with warheads kept banging into walls as they navigated the zigzag turns. Lives long governed by God's will, and the vagaries of weather and war, were clashing with the structures and systems of this modern hotel. It was also a moment of reckoning, an indictment of centuries of distorted development and decades of war, which had always kept Kabul ahead of the countryside.

Staff knew the drill. Paper photographs of Commander Massoud were soon tacked to walls, a temporary measure until proper portraits could be prepared. Every image of President Najibullah was quickly taken down. The leader once revered on state media was now reviled. After he had announced his readiness to step down, power had drained away from him. His own men had conspired against him, double-dealing with their erstwhile enemies and sinking the UN's blueprint. More territory fell to the *mujahideen*.

Najibullah had slipped away from his villa inside the old

royal palace in the dead of night on 17 April. Wearing a dark-grey pinstripe suit, sitting alongside his brother and a trusted aide, he moved in a three-car convoy including UN officials. A blue-flagged plane waited for them at the airport. But they were brought to a sudden stop at the last checkpoint by gun-toting militiamen who only answered to their own leader: General Abdul Rashid Dostum, who commanded loyalty among Afghanistan's Uzbek minority and had recently, and astonishingly, joined forces with Massoud. After urgent phone calls, loud shouts and threats, the convoy of the former leader was turned around and sped back into the city. Rumours swirled about Najibullah's whereabouts. The BBC reported that he had taken refuge inside the UN compound until the Afghan dust settled.

Amidst the hurly-burly, there was also hope. *The war is over.* Sharif at the front desk, his hair fashionably slicked with a side-parting, bounced through the lobby. Even Salem, his sombre sidekick, allowed himself a lopsided smile. They had all breathed a bit easier when the interim president selected by *mujahideen* leaders finally pulled into Kabul, three days after the fighters stormed in. The cavalcade had brought educated Afghans to the capital to make good on their promise to establish an effective Islamic government. They watched their new leader's first press conference on Afghan TV. The white-bearded, white-turbaned Islamic scholar Sibghatullah Mojaddedi grinned in the glare of the world's television lights, his outsized spectacles perched on his aquiline nose. Girded by a crush of aides and bodyguards, the cleric spoke of his joy to return to the motherland, his sadness to see how so many had suffered. 'Now we can dry the tears of widows and orphans.'

The Inter-Con staff dared to believe it marked a new start. New crockery was already being ordered. As the *mujahideen* meandered through the hotel, Sharif – ever the manager in his sombre grey suit and blue cardigan – cradled a sample plate; he was building spreadsheets in his head. 'We've got so many plans!' he said, his eyes twinkling with even greater sparkle. The hotel was full of his old journalist friends again, there to report on the birth of a new government; LyseDoucet of the BBC had recently travelled in on the new leader's convoy.

Mohammad Aqa's head was spinning, too. He had never been so pumped up with curiosity, so excited about the future, despite the chaos still coursing through Kabul. His hotel shone long into the night, a beacon in this city with only intermittent light. And it still had the best front-row seats to history. On the night of the *mujahideen*'s arrival the skies exploded with a spontaneous firework display staged by ecstatic fighters. Thousands of rounds of scarlet and emerald tracer fire arced across the sky. Flares cascaded in flashes of yellow and white. It was beautiful to behold. Darkly beautiful.

CHAPTER 9

The Agony

Spring 1992

Hazrat paced up and down his hallway. With every day there were more *mujahideen* in the hotel, occupying any rooms not snapped up by journalists. First the fighters crashed into vacant spaces on the first floor, tugging mattresses and pillows off the beds and onto the floor for a more comfortable sleep, twiddling the television dials to see what would appear on the screen. Then they scrambled onto the second floor, settling in on the wall-to-wall carpet in every room. Then they showed up on the third floor – *his* floor – coursing down the corridor, savouring their new fortune. Some even made their way up to the fifth floor to take over the spacious and still well-appointed Khyber Suite.

Some of the more recent arrivals were no strangers to modern lodgings. The latest *mujahideen* to arrive exuded a more urban, urbane air, some of them wearing khaki army jackets with 'US Army' patches on their sleeves: mementoes of their funders, even if they had spent more time plotting in princely villas in Pakistan than suffering the privations of the Afghan frontlines. Still, most fighters had lived hard lives where beds were, at best, thin blankets and fraying rugs on dirt floors. Toilets were holes in the ground, not these confusing white contraptions protruding from the floor tiles. Most Afghans lived with little. So did Hazrat and his family. But his job was to ensure sanitary conditions met the standards of this so-called five-star hotel, whoever happened to be in it.

Hazrat was growing accustomed to his new guests. After all, they were guests. And his Inter-Continental training still rang in his ears: 'Don't stare at the guests . . . The guest is always right.' But it took some getting used to. Downstairs, the Bamiyan Brasserie was heaving every morning with guests exploring this white-tableclothed land with its rolling hills of white plates. The fighters rowdily piled in for breakfast, after dawn prayers, before the journalists turned up. Platters of fried eggs swimming in oil, basins of snowy yogurt, a mountain of flatbread, a lake of green tea. And bowls brimming with the sweetest of treats – glittering sugar they could pour into their hands to eat. Many more men showed up for lunch. Waiters and busboys bustled back and forth, gripping buffet pans packed with fragrant rice freckled with chunks of potatoes or meat – until the food ran out, as it did at every meal. Staff struggled to communicate, courteously, that restaurant fare was meant to be paid for, not free for the taking. It was a task far beyond their purview, most of all for young waiters like Mohammad Aqa who could only focus on sprinting from one side of the restaurant to the other, clearing and cleaning. Managers possessing more authority eventually managed to convey to senior commanders that this was a national hotel – a government hotel. That meant it was now *their* hotel, which had to earn its keep. The journalists, the paying guests, found themselves jostling for space and food in a *mujahideen* mess hall; eventually they were moved to the smaller restaurant, the blue-carpeted Le Cavalier next door.

A new way of doing things soon fell into place. Some staff knew what had to be done, without being told. Many, including Hazrat, had already started growing their own beards. The music stopped. All of it: in the lobby, in the lifts, in the restaurants. The muzak was switched off; the musicians stayed home. The pianos disappeared, too. The otherworldly white one on the top floor in the Pamir Supper Club. The lustrous reddish-brown mahogany one in the Nuristan Cocktail Lounge. The piano the shade of Afghan walnuts, downstairs near the general manager's office. Someone said they had seen fighters sitting on the one in the lobby. They had never seen a piano before. Someone else even swore they saw a fighter toss rice on top of it. Nobody was sure where the pianos had all gone; one waiter said he spied them under the ballroom's sweeping stairs.

The alcohol also disappeared. Staff carted away boxes of beer, wine, spirits. Bottles were stashed in the basement, hidden away under wooden boards. At least that was what those in the know said. And it was better not to know. The journalists had known this day was coming. They were already coping with minor inconveniences – such as using the entrance around the back until the revolving front door was repaired after its first rendezvous with the rebels. Now their prized watering hole, the welcoming Nuristan Cocktail Lounge, was about to shut. It deserved a suitable send-off. Empty beer cans were piled high in precarious pyramids in a raucous tribute, wobbling towers collapsing with a shrill clatter and a rousing roar.

The bar was sorely missed, because the journalists' jobs were getting tougher. They were no longer just reporters. They also had to be scavengers. Time was spent scouring Kabul's twisting back alleys in a desperate daily hunt for ever-pricier diesel: the currency needed to secure a place in the queue that formed, night and day, at the top of the hotel for the satellite dish of the

Associated Press News Agency. A fuel-guzzling generator was rumbling on the roof strewn with spent bullet casings – the legacy of celebratory *mujahideen* gunfire. The lone telex in the lobby below still sometimes spluttered into life. More often it didn't.

Then came the day when the city, including the Inter-Con, was plunged into complete darkness. Rival fighters had knocked out the connection between the capital and its main power station some fifty miles away. Guests – media and *mujahideen* – found themselves trapped in the lifts, in their rooms. Journalists lit candles, desperate to keep writing. There was a story to tell. But they were unable to tell it. One enterprising British television engineer, Peter Heaps of ITV, came to the rescue. He managed to fire up his own smaller satellite dish and made it available to everyone. 'That's what it's all about,' he enthused, to his rivals' relief.

'Getting out' was getting harder, too. Every road out of Kabul was now in the hands of one band of brothers or another. Ragtag groups of gunmen, chests criss-crossed with bandoliers or pouches of ammunition, were high on the buzz of power, and sometimes Afghan weed as well. They were all kings of their own corner.

Kabul international airport often went dark. Gulbuddin Hekmatyar's men, now pushed out of the city to the south, fired barrages of long-range rockets across Kabul, including over the airfield. Not even Ariana Afghan Airlines – dubbed 'Scary-ana' by nervous travellers, and 'the bravest airline in the world' by its frequent flyers – was able to take off. Navigators not only had to make do with ageing American and Soviet-built aircraft, but their cars and buses were also being snatched by the *mujahideen*. Some days they couldn't even get to the airport.

However, one after another, the journalists checked out and

managed to get out, leaving only the most intrepid behind. And the day came when even the fighters were told it was time to pack up and leave. Like most government-owned lodgings, the Inter-Con had become a temporary hostel to house *mujahideen*, but it was long past time to make way for paying guests. Hapless housekeeping staff watched as corridors echoed with the clatter of a particular kind of checkout. Fighters bundled up their belongings, piling them into roomy shawls and carryalls, along with souvenirs of their stay. Blankets, lamps, cutlery, crockery, even taps from bathroom sinks were carted out of rooms, across the lobby and through the newly repaired revolving front door. Hotel accountants ruefully noted each day's tally of losses in their ledgers. That was the only power they had.

Some fighters moved next door, into vacant rooms in the student dormitories of the Polytechnic. More powerful commanders looked to the pleasant multi-storeyed villas in the neighbourhood of Kart-e Parwan on the other side. Most properties there were owned by Kabul's prosperous Hindus and Sikhs, who had long been part of this city's fabric, many of them corner-shop owners and trusted bankers working at the teeming money exchange in the old city. Some Hindu and Sikh families sold up to the incoming *mujahideen*. Others were forced to sell, their properties seized. Their owners fled across the city, some of them out of Kabul, some leaving the country.

At Kabul's finest hotel, rooms still cost $100 a night – only American dollars would do. But the services had taken a hit. The lifts didn't work. Electricity was rare. There was no hot water; only cold. Guests included occasional journalists, the odd gem dealer, Afghan commanders with means to pay, Arab fighters, Pakistanis advising the *mujahideen*. But for five dollars you could still get dinner. Waiters no longer handed out menus; they simply announced what had been bought in the bazaar that day. On a good day it was rice, maybe lamb kebabs, chicken, cucumbers and Afghan naan bread. On a bad day there was less. Not many dined anyway.

Hazrat mourned the unravelling of the place that had shaped his life. The soothing calm in the lobby. The music that made guests feel good about themselves, feel good about their stay. When he sensed he was out of everyone's earshot, he hummed old tunes to himself. With every day the well of loss ran deeper. The towels on his floor felt thinner to the touch. The pool was achingly empty of its perfect blue shimmer. His hotel was fading faster than his memories.

An Afghan spring always arrives with stunning bursts of new life pushing from bare trees and hard soil. But spring also brings the melting of snows that lay bare mucky layers of grime and dung and faecal dust. It unleashes streamlets of brown water, which muddy the lanes and streets. And in 1992 it brought with it the stinking sludge of a dark war, even dirtier than the last one.

Kabul was a war zone. The wide tree-lined boulevards and graceful palaces that had survived, remarkably unscathed, during two decades of upheaval were now a maze of competing fiefdoms in a bloody turf war. Different groups laid claim to entire neighbourhoods, sometimes just a few streets or a floor in a strategic building, stringing a rope or a chain across the gateway to their territory, setting up a table where portable rocket launchers perched, sometimes with a bunch of bright plastic flowers. Permissions and permits were often demanded, at gunpoint, to move from one neighbourhood to the next. Feuding factions fought from street to street, drawing and redrawing the city's map. The valley echoed to the thud of rockets, and even deeper thumps of tank fire.

In west Kabul you could never be sure when someone

would take a potshot, fling you to the ground, even rip your innards to shreds. The main thoroughfare running past the hotel was now too dangerous to use. Staff took a zigzag route, approaching the hotel from the back, around Cinema Aryub (now shut because it was deemed immoral), past the Bagh-e Bala palace that had now reopened as a guest house for *mujahideen* guests, through shrivelled vineyards no longer birthing grapes for wine, circling around the empty swimming pool and the silent tennis courts. Kabul residents, who had no other choice but to use the main road, marched into this maw. There was a hurry-scurry of people bent over bicycles, or skittering past with sad-eyed children in their arms or held tightly in their hands. Some wobbly wooden carts were packed with firewood from trees felled by hit-and-miss gunfire or chopped down for kindling. Others were a jumble of clothing and kitchenware as the homeless searched for safety. Some didn't find it. Bodies sprawled on the pitted road, faces bloodied, limbs twisted at odd angles, guts spilled – families too fearful to collect the remains of their loved ones until the guns fell silent in the dead of night. Even then, it was risky.

Hazrat made the perilous journey on foot, approaching the hotel from around the back. Staff like Amanullah who lived close by still speed-walked to work, too. Young Mohammad Aqa furiously cycled in and out, heart pounding as he raced past the Silo granary, skirting the edges of fiercely contested neighbourhoods. Little Sharif, the telephone operator, had to find a way in, too. His father had passed away after more than a decade of being laid up with illness; Sharif was now his extended family's only breadwinner. Almost everyone who worked at the hotel was. Big Sharif from the front desk jumped into a clapped-out taxi when one happened along. Afghans thrown together, squashed into back seats and front, took refuge in black humour and drew strength from their optimistic fatalism, rooted in an unshakable belief in God's grace. Everyone's time would be up, one day or the next. But treasured talismans – amulets empowered to keep evil spirits at bay – were tucked into pockets or dangled inside shirts, just in case.

Even Kabul's new leaders weren't taking any chances. Some of the business of government was now being conducted in one of the safest of places, the Inter-Con basement. The Afghan president was holding meetings in the executive suites that were once the domain of the hotel's most senior staff. Some days, when it felt safe enough to do so, the Cabinet convened in the ground-floor meeting rooms. With its solid 1960s build, nestled in a saddle between two hills, the hotel was partly shielded by mother nature. The real presidential palace, the centuries-old seat of power in the crenellated Arg citadel in the heart of Kabul, was far more exposed.

And there was already a new president. The first one, Sibghatullah Mojaddedi, who had driven into the city in triumph in late April, had schemed to stay on longer than the two months set out in the rebels' interim deal. He insisted, in his finger-wagging way, that the people wanted him. But that didn't last long. Another white-bearded Islamic leader, Burhanuddin Rabbani, with his own distinctive white turban with a thin blue stripe, wanted to take charge even earlier, arguing that the people preferred him. And he had more men under arms, including the forces of his top commander, defence minister Massoud.

Yet most Afghans felt defenceless. The distance between life and death was now measured in inches and minutes, by everyday choices to take one street or another, to stay in one place or leave, to go out or stay at home. In an unlucky land the odds of survival kept shrinking. And the day came when a random rocket, fired by someone at something, slammed into a scratched yellow taxi whose passengers had momentarily basked in their good fortune to flag down a vehicle. They were all slain in an instant, including Big Sharif with the biggest smile. His dream of a new era in hotel hospitality went with him.

Sorrow was a heavy cloak. It fell across everyone's shoulders when they walked past the front desk. First Najib. Then Big Sharif. But when positions suddenly went empty, they had to be filled. By summer Amanullah had been promoted. It felt like the saddest of successes. He moved up from room-service cashier to take over Big Sharif's responsibilities as the hotel's income auditor. That meant he moved down, too, to the basement, to take up his work. It no longer felt safe to sit in the lobby. His calculator's comforting click competed with the whoosh of rockets landing nearby, the gunfire cracking like monster crickets.

The certainty of statistics offered a refuge from a capital in chaos. The new leaders' first orders had been to shut cinemas, ban alcohol and command women to cover their heads. That had revealed some of their vision for a new Afghanistan. In practice, though, it had become a free-for-all. In some government ministries, including at Radio Television Afghanistan, women were sent home. Businesses were told to replace female employees with men. But in other ministries women were allowed to stay put; so, too, were male members of the old government. For the most part the routine business of government was paralysed as skilled civil servants fled and coffers became dry, and the issue that mattered was the battle for power.

For Inter-Con staff, as for all Afghans, what mattered most was inside their own homes. The patience of Hazrat had finally been rewarded. His lovely wife Laila had given birth to healthy, handsome children. God had tested them for many years. Their first-born, their first son, was Mehrabuddin. He had come into this world with the help of the midwife who rushed to their home and delivered him with difficulty. The Islamic *Azan*, the call to prayer, was whispered in his tiny right ear to ensure the first words he heard were those of his faith. 'God is the greatest. There is no God but Allah, and Mohammad is God's prophet.' And then, in his left ear the *Iqamah*, the call to prepare for prayer. But Mehrabuddin had died before his first year was out. Then came pretty little Huda. But she, too, passed away before she even toddled. And then baby Tamana, who lived a little longer, but not long enough to begin her second year.

It wasn't his Laila's fault, no matter what others said. Maybe it was the illiterate midwife, or their lack of good medical care, or perhaps they had not done enough or done what was right. *God works in ways beyond our understanding.* But at last their trials ended. When Soviet troops were still in Kabul, his lovely Laila had brought him beautiful healthy Sahida. And then, one after the other, his sons – Abdul Qadir, Ghulam Syed, Payman. *Patience is bitter, but the fruit is sweet,* he had said to himself, and to his dear Laila, so many times. Perhaps this was God's way. All would be well, in time.

For Amanullah, too, it was a year of new beginnings. He had just graduated from the Polytechnic. Now he was 'Engineer Amanullah'. He had fulfilled his own dream, and his dear mother's ambition for her last-born son. And his study had brought him another gift. He had met his sweetheart, Marzia. He was in his third year; she was in her second. He gave her a special name, calling her *Shala*, 'the most beautiful of eyes'. In the shade of the poplar-lined lanes on campus, and in crowded corridors between classes, their eyes would briefly lock. During breaks they would meet, sitting on benches an appropriate distance apart, sometimes so absorbed in conversation they would miss their next lessons. Shala was his distant cousin, and Afghans often married cousins, but this was about more than keeping things in the family. It was a decision made first by them.

They had both grown up in Kabul, the city where Afghans had more chances to be educated, and to dream, in their workaday world. And that meant there was only one place to hold his wedding: the Inter-Continental. And *mujahideen* or no *mujahideen*, it would be a mixed wedding. Amanullah honoured his country's traditions, with an open mind. He had of course requested his uncle to respectfully ask Shala's father for her family's permission to marry her. An observant, educated Muslim, he believed that all human beings – men and women – were equal. At the wedding of Amanullah and Shala, men and women would celebrate together in the ballroom. There would be music, too.

Hundreds of family and friends had to be invited, including from Paghman to the west of Kabul, Amanullah's ancestral village. Even *mujahideen* living there received the glittering cards. They showed up with assault rifles slung over their shoulders. 'Oh, we're sitting together,' they mumbled when they caught sight of the women in all their glitter. But to respect more conservative convictions, the women gathered at the back of the hall, the men suited and booted at the front, closer to the main door. Hospitality prevailed over ideology, in a very Afghan way.

The boom of the drums and fanfare of trumpets ushered a beaming Amanullah and his bride into the banquet hall. Two specially chosen bands brought melodies from East and West. Even Faiz Karizi, the Afghan king of folklore music, every Afghan's first choice – if they could afford him – graced the ballroom. The musicians served up strumming *rubabs*, tapping *tablas*, hands flying across the harmonium and fingering the trumpets. A tide of guests spilled onto the dance floor festooned with streamers, swaying to the music. Hotel chefs, so proud of their own Engineer Amanullah, outdid themselves: scented rice served piping hot with tender meat and soft pillows of bread. It was a day to cherish all the good in this life.

As the westering sun began to take its leave and guests savoured the last sips of cardamom-scented tea, a messenger discreetly entered the hall to whisper a message in Amanullah's ear. The groom's eyes narrowed. Fighters positioned on the heights of Koh-e Afshar, staring down on the ballroom from the mountain top, were about to start firing in this direction. Amanullah strained his ears to listen. A faint stammer of small arms was already seeping under the double doors. He looked around his wedding hall. He gazed lovingly at his bride. And then the tank in the hotel forecourt, guarding the grounds, discharged a warning shot.

The ballroom trembled. Wedding guests packed up in a panic, grabbing bags and coats and bundling out of the door. Everyone, from babbling babies to misty-eyed grandparents, hurtled down the hill. The banquet hall, which had, only moments ago, pulsed to a bouncy wedding beat, now shook to the shells belching back and forth. Most landed wide of the mark. The duel didn't last long. But the hotel once prized for being above the fray was slowly being sucked into it. Amanullah held his new wife close.

Plastic glue pots, cardboard pieces, stacks of matchsticks were all strewn across the carpet. This was where Hazrat now spent his days. He and his young family passed their hours making matchboxes in their spartan home in the neighbourhood of Shash Darak.

It was a long way from the hotel, in every way. By the winter of 1993 he could no longer make the journey there. It was too risky and there was no reward. The hotel had no money to pay anyone any more. Whatever his loyalty to the Inter-Continental, Hazrat couldn't work for nothing. So his family worked as one – oldest to youngest – smearing glue, bending cardboard, pressing pieces tightly together until they stuck, then stuffing them with matchsticks.

Night and day, every day, a thousand boxes a day. In a city mostly lit by hurricane lamps and candle wicks, matches were big business. The *paisadar*, the man with a lot of money who hired them, dropped off supplies, picked up his wares. He must have been raking it in. Hazrat's pop-up family firm earned a daily wage of seventy-five afghanis – a little more than one American dollar.

It wasn't enough. Like most Kabulis he scavenged through his own home, parting with whatever was of some value to barter for food. They often survived on *nan-e saboos* – leftover pieces of bread thrown or given away by those who didn't have to worry about their next meal. The man they called the *kharwala*, the donkey man, did brisk business combing the streets, burlap bags draped over his beast, calling out for scraps. This day-old bread had always fed cows and sheep and goats and chickens and, more and more, the poorest, too. These were the worst days of hand-to-mouth existence that Hazrat's family had ever known.

The donkey men dodged bullets as their animals trotted to their destination: Pul-e Khishti, the Brick Bridge Mosque. The donkeys instinctively knew their way to the Kabul river, now a slurry of excrement and rubbish, and to the oldest bridge, which gave its name to the magnificent blue-domed building. Created by a master tile maker in the late eighteenth-century and rebuilt under King Zahir Shah, the mosque was now pocked by bullet holes. But it still drew the pious and the poor, those seeking God's blessing and cheap grub.

Hazrat was among them. Every few days, in those pauses in a Kabul day when the guns fell silent, as fighters focused on foraging for food or fuel, he would trudge through shell-scarred streets, sometimes following the safest path through the gaping hollows in the blasted walls of buildings. In the mosque's orbit, the shops still standing were stocked with goods, many of them smuggled or stolen. And they were fronted by burlap sacks bulging with *nan-e saboos* and plastic buckets of *berenj-e-lok,* thin watery rice – a poor man's food that would have never seen the light of day at the Inter-Continental. But now Hazrat brought it home.

His family, like all families, pulled together, sharing what little food they had. Relatives – brothers and sisters, nieces and nephews – took refuge in Hazrat's humble home. One day started like any other. They all gathered for a poor man's meal, warming legs and feet under the long, low wooden *sandali* table set on a long rug. A thick blanket lay over it; a *manqal* charcoal brazier under it; men in one room and women in the other. Traditional Afghan heating and seating. Hazrat's eldest daughter, bright-eyed Sahida, and her best cousin Soraya skipped into the men's den, suppressing giggles, relishing their shared responsibility. A big task for little girls to carefully carry the water jug, basin and hand-towels, taking them to each person in turn so that they washed their hands before eating. Family chatter lifted heavy hearts and brought even more warmth to their room.

Then war arrived without warning. The biggest windows had been sandbagged to stop it from entering. That didn't stop it. A small random rocket smashed through a mud wall, shaking the cob house, sending shrapnel flying, pots and pans crashing, their midday calm shattered by shouts and crying. It took a moment for Hazrat to see Sahida and Soraya – best friends and cousins, born only days apart – standing not far apart from one another when the rocket struck. Sahida, slumped on the floor, bleeding, had been hit by slivers of steel. Soraya, folded in a heap, had been killed instantly. Hazrat, who was only slightly grazed, gently lifted his little niece, her body so limp it felt like an old rag doll, full of holes. He placed Soraya on the carpet, now coated with dust. His country had become a land without a last 'goodbye'; merely a sorrowful prayer.

Then he swept Sahida, his bleeding daughter, into his arms. They sprinted through the blighted streets to the nearest government hospital. A place overflowing with patients moaning in the corridor, floors slick with blood. But he found a kind doctor to care for Sahida, and to enable him to give some of his blood to boost the strength within her. Sahida, his first child to live long enough to grow up, had almost been snatched away. It left Hazrat breathless.

No one slept that night in his ruined home. They crouched by the flickering light of a storm lamp waiting for the moment when it felt safe to move. There were no free passes now, not even to bury the dead. Only when there was just the wail of stray dogs and a distant mumble of gunfire did the men take little Soraya on her last journey. Shrouded in white, she was carried through streets infused by the smoky incense of wood fires, the stink of rotting rubbish and sewage. Praying for the living as well as the dead, they crossed into the nearby neighbourhood of Macroyan 3, amid the comfortable Soviet-built residential blocks where some *mujahideen* commanders had settled after many of the old elite fled the city. Soraya was laid to rest next to a small shrine, a measure of dignity in a bleak little park criss-crossed by washing lines.

The next day Hazrat's family, and his brother Ghulam

Haider's, piled into taxis to head north to their sister's home in Tahiya-e Maskan, a burgeoning complex on the other side of Kabul. Her already-squeezed flat was instantly enlarged to make space for all of them. 'It doesn't matter how big your home is, it's how big your heart is,' they always said. They would have to live that maxim now. Only Hazrat and his brother stayed behind, packing their belongings in metal carts, then pushing them down cratered streets to reach their new refuge.

There were still traces of the old Kabul, the sloping roofs of elegant villas just visible behind high walls, the neon-lit pocket shops whose traders stoically made do with sputtering generators. They saluted each other in passing, knowing there was no certainty they would all still be here the next day. Even the avenues of grand old evergreens seemed sad, surrounded by rubbish and rusting metal poking from blotched snowbanks. But here and there charcoal braziers with skewered chunks of lamb and chicken still burned; Kabul's tenacious hospitality. One or other of the two brothers would be the first to notice a shuttered embassy with notices stuck to metal gates, a flagpole no longer flying its standard. Even the very last holdouts, including the Chinese, Iranian and Turkish missions, had been forced to pull out.

War was still on the brothers' trail. The far-off scrunches punctuating their hike sometimes seemed closer, as if to taunt them. And then it came for them. The rocket crashed into a stone wall along their path, hurling the two strapping men to the ground. Hazrat crawled towards his closest sibling, touched his hand to his mouth to see if he was still alive. Relief washed over him to feel warm breath.

They lay on cold cement. Hazrat, pain shooting through him, waited to see if another shell would strike, his brother Ghulam Haider unable to move. A clutch of young fighters slouched on a nearby tank noticed them and lunged to their side: a flash of empathy in this merciless conflict. They pulled Ghulam Haider into their metal beast to ferry him to the closest military hospital – the '400-bed' it was called, one of the best, built by the Russians two decades ago. Hazrat limped along behind the tank, his injured leg wrapped in a makeshift tourniquet.

War came along, too. Even hospitals weren't beyond its reach. Soon after Hazrat joined his brother inside the vast complex, a salvo of shellfire whistled into the yard, cracking windows, laying a crunching carpet of glass. Hazrat dropped once more to a cold muddied floor, pulling his brother with him; he reached once more, instinctively, to feel his warm breath. But this time it wasn't there. Shrapnel from the first attack had struck the back of his brother's head. In the rush, Hazrat hadn't noticed the gush of blood. His brother hadn't stood a chance.

The next day, woozy with grief and fatigue, Hazrat made his way back to the street where they had left their metal carts. They were still there, tied to a tree, under the watchful eyes of kind-hearted gunmen keeping the embers of a more civilised society alive.

Amanullah did what he could. He was Mr Fix-It now: the hotel's chief engineer. If water stopped running from the old taps, he patched up the source of the problem. If a creaking generator collapsed, he got it going again. If the rockets lit fires, he would holler to staff, 'Bring water and buckets!' They would all come running.

But sometimes even he couldn't fix it. And sometimes he wished he didn't have to. The hotel managers kept calling him in. They knew where he lived, just next door, on the Polytechnic campus in one of the comfy apartments reserved for lecturers. They would come and get him if he didn't show up. They needed him to keep this hotel going. More often than he liked, he spent the night in the basement, sleeping on a cot in the engineering department. Even there, where the clatter of shell-fire was all but shushed, he had to sometimes admit – if only to himself – that he was scared. It felt like a thick, prickly blanket he couldn't cast away.

But by the winter of 1995 the nerve-jangling crescendo of gunfire had become so quotidian he barely noticed it. These days it was the quiet Amanullah noticed most: that stillness which could end in an instant, sparking an infinite loop of worry for family, and friends who were like family.

It was risky even to make the short dash home. *Shukoor Khoda*, 'thanks be to God', he had only experienced one close call so far. He had been halfway up the hill on his way to work when a rocket slammed into the slope. In an instant, his military training came back. He threw himself down hard, face-first, tasting the dirt. Ears pricked. Body and soul braced for another salvo as he prayed silently that it wasn't his turn. His life had only just got going.

Shala was pregnant with their first child. His brothers and sisters, and their children, needed him, too; cancer had robbed him of his dear mother, exactly as it had stolen his father from them so long ago. And how would the Inter-Continental hotel survive without its Engineer Amanullah? On that day his prayers had been answered; no second rocket came.

His can-do spirit, his ready smile, helped him overpower his fear. He got on with it. He repaired the smashed concrete on the fifth-floor balcony, filled the ugly gap in the balustrade below, cleared away the twisted metal and splintered wood a few rooms down. He smoothed the stone wall peppered with holes at the entrance to the forecourt. He fixed the hotel's façade, the face it showed to the world. But when Amanullah walked down the room corridors, eyes looking westwards, his heart was so heavy it was like it was filled with cement. When he opened any of these doors along that side of the hotel, his heart broke. He couldn't fix all the darkness within. Ceilings were gaping black cavities, mirrors broken, carpets singed, porcelain toilets cracked. More than 100 rooms were like this – half of the hotel. Because of what happened next door in Afshar.

No one spoke openly of what had happened at the beginning of 1993. They didn't have to. It was there for everyone to see. The ruined hotel rooms on one side; what was left of Afshar on the other. It used to be such an ordinary place – a tightly packed quarter of mud-and-timber homes in the foothills of Koh-e Afshar, the mountain that gave it its name and faced the hotel. They were mostly the houses of the long-persecuted Hazara community, Shia Muslims. Their name Hazara, meaning 'a thousand' in Persian, could be traced back to the thirteenth-century garrisons in the Mongol empire of Genghis Khan. Their neighbourhood now looked as if it dated from that time, flattened like the crumbling ruins of a medieval civilisation. Biscuit-brown homes crushed into a jumble of clay, leaving only hunks of mud jutting like earthen flags of surrender.

Afshar's fate had been determined by its topography. The Hazara leader, Abdul Ali Mazari, had controlled the heights and the military base here in the foothills, just behind the Polytechnic. Once an ally of Ahmad Shah Massoud, who commanded forces around the hotel, Mazari had broken ties with him amid growing tension. On Massoud's side was the warlord who controlled the hills of Paghman a bit further west, Abdul Rasul Sayyaf, a tall Pashtun with a thick beard stretching to his chest, a devotee of an ultra-conservative Sunni Muslim sect. They cast Mazari's resistance as a threat to establishing state law and order. The battle for Afshar was political, personal, ethnic. It even drew in backing from foreign patrons such as mainly Sunni Saudi Arabia and Shia Iran.

It had dragged the Inter-Con onto the front line. Massoud's fighters positioned tanks next to the swimming pool, near the water tank, behind the staff quarters. A mighty Soviet-built machine gun was hoisted to the hilltop on the other side of the hotel. Smaller ones were mounted elsewhere. Week on week, the tensions escalated, until on 11 February at 5 a.m., at the first glimpse of light, Afshar was assaulted by barrages of rocket and artillery fire. The rolling thunder shook the Inter-Con, too. A terrified rush of people – those who had not already fled – surged towards the hotel, desperately hoping to seek sanctuary in another neighbourhood not far from its hill.

Hotel staff could not unsee what they had seen that day from the upper floors. The torrent of fear, the faces gouged, skulls smashed, blood spilled. And no one could unhear the accounts of frenzied pillage, of prisoners taken by both sides. And the stomach-churning whispers of rape. There were stories of benevolence and mercy, too, but many more of cruelty.

The next day, 12 February 1993, a hush had fallen over the hotel. Massoud, who rarely came to the Inter-Con, was here in his trademark round *pakol* cap. None of the waiters could remember ever having served Massoud more than an occasional cup of green tea. Now he was meeting with President Rabbani and his top military men behind the closed door of Le Cavalier restaurant. He had convened urgent talks: to bring an end to the mayhem, to exchange prisoners, to restore calm so that the people of Afshar could return, even if so little was left.

Some families cautiously came back, but only to retrieve the remains of their loved ones, interring them in the potato fields next to the Polytechnic. Both sides blamed the other. Yet what was done could not be undone. The Inter-Continental survived. But the darkness of this war was now sitting in its bedrooms.

What had once been the finest hotel in Kabul could now offer only the most basic of hospitality, sometimes not even that. Even the rooms on the other side of the hotel, looking over the pool and out towards the city centre, weren't in great shape. Some of their windows were cracked or blown out, covered with sheets of plastic, or criss-crossed with stripes of thick duct tape to provide a bit of protection, at best.

But there wasn't much more on offer anywhere else. The Inter-Con was one of the few places left in Kabul that still offered beds for the night, some food during the day. The Kabul Hotel in the city centre was shut. It sat in the middle of shifting frontlines, the city's maze of sandbagged checkpoints and make-shift bunkers. So the Inter-Con still hosted the most important visitors. The latest was the would-be UN peacemaker Mahmoud Mestiri, who sometimes came through the door to conduct his never ending-rounds of courtesies and consultations in one or another of the meeting rooms. On one occasion a gust blew in through broken windows, flurries of snowflakes settling on the shoulders of his fine winter coat, even on his bushy black eyebrows. Mestiri continued, unfazed, with the presentation of his latest report to the city's mayor.

There were also guests of the government. And intrepid journalists who specified they wanted a room facing the city; the mountains on the other side would block their satellite signal. They also wanted to see for themselves, from their balcony, what was being fired, where it was landing. Some, like Mr Bob, Robert Nickelsberg of *Time* magazine, even chose rooms where windows were simply plastic sheeting. It removed that risk of being showered with glass if something whacked it. The downside was that those rooms were like fridges, at least in winter. When someone checked out, a guest next door would steal into the room to pinch an extra blanket. Some even nicked leftovers lying on trays outside. Such was this catch-as-catch-can life.

The lobby felt ghostly, too. The tidy arrangement of cobalt-blue sofas, flanked by welcoming armchairs, silently waited for guests to come through the door. A bulbous turquoise vase with twirls of petite pink and white flowers stood upright in the corner, looking strangely out of place. Even the bookshop was now under lock and key, a management order scribbled on a scrap of paper stuck to its door. At the other end of the lobby, the Bamiyan Brasserie was serving day-old bread.

CHAPTER 10

Hope on the Hill

Summer 1996

Curved blades of butcher's knives swished through fatty lamb and lean cuts of beef. A gently boiling cauldron of water purred on the hob, harmonising with the rhythmic chopping of onions and carrots to make *qabuli pulao*, the national dish. Today, 26 June, white-bearded Inter-Con cooks in smudged chef's whites were immersed in their own domain, pushing away the world outside. They had been instructed to prepare special food for special guests. No more detail than that.

Down the corridor, in the Kandahar Ballroom, there was the clatter of chairs being lined up in rows. The pinkish-brown settees and matching armchairs were dragged onto the worn red carpet on the stage, a mess of wires drooping from a double microphone stand. A small official photograph of President Rabbani was fastened to the floor-to-ceiling backdrop, dwarfed by the voluminous, if somewhat faded, gold drapes.

It was a rare day when work absorbed this much attention and effort. But it was also the worst day in months, and that said a lot. Hundreds of missiles were pounding the wounded city. Front-desk staff idling in the lobby edged closer to the panoramic windows to sneak a peek. Columns of black and white smoke towered in warm summer skies, the mournful wail of sirens drowning out the sparrows' chirp.

The hotel was jumpier than usual, too, with guards circulating around its wooded perimeter, through the car park, across the forecourt. There was never any real respite.

As always, it was the radio that eventually told them what they needed to know. The BBC's Pashto and Persian news bulletins cut through the clang of pots and pans in the kitchen with startling news. Gulbuddin Hekmatyar was heading to the hotel. The warlord, whose forces had long been rocketing Kabul from the outskirts, was finally coming into the city. He was here to take up the post of prime minister, which he'd been offered so many times by other *mujahideen* leaders. He would swear his oath of office in the ballroom, the ceremony being touted as a rare step towards peace.

It was Hekmatyar's homecoming. He had not been seen in the city since his days studying engineering at Kabul University in the 1970s. Stories still abounded that, as a student, Hekmatyar had hurled acid in the faces of unveiled women on campus. His supporters batted away the charge as a communist smear. The BBC and other foreign radios often featured commentators describing him as a charismatic orator and an effective organiser, but also the most radical of *mujahideen* leaders – as well as the one who received the lion's share of resources provided by America and delivered to him by military spooks in Pakistan. He was accused of ordering countless murders, including that of a thirty-six-year-old cameraman, Andy Skrzypkowiak, who had been filming for the BBC and was found with his skull crushed by a rock in 1987. In 1994 it had been the Afghan journalist Mirwais Jalil, fondly remembered by hotel staff as a fresh-faced twenty-five-year-old who often accompanied foreign journalists on their forays. To this day, Inter-Con staff recalled Mirwais bounding into the hotel, flashing his infectious smile, always taking time for traditional courtesies. Even when he was in a rush, as on that day two years previously, just before his bullet-riddled body was found on the outskirts of Kabul.

Hekmatyar and his men always denied any responsibility for these crimes. But the accusations never went away. Some Kabulis also remembered one of Hekmatyar's *shabnama* night-letters in the harsh winter of 1989 as Soviet troops were pulling out of Afghanistan after a disastrous decade. In one leaflet bearing his signature, Hekmatyar declared that he would soon make his heroic return to Kabul on a white horse, like Islamic conquerors of old, and would pray in the historical Pul-e Khishti mosque.

The moment turned out to be more mundane. He entered the capital in a luxury SUV escorted by muscled motorcycle outriders in tailored white tunics. His titanic motorcade was fronted by a tank, his portrait draped across its turret. They had journeyed from his base in the east, about forty miles away, the potholed road ripped by shellfire and landmines and dotted by the rusting carcasses of Soviet tanks. The route snaked through terrain so tough that even war couldn't break it: staggering switchbacks ascending along sheer drops of grey-blue rock in the narrow gorge slicing through the Hindu Kush, the gateway to Kabul. Before they could parade through Kabul's largely deserted streets, Hekmatyar's convoy had come to a screeching halt, stopped by a barrage of missiles. It detoured through safer back roads, biding its time at a *mujahideen* safe house until the coast was clear.

Two hours before midnight, his moment came. The caval-cade roared up the hill, ferrying Hekmatyar and his new political partner President Rabbani into a forecourt flooded by bright-yellow light. Even the electricity showed up for the ceremony.

A red carpet stretched across the pavement, peopled by diplomats and senior officials from friendly nations like Pakistan,
Iran and Saudi Arabia, as well as high-ups in the Afghan government, who now governed mainly in name alone. Hekmatyar, in
a grey coat and trademark black turban – denoting that he was
a direct descendant of the holy prophet – observed an honour
guard by uniformed soldiers with peaked caps and red epaulettes, as a marching band played. Hotel staff watched, amazed,
from the hotel windows.

The pomp was swiftly shattered. A rocket struck the grounds
close by, forcing dignitaries to dive for cover in a rather undigni-
fied way. The lights went out. The hotel went black. There was a
rush to the front entrance; many got stuck in the revolving door,
unable to move in or out. Once they escaped, they were bundled
into the basement as more rockets whooshed in.

A short while later a who's-who of the *mujahideen* and their
friends piled into the ballroom with much vigorous shaking of
hands, gestures of hands on hearts, as if nothing had happened. On
the stage stood the turbaned President Rabbani, selected to lead
for four months in 1992 and still holding on to power four years
later. The swearing-in, witnessed by an Islamic cleric, was sealed
with smiles, even kisses on cheeks, between old arch-enemies.
Then it was time to tuck into the feast. Even Massoud, Hekmatyar's greatest rival, showed up – heading straight to the hotel's top
floor to continue the conversation long into the night. As part of
this deal he had agreed to formally relinquish his post. But no one
doubted that he was still the real power behind the throne.

Kabul's finest hotel had again set the stage. But Afghans
knew enmities weren't so easily forgotten, or forgiven. These
unlikely allies had been forced to make common cause by the
growing risk to their rule. A new force was rising from within
their very own ranks, rapidly taking ground: the Taliban. In

Arabic, *taliban* meant 'the students'. Many were young men, peasant farmers from eastern and southern Afghanistan who had come of age fighting against the Soviet invaders or studying in strict Deobandi *madrasas* in neighbouring Pakistan.

Now they were taking aim at their old *mujahideen* brothers-in-arms, repelled by their infighting, corruption and thievery, and offering salvation through the strictest interpretation of Islamic rules. By late 1994 the Taliban held sway over more than 40 per cent of the country, including Kandahar, their spiritual home. They were rolling into district after district, often not firing a single shot, welcomed by a people desperate to see an end to the anarchy.

Often advancing in convoys of dusty Toyota pickup trucks, the Taliban had recently reached the edge of Kabul before being beaten back. And they had closed in on Hekmatyar's headquarters in the rocky foothills south of the capital, forcing him to retreat in his fleet of sleek Japanese SUVs to another hideout further east. For a blissful while, Hekmatyar's attacks had stopped, roads had been unblocked, food trucks got through. A city that had been teetering on the brink of starvation revelled in this reprieve.

But the lull was short-lived. Now the Taliban were rocketing Kabul in a bid to topple the 'un-Islamic' government. It had been their barrage that briefly halted Hekmatyar's homecoming. Reports were also reaching the capital from districts under Taliban rule: of women ordered not to leave home unless accompanied by a *mahram*, a male relative, and to cover up completely inside the all-enveloping *chadri*. That changed little in the lives of women in the deeply conservative countryside. But Kabul was different. The *mujahideen*'s own directives on women's dress in the capital had eased over time into an order to cover their heads. The Taliban had a different vision.

Theirs was a moral mission, being played out in smashing televisions, yanking music tapes and videos out of cassette players. It weighed on the minds of some Kabulis. But for now, most simply worried about getting through the day, never mind the day after that.

Mohammad Aqa knew the drill by heart. Every day excluding Friday, the day of prayer, the longest table in the furthest corner had to be ready for service after noon prayers. White tablecloths, stains and holes hidden. Cutlery in straight lines. And a menu that varied from week to week.

It never varied that much, admittedly. Usually it was mounds of *qabuli pulao*, *qorma* lamb stew thick and oily with caramelised onions and sharp tomato purée, gently fried okra, some crunchy salad. When available, there was fruit. On special days *sheer birinj*, a milky rice pudding scented with cardamom. And green tea, of course.

The service was for the minister of the interior, Yunus Qanooni, and his department heads, about a dozen in all. Mohammad Aqa's job was to bring order to a disorderly time and to keep anything he heard to himself. Discretion and discipline were a waiter's bywords, especially in the cafeteria of the Ministry of the Interior.

He was proud to be seconded here. Serving in the hotel restaurant had been a job worth doing. But he stood even taller now in his black suit, white shirt, black bow tie. He was a proper waiter, an Inter-Continental waiter, assigned to this government cafeteria for which the hotel provided catering. The two-storey compound set behind thick stone walls and heavily guarded gates in the heart of Shahr-e Nau was not usually in the direct line of rocket fire. That was a good side of the job, too.

When the *mujahideen* took over in the spring of 1992 the hotel had originally sent Mohammad Aqa to serve at the Ministry of Defence; some cooks and waiters had fled when the rebels moved in. It was boiling hot in the kitchen, even hotter outside. The ministry, near the sprawling grounds of the presidential palace, was often in rebel sights. But waiters charged through kitchen doors without missing a beat. Old-timers zipped in and out of the heaving dining hall, expertly balancing a full platter on an open palm, their other hand steadying the heavy weight by tucking it into their shoulder. Novices gripped trays with both hands, trying to suppress nervous giggles, not always succeeding.

When Qanooni, then deputy defence minister, was appointed to head the Interior Ministry he asked the hotel to send Mohammad Aqa and others. Bespectacled Qanooni, with his trim black beard and a degree from the Faculty of Islamic Law, had a serious air and an intense stare. He was in the thick of it. He was a Massoud protégé, from the same Tajik ethnic group and the same picturesque Panjshir valley north of Kabul. They had fought the Soviets together. Now they were together in this mess of a civil war. In 1993 Qanooni's car had gone up in flames when someone tried to kill him. He blamed Hekmatyar. Now he walked with a cane. Afghanistan's tortuous history was in his bones.

His old foe, President Najibullah, was just streets away. Najibullah was still languishing inside the UN compound, along with his brother and an aide, four years after his attempt to leave Kabul was blown off-course by allies who betrayed him. He was said to be whiling the time away by reading voraciously, watching films beamed by satellite from Hong Kong and exercising on a treadmill. It was also reported that he was using his time to translate Peter Hopkirk's *The Great Game*, a chronicle of the nineteenth-century rivalry over Afghanistan between imperial Russia and Britain. Najibullah wanted Afghans to be able to read this text in their own language as new games unfolded all around him.

Mohammad Aqa still travelled back and forth to work on his trusty bicycle, taking different routes to and from his new temporary home to the north, in Khair Khana. This suburb of residential blocks, about three miles from the city centre, was still largely intact, a place of escape for many. His family had been forced to flee their home in Deh Mazang; it was now a muddy sprawl of rubble. The grand boulevard of Darulaman stretching from his old neighbourhood's roundabout was a woeful monument to war: the Soviet House of Science and Culture, once a modern angular block, was spotted with gaping black holes; the former Soviet embassy a mess of shattered masonry. At the very end of this sweeping avenue stood the skeletal remains of the Darulaman palace itself. *Darul Aman* had a double meaning: 'Abode of Peace' and 'Abode of Aman' – King Amanullah, who had ordered this palace built in the early 1920s; but he was ousted in 1929 and it never fulfilled its role as the seat of the Afghan parliament. Decades later it had become the offices of the Soviet-backed Defence Ministry. Now it was a blasted shell, its tall windows like dark eyes staring out onto Kabul. It looked as if Darulaman was crying.

Wherever he cycled, Mohammad Aqa saw the Interior Ministry police in their olive-green garb, hanging out with turbaned rebel fighters. There were soldiers in a strange mingling of American and Soviet camouflage fatigues. And there was even still a sprinkling of traffic police, in their enormous peaked caps and eye-catching white gloves, on duty at some roundabouts. There was something admirable about these traffic police. No matter who was in charge, no matter the weather, no matter the war and whatever the traffic, they were on the beat.

It was the human traffic that tugged at Mohammad Aqa's heart. Women beggars wailing under grimy blue burkas, bony hands outstretched and babies crying in their arms. Young boys and old men with leg stumps, hobbling on crutches, victims of landmines. And soot-faced street children plying their wares: matches and bobbing multicoloured balloons, bathroom scales and rusted tin cans of *spandi*, smoke twisting from the burning herb to ward off misfortune and evil spirits, for a tiny price. The street urchins danced around life and death, crossing front-lines with jerrycans to fetch water from hand-pumps, fuel from garages, goods from the shops. They knew the hours when the weapons fell silent, knew the safe routes through holes in the walls of hollowed-out shops and homes. They knew the detours around dark dangerous corners pungent with *charsi* weed, where knots of fighters quarrelled over stolen goods, where the djinns, the scary spirits, lurked.

Inside the Ministry of Interior cafeteria the focus was on far bigger threats. There was always a buzz around the high table. Mohammad Aqa dutifully focused on his table service, although he couldn't help but hear the thickening soup of names and numbers. Districts that had fallen to the Taliban; districts now at risk. Numbers of units; numbers of dead. And all the back and forth over politics. Pakistan was accused of backing the Taliban. India, and the Russians, had their own irons in this fire, as did Iran. And America seemed to be missing in action. Even its aid programmes had been shut down. Afghanistan's ethnic divides shot through these conversations, too. The Taliban were mainly Pashtuns, the majority ethnic group that provided Afghan rulers down through the centuries. The current government was dom-inated by ethnic Tajiks. It was a tense, turbulent time. Lunches were often abruptly cut short.

Today, 26 September 1996, had started as a day like any

other. Lunch had proceeded in the usual way, the tables tidied as normal. At the end of his shift Mohammad Aqa presented himself at the office manager's desk to check what should be purchased for tomorrow's breakfast. Often there were orders for cheese and jam, along with stacks of bread. No eggs. The minister did not eat eggs for breakfast.

'Don't worry about tomorrow,' the manager instructed Mohammad Aqa with a dismissive wave of his hand. 'Go and cook *halva*.' In Afghan tradition, *halva* – a dessert of wheat, mildly sweet, flavoured with cardamom and flaked nuts – was served the day after someone died. Mohammad Aqa shifted nervously, uncertain what to say. 'All the people here will escape,' the manager explained, looking him in the eye. 'But tomorrow the Taliban will be here.'

Mohammad Aqa vaulted up the stairs to join other spectators on the roof. From here they could see plumes of dark smoke drifting across the autumn expanse of sky. Fighting raged in the Pul-e Charkhi suburb on the eastern edge of the city. Government warplanes screeched overhead, spewing their deadly payload, a last-ditch effort to push back the Taliban. But some on this roof knew that the insurgents had advanced even further, driving troops from the shell-blasted customs building just six miles from the presidential palace.

Up the hill, on the Inter-Continental's top floor, Commander Massoud was watching, too. He stood alone in the gloom, walkie-talkie in hand, making and taking calls from his most loyal generals. Hotel staff hovered in the shadows, at a respectful distance. Snippets escaped through the squawk and static of his two-way radio set. 'The Taliban are coming . . . our soldiers are leaving.' And Massoud's reassuring replies. 'Don't worry . . . I'm sending more forces . . . we need to fight.' They had pushed the Taliban back the year before; he believed they could do so again.

The hotel manager instructed the most experienced waiter on duty to check if their esteemed guest would like tea or coffee. He quietly made his way into the red-curtained den, once the pinnacle of Kabul nightlife. Now it throbbed with tension. He cleared his voice to announce his presence. 'Coffee or tea, respected Commander?' Massoud glanced at him, still gripping his brick of a walkie-talkie. 'My son, do you have poison I could drink?' The waiter was knocked into silence. 'The situation is very bad,' Massoud wearily told him. 'How can I eat or drink?' He didn't expect a reply. The waiter nodded, unblinking, noticing how the legendary commander's trim black beard was now tinged with grey.

Massoud soon left in haste, his bodyguards and aides silently falling into line. Some Inter-Continental staff saw him charge through the lobby and down the hill in a small cortège of Russian jeeps and four-wheel-drives. Later that night they heard reports that he had headed north on the last road still in their hands, their ranks swelling into an ungainly procession of tanks and trucks and heavy artillery and armoured vehicles, tearing out of a city that was tumbling from their grasp. They were said to be barrelling towards Massoud's base in Jabal Saraj, the entrance to their stronghold in the Panjshir valley, their last redoubt. Later that night, foreign radios reported remarks from the *mujahideen* deputy foreign minister that Massoud retreated because 'he didn't want Kabul to be plunged into a bloodbath'. President Rabbani had joined him; he would decide the next day to make 'a transfer of power, to whom we do not know'.

A handful of hotel staff kept vigil on the top floor, staring into the night as Kabul's defences melted away. Fighter jets screamed out of Kabul, too, pilots taking themselves and their killing machines out of the capital and the Taliban's grasp. More unsettling was what the staff couldn't see: what would happen overnight on the city streets, what they would find when the first light crept over the Hindu Kush. But a faint hope burned. Perhaps tomorrow, at the very least, the guns would fall silent, the rockets would stop.

PART IV

The White Years

CHAPTER 11

Taliban Check-In

Autumn 1996

'What is a bellboy?'

Jamshid, a smooth-faced teenager in a dark tunic with yellow trim, pondered how best to answer the question. His job, he explained in some detail, stretched from welcoming guests with a smile to carrying their bags without complaint, to keeping a watchful eye out for anything untoward.

The black-bearded Talib before him seemed unimpressed. 'Show me where Naghma used to sing,' he said. 'And Ahmad Zahir. Where did he sing?'

Jamshid paused, wondering if any replies would carry risks. Naghma, the legendary songstress, was from Kandahar – like the inquisitive Talib, as it turned out, who confessed that he had occasionally caught snatches of her sweet voice singing Pashto folk songs on his transistor radio. By accident, of course. Jamshid was impressed that the Talib also knew of Ahmad Zahir, the music icon whose mysterious death in 1979 still caused Afghan eyes to well up. Like most Afghans of this city, Jamshid knew the pantheon of stars whose songs stirred Afghan hearts from one generation to the next. Some of the Taliban clearly did, too.

Jamshid beamed a cheeky grin, then quickly regretted it. The Talib, who seemed to have some authority in the hotel, didn't notice. So Jamshid began to take this inquisitive Afghan on a tour of the Inter-Con's glorious past. Pressing his face against the lobby's panoramic windows, he pointed to the empty space below, with its cavernous blue void of a swimming pool. There, once upon a time, the terrace had shivered with waves of swooning Ahmad Zahir fans. Such was the frenzy that the singer had been forced to escape through the staff entrance at the back. Jamshid had heard all about it from his father, who had worked at the Inter-Con, too, and got him this job.

Down the corridor they came to the biggest and best banquet hall, the Kandahar Ballroom. It was here that Naghma sometimes sang, to the delight of adoring concert-goers and wedding guests. The Talib and the teenager stood on the threshold, the young Afghan describing how the star's spectators would rise rapturously to their feet, gliding onto the dance floor, shaking away their cares. The Talib immediately shut down such thoughts. None of that tingle was allowed.

There were more questions on his list. 'Where did the girls who danced in the Pamir club stay for the night?' he demanded disapprovingly. Jamshid vigorously shook his head. The rumours of scantily dressed women engaging in all sorts of un-Islamic behaviour at a British-built, American-run hotel simply weren't true, Jamshid reassured him. But the truth fell on the floor.

The Talib wasn't alone in his investigations. On the floors above, the Taliban were eagerly bounding from room to room in search of taboo TV sets. Music systems, which had gone silent when the *mujahideen* moved in, were smashed in case anyone might be tempted to use them. And in the basement they struck gold: the stash of alcohol that staff had hidden away under thick wooden planks in 1992.

A raucous procession of Talibs marched up and down the stairs. This sinful poison had to be destroyed, not in a dark basement, but before the eyes of the world. Journalists were streaming into Kabul to report on the Taliban's astonishing ascent to power. They were soon summoned to a treeless waste-land north of the hotel. Dusty bottles of Afghan Nerone brandy and other spirits as well as imported beer cans were dumped on pebbly ground in a chorus of clinking glass and aluminium. A dirt-caked tank growled into position and began rolling back and forth across this booty. 'If anyone is caught drinking, they will be lashed according to the laws of Islam,' a black-turbaned Talib explained to the crowd. As pungent fumes wafted over the hill, the tanker seemed to steer an increasingly wobbly path through the mud.

The greatest reckoning came inside the hotel, in the Bamiyan Brasserie. Shortly after the Taliban's takeover, a Talib oozing authority, flanked by other *mullahs* – including some from Pakistan – stormed into the restaurant. They were there to see the big Buddha embedded in the clay frieze hugging the wall.

For these morality inspectors, this carving was a shameful relic of Afghanistan's idolatrous pre-Islamic history. Staff exchanged nervous looks. One brave worker plucked up courage. '*Maulavi Sahib*, please don't destroy the Buddha,' he implored him. 'This is part of our history, part of our hotel.'

His plea counted for little. 'Bring some tools!' the *mullah* ordered. Every hard implement to be found in the hotel was rushed into the restaurant: hammers and chisels from the engineering department, meat mallets from the kitchen, even shovels from gardening sheds outside. Eager Talibs leapt forward to give the sculpture the beating it deserved. *Allahu Akbar!* 'God is greatest. May God curse the creator!' Staff watched, hearts in mouths, as the restaurant filled with the clang of hammers and the chip of chisels. Then silence reigned, but for the breath-less panting of the exhausted henchmen. The buddha stared serenely, still largely intact. The workmen looked at one another sheepishly.

The head waiter, Marco, was summoned. Though his real name was Mohammad Daud, he had been christened 'Marco' long ago by a German tourist. No one knew exactly why, but the name had stuck. Some said it was a nod to the thirteenth-century Venetian explorer who travelled to the far reaches of Asia, including 'the very beautiful country of Afghanistan'. Or maybe he had been named after the nimble-footed Marco Polo sheep with their spiralling horns. Whatever the reason, everyone called him *Kaka Marco*, 'Uncle Marco'. And everyone agreed that he was the right man to take on the Buddha: a Pashto speaker hailing from Maidan Shahr in central Afghanistan, although he looked like an Uzbek from the north and was by far the most muscular man in the hotel.

Marco winced to see the target, stealing a glance at his fellow workers, who waited for him to finish this job. They offered wan smiles. Drawing a deep breath all the way to his belly, Marco wielded the biggest hammer in the hotel with all his might. The restaurant quivered as his blows fell. A fevered Talib sprung forward to add extra force, hurling his hammer so hard that it slipped from his grasp and flew across the room, sending everyone scrambling.

By the end of the day the Buddha was sufficiently defaced for the Taliban to declare their job done. A cloth was tacked to the wall to hide the rest. A silence fell over the restaurant like a shroud. The *mullahs* left.

No one spoke. Not even Engineer Amanullah, Mr Fix-It. When another hullabaloo subsided outside the entrance, where Talibs had been knocking down the statues of dancers and *buzkashi* horsemen covering the front façade, he quietly picked up the pieces and carefully carried them down the stairs to his engineering department. Perhaps one day he could put them back together again.

As-salaam alaikum. 'Peace be upon you, my brother.' No matter who showed up on his floor – the third floor – Hazrat always welcomed them with the same Inter-Continental warmth. But on this day it didn't land so well. 'You should say *Assalamu-alaikum Warahmatullahi Wabarakatuh.* "Peace be upon you and God's mercy and blessings",' the Talib chided him. Hazrat nodded politely and repeated the full Islamic salutation.

White-cloaked and white-bearded, with a barely concealed gun, the Talib eyed Hazrat up and down. He bore an air of judgement that conveyed he was a man of some standing in Taliban ranks. Hazrat proudly wore his own authority as a properly trained Inter-Continental employee. He still dressed in his housekeeping uniform, which was now as tired as he was. But his necktie was consigned to history. The Taliban had banned them as a symbol of the Christian cross. He still had his beard, in keeping with the times. By now it was black and long, touching the top of his shirt. Yet it was thin and wispy, not a patch on the bush of facial hair standing before him.

What mattered most to Hazrat was that he was back in his hotel. He had returned as soon as he was certain that the fighting had stopped – for now, at least. It became clear immediately that the Taliban were in control in the capital, and far beyond. The first sighting at the hotel had been a young fighter, spotted by staff on the morning shift, as he slept on top of the traffic booth at the bottom of the hill. Then another Talib had barrelled up the slope in a filched Russian jeep and marched into the hotel, demanding a white cloth. A waiter swiftly fetched a large cotton square. The Talib turned on his heel and legged it through the revolving door to the grassy triangle abutting the front entrance, yanking Afghanistan's black, red and green tri-colour down the flagpole's shiny steel shaft and replacing it with his make-do white Taliban flag – hoisted to bellows of *Allahu Akbar!* Then he sped back down the hill.

The Taliban entered the hotel without a shot fired. But the scene at another traffic booth in the city sent shockwaves through Kabul and far beyond. Afghans had thronged to the square next to the presidential palace to see if the rumours were true. They were. Two corpses dangled from wire nooses on the red-and-white traffic watchtower: one bloodied and bloated, limbs protruding at odd angles from a ripped tunic and trousers; the other, in jeans and a sports jacket, hanging straight down. One was Najibullah, the former president and spy chief. The other was his brother, Shahpur. Pakistani rupees were stuffed into their nostrils and pockets to mock them. Snippets about Najibullah's final hours shot through the crowds until a fuller story emerged. The Taliban had seized him from the UN compound where he had sheltered for the past four years. His pleas on shortwave radio, for UN protection, and offers from Massoud to rescue him, didn't save him. Beaten, castrated and shot in the head, Najibullah had been tied to the back of a jeep, dragged across stony ground in the dawn half-light. Now, in bright September sunshine, Taliban posed next to their prey, denouncing him as 'a murderer of our people'.

From that day forward, they pursued what they called their 'purifying mission'. Music and video cassettes were snatched from Kabul shops, ripped from car dashboards, cracked into pieces. Tangles of shiny tape dangled like tinsel from lamp posts and trees. Smashed TV sets were piled up on pavements along with jumbles of gouged paintings and photographs – of humans and animals alike – denounced as 'graven images' that gave rise to idolatry.

Hazrat observed it in the Inter-Con, too. On his floor the Talibs had broken objectionable paintings into pieces, taken away the TV sets and hacked at the bedside music systems. He lamented the loss of so much of what had made this Inter-Continental such a fine hotel. But his greatest disquiet was over what, if anything, would ever be done about the wrecked rooms all along one side of his floor: the black footprint of the civil war. The hotel had been storing disused furniture inside these locked rooms alongside the hotchpotch of broken beds, splintered mirrors and even stained blankets. Hazrat couldn't even bear to look at them.

But his guests were his priority. His Talib visitor had arrived to check on his son-in-law, his daughter and their two children, who were staying in one room. Food was brought for them three times a day. From where it came Hazrat did not know; he did not ask. But it was in such quantities that some of it would be offered to him and anyone else working that day. It was a blessing in hard times. Sometimes the Talib's daughter would open the door a crack to request more towels, clean sheets. As the days passed, the mood lightened. The children gambolled about in the corridor, filling the hallway with a warmth and energy that he had missed for years.

A few foreign journalists had come and gone shortly after the Taliban took over, leaving for other wars. Talibs still came in and out, sleeping with their weapons beside them. They would usually arrive late at night, leave early in the morning.

Hazrat tried to keep his floor as clean as he could, trying not to notice the smell and stains of the patterned carpet, the way it curled up in some corners. Every day Taliban hoteliers asked him to do whatever needed doing, whatever came to mind, not yet appreciating that hotels functioned best when each employee focused on a specific skill, in a particular department. Hazrat did his best to do what he was told. But sometimes he couldn't hold back his inner critic. He patiently tried to teach them the right way to do things.

Even in the gloom, he found calm. The sparrows alighting on the balconies, the butterflies flitting above potted red geraniums on the terrace. The Taliban had, at least, brought a quiet to this city. Hazrat also welcomed the edicts that stopped the crime and corruption that had cursed Kabul for so long. But the harsh Sharia Law punishments were repulsive: the amputations, the executions, the morbid scenes of limp bodies hanging in the squares, swinging from nooses. But crime and corruption seemed to have stopped. Senior Talibs kept showing up at the Inter-Con every day, to eat together, to pray together, to savour the satisfaction of knowing this was their hotel now.

The man who planted himself at the front desk had only one eye. The other was just an empty socket. It magnetically drew Amanullah's attention, though he quickly averted his gaze. One eye must have been lost in battle somewhere in all those years of fighting.

The Talib wanted to go to the roof. Amanullah discreetly took the measure of the man: younger than him, taller than him, his face framed by jet-black hair. His beard and bushy moustache intruded on his upper lip and reached up to those eyes. He wore a silver-coloured *perahan o tunban* and vest. His dark turban was wrapped loosely and largely. He must be from the south. Engineer Amanullah, duty manager on shift, didn't look much different. His white shirt and dark trousers had been banished to his staff locker in the basement. Now he, too, dressed like a man of this soil. But his striped turban was wrapped neatly, tightly, around his head. He flashed his Inter-Continental smile, leading his visitor across the lobby. The Talib didn't say much. But his presence was creating a buzz.

Another Talib sidled up beside Amanullah. He poked him sharply. 'Don't you know who he is?' he whispered tersely. Amanullah looked at him blankly. The Talib pulled him closer. 'He is Mullah Mohammad Omar.' Amanullah blinked, knowing the name, not knowing much more. 'He is the *Amir al-Mu'minin*, the "Commander of the Faithful".' Amanullah gulped, eyes widening, as he tried not to break his stride. He now understood the significance of this mysterious visitor, as the leader and spiritual guide of the movement that had just swept into power. He stepped more mindfully across the gleaming black and white marble.

The golden lift stood idly by, waiting for electricity, so they took the stairs, their sandals click-clacking up six flights – the same passageway that Commander Massoud had hastened up and down only weeks before. Some of the *amir*'s aides followed in their footsteps. When they reached the roof, the *amir* stopped for a moment to take in the view: the heights never failed to leave one breathless, and not just for the physical exertion required to get there. Kabul, the eternal. Then the *amir*'s questions began. 'Where is Koh-e Afshar?' he asked, peering into the distance. He would have heard of the ferocious battle that had been waged there. Amanullah pointed to the blighted landscape to the north-west. 'Where is the army school?' He wanted to look at one of Massoud's former bases. There was a lot he wanted to see. They stood there for some time.

'How do you connect with guests?' the *amir* enquired as they tripped back down the dimly lit stairs towards the sun-streaked lobby. Amanullah paused for a few seconds to give thought to his reply. He opted for the truth. '*Mullah Sahib*, we have almost no guests,' he said with a regretful smile. 'We have no telephones. We are here, cut off, on our own.' His special visitor said nothing. But when they reached the lobby the *amir* gestured to an aide hovering close by, instructing him to bring the new manager of Radio Television Afghanistan, now renamed Voice of Sharia Radio. They exchanged a few words.

Next the *amir* indicated that he wanted to meet the staff. Le Cavalier restaurant, with its royal-blue upholstered chairs, filled up in an instant, with many staff – from stooped white-bearded gardeners and cooks to wide-eyed teenage bellboys – deciding simply to sit on the fraying blue carpet. Everyone was bearded except for those in the first flush of manhood. There were no women.

Employees and their new employers eyed each other warily. The staff had heard so many stories about these men. They had risen through the ranks of the *mujahideen*, many of them schooled in *madrasas* in Pakistan. Allegations abounded that Pakistan's military intelligence had boosted their rapid rise, although the Taliban insisted they were home-grown.

They had heard their own stories about this hotel on the hill. Now they wanted to hear it from the staff themselves. The workforce reached back in time to recall the halcyon years of the Inter-Continental Kabul – the grand official banquets in the ballroom, the best shoe-shine in the city, an unrivalled business centre, cakes without compare. Amanullah recalled how everything once ran like clockwork. Hazrat reminisced about white sheets and soft towels in guest rooms, and those exciting days gone by when tourists travelled freely across the country. No one spoke of the music that once electrified the Pamir Supper Club, the fancy drinks in the cocktail lounges, the way men and women happily dined and danced together. They spoke of a national hotel, a house as familiar to them as their own home – a mirror of a nation on its knees, still refusing to call it quits. The *amir* mainly listened. The staff could only guess that he had a plan for the Inter-Con; that it would continue to provide hospitality to their most important guests.

As he rose to leave, there was a sharp clunk in the lobby. A pristine satellite telephone had been plonked on the front desk. Staff gathered round to ogle this very pricey gadget. Amanullah inspected it with a mixture of excitement and nervousness. 'But how should we pay for the calls?' he asked. 'We need American dollars. We don't have any.' His concern was batted away. This phone was theirs to use, and for their guests, too.

No one ever said where this satellite phone came from, who paid for the calls, how much it all cost. Some staff suspected a connection with wealthy sheikhs in Dubai. But what a gift it was. Until that point, anyone needing to make an urgent call had to travel down the cratered road, which couldn't even be called a road in some places, all the way to neighbouring Pakistan. Now they could speak to loved ones far and wide who had been forced to flee from their homeland. The Inter-Con was con-nected to the world again. All it needed now were some guests.

CHAPTER 12

Holy Hospitality

Winter 1996

The Inter-Continental Kabul was fully booked. *No vacancy*. Not a single one of the rooms fit for sleep was available. Staff were turning people away with apologies, sending them to the annexe next door in the empty student dormitories of the Polytechnic.

Amanullah beamed to see the wooden grid of pigeonholes emptied of keys. But he couldn't suppress a tiny twinge. It was true that, since November, guests had been beating a path to the front desk to book, even beg for, a room. But they were only doing it on Taliban orders.

Voice of Sharia Radio had put everyone on notice. 'They must move to the Inter-Continental hotel . . . Foreigners are not allowed to stay anywhere else.' All foreign nationals in Kabul – mostly aid workers and journalists – were told to pack up their rented houses and flats and move to the Taliban hotel on the hill. Visiting journalists weren't exempt, either. They were told they couldn't get exit visas if they didn't stay in the Inter-Con. Only the staff of international media organisations that had registered their offices in Kabul could continue to live and work from their own premises.

The Taliban press office issued a statement to explain their reasoning. The urgent imperative was to ensure the foreigners' safety and security, they said. They simply could not keep track of all the foreigners if they were scattered across this city. The journalists who trudged into reception had another theory. This was about money, they grumbled. The Taliban were eyeing the rent money filling the pockets of private landlords. They had realised that running a hotel required money – lots of it. And there were no funds to even start repairing the rooms that were still a woeful mess. The Taliban needed cash.

Still, in recent months some parts of the hotel had been knocked into better shape – all thanks to Engineer Amanullah. When the Inter-Con had come under its new Taliban management, he was dispatched to neighbouring Pakistan with the new general manager, and the head of the purchasing department, to buy whatever building supplies he needed. Much of it was available in shops across the border. But try as he might, Amanullah couldn't find the quality of glass to meet the standards of windows in his five-star hotel. He took that concern, among many others, with him when he was summoned to Kandahar in the south, the real seat of power, to present a report on the condition of the national hotel. The minister of civil aviation, now based at Kandahar airport, was responsible for all government lodgings. He wasn't well versed in the technicalities, but he knew how to make things happen. He picked up his satellite phone and called the Foreign Ministry in Kabul.

Lickety-split, Amanullah found himself being whisked away on a special plane, along with the Talib general manager, heading for the United Arab Emirates. There were no scheduled take-off times, no visas needed, no fuss at passport control. The aviation minister's man, an agent from the national Ariana Afghan Airlines, helped to smooth their passage. It was all quite dizzying for first-time flyer Amanullah. To sail high in the sky through cottony-white clouds above the angular peaks of the Hindu Kush. To see his city steadily shrink into tiny doll's houses and toy trucks, then disappear altogether in the blue. To gaze into the sparkly waters of the Persian Gulf, dotted with cargo ships and triangular white sails. To marvel at the forest of steel skyscrapers rising from the sand, glinting in the sun of the glittering city-state – and their first destination, Dubai. Amanullah steadied himself as he embarked on an engineer's shopping spree, purchasing panes of glass for the windows, copper pipes for the water, and more. All of it expertly packed and shipped back to Kabul on the national airline.

Over the next few months Amanullah's to-do list had kept growing. 'Why don't you repair the electricity?' the Taliban prodded him. In decades past, the hotel had run on the city's electricity – what Afghans called 'city power'. But during the civil war it was mostly replaced by coughing generators, hurricane lamps and candles. Amanullah had three asks to get the hotel's system up and running again: a car to keep him going back and forth to the relevant ministries; fuel to keep his vehicle going; and lunch to keep him going. And, of course, his salary. Once his wishes were granted, his work began in earnest: arriving at the ministry charged with sorting public services, glowing to say he was the chief engineer at the Inter-Continental Kabul and announcing that he was here to acquire electrical installation brackets, insulators, conductors, whatever he needed.

Next it was the plumbing. 'Can you fix the water now?' the Taliban demanded. Years earlier, Amanullah had overseen the drilling of a deep well a short distance from the hotel. The ground water on the hill wasn't up to scratch. But hotel pipes were broken, burst or stolen; water no longer flowed into taps and toilets on all the floors.

His Taliban bosses even asked the Inter-Con's chief engineer for advice on security. How to protect important buildings, in Kabul and Kandahar, in case they were attacked. Two walls of reinforced concrete, with clay in between, was his answer. Amanullah focused on doing his best to fix the worst of the hotel; his new managers gushed over every success.

The guts of the hotel were being fixed; so too was its face. The reception desk was now fronted by new Taliban recruits, an Inter-Continental welcome delivered with turbaned heads and bearded smiles. Experienced staff, including Salem who had run the show for years, were shunted from the front desk to back rooms, often to the kitchen, where they helped with whatever task needed doing, from peeling potatoes to washing up. The waiters did their best to hold onto some of their old polish, serving with a semblance of the manner in which they were accustomed to. They averted their gaze from the shrouded Buddha in the ruined frieze along the wall. Sometimes they even looked away from the food when guests complained the meat was as chewy as rubber, the vegetables overcooked, the chips stone-cold. They even noticed that their bread was being toasted on top of the heaters. In the lobby the bookshop had managed to stay open. The Taliban merely ordered the bookseller to cover up objectionable book covers, including images of women, Afghan royalty and each and every face. Old postcards were stuffed into boxes. The window display was carefully curated.

Amanullah tried to stay in his lane, to focus on his to-do list and the teaching he had started taking on at the Polytechnic. And last year his beloved Marzia had given birth to Rohullah, their first son; this year they were blessed by a second, Sami-ullah. Whatever the ups and downs of his country's political fortunes, the sacred cycles of life still spun forward.

★

The Interior Ministry's cafeteria was closed. Most employees now went home before lunch. Those who remained in the ministry ate as most Afghans did at home: lunch served on the office floor. The plastic *dastarkhwan* tablecloth was unfurled, metal bowls set down brimming with rice speckled with fat brown kidney beans or studded with potatoes – every so often even chunks of meat. One or another of the wizened cooks would scuttle in and out with a water jug and basin to wash everyone's hands. Cutlery wasn't needed; food tasted much better scooped with fingers from bowls.

Mohammad Aqa presided over the service. His waiter's uniform – black suit, white shirt, a tie – hung on a hanger at home. These days he wore traditional Afghan attire, like everyone else. The service was simple, effortless, but now there were new tasks and bigger tensions. He worried that he might get something wrong. One of the biggest responsibilities weighing on his shoulders was to ensure that no one dropped something into the minister's food. Mohammad Aqa brought in a bowl just for him. The minister and his entourage were vigilant about poison plots; history told them they had good cause to worry.

As with every shift at the top, it took time to earn trust. At the start, Mohammad Aqa's new bosses wouldn't share the night-password, which changed daily. It slowed his passage through checkpoints, especially in those nervous hours before the night curfew took hold. Kabul's new rulers were on the lookout for infiltrators – anyone spying for their enemies, who were now marshalling men and munitions in the north to mount a counterattack. Young men were being picked up in the streets. The putrid prison blocks of Pul-e Charkhi were filling up again.

Every night, late at night, Mohammad Aqa anxiously cycled

home. Every morning, before first light, he cycled back before almost everyone else to open the minister's office. His only company was someone from intelligence, there early to conduct a thorough security sweep before the minister arrived in his bubble of bodyguards, aides and hangers-on. Then the office would steadily fill up. Inconsequential chit-chat percolated in the waiting room, in the queues of visitors spilling into the portico and onto the lawns beyond. Afghans came from all around with a complaint, a concern, a question, many demanding to see the minister himself, once they had cleared every rig of security. Some brought before him, accused of one crime or another, were prescribed a punishment – sometimes harsh and physical – on the spot.

Mohammad Aqa stayed on his toes. One morning, after a day when he couldn't come to work, the minister asked where he'd been. 'Minister *Sahib*, I had to go to the dentist.' The minister cocked an eyebrow. 'Do you know this dentist well?' Mohammad Aqa was taken aback by what seemed like a loaded question. 'Yes, Minister *Sahib*, I do.' The minister grinned with pleasure. 'Then I will go to him too, tonight, at nine o'clock,' he said, before shifting his gaze to deal with someone else standing nervously in front of him.

Mohammad Aqa slipped out of the ministry and made haste to the clinic to inform his dentist of the minister's plan, urging him not to breathe a word to anyone. His dentist reassured him. Sure enough, the minister's teeth were treated in the same discreet professional way all patients were. The only difference occurred when it came to the bill. At the end of his appointment, the minister produced his thick notepad with *Ministry of the Interior Islamic Emirate of Afghanistan* printed at the top of each page, an official stamp at the bottom. The minister wrote down the cost of his dental work, scribbled his signature and tore that single sheet from his pad. A Taliban credit card. The dentist had only to take it to the ministry's Department of Finance in the morning. A neat solution in a capital without banks, accounting systems or much else by way of modernity.

The new Kabul was marked by absences and silences. Bright tissue paper kites stopped dancing in the sky. Pigeons didn't fly in flocks from rooftops at the whistle of their owner. Music no longer blared from cassette players propped on streetside stalls. Gone was the slap of playing cards on top of wooden tables in *chaikhana* teahouses. And schoolgirls no longer skipped down the street. They were all banned.

Fewer women ventured out, fearing the wrath of the morality police. Even hidden inside *chadris* they could still be whipped for some transgression. New rules kept being added. White stockings were now taboo. So were high heels, their seductive click certain to trigger impure thoughts in men. The radio often announced their tally of daily beatings. One day they proclaimed that 250 Kabul women had been whipped for un-Islamic behaviour. Voice of Sharia Radio also broadcast daily sermons explaining the obligations of both women and men. 'Satan urinates on the head of a woman who is not covering her head . . . A man looking at a woman, or a woman looking at a man, is the fornication of eyes.' There were episodes on music, also *haram* in the eyes of the Almighty. 'God will pour hot lead into the ears of those who listen to music.'

Inside the Ministry of the Interior the discussions also shifted to other issues of significance. The talk often turned to the spiralling drugs trade – a fixation for many in Western capitals, along with the rights of Afghan women. Opium-poppy cultivation had been climbing, year on year, through all the years of war, no matter who was in charge. Afghanistan was now rivalling the infamous Golden Triangle in South-East Asia. Farmers in the

Taliban's southern heartland, which grew almost all the crop, relied on these earnings to feed their families.

The outside world was also obsessed with their Saudi visitor Osama Bin Laden. He had been warmly welcomed to Afghanistan, when the old *mujahideen* were in charge, and he was in need of a new abode, out of America's long reach. The Taliban also regarded him as an honoured visitor, in keeping with the obligations of hospitality in their *Pashtunwali*, a tribal code that stipulated that guests should be protected, including from their enemies. But the West, and especially the United States, was accusing the Taliban of harbouring hundreds of foreign terrorists – chief among them the man who had once fought with the US-backed rebels against the Soviet occupation, but whose organisation, al-Qaeda, had now declared war on America. Mohammad Aqa didn't pay too much attention; it wasn't his world. He knew all that he needed to know about serving the people at his table.

As the world hailed the start of a new century, Kabul felt like it had been pulled backwards into centuries past. Streets echoed with the clopping of horse-carts, the hee-haw of donkeys, the dinging of bicycle bells. There weren't so many cars. The music of dusty villages had become the soundtrack of a capital largely cut off from the world. Landlines didn't work.

Televisions were still banned. Ariana Afghan Airlines flights were still grounded. Girls' schools were still shut. The last of the city's elite held on to the vestiges of their former life, hanging thick blankets over windows to hide the blue glow of their TV sets, to smother the sound of pirated videos and foreign radio stations. For most Afghans even simple pleasures like watching Bollywood movies were gone.

Even lifesaving foreign aid was being cut as sanctions multiplied over the Taliban's refusal to hand over Washington's most wanted man. Osama Bin Laden now stood accused of the bombings of US embassies in Kenya and Tanzania – attacks that had killed more 200 people. In August 1998 the United States hit back by firing dozens of Tomahawk cruise missiles into Afghanistan, into what were said to be Bin Laden training camps in the east.

The hotel was hollowed out, too. Despite Engineer Amanullah's best efforts, he couldn't keep the lights on for very long, the hot water flowing from taps, the rooms warm in winter, cool in summer. Next to the front desk an assortment of plastic tubs collected water dripping from the ceiling. Even the satellite phone on the front desk had been taken away.

There wasn't enough cash to do what was really needed: major surgery on the vital veins of the hotel that had lost so much of its lifeblood. And there wasn't much calm, either. By the turn of the millennium the war was back. Salvoes blasted by Massoud's forces from their bases north of Kabul were sometimes causing outages in the city's power. When the hotel went black, kerosene lamps were lit, stubby candles rushed to guests.

An oppressive miasma bore down on all the staff. On Hazrat's floor the occasional reassuring swish of the lifts or clatter from the stairwell sent a signal that guests were about to come down his corridor. He stood to attention outside his housekeeper's cubbyhole, his bearded face wearing a gentle smile. A glimmer of dignity came from doing what was expected of him in a hotel worthy of the Inter-Continental name. But at times he was seized by the painful thought that he was merely going through the motions.

Downstairs, the monotony was broken only by prayer times – bending and kneeling on the rugs laid out in the green-carpeted enclosure in the lobby between the arrangements of sofas and chairs. But wherever they wandered, bits of the past stared back at them. The odd Russian airline poster was still stuck inside a dusty glass poster frame. Some of the old hotel brochures promoting this 'enchanted land . . . where past and present meet' occasionally popped up in a drawer. Curious Talibs inspected them. The flyers' front cover showed what had been Afghanistan's most famous tourist attraction, one of the two standing Buddhas of Bamiyan – a miniature replica of which been whacked in the restaurant when the Taliban first took charge. By the time winter eased its grip in March 2001 the Taliban were ready to destroy the real ones. They attacked the statues, soaring 175 feet and 120 feet high in their niches, with rocket launchers, tank fire, even anti-aircraft guns – drowning out the cries of the world, above all Afghans in exile who mourned the loss of their precious heritage. The BBC's resident Afghanistan correspondent, Kate Clark, was kicked out of Kabul for broadcasting a critical interview.

More pragmatic thinkers in the Taliban ranks were urging the world to give them time and space, insisting that different policies would eventually prevail. There were signs they were easing up, ever so slightly, on some restrictions, even turning a blind eye to some of the secret schools for girls. And they called on governments to recognise and reward their new ban on opium-poppy farming – enforced through threats, compulsory eradication and the public punishment of culprits – which had nearly wiped out the crop in Taliban-controlled provinces.

But the gap between Kabul and the rest of the world's capitals kept growing. Only three countries had recognised the Taliban's rule: Pakistan, Saudi Arabia and the United Arab Emirates. And now the remaining aid agencies, the only remaining lifeline for hundreds of thousands of destitute Afghans, had pulled out. Some three dozen charities had headed to the Pakistan border in their bulky four-wheel-drive vehicles. They departed heavy-hearted, knowing what suffering they left behind. But they couldn't comply with a new raft of Taliban orders to relocate their offices to the crumbling student dormitories at the Polytechnic, without running water or electricity, just below the hotel. They had carried on, hoping the ultimatum would simply go away. It didn't. The Taliban sealed their offices, giving the charities no other choice but to leave. Only UN agencies and the International Committee of the Red Cross were exempted. They were overwhelmed as they struggled to help the many Afghans with nowhere else to turn.

Mother nature wasn't kind, either. For the fourth year in a row, the worst drought in decades was drying the fields, emptying the rivers, starving the animals, and the people. In ravaged villages, families piled what little they owned in the back of pickups, on top of flatbeds, across donkeys' backs, crossing the border into Pakistan or Iran, or heading to bigger towns and cities.

There were only a few foreign journalists based in Kabul to tell Afghanistan's story to the world. The Taliban let in a trickle more to see for themselves the 'ground realities'. But they had to stay in the Taliban-run Inter-Con. They had to move about in a Taliban-driven van and travel with a Taliban-approved translator. Those who managed to get in pushed back at their boundaries. The correspondent from the *Washington Post*, the smiley but serious-minded Pamela Constable, tried to sneak out of the hotel into her own waiting taxi. She was caught halfway down the hill and sent back inside. Her driver got pulled down to the basement and grilled in excruciating detail. At night, vigilant Taliban hotel clerks sometimes kept watch outside guest doors, rifles at the ready, usually dropping off to sleep in the small hours. It was a precaution described as the guests' 'protection'. Miss Pamela blocked her door with a bureau, just in case.

Other TV teams made it in, too, including British, German and American networks, who came to report on the trial of eight Christians accused of trying to convert Afghans, a crime punishable by death. Even after the media had been granted permission to cover the trial, they were detained for filming outside the courthouse. A Kalashnikov-carrying vice-and-virtue squad stormed into the Inter-Con and up the dark stairwell to search their rooms.

Kabul was suffocating. In the stifling summer heat of 2001, when even young Talibs began to wilt, the religious police agreed to let in a little breeze: they opened the Inter-Con swimming pool, the only one in the city. Exercise-minded Talibs had already converted the empty cavity into a pitch for five-a-side football matches. Now, for the first time in a decade, it was filled with lustrous blue water again. A list of rules was tacked to the wall of the poolside snack bar. No women. No boys under the age of fifteen. No tight swimming trunks; knee-length shorts obligatory. And everyone must get out of the water between 1 p.m. and 2 p.m. for prayers.

When the hotel was deathly quiet, there was an Arab guest who occasionally showed up. He never came through the front door, always entering from the back, through an emergency exit used only by him and those around him. He used a separate stairwell to reach his room at the end of an empty second floor. Those who caught a glimpse described him as tall and thin, towering above the other Arabs who travelled with him. His robe was long and white; sometimes he wore a khaki field jacket.

It was as if he had his own hotel within the hotel. His own Arab runners brought him his own specially prepared meals. He had his own cleaners. And his own men, with all manner of gadgets. Devices with antennae for communications. Even a telescope they would take to the roof, scanning east and west, on the lookout, it seemed, for enemies lurking in the surrounding hills, skulking in the streets below. Sometimes hotel staff and passers-by spied a mysterious motorcade snaking in and out, counting at least seven identical black Japanese jeeps with tinted windows, escorted by pickups bristling with weapons.

Someone heard from someone else that his name was Osama. The name rang a bell for certain staff. If it did, they said nothing more. For others, it didn't mean anything. He was merely another guest. And, besides, they weren't even serving him.

CHAPTER 13

The Tallest Towers

Autumn 2001

The swish and click of the revolving door jolted the front-desk staff. Hardly anyone ever showed up after curfew hours. But tonight the thin yellow light behind reception cast a glow on the round, bespectacled face of the Taliban foreign minister, Wakil Ahmed Muttawakil. The reception staff caught a glimpse of the troubled look on his face as he swept past.

Tonight a response to the news couldn't wait until morning. A few hours earlier the password to break the 9 p.m. curfew had been strictly shared with the few foreign journalists working from their offices in the capital. They had hurried up the hill, gripping notebooks and bulky camera bags, for an urgent press conference. Now the minister had joined them.

The handful of staff on duty already knew something terrible had happened. A few hours earlier, in the kitchen's half-light, the sound of knives on chopping boards had fallen silent as cooks and waiters collected around a worn transistor set. In the basement below, in the engineering department, Amanullah was doing the same – twisting his radio dial back and forth in search of the best signal. Word had gone around that something out of the ordinary had happened very far away.

Newsreaders on the BBC were relaying that two aeroplanes had flown into two tall buildings called the Twin Towers in New York. The office towers had collapsed. Many Americans were killed. It still wasn't clear how many.

Afghans knew what it was like to live in a city under attack. They knew about buildings buckling to the ground. They knew how it felt to emerge into the light, still breathing, grateful for God's grace. They knew that heart-stopping feeling of being swallowed up in grief when loved ones didn't emerge. Or at least, not alive.

But words like the World Trade Center – even New York – didn't mean much to most Afghans. The Twin Towers were an unfathomable 110 storeys high. The most head-turning sky-scraper in the city was the eighteen-storey Kabul Tower, built in the days of the king. It was even called *Hajhda Manzila*, 'Eighteen-Storey', in recognition of its unique scale. Even the Buddhas of Bamiyan, which the Taliban took days to destroy with all their firepower, were far shorter than New York's tallest towers. Only the Hindu Kush soared higher, its peaks poking through the clouds.

In the glass-walled meeting room in the lobby the crushing weight of what had happened filled the space. It was just big enough for a long white-clothed table, now lined by a few snaking cables connected to microphones, their heads pointed upwards at the foreign minister. He folded his arms across his Taliban uniform, white tunic and black waistcoat, flanked by his translator, dressed in an earthy brown. Other Talibs hovered, as did a handful of unsettled staff. Even the minister was burning with questions. He couldn't hide it. Perhaps he had even seen the images from New York on the television set in his ministry granted official approval; images that had by now also been seen by hundreds of millions around the world.

Like every well-informed Afghan, Muttawakil understood that his country, so cut off from so much for so long, was now being pushed to the centre of world attention. Worse, it seemed certain to be the focus of America's fury, whenever and however that came. From the first moment of realisation that this was not some terrible accident, suspicions mounted that the trail would lead to Afghanistan – to the guest house of America's greatest enemy.

The foreign minister cleared his throat to give the Taliban's first reply. 'We have criticised terrorism and will do so again,' he said carefully, pausing at paced intervals to allow for his Pashto to be translated into English. 'We have tried our best in the past, and we are willing in the future, to assure the United States in any kind of way we can that Osama is not involved in these kinds of activities.'

In a movement dominated by hardliners, Muttawakil was seen as a pragmatist. The son of a well-known Pashtun poet, he had risen through the ranks of the Taliban – starting as the driver of the Taliban's *amir*, becoming his translator, food taster and secretary, and rising to official spokesman and now their top diplomat. For years, behind the scenes, he had tried to find ways to resolve the tension around Bin Laden's presence. The Taliban kept insisting they needed to see proof of his crimes. The United States kept demanding that he was handed over.

Muttawakil had looked for ways out. He proposed a court with jurists from three Muslim nations, or a process supervised by a global body, the Organisation of the Islamic Conference. Just months earlier he had even secretly dispatched a courier to Pakistan to warn the United States and the United Nations of an imminent attack on American soil, having been tipped off by the leader of an Islamic movement from neighbouring Uzbekistan with links to al-Qaeda. No one heeded his message; they didn't trust the messenger.

The Taliban were in a bind. Their sights weren't set on global *jihad*. Bin Laden's ambition was to upend an American-dominated world order; the Taliban simply wanted to consolidate their power in Afghanistan and defeat their rivals, who still controlled 10 per cent of the territory. Their Arab guests adhered to a different interpretation of Islam, spoke a different language, had their own distinct culture. But they were guests. And guests had to be respected. Yet their tribal code also expected reciprocity. It now looked as if their most famous guest was about to destroy his host's house.

Two years earlier, shortly after the US had tightened sanctions again, it was Muttawakil who admitted that Bin Laden was in Afghanistan under the protection of a special commission. Only its members knew where he was; no one would reveal their names. Now the journalists pressed the minister about the Saudi's whereabouts. 'I don't know where he is,' he insisted. 'But I can tell you – he isn't in this hotel.' For a moment he couldn't resist a grin.

Hotel staff spent the next few days quietly trawling through their memories. They recalled the glimpses of bearded men in the halls, the sophisticated gadgetry, the blacked-out windows. And now there were whispers that the al-Qaeda leader even had a safe house in a villa in the neighbourhood of Kart-e Parwan, below this hotel, right under their noses. Now they understood why there had been such secrecy. But they couldn't fathom how such an audacious assault could have been planned in a country with no landlines, not many satellite phones, hardly any computers and erratic electricity – a world almost completely unplugged from the twenty-first century.

Rumours followed everyone around like shadows. The Taliban general manager pulled Amanullah into a quiet corner, peppering his chief engineer with questions. 'What is this 9/11? What about Osama? What does this mean for Afghanistan? What will it mean for the Taliban?' Engineer Amanullah, the most educated man among the staff, didn't know all the answers. He knew one thing, though: it would mean more war. Every Afghan knew what war looked like, sounded like, felt like. But this would be different. It would be an American war.

The world as they knew it seemed to be teetering. Just a few nights earlier there had been shocking news about Commander Massoud, who had been leading the anti-Taliban resistance. The former defence minister, to whom they had occasionally served green tea, was dead – killed in a suicide bombing in his own heavily guarded base in the east of the country. Two al-Qaeda assassins, posing as Arab TV journalists, had detonated a bomb inside the camera that was filming him.

Foreign radios sizzled with speculation that the two spectacular events were linked. Perhaps Bin Laden knew that his attack on America would unleash hellfire on the Taliban, on Afghanistan. Massoud, certain to be the United States' ally of choice, had to be eliminated. Some even suspected that his assassination sent a signal to the aeroplane bombers: *start your mission.*

The buzz in the lobby intensified like a swarm of angry bees. The Taliban congregated in tight huddles, squatting on haunches or squeezed into the sofas in front of the floor-to-ceiling windows to keep an eye on the city. Some marvelled at the victory of their Muslim brothers, revelling in news that the enemy infidels had been so dramatically smacked. Some Talibs even managed to slip inside the marbled Foreign Ministry to steal a glance at the authorised television set, flickering in and out on a weak signal, which was playing the same images over and over again. Silver planes slicing into office blocks like mega-missiles. Dark smoke blotting the sky. Tall towers collapsing. People running, screaming, weeping. And the script at the bottom, with the words of US president George W. Bush: 'We will find those responsible and bring them to justice . . . no distinction between the terrorists who committed these acts and those who harbour them.'

His words were translated for Talibs who couldn't read them. But they all knew the grammar of war, and they didn't fear it. After all, they had survived the onslaught of America's Tomahawk missiles just a few years earlier. America might be called a superpower. But they believed God was on their side.

A stream of white and black flowed up the hill. A thousand turbaned clerics, dust on their sandals and Islamic law in their heads, had journeyed from modest village mosques across the land to its biggest hotel. The *mullahs*, most unaccustomed to buildings of such grand proportions, slid across the marble, marvelling at the glittering chandeliers and shimmering lifts.

These were the learned men who were called upon at moments of truth. Their last major judgement had been to rule that the Buddhas of Bamiyan should be destroyed in the spring. Now, as cooler winds blew in and war clouds gathered, they were summoned for an even weightier decision. More than a week had passed since the attack in New York. America's impatience was growing. The Taliban *amir*, Mullah Mohammad Omar, had tasked his Supreme Council of the Islamic Clergy to reach a verdict: should they hand over Osama Bin Laden? 'Veteran honourable *ulemas* should come to Kabul for a Sharia decision,' he announced through Voice of Sharia radio. 'The valorous nation can defend Islam and their country in the light of the verdict.'

Hotel workmen had quickly patched up some of the ball-room's ugliest war scars to provide a respectable setting for such a distinguished assembly. Soon the *mullahs* were sitting turban-to-turban in the hall, their conversation going over and over seventh-century Quranic verses, centuries-old tribal traditions and the various perceived plots in Western capitals – as well as any possible scheming by countries next door. Pakistan, now led by its military strongman General Pervez Musharraf, was suspected of playing a double game: officials were publicly standing shoulder-to-shoulder with their American allies while spooks in the shadows were telling their Taliban friends not to give in.

Hotel staff hovered at the ballroom doors and paused while pouring tea, drinking in the grandstanding speeches and inter-jections from wizened *mullahs*. The most talkative even held court during their breaks, engaging staff in conversations about the contours of Islamic law. Of course there was the age-old suspicion that this traditional assembly was merely an elabo-rate façade, concealing decisions already taken in the real seat of power. In this case, that meant inside the high, thick walls of the reclusive Mullah Omar's compound in Kandahar. On this occasion, though, there was a growing sense that the Taliban were at a loss over what to do. That or they simply didn't grasp the enormity of what had happened on the other side of the world.

At the end of two intense days, which included a conclave in the even more imposing presidential palace, they settled on a compromise between hardline clerics braced for war and those who believed it was time for their guest to leave. Their decree was announced in detail on Taliban media. 'To avoid the current tumult, and also to allay future suspicions, the Supreme Council of the Islamic Clergy recommends to the Islamic Emirate of Afghanistan to persuade Osama Bin Laden to leave Afghanistan whenever possible,' they said. It was the gentlest of nudges to their guest that he might consider that, after five years in Afghanistan, he had overstayed his welcome. There was also a conciliatory nod to America for the loss of lives in the September attack. 'The *ulema* voice their sadness over American deaths and hope America does not attack Afghanistan.'

But they would also hold firm in the event of a holy war. 'If infidels invade an Islamic country and that country does not have the ability to defend itself, it becomes the binding obligation of all the world's Muslims to declare a holy war.'

The clerics also reiterated Taliban demands to see proof of Bin Laden's alleged crimes. But, in truth, there was little hope this last-ditch effort would succeed. America wanted Bin Laden and other al-Qaeda high-ups handed over, their terrorist training camps closed down and all foreign nationals freed. That included the eight Christians now on trial in Kabul.

The decree was issued about ten hours after President Bush had ordered his biggest bombers and more forces to military bases in the region, within striking distance of Afghanistan. The clerics had no desire to hang around. Their task completed, a thousand *mullahs* streamed through the hotel's revolving front door, a throng of white and black turbans sprinkled with greys and browns, bobbing back down the hill.

Yek, do, seh, char, panj. 'One, two, three, four, five.' Amanullah counted the crump of every shell. Even in the engineers' room in the basement, its door tightly shut, he could feel each one.

It made his legs, his teeth, shake. The hotel trembled with each crash. Amanullah counted every one, unable to shake his book-keeper's instinct. The precision of numbers helped calm his pounding heart.

On 7 October 2001 a new word entered Afghans' vocabulary of war: 'B-52'. America's powerful warplanes were spitting bombs on Afghanistan. The most daring staff crept closer to the windows, the front row on this war, to see a half-moon night illuminated by the bombs' blinding white flashes. The spritz of tracer fire from Taliban anti-aircraft guns soon lit the sky like shooting stars. Soviet-made rockets started whizzing into the city, too: salvoes fired by America's allies, the *mujahideen* of the Northern Alliance, dug in north of Kabul. Black-and-white smoke billowed from Kabul's airport. Then quiet reigned, punctured only by the cries of distressed stray dogs. And the electricity returned.

Night after night, it was the same. The bombs seemed to be the preserve of the dark. Warplanes and cruise missiles streaked like silver bullets across the black. The Taliban started shutting down the electricity themselves, believing darkness would be their friend. But there was no hiding from the most modern machinery of war. Kabul, Kandahar, Jalalabad and more were in the sights of America and its allies, including Britain. Taliban military bases, arms depots, communication towers, the Defence Ministry: anything, and anyone, they said was connected to al-Qaeda. All the while Taliban fighters prowled the streets in pickups mounted with anti-aircraft guns, their shouts of *Allahu Akbar* – and the scent of risk – carrying right up the hill to the Inter-Continental.

Like most Afghans, Amanullah only had his radio sets as guides. After dark, the BBC and VOA filled in the names and numbers: B-52, B-1, B-2. Tomahawk cruise missiles launched from American and British warships and submarines. Promises of extra forces from Canada, Australia, Germany, France. But sometimes there was only the static of radio, and the rumble of explosions echoing across the city. A legion of foreign journalists gathered on the other side of the mountains, too, alongside the *mujahideen*, reporting what they were seeing and hearing in the skies, some of them close enough to witness the eye-popping spectacle. Foreign radios carried their stories, too. Like the rebels, they were raring to enter Kabul.

It was said in America that the bombing would only last about a week. But as the weeks went by and the half-moon inched towards its full shine, the hail of missiles only intensified. The bombers seemed to circle ever lower in the skies, throwing down colossal fireballs. A military compound close to the long-abandoned US embassy went up in flames. An ammunition dump on Kabul's eastern rim set off a shower of explosions. Hospitals were hit, too, and fragile mud homes. The city was cut off; even food wasn't getting in. Weeks beforehand, the Taliban had ordered all foreigners, including aid workers, to leave the city. Many had already left.

Then another new term entered the Afghan lexicon: 'Daisy Cutter'. The bomb of all bombs was said to be as big as a small car. The BBC and VOA explained that these had also been used in the Vietnam War in the 1970s. That they tumbled to the ground on parachutes and incinerated everything in reach. And they were being dropped in northern Afghanistan and even closer to Kabul, to pave the way for the West's Afghan allies to re-enter the city. To take back what they lost to the Taliban five years earlier.

Every evening Amanullah sat tight. Every afternoon Hazrat went home at the end of his shift and pulled his family close, eight children huddled within their smashable walls. Every morning Mohammad Aqa stayed put with his two dear daughters and his wife: no one, not even the interior minister, was turning up at the office. And every day they all felt the panic rising in their chests as they waited for the return of the B-52s, and maybe the Daisy Cutter too.

CHAPTER 14

A New Day

Autumn 2001

Arab fighters hugged the wall. Their mottled green uniforms caked with days of dirt, they gripped their Kalashnikovs and inched around the hotel, eyes darting to and fro. But none looked up to see the tall Mr John – John Simpson from the BBC. Standing at the picture window at the end of the second-floor corridor, the one he always stayed in, he spotted them from above.

His team had burst through the front door of the Inter-Con just as a new day was breaking. They had reached the edge of Kabul at first light in an armoured convoy of *mujahideen* known as the Northern Alliance. The men with guns stopped there, mindful of a promise to Western allies not to storm into the city. But they assigned one of their fighters to accompany the BBC team as they went ahead on foot into the capital. Hitching rides on rusty bicycles and in dilapidated taxis, they pushed through streets fast filling with celebratory crowds. Their most pressing concern was getting to the Inter-Continental hotel, the place from which they hoped to send their story to the world.

The old order had melted away. The last remnants of the

Taliban had slipped out of Kabul in the dead of night. Osama Bin Laden and his al-Qaeda aides were said to have left even earlier, disappearing into the labyrinth of caves and tunnels in eastern Afghanistan, which the Saudi engineer had helped fortify during the 1980s war against the Soviets. The only foot soldiers still in the capital were clusters of diehard foreign fighters – including the Arabs stealing around the hotel wall, resolved to resist to their last bullet. Nameless bodies sprawled in nameless ditches across the city, Afghans taking their revenge on fighters who had terrorised a city that wasn't their own.

Before the high noon sun warmed the November chill, some Northern Alliance soldiers, who quickly broke their promise to pause on the rim of the city, were combing the grounds around the hotel in search of the last enemy holdouts: they could be hiding in the parched shrubbery or rusted military vehicles flipped on their side. Mr Peter, the BBC's cameraman, came upon a tense scene on the threshold of a crumbling mud property and filmed it all. Half a dozen foreign fighters were refusing to leave their last redoubt, even when bullets were shot in. The soldiers soon found a secret weapon. Another Arab fighter, captured by Afghans as he tried to escape, was dragged to this spot. They roughed him up, then forced him to shout to his fellow fighters. They emerged one by one, hands high in the air. A grey-bearded Pakistani in a grimy green tunic was stripped of anything of value. A handful of Arabs were whipped with rifle butts and shoved into a military jeep with other captives. One cowered in the corner, a defeated man with scared eyes and a bloodied nose.

The hotel's invasion by foreign media had begun the night before, with the arrival of a clutch of journalists who had secured rare Taliban permission to enter Kabul. Until now teams from the BBC and Associated Press (AP) had been working from their offices in the city centre. But on the thirty-seventh night of the US-led assault they had decided the Inter-Con was a much safer bet, after a bomb slammed into the road next to the BBC office. Correspondent William Reeve had been live on air, being filmed by veteran cameraman Phil Goodwin, when the blast jolted him out of his chair.

As B-52s shrieked overhead, the BBC and AP teams set off on what should have been a fifteen-minute drive to the Inter-Con. The AP's impressive Canadian journalist Kathy Gannon, the first to get into Kabul at the peak of the war, kept her eyes on the sky and the road until they came to a juddering halt at a Taliban roadblock. Jittery fighters bellowed into their car, demanding to know what these foreigners were up to. The AP's widely respected Afghan reporter Amir Shah softly talked them down. The BBC's ordeal was captured on calm Fred Scott's camera. After an agonisingly long delay they pulled into the Inter-Con portico before 9 p.m. News reached them that the Al Jazeera office had taken a direct hit, although none of their journalists were harmed. Never had a limping hotel lit by candles seemed so welcoming.

Hour after hour, day after day, journalists pitched up at the front desk, pleading for a room: correspondents, camera operators, producers, satellite engineers. Every room – even ones with toilets blocked, ceiling beams exposed, windows plastered with plastic – was gratefully taken. When more BBC teams piled in, including one with LyseDoucet, five women squeezed into a single room. Journalists bedded down in banquet rooms and in the halls. The BBC took over the entire second floor, CNN the fourth. There was even a waiting list for rooms. Kabul was again the world's most important dateline.

Most journalists had travelled from the north, through

territory controlled by the Northern Alliance, on a clear run to the capital. Hundreds more had been furiously kicking their heels at the Pakistan border, surging across the frontier once the gate finally swung open. But danger still lurked. On 19 November four journalists – two Italians, one Spaniard and an Afghan – were murdered in an ambush on the route to Kabul. They were stopped by what seemed to be Taliban stragglers in black turbans, bludgeoned with rifle butts and rocks, some shot dead as they tried to flee.

Still more journalists kept coming. The Inter-Con's media hub had soon pulled taxi drivers and English speakers to the hill. Afghans who had anything to offer loitered in the lobby. They all wanted a piece of the action; everyone needed work. The influx stoked the suspicions of the Northern Alliance fighters now tasked with surveilling the hotel. They began picking up Afghans at will and taking them away for questioning. Old warlords from various *mujahideen* factions also began holding court everywhere from the ballroom to the Bamiyan Brasserie, not hiding that they too had been bowled over by the might of America's B-52 bombers. Their power in the emerging political order was still to be decided.

For hotel staff, it was a good chaos. In lives forever ambushed by the past, they allowed themselves to look ahead for the first time in so long. The new general manager, Sher Babarkhel, sounded a call to arms to staff who had slipped away during one war or another. He had been part of this hotel since its first years, when he waited on tables at the Pamir Supper Club in white gloves. Now there was a chance to bring back some of the sparkle of its glorious past. His missive – 'Come back. We need you!' – was a call for help and a cry of joy. It travelled by word of mouth, knocks on doors and quick calls on a satellite phone, when someone kindly lent him theirs for a moment.

Naser Ali, the pastry chef, immediately quit his cook's job in Pakistan and came flying through the door. 'I am back in my country, my hotel, my kitchen. I am home.' The response was so enthusiastic that Sher Babarkhel couldn't resist a very Afghan poke at those who took a bit longer to arrive. 'You're too late,' he regretfully informed the smily waiter Sadozai, who had packed up his life in Pakistan and charged into the lobby just ten days after the Taliban fled. 'We don't need you any more.' Sadozai was left speechless. Silence thundered for a moment. Then Sher Babarkhel and everyone else exploded with laughter. Sadozai bent double with relief and glee.

Staff who had been consigned to back rooms returned to front offices. Salem, who had spent years peeling potatoes in dark corners of the kitchen, emerged into the light – taking off his turban, taking out his tie and joining the multitude of men who shaved their beards, blissfully running their fingers over smooth chins they hadn't touched in years. Others cautiously kept theirs, just in case. Bellboys and housekeepers, including Hazrat, trudged up and down the stairs, carting hefty suitcases and luggage and earning handsome tips. Some equipment needed to be carried to the icy, wind-blown roof, now dotted with cameras that were putting Kabul in the eyes of the world again.

Everyone had a dream. *The war was over.* Engineer Amanullah doodled designs for a reimagined Polytechnic, even a private university to educate the next generation of engineers, including women. Naser Ali was excitedly developing plans for a modern hotel bakery. Waiters daydreamed about purchasing comfortable little houses instead of living at the mercy of greedy landlords. And maybe they would be able to buy motorcycles – or a second-hand car – even if most were still partial to their trusty bicycles.

Mohammad Aqa was beside himself that his two girls could now enter classrooms. He hugged his daughters close: 'It's going to be OK!' He, too, had happily returned to the hotel and his restaurant. The day he showed up at the Inter-Con he had found himself vouching for the old Taliban general manager, who had suddenly driven up the hill in a hotel car carrying a large stash of money. He explained that he had taken the money with him to keep it safe in the first uncertain days and was now bringing it back to the hotel, along with the car. Mohammad Aqa's reference ensured that he was able to leave safely.

Even Hazrat allowed himself to hope. They had reached rock bottom. 'It can only get better now' became his new mantra. 'It's not just me who thinks that,' he told anyone who would listen, and many did. 'A lot of Afghans feel the same.'

Kabul cautiously peered above the parapet. Centuries-old palaces and grand merchant houses were now blackened shells. Even the elegant Bagh-e Bala next to the hotel had partly crumbled after being hit by an American missile meant for al-Qaeda. In the city centre a section of the Kabul Hotel was a dark maw, blown wide open by a bomb. The entrance to the stately Central Bank was a tatty brown blanket; the Ministry of Public Health a metal skeleton without doors, windows or many walls, rattling in the winter winds.

But a new system was slowly taking shape. In an imposing castle in the far-away German city of Bonn an agreement on a post-Taliban arrangement was finally reached after a week of impassioned back and forth. Hamid Karzai, a former *muja-hideen* spokesperson and distant relative of the former king, was selected as its chairman while he was still battling the last remnants of Taliban rule in southern Afghanistan. LyseDoucet was the first to tell him the news, when she called him on her satellite phone from Kabul to ask for his response. 'That's nice,' he exclaimed, with modest understatement.

As another winter roared in, UN envoys went in and out of the Inter-Con, holding press conferences in chilly rooms where everyone kept their coats on, hats pulled over ears. There would be five deputies and twenty-three ministers, and an interim Cabinet meant to represent all of Afghanistan – though worries were already seeping through as to whether it actually did. The UN spokesman, Ahmad Fawzi, kept sending messages from the Inter-Con's pulpit to the press: *Afghanistan's new government needs everything.* Desks, chairs, windows, doors, paper clips – you name it, they needed it. But new ministers were dreaming big, too. 'Afghanistan is now open to tourism for the first time in twenty-three years,' declared the new interim tourism minister. 'Many people will be curious to see it first-hand especially since it has been on television so much lately.' He predicted that tourists would start arriving within months, and revealed that he was already looking for partners to upgrade the Inter-Continental Kabul to its past splendour.

The hotel sat waiting. Its blue signboard was now scratched, pockmarked by shrapnel, letters punched into black holes. There was no letter o in 'Hotel'. There was no letter o in 'Continental'. There was not even an 'Inter', the word painted over long ago with a thick white stripe after the luxury international chain pulled out.

But its iconic letter K still danced on the glass of the revolving front door, and on the roof in a most beautiful blue. After multiple bloody coups, two invasions, a grievous civil war and strict Islamist rule, the Inter-Continental Kabul was bowed, but not broken. It was still the city's finest hotel. It had never shut its doors.

PART V

The Years of Light and Dark

CHAPTER 15

Abida's *Ashak*

Spring 2002

The kitchen didn't have the right pots. It didn't have all the right ingredients. The hotel's new manager and deputy manager didn't know a thing about Afghan food; they were both foreigners. But Abida knew. In the kitchen of the Kabul Hotel in the city centre, before the *mujahideen* and Taliban forced her to sit at home, she had been famous for it. 'Bring us Abida's delicious *mantu* and *ashak*!' her guests would shout. 'Bring those tasty *sambosas*!'

Now she was being tested for a job at the Inter-Con. 'What can you cook?' the hotel's new bosses asked her. Abida had the answer. It had to be dumplings. Plump *mantu* stuffed with delicately seasoned meat. *Ashak* puffed with sweet *gandana* leeks, both smothered in a garlicky or tomatoey yogurt. Warm dumplings. Cool yogurt. Not too spicy, but not bland. Afghan food. *Ashak* and *mantu* took skill, time, patience and love to prepare – a food for feasts and celebrations. If Abida passed this test, they would join the menu of Kabul's finest hotel.

She wasn't nervous. Life had never given her the gift of learning to write. She could only read a little bit. But *Shukoor*

243

Khoda, 'thanks be to God', the skill she did have was a super-power. It wouldn't be easy, though. What had once been the kitchen of kitchens in Kabul had been devoured during the decades of flying rockets and power cuts. All that remained were the two white-bearded cooks, bent over by too much back-breaking work, shuffling about in an ill-lit corner. Survivors, still cooking. War couldn't steal all their recipes kept safe in memory.

The hotel's new managers had started to fix the kitchen, but it still wasn't up to scratch. Abida would need to improvise. She sifted flour and salt into the best bowl she could find, adding eggs and oil, then water, making a smooth dough, dividing it into smaller balls, pushing her palms into this soft squishy mix, firmly rolling it forward and back, turning it round and round. Strong fingers dusted with flour and dotted with callouses. Abida was a maestro conducting a kitchen concerto. She knew every note by heart.

As she cooked, Abida allowed her mind to wander in a past that would never be past. She had come into this world during the days of the king, in an ordinary poor Kabul family. Her father, like many fathers then, had pulled her out of school when she was only in grade four, around fourteen years old. She was a beautiful girl, quick to learn, with a glossy mane of walnut-brown hair and striking doe-eyes. And it was time to marry.

Abida didn't know a thing about marriage, not even much about life. But she had to honour her father. And honour her husband Qasim, a distant relative, forty-five years old. He was not too kind. But not too unkind, she believed. Sometimes it was his words that were harsh, sometimes his actions: a slap if he was next to her, a thrown object – a cup, a bowl – when he was far from her. Sometimes she would wince, and sometimes she would weep. She had no choice but to love him, to have children, to honour her father's name.

Besides, it could be worse. It was said that husbands had improved. And Qasim was a very good tailor. There was no one like him when it came to turning out a fine waistcoat and *perahan o tunban* trousers and tunics. Afghans would buy his finely stitched clothes to send to their family members in Europe. That made her proud. Within two years she gave birth to their first child, a beautiful daughter, Anissa. Almost every year, for many years, she bore another.

Abida had to work. By the time she was in her twenties the communists had taken over; that meant there were more opportunities for women, even if there were worries, too. Someone she knew who knew someone got her a job in the Kabul Hotel. She became the first woman to work alongside the men in their kitchen. Abida produced *mantu* and *ashak*, as well as crispy fried Afghan *sambosas* stuffed with minced meat. And for the biggest weddings, with more than 500 guests and all too much food to prepare, two other women working in the laundry pitched in to help her. They made quick work, weaving together.

There were rowdy official occasions when comrades in the Soviet-backed party raised glasses of vodka high above the tables to celebrate something to do with their revolution. And there was the whirl of weddings with Kabulis in nice suits and sparkly dresses. Their happiness made Abida happy, too. But families' tears of joy were often mixed with sorrow. Sometimes weddings only had a groom, or a bride – their betrothed far away, already living in exile, and they too would leave their own family behind to join them, perhaps never to return. That was marriage in Afghanistan then.

On nights when she worked late, the hotel manager on duty would put her in a car to make sure she reached home safely.

Kind-hearted security guards also kept a watchful eye on Abida –
she was so young, after all – one of them always telling her what
to say if she was stopped at a checkpoint by soldiers demanding to know where she was going at that hour. 'Where are you
going so late, *siah sar* – "black-headed one"?', that casual way in
which Afghan men sometimes addressed women. She was to
say she was at the hospital with a family member, not working
evening shifts at a hotel, they told her. Women shouldn't be out
so late.

Qasim helped out at home, sewing his clothes there instead of
in his shop. Her eldest Anissa looked out for the youngest. Four
daughters, three sons, and a life of toggling between hotel
and home. Life as Abida knew it was always a juggle, always
demanding attention to every detail, and there were so many.

She carefully cleaned the *gandana*, Afghan leeks that were
long and green like chives, rinsing them of soil and chopping
them into pieces. The onions needed to be finely chopped, too,
the meat minced, thrown together with tomatoes to sizzle in the
pan. The aromas offered a path to the past, lifting her from
the kitchen to other places and times. To happy memories that
boosted her spirits like yellow butterflies flitting across flowers.
To sad ones that stung like a hot pot on her skin.

When the civil war had exploded in the 1990s their home in
Kabul, as humble as humble could get, had been looted by a
group of rampaging fighters. She didn't know which; they all
seemed the same. Qasim's shop was cleared out, too. They even
took his sewing machines. So they moved from house to house
until they had no choice but to melt into the tide of people
escaping to Pakistan. But after twenty days Abida knew she
couldn't live in a land that wasn't their own. She urged Qasim
to take them back to Kabul. Eventually he listened and agreed.
It wasn't like he had any work in Pakistan anyway. How she

wished Qasim hadn't given in to her that time. It brought tears to her eyes; it always did.

Abida wiped them away. This was no time to cry. She cut squares of dough for the *mantu*, placed a heaping spoonful of minced-meat mixture on each one, and pinched two diagonal corners together. She gently set the dumplings inside her improvised steamer. Then she traced rounds in the dough for *ashak*, dropping a dollop of softened leeks on a circle, tightly sealing it with another, popping each morsel, one by one, into a pot of raging water. She stared into its tempest.

The details of the day that changed her life for ever were burned in her memory like an old family recipe. It was the fourth day of the fourth month. They had returned to Kabul, on her urging, to become refugees in their own city. They were living in someone else's house in the neighbourhood of Kart-e Parwan, just below the Inter-Con. The owner provided them with mattresses to spread on the floor to sleep, and appliances in the kitchen to cook. In return, they protected his premises as best they could. Time in Kabul was now marked by the ebb and flow of the fighting. It unfolded like clockwork – the hours of quiet but for the birdsong, the hours of whistling bullets and crashing shellfire. They knew the schedule. In the morning the rockets fell.

On one of these mornings, as Abida bustled about the kitchen, heavily pregnant again, scrambling eggs with tomatoes for breakfast, she realised that one of their children had wandered outside. She asked Qasim to please go and find him. And he did. Minutes later a rocket slammed into their street, hitting him smack on the head. He came back dead. Their youngest son, Suleiman, born not long after, never got to see his father. The shrapnel wounded one of their daughters, too.

Everyone blamed Abida. 'Why did you insist on going back

to Kabul? If you hadn't gone back, your husband would not have been martyred.' Grief and guilt had threaded together. A wife, mother, woman, upbraided for the choices she had made. *Zana bad bakht* – 'the woman's fault'. But in moments when she pulled herself together, Abida accepted her fate. *Kismat.* 'Written by God.' God had taken Qasim away; God would provide. Her children were going to bed hungry, but she didn't want to ask her family, or his family, for help. She didn't want to join the queues for a UN ration card to receive free bread from the bakery. Begging felt dishonourable. And she would be harassed in the streets. She was still young, still strong. Her oldest daughter, Anissa, now a teenager, could do her part.

They turned to what her Qasim had taught her: to sew. Abida and Anissa would sit cross-legged on their *toshak* mattress on the hard mud floor, stitching by sunlight, by moonlight, by flickering oil lamps. Her littlest toddled and tumbled around them.

Fine needlework was the way that illiterate women of Kandahar had always told the stories they couldn't write into words. *Khamak* was a language of delicate flowers and geometrical shapes, stitched in silky symmetry onto men's tunics and women's dresses, tablecloths and cushions. A tradition from the heartland of the Pashtuns, needlework sharpened Abida's mind and brought her money. Her customers were wealthy businessmen or local charities who brought them the materials, then picked up their wares. She didn't know where her handiwork was sold, whose homes it ended up in. But she wanted to believe it brought joy.

Abida kept stitching her family together. Her babies began to walk, her toddlers grew into teenagers, and Raisa and Safina became big enough to lend a hand alongside Anissa. Abida did what she could. When her children's classrooms were closed by the shellfire of the *mujahideen* or the strictures of the Taliban, Abida managed as best she could. She tried to open up the world for her children, even as she felt her own walls closing in, more with each year that passed. She longed to become Chef Abida again, to feel the silken flour between her fingers, see her dishes steaming on big kitchen counters. For so long it seemed like the day would never come. And then it did.

In late 2001, on a bitterly cold winter's day when trees were bare and the hills blanketed with snow, weeks after the Taliban were toppled, Abida gripped her radio, pressing it to her ear so that she heard every word of this first speech from her new leader, Hamid Karzai, on the Voice of Sharia Radio – now rebranded again as Radio and Television Afghanistan.

'I hope God will give our country a bright future,' Karzai's voice boomed from inside the heavily guarded Interior Ministry. 'What our country and its people have suffered over twenty-three years cannot be described or written.' Abida's eyes welled up again. They were like the leaky *bambah* pumps at the end of her road. But on this day she let her tears spill. They were drops of joy. 'Today we are happy that we can see the sun rising again on our land. I think a wave of peace and unity is coming to our country,' Karzai continued.

Her new leader was announcing a thirteen-point plan for his new government. Her hand tightened around the radio. It started with Islam. Shouts of *Allahu Akbar* rose from the hall where he spoke. Then Karzai moved on to points about protecting the territory, fighting terrorism, freedom of speech and belief, obeying the laws. At last he came to point number five. 'We respect Afghan women, who are half of our country's population,' he began, with thunderous applause almost drowning out the rest of his pledge, 'and we give the rights to them under the country's law.'

Abida squeezed Anissa's hands, already indented by the telltale signs of a seamstress. She still wasn't sure what Karzai's words would mean, but something that she had feared was long dead tingled within her again. Not long afterwards, her radio brought her more news: 'Women who work outside the home can return to their jobs.' An office for jobs in the government-owned hotels had opened. She turned to her Anissa. 'What should I do?' Her eldest answered without the slightest hesitation: 'Yes, *Maman*! You should go!'

It was like the shot of a starting gun. Abida reached for her washed-out blue *chadri* and bolted out of the door of their four-room mud-and-timber house, leaping into the first shared yellow taxi that trundled by. The head-to-toe burka was no longer obligatory – but Abida was still nervous that this good news, like most good news in her life, would not last long, and that women would again be pushed back into the cages of their lives.

Yet Kabul was already starting to sound and look different. There were the old problems, of course: the fetid open gutters running along pavements, and the buildings scarred by war; the soot-faced urchins scooting through traffic, waving packets of cigarettes and smoking tins of *spandi* herbs. But so much had already changed, in just a few months. It was still startling to hear music blaring from shops, to see men's clean-shaven faces, to see women's heads uncovered, even the astonishing sight of glossy red lipstick. And the streets had been heaving with a new kind of traffic. Shiny new SUVs, plastic coverings still on their seats, were crowding out the rickety old bicycles. More beat-up taxis were jostling for space. Vehicles of all styles were streaming across the border from Pakistan, identifiable by the steering wheel on the right side, the legacy of their British colonial history: the wrong side for Kabul, a city that still prided itself on never being colonised, despite countless invasions.

Abida's eyes had shone like stars as she strode through the open door to make her own history: the first woman to register her name at the office for the Department of Government Hotels. The ministry had just restarted work on Ariana Square, the central piazza where the battered body of President Najibullah had dangled from the traffic post in 1996. Abida scribbled her signature – some of the few words she could write – on the first blank page in the register. She was going to return to her old job in the Kabul Hotel, to restart her life. Her city pulsed with a new sense of purpose.

Carefully removing the *mantu* from her makeshift steamer, Abida placed each moist dumpling on a dish, slathering them with a tomato sauce seasoned with coriander. The *ashak* were tenderly lifted from the boiling pot and set on a plate of garlicky yogurt, although she couldn't find any sprigs of mint to sprinkle on top.

In the days after she had put her name down to return to work, Abida had lain awake at night. She couldn't wait to get back to the big kitchen. It didn't matter that the Kabul Hotel was a shambles, its grungy yellow-and-lime exterior blotted by black smudges and shrapnel holes. Its garden stank. The interior was dank and dark, layered with years of dust and debris, fallen beams, furniture turned topsy-turvy. The lovely lounge, which once seated the wealthy and connected, was now stacked with broken sofas bursting with stuffing, chipped sinks and beds dragged from derelict guest rooms. There wasn't even a place to sit. But they all set to work, scrubbing floors and sorting furniture, cleaning cutlery, polishing glasses. Soon the kitchen was infused with the warming steam and smells of cooking. And then the words she had longed for. 'Bring us Abida's delicious *mantu* and *ashak*!' the guests called out. 'Bring those tasty *sambosas*!'

When the bad news came, months later, it was like a rocket crashing into her life. The Kabul Hotel would shut for a long time, to give it a complete makeover. It had been leased to Prince Aga Khan, the worldwide leader of the Ismailis, a branch of Shia Islam, who was also known for his exquisite Serena chain of luxury hotels. Abida was crushed. But not for long. Her wishes were delayed, not denied. In the bazaar she bumped into a former colleague who told her about a job opening in the Inter-Con kitchen. She made haste to the hill the very next day, taking in the tree-lined path sweeping up the hill, the splashing fountain, the famous entrance, the chandeliered lobby. The hotel she had heard so much about, but never seen. She was soon whisked away to the manager's office down the winding stairs. 'What can you cook?' he asked her.

With Abida's *mantu* and *ashak* completed, and taste-tested, the managers summoned her. 'Delicious!' They loved it. Her eyes crinkled with delight. They wanted more. But they had one last question. 'Do you have any worries about working alongside the men?' Abida shook her head emphatically. She had worked with men at the Kabul Hotel. Now she would be the first female sous-chef at an even more famous hotel, the Inter-Continental Kabul.

Abida Nazari – chef, seamstress, widow, mother of eight children – was back where she belonged. She would start work the very next day. And she had already made her mark. An Afghan woman had changed the menu.

CHAPTER 16

A Royal Return

Spring 2002

Something was in the air. Mohammad Aqa could feel it as he perched on the elevated wooden chair at the entrance to the Bamiyan Brasserie. A lemony spring light streamed through the wraparound windows on the far side of a room that he knew like his own home. From here he could see his favourite place in this hotel: the terrace, with its sweeping view of the city's vast sky. And his favourite piece of furniture was in front of him again: the scuffed waiter's cabinet, dimpled by history, from the king's time.

Mohammad Aqa was finally back from his secondment to the Interior Ministry. Back where he belonged. He got up to push open the kitchen's flip-flap door. 'What's going on?' he asked the young waiter stacking saucers and teacups. 'There's a special event today,' the boy replied matter-of-factly. 'Karzai *Sahib* is coming. He's going to make the first telephone call.' Mohammad Aqa took a moment to savour the self-confidence of a boy born into a land without working telephones, who had no experience – not even the least bit of knowledge – about what that would entail. He felt a frisson of anticipation. *The new leader was here.*

Mohammad Aqa knew little about Hamid Karzai. People were saying that he had been deputy foreign minister when the *mujahideen* were in power the first time around, but Mohammad Aqa hadn't known that. In that time, Karzai had fled the capital amid rumours of plots against him, fearing for his life and infuriated by the infighting, just as Kabul was plunged into civil war. Now Karzai was back. Mohammad Aqa felt proud there was now an Afghan leader who spoke so well in Afghanistan's two main languages, Dari and Pashto, as well as foreign ones, including Urdu, Hindi and English. Better still, he spoke a language of peace.

Mohammad Aqa stepped out of the kitchen and into the lobby, where a rare surge of electricity was lending the chandeliers a celebratory sparkle. Besuited Afghans with curly wires coming out of their ears – giving away that they were those not-so-secret security types – were prowling the ground floor. They were barking at staff to stay in place, not to move even an inch in the direction of the ballroom. Mohammad Aqa turned on his heel and headed towards the staff passageway connecting the kitchen to the banquet hall, skipping quickly through the dimly lit corridor without attracting anyone's attention.

He nudged open the ballroom's side-door. The banquet hall was abuzz with expectant chatter. Mohammad Aqa noted the table-setting approvingly: the round tables draped in white tablecloths, with white napkins folded into standing fans. Every seat was occupied: men and women, Afghans and foreigners, tunics and turbans and Western suits, a sprinkling of women's headscarves. They were all waiting.

The new leader strode in. Karzai was here. The room exploded with applause. Here he was, in a swarm of aides and hangers-on, waving and smiling, wearing the Afghan clothes the world was making such a fuss about. A striped green silk Uzbek *chapan* cloak draped over a dark blazer, matched with a finely tailored grey tunic. A trim grey *karakul* sheepskin hat. And his grey-flecked, neatly clipped beard. Karzai's East–West style.

He was handed a shiny telephone that fitted neatly in the palm of his hand. 'We used to only have telephones on tables,' Karzai quipped with a hint of a grin. 'Are you Shaida?' he asked cheerily as he pressed the mouthpiece against his bearded face. 'I gave them the number of a friend, so I hope it's the right one,' he joked. Laughter rippled through the hall. Mohammad Aqa smiled, too. How nice to have something to smile about. Foreign radios were talking about it as well: Afghanistan's new leader, charming the world with his folksy style.

The Afghan chosen for the honour of this first call was a war widow, one of millions of refugees forced to flee their homeland. 'I'm very happy to talk to you today because we're launching, for the first time, a new mobile-phone system, and there are a lot of people here to witness this call,' Karzai told her. He didn't share what she said. Perhaps putting her voice on speakerphone was a technical step too far.

Karzai handed back the mobile phone. 'It's working!' he declared, sparking another delighted ovation. Of course it wouldn't be working any time soon, for almost all Afghans. A new handset cost between $350 and $450, an unimaginable sum. Still, the thought of it was tantalising. Afghanistan was returning to the twenty-first century.

Mohammad Aqa looked around the room, spotting other officials in the new interim government. He could see the foreign minister, Dr Abdullah Abdullah, who was also being noticed for his sartorial flair. And there was the boyish-faced Afghan-American businessman Ehsan Bayat, standing right next to Karzai. He had grinned a Cheshire-cat smile when Karzai handed back the telephone. The stage was decorated with banners advertising his company, AWCC, the Afghan Wireless Communication Company: Afghanistan's first mobile-telephone network. Bayat had been to the hotel many times, including in the Taliban days, when he was given an exclusive licence to establish the first wireless telephone network. Now, with the Taliban gone and the international trade embargo lifted, he had already brought in the latest US technology.

It felt like a miracle. The hotel still had its old telephone exchange in the basement, an antique Siemens switchboard with its grid of jacks and cords. But most of the old telephones had stopped working long ago. For years most Afghans had had to make the journey across the risky, rutted land routes to Pakistan simply to make a call. Phone lines were shredded when fighters dug trenches; others were stripped for copper to sell. Even Afghanistan's 93 international dialling code had been sold off; Bayat had only just managed to buy it back. Mohammad Aqa headed back to the restaurant with a spring in his step. Afghanistan was connecting to the world; the world was coming to the hotel. It was all happening so quickly.

In no time at all, Bayat's AWCC had opened a shiny glass-fronted shop in the lobby. Staff shook their heads in amazement. The queues stretched right across the floor from morning to night. Some of these phones were now a bit cheaper, costing $250, although even that was more than triple Mohammad Aqa's monthly salary. The staff eyed the customers going in and out, gingerly lifting their first phone from its pillow of thin tissue paper inside its cardboard box. And then these mobile phones started ringing – and what music it was! There were new tunes every day. A lively *Lambada* from Brazil.

Intriguing *James Bond* music from Britain. Ringtones no one in the hotel had ever heard before, on mobile phones that no one could afford to buy.

Until one of their own bought one, that is. Head waiter Haji Noorullah had a brother in Ukraine who sent him some money. Mohammad Aqa watched with a barely concealed smile to see how Haji took such care with his new possession, even wrapping it in tissue paper when he charged its battery. How they teased him. 'Haji Noorullah, you love this phone more than your children!' There was much laughter about the indulgence of it. How could any of them afford to use such expensive phones, when just saying hello in Dari or Pashto would consume all the data in the wave of customary greetings: 'How is your family, how is your health, how is your life? God bless you, God bless them, God bless Afghanistan', and on and on. They would be cut off before they even got to the real point of the call, Afghans joked, with delicious glee.

A few months later, in the basement, a spacious room was painted white and its long wooden tables were also decorated in white and installed with white dividers. Soon eleven bulky screens and keyboards were carted in: *computers*. It was the same word, albeit pronounced a bit differently, in English, Dari and Pashto. A *worldwide web* promised to connect them to anyone, anywhere. This was Bayat's latest scheme: what he was calling Kabul's first internet café.

The hotel needed this service more than ever. Once again journalists and other guests were pouring into the city and checking into the hotel. The Inter-Con felt alive for the first time in so long. On the floor above, Mohammad Aqa would steal moments to stand on his favourite terrace. The gentle breeze of spring no longer carried the whistle of missiles and the growl of warplanes to the hill. The skies opened for kites to fly, children to laugh, dreams to soar. He filled his lungs. A new time was starting – for his country, for his hotel.

There were even new leaders for the Inter-Con. He had watched the signing ceremony in the Nuristan Cocktail Lounge for an agreement between a Dubai company, the Al Yaquob Group, owned by a wealthy Arab sheikh, and the new Afghan government. Their enterprise, Freecom Trading, was awarded a lease to run the Inter-Con for the next fifteen years. They promised to spend more than $10 million to restore the hotel to its five-star glory. 'Afghanistan has become the focal point of business, following the prevailing stable environment in the country,' the sheikh enthused. 'For us, it is a quantum leap towards investing in the leisure and hotel industry in Afghanistan.' Mohammad Aqa wanted to believe him.

Ruddy-faced German soldiers patrolled the premises, rifles and machine guns at the ready. British troops in sand-coloured berets had set up a base on the roof, their shimmering Union Jacks fluttering on high as snipers trained their binoculars on the grounds below. In war and peace the Inter-Continental Kabul was still, beyond doubt, the country's lookout of lookouts. In June 2002 it became a watch-post for ISAF, the International Security Assistance Force, tasked with helping Afghans keep the peace. They were there in Kabul: 3,500 soldiers from nineteen nations' armies, as part of the world's promise to 'stand with Afghans for the long run'.

Their Inter-Con deployment mattered, a lot. Just below the hotel, a glossy white pavilion rose from the playing fields of the Kabul Polytechnic: a voluminous Bavarian-style beer tent, provided by Germany and repurposed for an old Afghan tradition. A *Loya Jirga* had been summoned. In fact it was an *Emergency Loya Jirga*, tasked with urgently choosing a leader and

![Colour returns to the streets outside the Inter-Con]

Colour returns to the streets outside the Inter-Con after the US-led invasion which toppled the Taliban, November 2001.

At the 2002 *Loya Jirga*, former king Zahir Shah (*left*), accompanied by the interim president Hamid Karzai, announces that he has no intention of returning to the throne.

Police officers watch proceedings from a television in the Inter-Con, just up the hill from the *Loya Jirga* site.

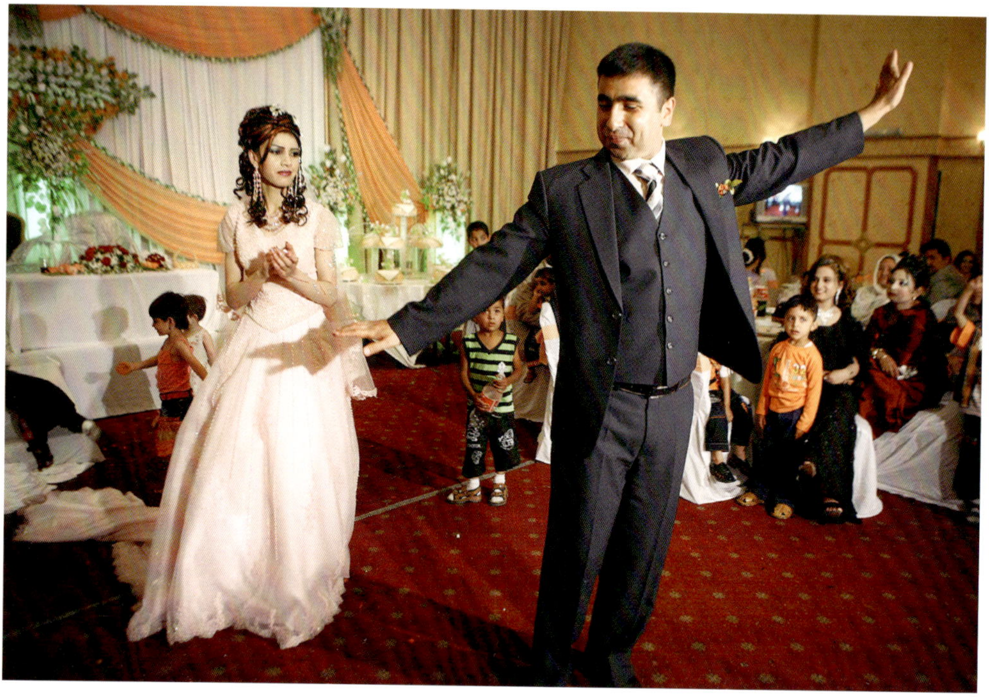

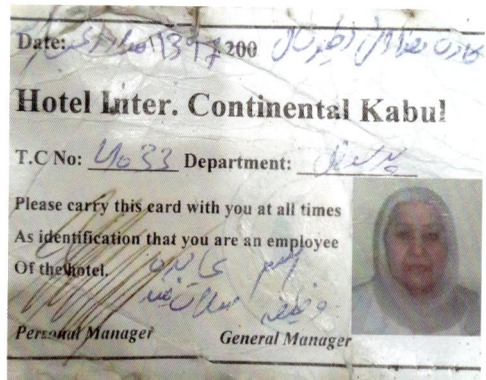

Young love in the Kandahar Ballroom, August 2007.

Date: 200

Hotel Inter. Continental Kabul

T.C No: Department:

Please carry this card with you at all times
As identification that you are an employee
Of the Hotel.

Personal Manager General Manager

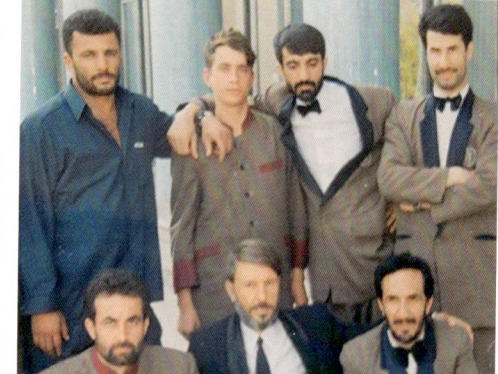

An identity card grants hotel access to Abida, the first female chef to work in the Inter-Con's famous kitchen following the fall of the Taliban.

Mohammad Aqa (*top right*) has a moment of downtime with his fellow waiters outside the Inter-Con.

A thick cloud of smoke billows from the Inter-Continental during the January 2018 attack.

The Inter-Continental ablaze in the wake of the June 2011 suicide bombing.

Relatives of a victim of the second major suicide attack collect his belongings from a burnt-out Inter-Con, January 2018.

Pop superstar Aryana Sayeed enthrals young Afghans at her Independence Day performance in the Inter-Con, August 2017.

A chef prays at the hotel during a break in his shift, 2015.

Qudus, who spent his entire working life cycling to and from the Inter-Con, poses in the foyer, September 2018.

The Inter-Con under new management in the years following the Taliban's return in August 2021.

The front desk of the Inter-Con, now on Taliban time.

A hotel employee prepares the Kandahar Ballroom for one of its famous feasts.

Housekeeper Hazrat on the third-floor corridor – his corridor – in the hotel he has proudly served since 1971.

Amanullah, former Chief Engineer, is today Dr Faqiri, dean of engineering at Kabul Polytechnic.

Restaurant Manager Mohammad Aqa stands ready to serve in the Bukhara Restaurant, formerly the Bamiyan Brasserie.

Abida holds her 'Employee of the Month' certificate, hard-won during two decades' work in the Inter-Con kitchen.

Sadeq, the Acting Front Desk Manager with a megawatt smile.

Malalai quietly makes history as one of the Inter-Con's first female waiters.

The Taliban-rebranded entrance sign at the bottom of the hill proclaims the hotel to be an 'Intercontinental for Everyone'.

Hazrat, now formerly of the Inter-Con, looks out on Kabul from the cracked window of Room 319.

a Cabinet. The interim authority headed by Hamid Karzai had been selected at speed, thousands of miles away, in the dead of winter when the Taliban were on the run. Now there would be a transitional authority to run Afghanistan for two years. If all went to plan, UN-backed elections would then be held – the first time in history that Afghans would directly elect their president.

And so 1,600 delegates, chosen by their communities or selected by the *Loya Jirga* commission for special seats, converged on the big tent. Their head coverings were their business cards. Tribal elders from the south and east sported turbans so loose and large it looked as if they might tumble to the ground. Kabul turbans were wound tightly, neatly. Many men wore rolled-up wool *pakol* caps, the mark of the *mujahideen*. But some of the old warlords – wannabe democrats – were in Western suits with ties, a few of them matched with comfy white sneakers. There was a rainbow of headscarves, too; the more conservative a delegate's home, the longer and more sombre her head covering. Simply being there was a badge of honour. It was the first time in Afghan history that women sat in a *Jirga*.

The hotel had its eyes inside that tent, too. A giant video screen had been erected in the ballroom, the centrepiece of a quickly built press centre for the media – to keep them from the heavily fortified venue, except on escorted visits. Journalists hammered out copy on their keyboards or broadcast live from the forecourt. The BBC even hoisted its own yellow-and-black marquee on the cement platform where a bandstand had once stood, providing a splendid view of the setting below.

In the lobby, in front of the tall blue urn decorated with tiny pink flowers, another television set had been placed on a high cabinet, so that everyone could watch. In fact every TV set anyone could find – old ones rescued from the basement where they had been hidden from the Taliban, new ones purchased in haste – was switched to Afghan state TV. In back rooms behind the front desk, in a corner of the kitchen, in management offices below, in guest rooms above, everyone wanted to see for themselves. They had waited long enough: for years, and then for another twenty-four hours when the *Jirga* was abruptly delayed at the last minute. No one could say why.

On the morning of the *Jirga* a blinding wind swept sheets of sand and dust across the city. The tall pines bowed before its force. Blue skies turned black, white flashes zigzagging across slate. Birds shrieked. The BBC tent was knocked from its moorings, tearing strips of tarpaulin from their metal pegs and sending LyseDoucet and her BBC team running for cover. *Patsha gardeshi*, hotel staff whispered knowingly. 'When a strong wind blows with the dust, the king changes.'

When the flags fell back into silent folds and the trees were still, a sleek black limousine, bulletproof with tinted windows, swished past the hotel on the empty road below. Flanked by escort cars and armoured vehicles, it swung through the open gates of the Polytechnic next door. Sentries stood in salute as it rolled through the heavily guarded grounds now dotted with all manner of small tents, towards the biggest pavilion of all, the *Loya Jirga* site. When it pulled to a stop, bodyguards sprinted into position to pull open the heavy doors. *Ala'Hazrat.* 'Your Majesty.' The exiled king had come home.

Eighty-seven-year-old Zahir Shah, his dark moustache now silvery grey, shuffled towards the entrance in his tailored Italian suit, a traditional grey *karakul* hat on his head. He had spent almost three decades in exile, ever since being toppled by his cousin in the 1973 coup. Now, in keeping with tradition, he had been invited to open the grand assembly. The big tent below filled with thunderous applause at the sight of the king.

All eyes in the hotel were on the screens. Every seat of the media hub in the ballroom was occupied – rows of straight-backed chairs carpeting the floor and the upper gallery. Down the corridor, in the lobby's ersatz cinema, Afghans sat squished together on the sofas or sprawled across the floor: policemen in green serge uniforms and caps, Afghan journalists with their Handycams, young boys who sat cross-legged on the carpet, watching wide-eyed. Cooks stopped chopping. Waiters waited. Even the doorman had abandoned his post. Only the cauldrons of rice on a low heat kept up their babbling.

They watched the delegates rise, almost as one, as the frail king stepped haltingly across the stage towards a table draped in royal blue and gold, steadied by an official's arm. 'I'm so happy to be close to you again,' he whispered, his thinning voice boosted by the microphones. Many Afghans felt the same. Zahir Shah was, in law, merely a normal citizen. But in the hearts and minds of many Afghans, he was still their king, the living embodiment of the golden years before coups and conflict shredded their country.

The king was reading from a Dari script, held fast in shaking, translucent hands. But he had only just started when the hush in the ballroom was shattered. The big screen had gone black, sparking a wave of indignant cries from the journalists. On his stage the king kept reading sotto voce, oblivious to the drama. Only as he completed his address and the assembly filled with applause did the audio return to the hill.

The ballroom was filled with angry head-shaking. UN officials were quick to blame a blown fuse. But no one believed the technical excuses. After all, the same thing had happened when Zahir Shah's plane had touched down in Kabul only weeks before. *Someone was silencing* Ala'Hazrat. *Someone was humiliating the king.* There was no shortage of motive, after all. As much as

Zahir Shah was loved, he was also feared: seen as a threat by the many pretenders to the new thrones.

In the run-up to the *Jirga*, many had worried that some in the assembly would nominate him to be the new president – even the new king. In decades gone by, during his exile, Zahir Shah had occasionally been asked if he had any desire to reclaim his throne. 'It's not something I seek for myself,' he would say, with the wave of a knobbly hand. 'But if my people ask me, I cannot refuse.' That ambiguity had been squashed the day before; some said it was what had delayed this historic gathering. Many suspected it was the doing of Zalmay Khalilzad, the US special envoy with Afghan ancestry, who had met the ex-monarch, who was wearing his pyjamas, in his bedroom. Khalilzad revealed to confidants that Zahir Shah had poured out his woe that he was being pressured to take on a role that, at his age, he couldn't possibly perform.

With the big screen back in action, the journalists in the media hub gradually pieced together what had been said. 'Think of peace in the country,' the ageing king had said. 'I never came to be king, just to serve Afghanistan and the nation, and to bring peace to the country, national unity and reconciliation.' He urged his people to move towards a democratic system based on Islam. And he expressed his support for the man now leading the nation, Hamid Karzai.

Now Karzai took the stage. Sporting an impressive grey-and-black turban – one tuft jutting from its folds, another falling on his shoulder – the interim leader addressed the assembly as the king sat silently at the table. 'We want to start our *Jirga* with beautiful words,' Karzai proclaimed. 'In the name of God, I want to introduce Mohammad Zahir Shah as *Baba-i-Millat*, "Father of the nation".' A ceremonial role, but an honourable one. A shrewd move. Even Karzai could not compete with a celebrated king.

*

Not only *Jirga* delegates were descending on Kabul. That spring and summer a wave of Afghan exiles was surging into the city from all corners of the world. The Inter-Continental was one of the only places seen as suitable lodgings until they managed to find long-term accommodation. Hazrat's floor was humming with guests thrilled to be home – ex-diplomats, ministers, business types.

The happiest guest was residing in one of the suites at the end of the corridor. Prince Ali Seraj – businessman, philanthropist, self-styled 'King of Kabul Nightlife' – was back. Most mornings he emerged from his suite to beckon housekeeping staff on the floor, including Hazrat. 'Let's have a chat!' his gravelly voice would boom down the hall. The prince with the distinctive goatee wanted to know everything there was to know about life in a country whose air he had not breathed since he fled on a bus, disguised as a hippy, after the 1978 coup.

Hazrat was elated. It wasn't just that Prince Ali would finish each chat by pulling out his bundle of crisp American bills, peeling them off one by one for his audience. And it wasn't just that Hazrat could toss in a French word or two: after all, he and the prince had both been schoolboys at Kabul's French academy, the Lycée Esteqlal. It was that the prince's return was a tonic. Of course the former king's homecoming had gladdened his heart. But time travel with Prince Ali was a completely different ticket. The king's distant cousin was part of the hotel's storied past. The *enfant terrible* of the royal family – Prince Ali's words – had been a regular fixture on the tennis courts in his white kit, and by night had danced the hours away in the Pamir Supper Club. He even had his wedding reception there when he married his American sweetheart, Maribeth.

Now Prince Ali was living in two rooms with pitted walls and splintered windows criss-crossed by strips of tape. There was no hot water; some days no water at all. The lifts were broken. But the way Prince Ali gushed, you'd think he was staying in a palace. He enthused about his spacious rooms with Afghan rugs rolled across the floor, and the spectacular view of the city he had longed to see for so long. His Kabul was gone, but it was still home.

Hazrat was one of the only staff on his floor old enough to recognise the hotel that was inside Prince Ali's head. He remembered everything. The boxy meeting room in the lobby had once been the legendary Nuristan Cocktail Lounge where Afghan wine and brandy flowed. The cold shell of a suite on the fifth floor had been the Pamir Supper Club, graced by waiters in smart dinner jackets serving *escargots* and the finest steaks. The lobby had sparkled with its parade of glass-fronted shops.

Now most of the glass was plastered with cardboard or covered by dust. Only one of the old stores was still there: a shop selling jewellery studded with Afghan gems, antique holy Qurans and old and new carpets. The bookshop, manned by the eager bookseller or one of his young sons, was almost always open; Snickers and Bounty bars smuggled from Pakistan were as popular as the books – all obtainable for a price.

Just outside the shop, at the front entrance, the doorman kept tearfully reaching into his pocket for a creased photograph: a snapshot of a clean-shaven Inter-Continental doorman standing in the exact same spot, in his crimson blazer with black piping and shiny buttons. It was snapped only months before the coup in 1973.

The return of familiar faces fuelled Hazrat's hope. He felt that lightness of a new start on his floor, and on the ground floor – even if five-star hospitality still seemed like a different galaxy. The Bamiyan Brasserie was brimming with guests again. Night after night, Afghans returning from around the world sat down to eat the same meals. There wasn't a menu to peruse any more. No point even asking, although sometimes they did, in jest: 'What's for dinner tonight?' The waiting staff were in on the joke. But it was always grilled chicken and rice, hamburgers and fries, or spinach and meat stew. 'The worst food in Kabul, but the nicest waiters' was how some put it. One night Prince Ali went into the kitchen himself to prepare a *qorma chalow* meat stew worthy of its name, though even he struggled to cook in the blackened pots perched on burners held up by bricks.

The prince's next project was the missing music. The entertainment system had been ripped out years earlier, but its wiring was more or less intact. He whipped around the bazaar, stopping at music shops that were now doing brisk business, and returned to the hotel with a CD player and a stack of Afghan classics. With the boombox connected, the dials were pushed to top volume. The velvety voice of Ahmad Zahir, Afghanistan's star of stars, suddenly caressed the hotel. Startled staff and curious guests streamed into the lobby-cum-pop-up-music-hall. Even the security guards rushed in. And they danced. 'This is how the Inter-Continental Kabul used to sound,' the Afghan general manager exclaimed.

With every day the hotel was sounding more like it did before. From the third-floor balconies Hazrat could hear the thwack-thwack again: the tennis court was back in action. Even Daoud, the former national tennis champion, was where he belonged. Forced by the fighting to put down his racket and take up needle and thread as the hotel tailor, Daoud had returned to his true calling. His racket strings were frayed, the green net tangled and torn. But his Taliban-era bushy beard and baggy trousers were history; he had re-emerged with his hair and moustache dyed a more youthful black. Ageing, yes, but still master of the forehand, the lob and the serve. He was giving tennis lessons again, or whacking balls back and forth in fast-paced matches with hotel guests. He always won.

Hazrat smiled from the balcony. The splash was back in the pool, too. Its paint was peeling, its water a greenish hue and it was still male-only. And drinks were certainly not served. But the knee-length shorts of Taliban swim-style were no longer obligatory. Western-style trunks were back in vogue, along with an eye-catching assortment of improvised costumes that elicited a bemused look from Sultan, the white-bearded attendant. Hazrat could still conjure up the plush towels he'd prized when he first arrived here, fresh out of hotel school, not much older than the biggest boys now splashing around wildly – the ones who could afford the $3 entrance fee. Some of those original towels were still stacked in the cabanas, their Inter-Continental insignia now faded, their thinning fabric trailing loose threads.

It wasn't just in the Inter-Con where old times were inching back. In Shahr-e Nau in the city centre the New Marco Polo was serving up its famous hamburgers. Its owner Sultan Malikyar, another derring-do entrepreneur of the 1970s, was also back in town. Prince Ali's Golden Lotus had reopened its doors although someone else now owned it. Even the iconic Khyber restaurant, where Hazrat also worked for a while, was serving up a popular buffet on the bustling square abutting the presidential palace, which kept building new rings of security.

By the summer of 2003 affluent corners of Kabul were transforming into a mini-mecca of world cuisine – German, Italian, French, Iranian, Indian, Thai, even a Croatian restaurant alongside the multiplying kebab kiosks, juice stands and pizza parlours. New places kept popping up. The Elbow Room, a den pulsing with light and sound, was the 2000s' answer to the Twenty-Five Hour Club: the brainchild of young Brits, not young Afghans. It was discreetly hidden from public view down a long alley next to the Chinese embassy, not far from the Foreign Ministry, with a security guard at its door, and the word in certain sets was that it served the best cocktails and club steaks in Kabul, at a steep price. Even here the curfew sent everyone speeding home before 10 p.m.

A capital that had been yanked back into medieval times was now pushing into the future at breakneck speed. Internet cafés, English-language schools and computer centres were springing up across the city, as well as in provincial capitals, as Afghans seized the new opportunities opening up. Even tourists were trickling back in, mostly adventurous travellers raring to explore. The quarter known as Chicken Street, once a magnet for hippies and travellers living on the cheap, was still trading in everything from old coins to new carpets, with a few sellers still killing chickens at the very end. But now its regular customers included foreign soldiers with the security mission and the aid workers turning streets white in their parade of luxury 4x4s. Some of the Afghan drivers at the wheel were earning ten times more than government ministers. Even street urchins were moving through the traffic peddling copies of a new handbook for a new city: *The Survival Guide to Kabul*, a guidebook for moneyed foreigners and Afghans, the first book of its kind since the 1970s. At the most popular hangouts, beggars huddled by the door or pressed their faces against the glass.

The president wasn't happy. Hamid Karzai – whom the *Jirga* had overwhelmingly chosen as head of state, over two challengers – was proving more conservative than his urbane air suggested and made it known that he didn't like all the carousing. Especially when he received reports that his own young Afghan staff, many having grown up in Western capitals, were also moving in the fast lane. Alcohol was still officially banned, although discreet drinking by non-Muslims was tolerated. Embassies and aid agencies urged staff to be respectful of local customs.

At the Inter-Con the staff were all too aware they had competition. New hotels were bursting onto the scene. Places like the Mustafa Hotel, popular with some journalists due to its American feel – a New York Yankees logo and a basketball court at the back, darts and pool tables, pizzas and beer, all curated by its charismatic Afghan manager, who was born in Germany and raised in New Jersey. And the Gandamack Lodge, named for Britain's defeat in the First Anglo-Afghan War, which was run by the former BBC cameraman Peter Jouvenal in the villa that used to belong to Osama Bin Laden's fourth wife. At the top of the scale, the Kabul Hotel was rising from its ruins as a five-star Serena, its renovations continuing apace. There was even talk that, for the first time since the 1960s, another international hotel chain, the Hyatt, would go up, right across from the American embassy.

But guests still kept coming to the Inter-Continental, and still kept complaining. Hazrat kept watch from the hard-backed chair just outside his housekeeping cubbyhole on the third floor. Some days it was the water: 'Please bring me water for a shower!' guests would shout desperately from their rooms. On other days it was the electricity, power cuts rendering the rooms insufferably hot in summer, freezing cold in winter; some guests told him they were sleeping in their boots and socks. Everyone at housekeeping did what they could. It was never good enough. 'The worst hotel in the world' is what some people called it. Especially the journalists.

Maybe they were only joking. Still, it hurt to hear it. Hazrat told anyone who had the time and interest to listen that the Inter-Continental Kabul used to be one of the best hotels anywhere on Earth. Maybe it would be again. There were whispers that the Inter-Continental chain might return; there had been a flutter when the polished Swiss hotelier Pierre Martinet, one of the hotel's first general managers, had come through the door one day on 'just a personal visit' and had gushed how his Afghan staff of old had been 'so easy to train'. But his homecoming was bittersweet. 'It's such a disappointment,' he later confided to friends, 'but I was expecting as least as bad, or worse.' He concluded that renewing the relationship with the Inter-Con was not on the agenda – it was far too big an investment to repair all its broken bones, he regretted. The hotel would have to make do with its new managers and the company funded by a wealthy Arab investor, who was, it was said, the only bidder. There were whispers that a certain warlord had profited handsomely from the deal.

Hazrat resolved to do his part to make his hotel great again. But some of the most loyal of staff were slipping away. The former Afghan general manager Sher Babarkhel, who had starred in the hotel's very first brochures, had moved on to work in the presidential palace. Even Engineer Amanullah had decided it was time to move on, leaving to study for his doctorate in engineering and to help educate the next generation of engineers; he was teaching at the Polytechnic and had helped to launch a private university, where he was now delivering classes. At least Amanullah wouldn't go far. He was still living on the grounds of the Polytechnic below this hotel, his second home.

CHAPTER 17

Abida's Elections

Autumn 2005

Abida liked his biscuits best; the ones shaped like birds, rabbits and ducks. Naser Ali, the head pastry chef, cut his cookies with surgical precision, sliding them on outsized trays into the mouth of the waiting oven. When they emerged, piping hot, the aroma was so sweet it could make you swoon. They called him *Kolcha Paz*, the 'Cook of Cookies'.

Abida watched every step of the master baker in his jaunty white toque and chef's coat, a double row of petite black buttons resting on his rounded belly. Naser Ali bounced with a little limp and a smile as warm as his fresh biscuits. He caringly sliced thick biscuits in two, slathered them with sticky jam, smooched them into sweet sandwiches, sprinkled with snowy sugar. He didn't mind a bit when Abida peeked over his shoulder. After a while she even pitched in to help. That's how Naser Ali had learned when he first entered the Inter-Continental Kabul kitchen as an illiterate labourer who couldn't read a single word in any cookbook, working under a genial German chef who patiently showed him how to bake the best of pastries.

Naser Ali loved it when his sweets were loved. Even Hamid

Karzai was asking for his cake. Or at least the president's staff were, calling the hotel to order Karzai's favourite, a simple traditional vanilla loaf. Slices sat on the palace's fine porcelain plates, served with quality tea and sometimes coffee in dainty ceramic cups. Offering sweets to guests was a sacred part of Afghan hospitality, even if it was simply toffees in bright foil. Vanilla loaf had been served down the centuries to everyone from peasants to royalty. Now it was on the table of Afghanistan's first president to be directly elected by the people. There were so many who wanted to take tea with him. Naser Ali and Abida would, if they could. They had voted for him in October 2004. All their older children did, too. Like many other Afghans, Abida slipped her ballot into the box with tears in her eyes. It seemed to be yet more proof that a brighter future lay ahead.

Today the treats weren't being sent down to the palace. They were to be eaten right here in the Inter-Con. Almost all 351 members elected to the National Assembly – the first in more than thirty years – had descended on the hotel. They were here for Orientation Week: a week in which to learn how to be lawmakers. Turning a land governed by guns into a land governed by the people's representatives wouldn't come easily. It took great effort. The newbie MPs were beginning their days in the Kandahar Ballroom, now converted into a classroom, before ploughing through the lunch buffet in the Bamiyan Brasserie, congregating in the coffee shop to talk politics, followed by another epic buffet in the Bamiyan and then *gupshup* into the early hours. The next day they started all over again, most of them rising in the twilight for morning prayers.

Staff beamed to hear their visitors exclaim, 'What a nice hotel!' Some, from more privileged families, recounted childhood memories of travelling up the big hill to gorge on cake, paddle in the pool, ride in the lifts. But the hotel wasn't merely the domain of the upper classes any more. All of Afghanistan's chequered history had gathered within its walls this week: royals, communists and warlords; men and women; even a fistful of former Taliban. In the heaving lobby the legendary Taliban fighter known as Mullah Rocketi – famed for annihilating his enemies with rocket-propelled grenades – stood making small-talk and big promises to fellow politicians. Standing right next to him was the smiley-faced MP and journalist Shukria Barakzai, often dressed in the bright colours of the Afghan flag, including headscarves with a habit of slipping onto her shoulders. Ms Barakzai's laughter rippled through the room like gurgling water. The bearded commander, as big as a bear, was overheard telling journalists that Ms Barakzai was 'my new friend'. She didn't object. 'If people want to change their ideas, we should give them a chance,' she told a sceptical journalist. 'But they must remember the past is the past.'

But the past was not past. Staff hovering around the ballroom door held their breath when Ms Barakzai stood her ground, insisting that the front-row seats should be reserved for women. Sixty-eight women were part of this new parliament, many chosen through a quota system to ensure that their voices were heard. But another female MP felt obliged to offer her place to a well-known political leader of advancing age. And before you knew it, all the usual suspects had plonked themselves down at the front. About two-thirds of this new assembly had been men of guns, or linked to them. One of them even sent a message to Ms Barakzai scribbled on a piece of paper telling her that she should wear suitable Afghan clothing rather than Western-style trouser suits, not to mention a bigger scarf. One that would stay on her head.

Waiters nudged each other knowingly as they watched people they had served in this very hall during the civil war wearing different clothes, using different words. Men who had once called the shots were sitting like students, listening to Afghan and foreign experts in political science, constitutional law, parliamentary procedures and more. The subjects were brain-bending: the complexities of the constitution forged two years before, which was now meant to govern their lives; the rules and regulations of making new laws; the budgets, committees and parliamentary groups. And they were all lectured on what was called a 'code of conduct'. Law-makers didn't just make laws, they heard. They also shouldn't break them.

In tea breaks, waiters juggled urns of hot liquids and plates of biscuits and vanilla loaf as they steered a path through the packed ballroom. Warlord-turned-defence-minister General Mohammad Fahim was heard protesting that '"warlord" was an insulting word and was being used against the *mujahideen* who were the heroes of the resistance. No one was being allowed to forget that – certainly not in this city, and not in this hotel. The face of the legendary commander Ahmad Shah Massoud, staring into the distance, dominated the exterior façade of the ballroom. Smaller portraits of the slain fighter were stuck to the walls inside.

But Afghans were also looking to the future. The Inter-Continental was serving up the first taste of a new time. MPs dared to believe in this budding democracy. One woman, her black headscarf safely kept in place by a second black shawl on top, hailed the new dawn to Afghan journalists: 'Representatives from all parties and groups are now under one roof to rebuild and serve their country . . . the future of our parliament is bright.'

The hotel felt brighter, too. Abida looked for reasons to walk through the lobby and sneak peeks into the ballroom, the restaurant, the coffee shop. More glass-fronted shops, gleaming with curiosities, had opened – even an office emblazoned with the bold blue-and-white branding of Ariana Afghan Airlines. Floor by floor, starting at the top, guest rooms were slowly being fixed and furnished. The loveliest refurbished space, the fifth-floor Khyber Suite, was being rented for nearly $500 a night. Below, a steady trickle of guests skipped down the stairs to the fragrant beauty salon and spa, where young women from Thailand were offering massages; or to the fitness centre, newly kitted out with mighty exercise machines.

There was some grumbling among managers and official visitors about the quality of the ongoing refurbishment, the materials that were being imported, even complaints it wasn't really of a five-star standard. But for staff like Abida the rooms were beautiful to behold. Pale wooden surfaces. Shiny new TVs. A dreamscape.

Abida felt at ease. The Inter-Continental was like an international city within the city, filled with Afghan and foreign managers, Afghan and foreign guests. And now this gaggle of politicians. In their ballroom classroom, male and female MPs, some with their children, shared tables as they tackled big topics. When they sat down for meals, old enemies congregated together, even if men and women still mostly ate separately. Tradition was still stickier than old political scores. It was much the same in the staff cafeteria. Abida usually sat down with the women working in other departments. In truth, they liked it that way. They had their own kind of talk.

A new kind of chatter was everywhere. Prominent politicians brought their staff: bored bodyguards lounging in the lobby, drivers idling in the parking lot, now chock-a-block with the latest model luxury SUVs. With them came the stories. If they knew you, they would share them in whispers. 'There's business going on,' they confided. 'Deals being done.' Deals involving the dark arts. The most affluent and ambitious had snapped up the hotel's priciest suites, bases from which to vie for votes for the parliament's top jobs. You could see the suitors queuing outside their doors or squeezed together on sofas, waiting their turn. Staff couldn't close their ears to bits of back-and-forth. 'Vote for me and I can arrange a new car . . . which model do you like?' One Western diplomat involved in the education of the newly elected was seen going door-to-door on every floor, urging MPs to act on their conscience. Hotel staff tried to mind their own business. But, in this new time, some MPs were forgetting the old proverb: 'Walls have mice, and the mice have ears.'

It wasn't only the parliamentarians bending the rules. There was the mysterious shootout in a guest room, where a British guest took out his pistol and shot dead two Afghans. There were the rowdy parties of foreigners and Afghans in the penthouse suite, where music blasted and alcohol flowed. And there was the revolving door for the hotel's foreign managers. The German general manager was said to have fallen out with the Dubai company over the renovations; he left after a few months in the job. His Indian successor stayed only just as long, after quarrelling over his salary. The South African front-office manager also made a swift exit. But the hotel still had a kind and knowledgeable British-Iranian lady called Leila in the general manager's chair, and Albert from South Africa was still looking after the food and beverages.

Then, one winter's day in late 2003, the wall of lobby windows had shattered, raining glass across the floor and knocking diners off their chairs. The hotel shook. The lights went out. Afghan and foreign soldiers rushed to the scene, encircling the grounds. A rocket had slammed into the garden, creating a little crater.

It was quickly covered over. New panes of glass were installed. No one admitted they did it, but everyone suspected the Taliban; their attacks were on the rise in the provinces, far from Kabul.

Through it all, Abida kept cooking. The kitchen was a world of its own, filled with smoking pots, scraping knives and dripping sweat. She kept preparing her specialities – *ashak* and *mantu* dumplings – but was always adding new dishes to her repertoire, from her aubergine-and-tomato *borani banjan* with its swirls of creamy, garlicky yogurt to her sweet-and-sour rice dish, *zereshk pulao*. She kept making her mark, too. When the hotel decided to bake its own bread, rather than keep bringing it in, with the risk that someone might tamper with it, she put her sandalled foot down. They shouldn't try to wedge the baker's oven into her space. Bread needed its own kitchen, so that its heady scent and smoke didn't overwhelm the main one. She won that battle too.

At the end of every shift, when the din subsided, the staff fed themselves. New managers always meant new rules: these days the restaurant food was just for guests. Separate food was brought in for them, to be eaten downstairs in their cafeteria. But no one noticed a quick bite here and there, a little treat slipped into a pocket. This was Afghanistan now. You got the sweet as well as the sour: *zereshk pulao*.

The Taliban had banned *Nowruz* as pagan worship. But on the first day of spring 2008, the first day of the Afghan new year, Kabul's skies were dotted with dancing kites as Afghans celebrated the festival that the Taliban hadn't been able to destroy.

People thought about the Taliban a lot, these days. Their attacks were creeping back, despite the more than 50,000 international troops now on the ground across the country. Still, the spirit of *Nowruz* could not be stolen. Families clutching bouquets of flowers and bags of sweets thronged to cemeteries and shrines to offer prayers to precious saints and lost loved ones. Blankets were flung across the endless carpets of grass in the magnificent Bagh-e Babur gardens and other emerald spaces, including the ever-popular Bagh-e Bala next to the hotel. Picnics were the people's banquet.

For Afghans who could afford an Inter-Con life, a feast awaited. Women's high heels click-clacked across the marble floor, children in new clothes skipped to the muzak and a choir of competing telephone ringtones. For days Abida and her fellow cooks had joined hands to prepare the traditional compote *Haft Seen*, 'Seven Fruits': plump apricots, sweet yellow raisins and large black seeded ones, crunchy walnuts, pistachios and almonds, as well as *sinjed*, the round red fruit of the oleaster tree, were all left to soak and sweeten in bowls of cold water. It was part of a spread meant to symbolise new hope and prosperity. The buffet tables groaned. But as the day drew on, the kitchen crew seemed more and more distracted. A crescendo of clapping and joyous screams were seeping from the ballroom, drifting down the hall. Abida wiggled her toes. *Afghan Star!*

The hotel was hosting the grand finale of the TV show that everyone was talking about. Eleven million Afghans, one-third of the population, had been tuning in to TOLO TV every week to watch, and to vote for their favourite singers via text message. It was more exciting than the parliamentary elections, and the campaigning was just as lively. Posters of contestants, catapulted into overnight fame, were plastered across vehicles and shop fronts. Their backers, including wealthy merchants seeking to cash in, were taking to the streets with megaphones: 'Your vote can decide their fate . . . your vote will take them to the mountain of success.' The queues to watch the pre-taped finale at the Inter-Con stretched up the hill, across the forecourt and through the ballroom doors.

When her shift ended Abida made haste, slowing her steps slightly when she spotted some now-famous faces still lingering in the lobby. But there was no time to waste; her whole family was waiting. Everyone knew the drill. Dinner had to be done with quickly. Abida, her children and her grandchildren needed to be in place, everyone dressed in their best as if it was a night out, sitting comfortably on the carpet in front of the TV by start-time, 7.30 p.m. It was the same every week. But especially for the grand finale.

Tonight they only just made it in time for the opening credits. The music rolled. Lights flashed. The audience roared as the camera swooped over their heads. 'Who do you think will be the Afghan Star?' The host, Daoud Sediqi, resplendent in a pistachio-green shirt and tie, teased the crowd packed into the Kandahar Ballroom. They screamed in reply. So too did Abida's family in their mud-walled living room.

The real Afghan Stars in Abida's life were sitting with her. Her eldest daughter, Anissa, was working at a school in the morning, studying law and political science at university in the afternoon. Mohammad Najib was learning Arabic. Mustapha would soon enrol in dentistry. Mariam was studying journalism at one of the new private universities. And little Suleiman was now in high school. Abida's daughters Raisa and Safina had made it to university, too, although the fighting had long ago forced them to stop and now they were focused on raising their families. To all of them she had recited the same proverb: *Qatra, qatra, darya mesha*, 'Drop by drop, a river is made.' Studying was everything. 'It doesn't matter what kind of shoes you wear,' she would scold them. 'Study! If there's no electricity, study in the sunlight! Study by the moonlight!' This show had become the family's weekly respite from all their studying. Every week they argued good-naturedly over who should win. But they agreed on what mattered. How wonderful it was to have fun, to embrace this light after enduring all the dark. And to see Afghan women singing on the stage.

Abida had wanted Lima Sahar, the first woman to reach the top three, to be crowned this year's Afghan Star. Her voice wasn't the best, it had to be said, but millions of Afghans weren't simply voting for her voice; they were voting for her courage in a country where it was still controversial – even a crime, in the eyes of some – for women to sing in public. Twenty-five-year-old Lima had to learn to sing in secret in her home in conservative Kandahar, the birthplace of the Taliban. When she emerged from her house – and she only did so when it was absolutely necessary – she wore the all-enveloping blue burka to avoid intrusive stares, and worse. She had received a deluge of hate-mail for daring to appear on the show. The Afghan Council of Scholars had denounced *Afghan Star* as 'immoral and un-Islamic'. But Lima was as demure and modest as a female singer could be, in her floor-length embroidered traditional dress. When she sang, her body barely moved. Abida had shed a tear to see her voted out last week.

The performance of twenty-two-year-old Setara Hussain-zada, another female contestant, had been far more explosive. When she was voted out earlier in the series, she had twirled across the stage in her farewell dance. The audience had gasped when her headscarf slipped, revealing her hair. Setara just kept dancing. She became the talk of the town. And there was a wave of death-threats. She even had to flee her home city, Herat in the west, regarded as the country's cultural heart, and go into hiding.

Abida watched, rapt, as the two finalists in season four – two young men in snazzy white suits – stood next to the host. 'First Hameed Sakhizada will sing for you,' announced Daoud. Hameed, who was trained as a classical musician, took to the octagonal stage, pulsing with red-and-yellow light. With his jet-black hair curled around the edge of his collar, he crooned:

'If you are from Bamiyan or Kandahar, we are one brother,
If you are from Kabul, Balkh or Takhar, we are one brother . . .
We are all one brother.'

His ode to national unity was particularly poignant because of his background: Hameed came from the minority Hazara community, which had long suffered discrimination. He ended his bid for the top prize with a shy smile and a half-bow in his pinstripe white. The host asked the audience for another round of applause; the hall thundered.

Next came Rafi Naabzada, a nineteen-year-old ethnic Tajik from the northern city of Mazar-i-Sharif, already very much the pop star with his smooth good looks. In brilliant white attire matched with a soft pink shirt, Rafi lifted his microphone and leaned in to a traditional Persian love song:

'May the length of my existence be as short as her faithfulness . . .
My glass of wine is now empty.
It will break by the weight of this life.'

Green glowsticks dotting the crowd swung softly to his rhythm. Rafi's song stirred a sadness in Abida. She thought of her Qasim. Theirs had not been that kind of aching love. But she had loved him, as her husband, the father of their children; she still did. She gazed at her children sitting all around her, shrieking with laughter as they punched their votes into their mobile phones, unsuccessfully trying to hide their choices from one another. She had learned to fill Qasim's absence with their presence.

'Should we announce the result?' shouted Daoud. His question jolted Abida from her musings. 'Who is the Afghan Star?' he baited the crowd, as rival fans began calling out their favourite when a judge emerged on the stage, holding a piece of paper in his hand.

Abida's family, like millions across Afghanistan, locked eyes on the TV's split screen. Music heightened the suspense. Hameed looked down nervously, his forehead glistening. Rafi stared into the middle distance. Abida gripped her cushion.

'The person people have voted for – the person who's won the title – is . . . Rafi *jaan*!'

Whoops and wails erupted in front of TV sets across the country. The Inter-Con audience rose to its feet. Rafi's supporters waved photos of their star. Even Hameed's backers tried to mask their disappointment, knowing that the nation was watching. 'Long live *Afghan Star*. Long live Afghanistan!' The rivals embraced. Afghan flags rippled across the hall.

Rafi Naabzada had earned the title, along with an eye-watering $5,000, ten times the average annual Afghan salary. Hameed Sakhizada was gracious in defeat. 'I do not feel I am defeated today,' he reflected. 'I think I am a lucky man.' So many Afghans felt a bit lucky, too, as a new year began in a land where, all too often, luck ran out.

After the music died down and the lights went out, Abida lay on her mattress, her mind still dancing. She loved the thrill of elections. She could still remember the excitement of casting her ballot in the presidential and parliamentary elections. If only those votes were as seamless as *Afghan Star*. In the new Afghanistan, stories were already multiplying about bribery, even ballot-box stuffing. The popularity of President Karzai, who would

look for their votes again next year, was slipping amidst accusations of government corruption and an escalating insurgency.
Karzai pointed the finger of blame at his allies, especially the
Americans, who were spending millions in aid, and sending
more and more troops into the countryside.

Abida knew she would vote for Karzai again. He had changed
her life; she would never forget that. But even the Inter-Con
had new leaders again. The Dubai company Freecom Trading
had pulled out of its fifteen-year lease; there had been disappointment on all sides. The contract had then been given to a
company owned by Afghans with foreign passports. But a messy
back and forth followed, laced with accusations of wrongdoing.
Even Leila, the British-Iranian general manager, finally left in
protest. The Afghan government decided it would run the Inter-
Con itself.

Sometimes late at night, staring into the dark, Abida allowed
herself to dream of how, if she could read and write, she would
write a book about her life.

CHAPTER 18

Mohammad's Mourning

Spring 2012

Mohammad Aqa stared at the ceiling, his head in the clouds. The restaurant ceiling was now painted in a dreamy blue dappled with white. And it was curved, with spotlights on its beams, like a spaceship. The old vista was gone. The restaurant balcony had been demolished and, with it, his bird's-eye view of Kabul: the space where he had embraced the brisk winds of winter and the warm breath of spring, and had seen guests gather to sit above the city. It had been shaved off to make room for more tables in the dining room.

The Inter-Con had been renovated. The restaurant wasn't even called the Bamiyan Brasserie any more. It was the Bukhara now, harking back to the eighth-century centre of Islamic culture, now part of neighbouring Uzbekistan. A separate room next to it kept the Bamiyan name, blushed in shades of pink. Every area was drawn from the same soft palette.

It felt like a different hotel. When Mohammad Aqa stepped out of the Bukhara, it was as if the spaceship had dropped him in Dubai – the megalopolis a short flight away and a whole world apart. Decorative capitals glinted at the top of the lobby pillars. Stuffed sofas shimmered with scrolled armrests. The reception had been shifted to the opposite side, the same side as the restaurant, the front desk now washed in gold and taupe and set against a geometric backdrop in matching hues. It took pride of place where the legendary Nuristan Cocktail Lounge, and the cosy Le Cavalier restaurant, had once stood. They were gone too.

The project had taken two years, and was said to have cost the government many millions of dollars. A Dubai-based design team had come up with the new layout, with sign-off from the Finance Ministry. There had been other ideas. The general manager, an Afghan-Australian businessman, Mr Sarwary, had suggested that the Inter-Con should be shut, for a year or perhaps even two, for a proper refurbishment. He had recommended more research into international standards of hospitality for a hotel that had to cater to Afghans from across this country, as well as foreigners. But a Dubai refit had won the day. The new hotel had been ceremonially opened this year by the white-bearded, black-cloaked political leader Sibghatullah Mojaddedi, who had briefly captured the world's attention when he served as president for a few months in the spring of 1992. As the eighty-seven-year-old cut the bright-blue ribbon and ambled across the threshold, aided by his cane, he led the assembled bigwigs into the Inter-Continental Kabul's new era. It was only the second grand opening in the hotel's history; the first since the king's prime minister had cut the last ribbon in 1969.

In all the gold, there was some mud and dust. The first decoration flanking the front door was a mural portraying a camel caravan plodding through the eleventh-century arch of Qala-e-Bost fortress in southern Helmand province. Tucked behind the front desk was an image of the baked-brick Minaret of Jam etched with intricate artwork, recognised as a World Heritage Site. Hangings honouring Afghanistan's storied past hung here and there. Yet it was, above all, a hotel that had been pulled into modernity. Water flowed through new pipes. Up-to-date wiring powered everything from light switches to the multiplying banks of security cameras. The internet was finally available in guest rooms. The poolside space was expanded to entertain more than a thousand guests – more than three times as many as before. And in front of the hotel entrance, water splashed from a new fountain twinkling with pink-and-white fairy lights. Only the hotel's façade remained unchanged. That and its aura of wealth. But now it was the Dubai dream: that anyone could get rich quick, especially with the right connections and the right access to the eye-watering sums now washing through Kabul.

Some staff liked the new bling, as did many guests. Abida took a shine to the glitter, as well as to her much better kitchen. But Hazrat strode back and forth across the new floor, har-rumphing each time, upset that a lesser stone had replaced the original black-and-white marble quarried nearby. To his dis-cerning eye, most of the new material seemed to be of inferior quality. Even government officials who later sailed through the door for meetings were aghast. 'An insult to the Inter-Continental,' one minister was heard to mutter.

For his part, Mohammad Aqa had managed to convince his bosses not to remove the poolside cabanas – the one with its peak shaped like the nib of a pen, the other like an open book – insisting they were an iconic part of this Inter-Continental. And he also held on to the worn waiter's station from the king's time. During quiet pauses in the day he stared at the dreamy blue ceiling, into the make-believe clouds. The new paint could not gloss over all that had happened here, and especially the events of the last year, when the hotel was in the midst of its makeover. The black still seeped through.

He couldn't forget the hands. The big, strong hands with a warm, snug grip; he had clasped them so many times. They were the hands of Tony, the tall, gentle pilot from Spain who had told Mohammad Aqa that he, too, had been a waiter to help pay for his pilot's lessons. The last time Mohammad Aqa held Tony's hands they were cold and hard, like wood, just hours after he was killed by a suicide bomber.

Mohammad Aqa could have been in the hotel that night, too: 28 June 2011. His manager had recently moved him to the day-shift, but his young nephew, who worked at the reception desk, had been present. By God's grace, he was still alive. The youngster had just pulled into the parking lot when he saw the attackers barrelling up the steep rocky slope. He sat, frozen in his seat, then slid from his car and crawled along the ground to hide in the trees until morning. He called his uncle. And his Uncle Mohammad Aqa had kept calling him, hour after hour, to hear his voice: 'Kaka, "Uncle", I am still here. I am still alive.'

There had been nine suicide bombers in all. Not that anyone knew that at the time. There weren't even any images to watch on Afghan television. The year before, the Afghan intelligence agency had banned any live reporting of attacks when they were in progress, saying that it only served their enemies. So Mohammad Aqa had hurried to the hotel at first light. Thick grey smoke still poured from the roof. Knotted bedsheets dangled from balconies on upper floors, the escape routes of panicked guests who had jumped to safety. Security forces swarmed around and inside the hotel. It was one of the cooks who had identified Tony for the Kabul police. His body was brought to the lobby and laid out on a sofa. *The body of a person with black hair* was how the police first described Tony. Then his corpse was labelled *Antonio Planas, from Spain.*

Tony, who had seven brothers and sisters. A big family, like an Afghan. Tony who was always smiling, even though he was only in Kabul to wait for his last salary, because he hadn't been paid for months. He had been flying the Frankfurt–Istanbul–Kabul route for Ariana Afghan Airlines. Tony kept saying that he loved to fly. And he loved Afghanistan. The day his life ended was the day his new life was about to begin. The morning when he lay cold and hard on the sofa was the morning he was supposed to fly home to join his wife, dear Manuela, and their nine-year-old daughter, to celebrate the new life they would start in Dubai the week after. The moment he was meant to land was the moment they were told he was dead.

Tony's bags had been packed; he had been ready to go. He had been in the lobby with his suitcases, checking out, when the attackers stormed in, in a blaze of bullets and bombs. He had been taken somewhere safe. The Kabul police chief later said Tony had tried to return to his room when the assault, which raged for five hours, seemed to be over. But the last of the bombers was hiding. When Afghan special forces went from room to room at dawn, the attacker ignited his vest, killing two policemen and Tony. The head of the last bomber was found in the hallway.

Hotel staff were numb. The security guard, Kaka Sher, had been shot dead on his mat as he bowed in prayer at the first security gate. The kind cook from Pakistan was killed in the kitchen when the bombers burst in. The quiet old man who arranged flowers was cut down outside the ballroom as a wedding party jolted to a halt. Shir Hussein of housekeeping was lucky. He had come down to the lobby in the lift, not knowing what was happening. When the door swished open, he saw the guns, the vests bulging with explosives, and thwacked the lift button to speed back up. Hafiz, the old night-guard around the swimming pool, also lived to tell his story. He had told Mohammad Aqa everything, or at least what he remembered. Mohammad Aqa held fast to every detail.

It had started around ten o'clock at night. The poolside restaurant was heaving with hundreds of diners: Afghan businessmen with their bodyguards, and government officials with their aides, there for a conference about the future security arrangements for Afghanistan. The music flowing from the loudspeakers had been soft and sweet. It was that time of night when guests had filled their plates, most of them more than once, and were heading back to the buffet, to the very end of the table, where the chef in his towering white toque was scooping creamy *sheer yakh*, Afghan ice cream, with its tastes of cardamom, pistachios and rose water.

Suddenly gunfire rang out. A man with an AK-47 rifle, and another, dressed in white with a PK machine gun. The armed guard next to the ice-cream maker collapsed. Women and children screamed. Guests leapt in horror. Chairs tipped over. Tables turned. Bowls and plates of half-eaten food crashed to the ground. Hafiz saw them pump bullets into the bodyguard of a well-known businessman. 'Don't kill me, I have children!' he had cried. They didn't spare him. His blood ran rivers under the table. His mobile phone kept ringing. The attackers shot a hail of bullets in the air. 'Why are you staying here, you stupid people?' one shouted. Guests tumbled over each other to escape, some sprinting to a small exit door nearby, others scrambling over the low boundary wall, sinking into the ditch; still more scurrying down the hill.

Hafiz crouched, trembling, behind the refrigerator close to the ice-cream stand. The attackers found him. 'Don't kill me,' he pleaded. 'I am only a poor man with a family.' They forced him to go with them around the pool, up the stairs, into the hotel; he had no choice. In the lobby there was a shootout between attackers and hotel guards. 'O son of Obama, I will not leave you alive, I will kill you,' one bomber shouted, before a hotel guard shot him dead. But the others dragged Hafiz with them to the fourth floor. As they stood on a room balcony, loading their guns, the hotel was suddenly plunged into darkness. The Kabul police had shut off the power. Hafiz seized his lucky break, pelting along the corridor and clattering down the stairwell, willing his feet to go faster. They hurled a grenade down the stairs after him, knocking him unconscious. Hafiz was found later by the police chief. He survived.

Wherever Mohammad Aqa looked that day, he had to look away from. Blood at the door, in the lobby, on the floor, on the walls. Fragments of human flesh. Body parts – hands, legs, feet – strewn around. And the stories of other survivors, recounted breathlessly. Almost all the guests had scattered into the night, making their own escape or being escorted to safety by Afghan security forces. Governors from distant Afghan provinces and their aides. A Lady from London. A young Afghan-American graduate student. An elderly Afghan judge. Wedding guests had clambered down the hill, as fast as they could in their finery. Some had jumped from the windows. Guests in the restaurant had fled to their rooms, cowering in wardrobes and cupboards, hearing gunfire ricocheting in the corridors, attackers knocking on doors, the firefights with Afghan special forces.

Once the attack ended, Afghan media started broadcasting footage of the horror. Mohammad Aqa had watched, transfixed, the images of bright-orange flames licking the black sky. They tore through the top floor. Scenes of police vans and ambulances encircling the area, and a US drone buzzing overhead. Eventually helicopter gunships, piloted by New Zealand special forces of the ISAF mission, had swooped in to finish off the fighters on the roof. The night had finally gone quiet at about 3 a.m. Until, hours later, the last blow: the lone attacker who blew himself up, taking Tony with him.

For the next few days journalists swarmed around the security barriers that blocked entry to the hotel. They quoted the Taliban spokesman, Zabihullah Mujahid, who said it was their men who 'took advantage of the meeting of 300 Afghan and foreign officers' at the hotel. His statement boasted of 'dozens of casualties'. In the end, the attack took the lives of ten civilians, two police and nine bombers, and wounded many more. There was such a global spotlight that the Inter-Continental chain issued a press release saying that the Inter-Continental Kabul was not actually an Inter-Continental hotel. 'In light of this fact, we respectfully request that future reports, where possible, make this clear.' But they expressed concern for a place that had once belonged to their exclusive club. 'Our thoughts at this time are with all of the people affected by this tragedy.'

The hotel hummed with speculation. How did the attackers get through the rings of steel guarding what was said to be one of the most fortified buildings in Kabul? A hundred guards from the Ministry of the Interior and sixty security cameras were meant to keep this national hotel safe. Who informed the Taliban that a major security conference, with governors from across the country, was taking place? Security officials were investigating whether some attackers had worn Afghan army or police uniforms, or had disguised themselves as the labourers working to renovate the hotel.

And guests and staff were asking why some police held back from entering the hotel. Some even ran away. The conference had been organised to discuss the transfer of security to Afghan forces. US president Barack Obama had even been saying that his forces had inflicted so much damage on the Taliban that his troops could start coming home. They had got the man at the top of their Wanted list: the al-Qaeda leader, Osama Bin Laden, had been shot dead in a raid by US special forces on a villa in Pakistan the previous month. Some of the forty-five NATO armies with boots on the ground had already pulled their men and women out, saying they had done a decade of duty.

Afghans knew the foreign troops had to go home some day, but kept asking if the time was right, especially after this. But life had to go on. The security conference was moved to the presidential palace. The hotel got back to work. Everyone was on their knees or up on ladders to scrub walls and floors; even the general manager, who had left the poolside restaurant that night just minutes before the bombers arrived. Staff cringed as they kept finding body parts. They came upon hand-grenades tucked into chairs, ready to explode when the seats were pulled out. Hazrat's housekeeping boss was injured when he opened a door and a 'sticky bomb' exploded. Abida's kitchen counter was peppered with bullet holes. Her workmates teased her that, had she been there that night, she wouldn't have lived to cook another meal – that Afghan way of using humour to ease the horror.

Mohammad Aqa mourned the loss of the fifth-floor Khyber Suite with the biggest balcony, the best view. The rooms of a thousand stories and more – of princes, politicians, foreign leaders, military commanders, brides and grooms – had gone up in flames. Now some staff were refusing to go up to the fifth floor on their own, fearing that the djinns, the dark spirits, now dwelled there.

But the din of diggers and drills, painters and builders, had swiftly resumed. Now there was even more to repair. A people who had survived decades of war, who knew how swiftly the living could become the dead, knew that the only solution was to live. Live as if it was your last day. It could be.

CHAPTER 19

Collapse

Autumn 2016

Time crawled. It had been another long day in another long week, the rhythms of the restaurant following their predictable flow. Swells of diners had just finished vacuuming up buffet offerings and piling out the door. After a pause, another wave would arrive.

Mohammad Aqa cast his eye across the room as waiting staff set tables for the evening. He had recently been promoted to restaurant manager; it was his job to make sure everything was as perfect as possible. It sounded as if it was. The muffled thumps of tissue boxes with old Inter-Continental branding being dropped. The sharp clunks of plates being plonked on buffet counters. The pitter-patter from the trio of musicians tuning their traditional instruments as they sat cross-legged along the wall. And the hubbub from the lobby drifting into the restaurant. Down the hall they were preparing for another wedding party for the son of a *paisadar*, a very wealthy politician; his invitation list would not only celebrate a family's joy, but would also confirm their connections with the powerful and prosperous.

Mohammad Aqa absorbed all these reassuring Inter-Con

rituals. But he wasn't himself today. He stared into the middle distance, instinctively brushing a tablecloth with the back of his hand in search of any crumbs. As the buzz built, he could feel his energy slipping away. Something caught in his throat. He rested his hand on the back of a chair to steady himself. A great swallow should sort it. He glanced around the room again to see how the waiters were faring. Nothing was amiss. But his throat was blocked. It felt like a lump of rock. He clenched his jaw, tightened his grip on the chair. Yet still he felt unsteady on his feet, could feel himself swaying. He tried to say something. He couldn't.

The loud thud startled his colleagues. They bolted to his side. Mohammad Aqa, the one who always knew what to do, had crumpled in a heap. They shouted for help, one waiter sprinting into the kitchen. Mohammad Aqa was soon lifted from the floor, his work fellows moving him as quickly and carefully as they could. A hotel car idling at the entrance was commandeered to hurry him down the hill, careening around security barriers, swinging left at the bottom to a private clinic just down the road. The glass doors opened with a swish. Mohammad Aqa's colleagues hurried in, beseeching the front desk to bring help.

A doctor placed a monitor over the main artery in Mohammad Aqa's upper arm, squeezing it as he inflated the cuff with his small hand-pump. The doctor's expression registered more loudly than the numbers. The blood-pressure reading was more than 200. 'We don't have the facilities to treat him,' he said apologetically. Mohammad Aqa, drifting in and out, caught snippets of their conversation and summoned up all his energy to speak. 'My cousin works at the two-hundred-bed police hospital,' he said. 'Take me there. The deputy director, a general, is my friend.'

They raced to the hospital, where Mohammad Aqa's

general-friend rushed him into the Intensive Care Unit with a shout of 'Emergency!' A specialist doctor removed Mohammad Aqa's black hotel tie, undid his shirt buttons to help him breathe. 'How is he?' his general-friend enquired impatiently against the ominous beep-beep-beep of the monitors. The doctor cautioned him to remain quiet. His new patient was in very bad shape. Mohammad Aqa could hardly hear; he couldn't see. He was too weak to walk. Then, he lost consciousness.

For fourteen days and nights Mohammad Aqa lay on a hospital bed, his distraught family crouching by his side. His daughters Yalda, Mursal and Fatima, his son Abdullah and his wife Aziza visited daily. When he was finally discharged, his blood pressure back under control, they brought him home to care for him there. But Mohammad Aqa was restless, seized by a pang to return to work, to be himself again. He tried to put on his uniform. He couldn't do it. He still wobbled on his feet, his vision was fuzzy, his hearing weak.

So he yielded to his fate. Every morning his youngest daughter, ten-year-old Fatima, would take her father's hand to help him take the small number of steps to his brother's house next door. 'Keep going, *baba*,' she would urge him. 'You can do it.' Some days Mohammad Aqa placed one hand on the wall, the other on her little shoulder, cautiously putting one foot ahead of the other. Weeks on, he tenderly told his doting daughter, 'Don't help me. Even if I fall, let me. I must stand on my own feet again.'

The next two months were slow going. By God's grace, he slowly regained his strength. His hearing improved. One of his nephews, an ophthalmologist, reassured him that his eyesight would eventually return to normal, too. But when Mohammad Aqa looked at something like his mobile phone, close up, his eyes took time to focus. Perhaps he had seen too much, too close, for too long. War had consumed him for decades. The gunfire in the early 1990s that rattled around his home. The attacks all around the hotel, including the times when he had been sent running from a hail of rockets. And the suicide bombing of 2011, which stole his friends and fellow workers and wrecked the hotel's special spaces.

But what finally broke him was what he had seen on a summer's day in July 2016. It happened in his own neighbourhood, Nowabad Deh Mazang. Decades ago this quarter had been known for its charming ateliers, which created the embroidered fur-lined leather coats: the *pustinchas* beloved of Western fashionistas. Its namesake was the potter Mazang Khan Hilal, who had settled here in the 1700s, crafting clay pots, cups and suchlike. *Deh Mazang* –'Mazang's village'. Over the years Mohammad Aqa had witnessed its pastel-yellow merchant houses reduced to blackened teeth of timber. The district had been wrecked by fighting; it raged from street to street, at one point forcing Mohammad Aqa and his family to take refuge with relatives in the north of the city. By the middle of the 2010s, half-finished rebuilding projects scarred its skyline, a sign of the city's economic malaise, its corruption. Mud-and-wood shacks hugged the hillsides as they always did, the neighbourhoods of those with nothing. Still, it felt like home. Until that day of 23 July 2016.

The two blasts in the early afternoon had shaken Mohammad Aqa's house. He sprinted from his home, behind the traffic department on the edge of the main roundabout, towards the direction of the noise, then wished he hadn't. The police had quickly cordoned off the area; he could only watch in horror. Dazed witnesses, some splattered with blood, wandered at the roundabout. Others hobbled, groaning in pain. The dying and the dead. Sandals and shoes scattered like pebbles around the junction. The ice-cream man and his metal cart washed in red.

It was the bloodiest attack in the capital since the Taliban were toppled in 2001; the first assault by the extremist Islamic State group. The attackers wielded axes, knives and other weapons. Two suicide bombers blew themselves up. The third attacker was shot dead by security forces before he detonated his vest. The Islamic State group called it a 'martyrdom attack' on the Shiite Islamic sect, the Hazara community, some of whom had been protesting at the roundabout for greater rights.

Month after month, Mohammad Aqa's mind kept taking him back to that day. He couldn't sleep. His neighbourhood had again become a byword for a savagery that spared no one. Was this his country's future? Afghanistan's commander-in-chief, President Ashraf Ghani, who had come to power in disputed elections in 2014, had declared only months earlier that the Islamic State group had been defeated in Afghanistan. American airstrikes and Afghan ground attacks had pummelled their stronghold in eastern Afghanistan, the old stomping ground of Osama Bin Laden. But at the beginning of July, US president Barack Obama had described the situation as 'precarious' and announced he was postponing the pull-out of nearly 9,000 American forces.

Mohammad Aqa's memories of the assault in Deh Mazang kept assaulting him. In his dreams and during his days he kept seeing the blood-soaked streets and ditches, the contorted corpses. Until that day came when he could fight them no more and he fell to the floor.

Abida bustled about her kitchen, oblivious to the din of crashing pans and clanging plates. She placed her perfect plump packages of *ashak* and *mantu* on flat serving platters, fried just a few more *sambosas* to a crisp golden brown, slid plates of crunchy vegetables into the humming fridge. And she couldn't stop smiling. All day long an excitement had rippled through the hotel as shafts of an amber autumn sun inched across the floor and up the wall. Aryana Sayeed was coming to the hotel tonight.

It was all anyone could talk about. Afghanistan's superstar would twirl on the terrace around the pool. And in her performance she would turn a page of history: the first live music concert to celebrate Independence Day since the Taliban were ousted. Abida hoped she might catch some clips on the last news bulletins of the night. She couldn't linger in the hotel to steal a watch through the windows. She lived with a rule: when the dark closed in, she had to be with her family as soon as she possibly could.

Abida had seen Aryana Sayeed on her TV screen last night. The pop star, just thirty-two years old, had appeared on TOLOnews in a sombre grey-checked blazer – a stark contrast to the sparkly, curve-hugging costumes that had led some people to call her the Afghan Kim Kardashian. 'People in Afghanistan are sad,' the singer had said. 'On Independence Day, I think it is good for everyone to be happy and nobody to be thinking about war.' Abida had quietly cheered from her front-row seat at home. Her life was as different from the superstar's as the day was from the night. But she appreciated Aryana: as a female singer, as a woman who spoke up for women and as an Afghan who radiated happiness and hope, even now.

The Inter-Con needed Aryana's positive vibes, too. There was all too much chatter about *garang* – the scary things – these days. Some staff talked, and others jested, about the djinns: the spirits inhabiting the dusty storage rooms stuffed with discarded furniture around the back of the hotel. The rooms were said to be built on top of graves. There was an Afghan saying: 'In places where there are graves, the places become scary at night.' Some of Abida's colleagues were making too much of a joke about it, trying to frighten new staff with tales of a haunted hotel. They would speak in hushed tones of the creepy feeling of being watched, being followed, of voices whispering into the night, a sudden chill in a warm wind. Abida rarely ventured around the back to check those rooms. But she never ever saw anything, never ever felt anything, even on nights when she had to work late. She was sure of it. Thank God for that.

At the end of her shift Abida made haste down the hill, past the dangling red orbs of the pomegranate trees. But as she reached the bottom she noticed the main lane was blocked. Hundreds of young Afghan men, along with a smaller number of women, were trying to move up the incline, chanting as they went, waggling mini Afghan flags. Another group, mainly older bearded men, was trying to stop them and shouting back. Riot police, bulked up in battle gear, batons and rifles at the ready, struggled to keep them apart.

Not everybody was an Aryana Sayeed fan. Months earlier, as a judge on the *Afghan Star* contest, she had cavorted on the stage with a male singer. Even TOLO TV, known for pushing the envelope, didn't broadcast it. But they posted it on their YouTube channel, sparking both adulation and outrage. Aryana Sayeed then lit another flame when she wore a beige skin-tight dress at a concert in Paris; her critics condemned her, saying it looked as if she was naked. 'Why do you care more about what women wear than how they are treated?' she hit back on social media. She set fire to the dress to make her point.

Now the showdown had come to the gates of the Inter-Continental. Insults were hurled back and forth. 'Don't allow this international whore to dance and sing,' bellowed one big-bearded protestor. 'It's our right to celebrate with our music,' another yelled back. The police did what they could, which wasn't much. The two groups were in gridlock. Only when the last of the day's light began to slip behind the hills, and the call to prayer wailed from the loudspeakers crowning the mosques nearby, did one group spot an opportunity. The anti-concert crowd fell to their knees to pray, and single-minded Aryana fans seized the moment to push past them. Not since the days of Ahmad Zahir in the 1970s had the Inter-Continental witnessed such high-octane fandom.

Aryana Sayeed had originally been booked to perform in the Ghazi Stadium, the city's biggest outdoor venue. She had chosen that site not only for its size, but also for its symbolism. It was once the stage for the Taliban's grisly executions. She wanted her concert to highlight that, ninety-eight years after independence, Afghan women were still not completely free. But powerful forces tried to stop her. 'Vulgar' was the verdict of conservative clerics. 'The fighting goes on, lives are being lost every day. This is no time to sing and dance!' protested Mullah Attaullah Faizani, the head of Kabul's clerical body, the Ulema Council. 'They came from the West and want to stand against our religion,' he said, in a nod to Aryana Sayeed's decision to leave Kabul to live in London for her own safety. When officials cancelled the stadium event, they insisted it wasn't because they were under pressure; they were simply worried about security. Not everyone was convinced they were telling the truth. But security certainly was an issue in Kabul, now more than ever. There were fears that a Taliban attack, at the peak of the summer fighting season, would shatter this year's independence celebrations on 19 August.

That night Abida switched on her TV precisely at ten o'clock to watch TOLOnews. The Afghan flag rippled across her screen, signalling a special programme dedicated to Independence Day. Grainy black-and-white photographs of King

Amanullah, the modernising monarch who had led Afghanistan to independence in 1919, mixed with the day's images of solemn wreath-laying, flag-waving from honking cars and roaring motorcycles, and men dancing joyously their traditional *attan* in the streets. Abida felt a feel-good glow. Even her doctor would approve. 'Don't watch the news!' he always chided her. Bad news sent her blood pressure soaring. But this was nice news.

'In the name of God, greetings to you all,' said the presenter. 'Welcome to the ten o'clock news programme. I am Fawad Aman.' Abida eyed him – baby-blue eyes and baby-blue striped tie against a blue screen behind him, pulsing with white dots. Smart young man. So calm. She slid deeper into the cushions.

Moments later, the screen cut to President Ghani. 'Today is the day to show our national unity!' he shouted croakily, his fingers stabbing the air in his signature style. The TV was highlighting the immense crowds who had packed the parade grounds in Kabul, and in the western city of Herat, as the president laid enormous wreaths of red and white flowers at monuments honouring the country's freedom. Military officers looked on in full regalia, golden epaulettes and braid draped across rounded bellies, saluting their commander-in-chief. Even the TV reporters succumbed to the spirit of the day. One extolled the virtues of all the new flag-sellers, who weren't in it just for the money, but for 'today's celebration and dreams of a future where the city and country bear the name of peace'.

Abida was mesmerised by all the pomp and ceremony. But there was one place – one person – she particularly wanted to see. After fifteen minutes her wait was rewarded. She locked her rough-skinned fingers around her teacup, smiling. The Inter-Con's poolside terrace had been utterly transformed. Towering metal girders buttressed a wall of pulsing striplights criss-crossed by flashes of stark white-and-yellow beams. Smoke canisters exploded on the edges of the stage, creating an ethereal haze. And there she was: Aryana Sayeed, her flowing cape twirling in the colours of the Afghan flag, her long, straight black hair swinging with the music. 'I want to sing a romantic song, should I sing it for you?' The crowds swayed and sang and shouted – Afghan flags fluttering in one hand, mobile phones filming in the other.

> *'Afghan boy, you are tall, you have intoxicating eyes,*
>   *and a beautiful face.*
> *Oh, I may die for your ancestor . . .*
> *You have such a great loyal heart when it comes to love.'*

The TV news cut to some vox pops. A young woman, her stylish glasses matching her dark-brown hair, a honey-yellow scarf draped across her shoulders, talked of how Aryana Sayeed 'brings smiles to the faces of Kabul residents who have endured the most challenging of times'. A man in a white T-shirt and a trendy haircut insisted that 'being happy on this day is every citizen's right'.

Abida felt happy – happy for everyone's happiness. Aryana Sayeed was otherworldly, but her traditional songs with a modern twist mirrored the aspirations of her own children: their desire to stay rooted in Afghan culture, while reaching out to a new and much wider world. Abida shimmied to the music, too, just a little.

Even the presenter, Fawad Aman, beamed for a second when the report ended. Then it was back to the news and his professional face. Donald Trump had recently been inaugurated as US president and was deliberating on the situation in Afghanistan. 'American security and intelligence officials met with President Trump at Camp David today,' the newsreader said. 'After the meeting President Trump tweeted, saying, "Important day spent at Camp David . . . Many decisions made, including on Afghanistan." ' No details were made public about whether the president would send more troops to Afghanistan, Fawad Aman informed them.

It was time to turn off the TV and turn in. Night after night there were reports of the Taliban's advances, the army's attacks; of Afghan civilians losing their lives in ever-greater numbers. Abida's mood darkened. The suicide attacks in Kabul were multiplying, too. The Serena Hotel, which used to be her Kabul Hotel, had been assaulted not once, but twice – even with its high walls, fancy security cameras and multiple guard-posts. Some of her former colleagues told her that the blood on their beautiful lobby floor ran all the way to the kitchen. Abida squeezed her eyes shut and pushed those thoughts away. She could hear her doctor's reprimand ringing in her ears: 'Turn off your TV!' Bad news was bad for her health. But now the newsreader Fawad Aman was asking her to stay put. 'Please stay tuned for a special report on the restoration of Afghanistan's independence. God bless you.'

Abida found herself lingering a bit longer, watching the footage of her country from 100 years ago. Afghanistan's past was not so different, with its tug-of-war between a reforming king along with his pioneering wife, Queen Soraya, and conservative forces. Everything had changed; nothing had changed. The programme showed images marking the many steps on Afghanistan's road to the future: the country's first newspapers, the first girls' schools, the building of factories, a railway and telephone and telegraph lines connecting its people. Then the images caught Abida's eye: black-and-white footage from the evening in 1969 when the Hotel Inter-Continental Kabul was officially opened amid a splash of lights in the forecourt. Then, the hotel had been filled with Afghan and foreign glitterati clapping with reserved excitement. Tonight it had been bathed in throbbing lights and the wild applause of young Afghans daring to dream.

Mohammad Aqa returned to work feeling like a different Mohammad Aqa. He was older, less energetic. He noticed the grey at his temples, his receding hairline. He had been in the hospital for nearly two weeks and had rested at home for a few months. But he eased back into the routines, which he could now do without even thinking. And he still kept his waiter's graceful bearing, that air of authority no one could take away.

The hotel was a balm. But it felt different, too. All his waiters felt it – that tightening grip of security. And sometimes it pulled some of the pride and dignity from their sense of self, from their profession.

When Hamid Karzai was president, security had been tight too. But in those days there had been a more relaxed air, even at the most formal dinners. On one occasion Mohammad Aqa had been assigned to work at a dinner in the Foreign Ministry attended by important American visitors. The honour was even bestowed upon him to serve the Afghan leader. Mohammad Aqa had tugged at the edges of the special gold waistcoats they wore in this setting, straightened his shoulders and kept a respectful distance, serving from the left, offering a heaping spoonful of *qabuli pulao*. 'I've eaten lunch at the US embassy and they also served a delicious *qabuli pulao*,' the president had protested with a smile. Mohammad Aqa had leaned in, just a bit closer, knowing that true Afghan hospitality had no hierarchy. 'President Karzai *Sahib*, our *qabuli pulao* is even more delicious.'

Karzai had chuckled, unable to resist an Afghan quip. 'Every shopkeeper says the goods in his shop are much better than in the others.'

Things were different now. At official dinners hosted by President Ghani you could cut the tension with one of the fine silver knives. When the leader was in the room no one could move an inch, not even the waiters, without permission from unsmiling bodyguards. *Gul-e babona*, Mohammad Aqa thought. *We are like the unwelcome weed standing in the midst of all the flowers.*

How all their lives had changed. It hurt to remember how, in 2002, he had even been able to sit down with Ashraf Ghani when he returned from America, leaving his World Bank and academic life behind, to join the interim government as a financial advisor. An easy optimistic air had permeated the Bamiyan Hall, a hub in those times. When the hullabaloo subsided after lunch, and most players, politicians, pundits and the press dashed to their next meetings, it was possible to approach almost anyone, even sit at their table. A fellow waiter even took a photo with the man who would later become their president. Mohammad Aqa still regretted he had not done the same.

At work Mohammad Aqa tried to remain focused on all his regular, well-rehearsed rituals. But the past was everywhere in the hotel, too. There were mementoes within the walls, inside the rooms. The memories of all the dear people he had lost, without ever saying goodbye. Among the last to be snatched away was Ahmad Sardar, the young journalist who had managed the hotel bookshop in the 1990s and who often stayed at the hotel. They had spent so many moments together, whiling those hours away when no one came to buy books or to eat in the Bamiyan Brasserie. Sardar was slain in 2014, along with his wife and two daughters, in the second Taliban suicide bombing at the Serena Hotel; only his young son had survived. They had been sitting in the restaurant, enjoying a *Nowruz* dinner. And their family bookshop no longer featured in the Inter-Con lobby, as business was no longer brisk enough to justify keeping it open. The family's focus shifted to their shop in the city centre.

For all his love of the hotel, even Mohammad Aqa stayed away from certain areas – the fifth-floor Khyber Suite, the bride's room at the back of the ballroom, the storerooms behind the hotel – where the djinns dwelled. He tried to make light of such stories. But there were incontrovertible truths. On so many nights there had been a banging noise in the corridors, but whenever someone went to check, there was nothing to be found. And there was the story told time and again by a waiter in room service. He swore that he saw a woman walk into their station just past midnight and say, 'If you want to leave, I'll do your job for you.' When he stood up, rubbing his eyes, she was gone – sending him fleeing, terrified, into the lobby. And there was Sayid Jan, a healthy man with no medical issues, found dead in a room. Some staff believed the djinns had killed him.

Maybe the trauma magnified all these frights. Maybe it even created them. But a djinn had even grabbed Mohammad Aqa by the throat when he slept one night in a room under the ballroom. He had leapt from his bed, flung open the door and run away. The djinns seemed to be inescapable. They were the Inter-Con's uninvited guests. And they never checked out.

But Mohammad Aqa wasn't leaving. The Inter-Con was his home, the place where he had eaten most of his meals, laundered his uniforms, spent decades of his life. He had invested so much in this hotel that he could imagine no other. He had risen through the ranks from busboy to waiter, to captain, head waiter, restaurant manager. In those moments when he felt that darkness gathering within, he held his family close, remembered how far he had come, what they had been through, how his life had been spared so many times, *Shukoor Khoda*, 'thanks be to God'. He could still conjure up the taste of the delicious freshly squeezed orange juice they served him at the hospital that day he was discharged, the day he knew he would be OK.

CHAPTER 20

Inside the Cleaners' Closet

Winter 2018

The Afghan minute-hand that crowned the wall of world clocks in the lobby crept towards nine o'clock. Hazrat was preparing for the end of his late shift; only one hour left. When the day was busy, the hours whizzed by. And today was very busy. Almost every room was full, after more than 100 telecom bigwigs and dozens of senior officials from the provinces had checked in for a major conference in the ballroom, organised by the Ministry of Communications and Information Technology.

Hazrat felt the tension in his shoulders ease as the melody from *Romeo and Juliet* – Richard Clayderman's version – filled the mirrored lift. The soft muzak always awakened old memories: the sounds of the radio filling the Inter-Continental's guest rooms as he snapped crisp white sheets across the beds, hung fresh white towels on the rails.

The lift juddered slightly as it drew level with the ground floor. As the doors shut behind Hazrat, the love theme from *Romeo and Juliet* was replaced by Afghan music and the murmur of table talk drifting in from the Bukhara Restaurant. It was peak time at the buffet. Hazrat had one last task weighing on his mind. He had recently become the housekeeping department's lobby supervisor. And he had noticed that the floor-to-ceiling curtains, smudged by cigarette smoke and the many hands that tugged at them, needed a good cleaning. His co-workers – smiley pint-sized Barat, a cleaner from the Hazara community, and twenty-something Hassan, also Hazara, who had just been seconded to housekeeping – joined him with the hotel's tallest ladder to take them down.

The trio sized up the thick golden drapes, the lights of Kabul winking through the gaps. From this distance it could deceive you; it looked so peaceable. Close up, Kabul was morphing into a fortress. The streets were planted with forests of T-walls, the forbidding cement blocks shaped like an upside-down T that were designed to withstand explosions. A section of streets populated by embassies and aid offices – the 'Green Zone' – was now completely ringed by concrete and steel, a no-go area for anyone who didn't have the right permissions. There were no-go areas for foreigners, too, including the once-popular restaurants in Shahr-e Nau now seen as tempting targets for suicide bombers. The Inter-Continental was also on the blacklist of the most high-profile embassies and agencies. But for others the hotel was still seen as relatively safe, set apart from the city centre. Since the terrible assault of 2011 it had reinforced its defences with more guards, more rings of steel, even sniffer dogs trained to smell explosives.

Hazrat propped up the ladder beside the windows: close to the glass, but not so close that it might tip over. He eyed the bottom rungs, then gripped the metal side-rails, preparing to climb. And then he heard it. They all did.

Rat-a-tat.

A staccato burst rang out. They all froze beside the lobby

windows, eyes darting in every direction. *Rat-a-tat-tat*. It was unmistakable the second time. Gunfire – in the restaurant.

Suddenly there came the crash of tables and chairs, spine-chilling screams. A colleague's cry rang out from the terrace below, 'Call the police! The suicide bombers are here.' Then a shout from the restaurant: 'Which ones are foreigners?'

The three housekeepers, their panic rising, darted in the direction of the front desk. Guests and staff were stampeding through the lobby, chased by gunfire. Bullets ricocheted off marble. A handful of attackers, brandishing guns, were striding towards the lifts. The strains of *Romeo and Juliet* hung briefly in the air as the golden doors slid open and shut. The men were heading to the guest floors.

Hazrat and his colleagues scarpered immediately to the closest shelter, the cleaners' closet at the far end of the lobby. An immense pipe, as thick as a tree, took up most of the space inside. There was barely room to move, barely air to breathe. But there was nowhere else. The three men squashed together: one tall, one short, one in between. All they could do was listen. The screams and cries just outside their door invaded their bolthole. And the attackers' commands: 'Don't leave any of them alive, good or bad. Shoot and kill them all.'

Hearts pounded in the dark of the closet. The doorknob rattled. Someone shouted in Pashto, then Persian, 'Come out! Come out!' Hazrat pressed his face into the rough surface of the pipe, wrapping his arms around it. They all did. Three men hugging a steel cylinder as if, somehow, it could save them. They didn't even dare breathe. The doorknob jiggled again. Then another voice: 'There's no one. Let's go upstairs.' Hazrat let out a long sigh as he heard the receding footfall.

As the minutes turned to hours, the terrifying sounds outside came in and out of earshot. The crackle of rifles, the cries and moans and the occasional ear-piercing explosion. The closet shuddered with every blast, sending chunks of plaster flying to the floor. Hazrat peered into a dark so complete that his imagination took over; he struggled to shut down the thought of his anxious family, glued to their phones, who by now would know more than he did of what was happening outside their closet door. A truth was taking hold: tonight his time could come. Faith in God's mercy was a mighty sedative. But he could still feel the cold hands of fear grasping at his throat.

Twenty-something Hassan nodded off to sleep, his head cushioned by Hazrat's arms. Hazrat's eyes never shut.

Mohammad Aqa's phone jangled, jolting him from a deep sleep. 'Have you heard about the attack on the hotel?'

The hotel driver's words shocked Mohammad Aqa out of his grogginess. He stumbled in the dark to turn on his TV. These days the media had permission to report on ongoing attacks; they were back to broadcasting live from scenes of carnage. A reporter for TOLOnews, a stony-faced Gulabuddin Ghubar, stood in the pitch-black, his face fragmenting in and out of pixelation because of the awful signal close to the hotel. But his words came through, all too loud and clear: 'Around three or four attackers . . . Reports suggest they have taken hostages on the second and third floors, as well as in the kitchen and some other rooms where people were present.'

Mohammad Aqa dialled a friend staying at the Inter-Con who had just returned from America. 'Haji *Sahib*, how are you? Where are you?' His friend happily informed him that he was at a party in the city. 'Do you know that suicide bombers have gone into the hotel?' His friend didn't. But his brother was there. He ended the call abruptly.

Mohammad Aqa turned to the TV again. The presenter,

Fawad Aman, had gone back to their reporter not far from the hotel, behind a security cordon. 'The attack has not been contained . . . It may be more difficult than initially expected . . . A similar attack took place here in 2011 . . . People are really questioning how the attackers managed to get past the security checkpoints.' Mohammad Aqa checked the time; it was just past ten-thirty. Sleep wouldn't come now, he knew; too many thoughts chasing each other in his head.

He lay awake for an agonisingly long time. At the first glimpse of light around 5 a.m., after morning prayers, he couldn't wait a moment longer. He jumped into the first minivan he saw and alighted close to the hotel. The cold winter air pinched his skin. The scene took his breath away. A mass of black smoke poured from the Inter-Con's roof, a tongue of orange flame flicking from the top floor. Long strips of the hotel's white façade were blackened. The walls were filled with dark, gaping holes where balconies had once perched. But even now, at the highest point of the smouldering roof, the kicking blue letter K was still visible: dusted by soot, but still standing.

American armoured vehicles mounted with heavy machine guns blocked the main road, the tarmac beyond covered in wailing police vans and ambulances. Afghan special forces in combat gear formed an impenetrable circle around the entrance, stopping almost everyone from advancing beyond the first boom-barrier and metal gate. No one, except for security forces and medical teams, was moving up the hill.

The crowd kept swelling: distraught family members, journalists, staff and stunned bystanders all clamouring to find out what was happening. They watched, stunned, as guests on upper floors flung bedsheets, tied together in makeshift ropes, over balcony rails to try to escape. One man lost his grip and fell to the ground. A collective gasp rose from the melee. Gunfire was still occasionally crackling from inside.

Every so often a new shred of information shot like a current of electricity through the throng. *There are six suicide bombers. The Taliban say they were their men.* From some vantage points, at some moments, they could spot moving shapes on the roof – the troops said to be part of an elite anti-terrorism unit. They had been lowered onto the hotel by helicopters in the heat of the siege. Units were now said to be going from floor to floor, working with Western special forces to bring an end to the assault. Then word went round that Afghan special forces had killed the last of the attackers. *The government says more than 150 people were rescued, including forty foreigners. Six people are dead.* The attack was over.

Mohammad Aqa took solace in a circle of staff congregating together on the edge of the crowd. Their world had been reduced to this burning square. After a few hours the general manager appeared, gently but firmly telling them to go home. No one would be allowed inside today. Many, including Sadozai – a colleague who had just been promoted to Mohammad Aqa's old job of banquet manager – reluctantly mounted their bicycles. Earlier Sadozai had told his colleagues how he had tried to cycle here in the dead of night, in a flood of tears, fearing his beloved Inter-Con was gone; his wife had wisely stopped him, telling him to wait until morning.

Mohammad Aqa loitered for another half-hour, a short distance from the hotel, unable to pull himself away. On an impulse, he went to the back road to see if he could slip inside from there. But he was stopped again, told to go home, told not to worry, that everything that could be done was being done – to save the guests, to save the hotel. He made his way back to the main road, anxious about his friends, about the Inter-Con, about everything.

Hazrat was still pressed against the pipe in the chill of the cleaners' closet. All three of them were: Hazrat, Barat, Hassan. As the half-light slipped through the cracks, they exchanged wan smiles. They had made it through the longest, darkest night they had ever known. *Shukoor Khoda*. 'By God's grace', they had survived.

'You can come out.' The words shattered the eerie quiet. They didn't move. 'Please take care. Our staff are in there.' Relief washed over them. These were voices they recognised. It was hotel staff warning Afghan special forces that the stragglers now surfacing from closets and cupboards were colleagues, not killers. They could hear people wriggling out of concealed spaces in the ceiling, landing with loud thuds. It was over.

Hazrat stretched his aching arm to unlock the door. He was the first to step out. *Dresh!* 'Stop!' a soldier barked. On seeing a stooped man in a wrinkled hotel uniform, he lowered his rifle. The housekeepers, glued together for more than ten hours, tumbled into the lobby, dazed. Men in uniform – police, army, hotel guards, special forces, spooks – swarmed all around them. The walls, the floor and the ceiling were splattered with blood. Bodies sprawled around them, lifeless. The housekeepers picked their way through the carnage.

'Would you mind being interviewed by the media?' an official tentatively asked Hazrat as he approached the front door. 'What interview?' he replied incredulously. 'I haven't slept a minute; my family is desperate to see me.'

He walked haltingly down the hill, shoes crunching on cold ground, his heavy breath forming puffs of white smoke. Beyond the pine trees he saw a sea of people milling about, beyond the blue-and-white boom-barrier at the bottom of the hill. Phalanxes of armoured vehicles came into view as he rounded the bend in the road. He scanned the faces in the crowd. The clamour was disorienting. He seemed to be deaf in one ear after his night pressed against the pipe. As he moved towards the crowd, he could make out the words of the journalists. 'What happened to you? Can you tell us your story?'

He kept shaking his head, kept touching his hand on his heart, kept looking into the multitude, seeking out the faces he knew. Then he saw them. His sons. All six, Abdul Qadir, Ghulam Syed, Payman, Zaki, Tamim, Samir. And they saw him, too. They pushed their way through the security cordon. 'That's our father!' Startled soldiers gave way. His sons tumbled into his arms. 'You're alive!' None of them had slept that night, either, crouching around a fire they had built from twigs and branches outside the bakery at the bottom of the hill, praying to see their father again. It was time to go home.

Mohammad Aqa heard they found Brigitte's body on the restaurant floor, next to the table to the right of the door. It was where she always sat, usually on her own, so that she could listen to the musicians play. The German nurse had been coming to Afghanistan since the 1980s. She even spoke Pashto. She had always been so calm, so kind. Sometimes she stayed with friends in the city, but this time she had been told it would be safer to stay in the Inter-Con. She was the first person to be shot dead. It was her birthday.

Two more bodies had been found on the third floor, even after the security sweep ended. They were so badly burned no one could immediately say who they were. As Mohammad Aqa worked his way around the hotel, sweeping shards of glass, clumps of plaster and hunks of wood into neat piles, he steeled himself to find more. Whole floors had become a ghoulish hell-scape. Incinerated corridors with every surface charred, strips of plaster dangling from blasted ceilings. In just one night, more of the hotel had been destroyed than in all the war-torn decades gone by. The golden hotel turned black.

The ruin didn't stop at marble, wood and steel. The hotel's people were broken. Waiters in brightly trimmed waistcoats had become white-bandaged patients in blue hospital tunics. Staff watched, shocked, as they saw their colleagues recounting their stories to reporters on all the Afghan TV channels. Twenty-year-old Haseeb, who had started waiting on tables only four months earlier, had witnessed the attack from its very start. He described how two young Afghan men had come into the res-taurant shortly before 9 p.m. 'They were wearing very stylish clothes,' he recalled. 'They came to me and asked for food. I served them and they thanked me as they sat in their seats. Then they took out their weapons and started shooting people. There were dozens of dead bodies lying around me.'

Haseeb and eleven colleagues had fled to a suite on an upper floor, banging on its door with all their might. A group of Afghans, including a TOLOnews reporter and a diplomat, were inside and, by God's grace, had let them in. The group had barri-caded themselves in with everything at hand. But within an hour the attackers were charging down their floor, smashing doors, hurling firebombs. And then they came to that suite, blasting through the locked door.

Many didn't make it. Some escaped by scrambling onto the adjacent balcony. Others jumped. Two waiters died instantly when they hit the cement. But Noorullah, another young waiter, fell into trees that broke his fall and saved his life. Writhing in pain, barely able to speak, his jaw, arms and legs swathed in white bandages, he also shared his story with the journalists.

Hasibullah from the bakery also jumped, breaking his legs and his back when he landed.

Later on TOLOnews, the journalist who was in the room, Abdulhaq Omeri, gave his account of what happened. He was known for his news reports from dangerous frontlines in the provinces. Now the hotel had become his war zone. He had spent the night hiding on a balcony in sub-zero temperatures. 'We sat there for the entire night. During that time I heard women and children screaming, men begging the attackers to spare their lives.' Three friends with him never lived to tell their stories. And he shed some light on what had happened earlier in the day, gleaned from a waiter who had hidden with him. A big box had been brought into the hotel that morning through the kitchen. The waiter revealed to Omeri that 'It looked suspicious, but he was told by one of his seniors that it was none of his business to ask questions about that box.'

Within hours this was all anyone could talk about. *An insider attack?* Two, maybe three bombers were said to have checked into the hotel two days earlier, their suitcases packed with weapons and equipment. How did they get through three checkpoints? How did they know so much about the hotel? They had known the layout of every floor, the emergency exits, the biggest suites. Some of the bombers were even wearing Afghan army uniforms. Where did they get them?

The blame game began. A private security company, the Kabul Balkh Safety and Security Organisation, had won the government contract to secure the grounds three weeks earlier. It accused the hotel of not fixing broken metal detectors and other safety equipment. 'It was always tomorrow, tomorrow.' It blamed hotel security for failings inside the building. Even for complicity.

The government blamed Kabul Balkh. Guests had been

complaining, 'They didn't check our luggage . . . there were no body searches.' Most private security companies had been dismantled under the last government. But not Kabul Balkh. 'It had been a mistake to hire them,' some government officials said. Hotel staff on duty that night expressed disbelief, alleging that the security guards were blindsided and hadn't known what to do.

Many others blamed the Haqqani Network. The group, aligned with the Taliban, was already on the West's terrorism blacklists and had been tied to other deadly attacks in the city – including the 2011 assault on the Inter-Con. Months after that attack, Afghan intelligence had released details of calls between the bombers in the hotel and a phone in Pakistan that was linked to one of the brothers of the Haqqani family, whose father founded the group. Were they involved in the 2018 attack, too?

Certain staff from the hotel, and the Kabul Balkh security company, were taken in for questioning; some were detained, some placed on a travel ban so they wouldn't leave the country; others escaped anyway. Most simply kept their heads down, trying to put their hotel back together. Everyone talked about the story of Hashmat, the security guard, who found a huge wad of money, more than 50,000 euros, in Room 408, the room of the German nurse Brigitte who was shot dead in the restaurant. There was a note saying that it had been donated for Afghan widows. Everyone was impressed that Hashmat handed the money over to hotel managers, even though he had started to dwell on how it could have changed his life.

They were still scrubbing blood from the walls and ceilings two weeks on, when Hazrat felt well enough to return, although his hearing was still impaired. Barat the cleaner came back, too. Twenty-something Hassan, their fellow survivor, never showed up again.

⋆

Hazrat kept finding clumps of hair and flesh in the rooms. For weeks he would flinch as he discovered what had happened to guests that night, including to those he saw as his *special guests*.

Like Mohammad Aqa, he missed Brigitte. He also missed Soraya in Room 312, killed after hiding in a cupboard that attackers sprayed with bullets. She hailed from the old Afghan royal family; he had loved hearing her stories. And then there had been the pilot in Room 516. Hazrat couldn't remember his name, but he was one of many; nine pilots with Kam Air were killed in all. They had put their trust in this hotel even after Tony, the Spanish pilot, had perished in the 2011 attack. Seven of the dead were Ukrainian. Hazrat kept thinking about how in the morning, at breakfast, they would sit at the same tables near the windows, sometimes speaking Russian, sometimes Ukrainian – tall and muscular, as pilots flying in and out of tough places should be. One of them had been killed while dining in the restaurant. Two other pilots who had lost their lives were from Venezuela. A Greek aviator was lucky – he pulled the stuffing from his mattress and hid inside as the attackers went from room to room, blasting away the electronic locks.

The presence of those pilots showed how the Kabul Inter-Continental had changed. This was no longer a hotel just for the posh and the privileged. The wealthiest usually headed now to the more elegant, more expensive Serena Hotel in the city centre. Visiting politicians stayed there, too, or in their own heavily fortified embassies. Most Inter-Con guests were neither very rich nor very poor. It had become a gathering place for everyday people trying to make this country work.

And how the staff hoped it could be that place again. Two months after the attack the hotel's doors opened again. The lobby had been repainted, refurbished. Its shiny golden renovation was gone. The promenade of pillars had returned to their traditional wood. The sofas and chairs were less stuffed, less shiny. Gilded hangings gave way to blue patterned curtains with touches of gold in fringed valances and tiebacks. Sheer white curtains skimming the glass let the light in. Down the hall, the Bukhara Restaurant was refreshed, retaining its blue-and-gold flourish as if nothing had happened.

Yet the guests still wouldn't come. Mohammad Aqa stood at the restaurant door as every day steaming serving pans were ferried to the buffet table. But few diners came to eat. He tried not to look at the stubborn bullet holes in the floor. Hazrat was proud that the first floor, relatively unscathed, was ready and waiting for guests. But not a single room was booked. And the floors above still reeked of smoke. Door locks were still smashed. Carpets blackened. Mirrors and windows pockmarked by bullet holes.

Floor by floor, room by room, the rebuild was under way. But there wasn't enough money to fix everything at once. And the Inter-Continental's tarnished image would take even longer to repair. From the door of the restaurant, Mohammad Aqa could still hear the soothing strains of *Romeo and Juliet* playing on a loop whenever the golden lifts opened.

PART VI

The Year of a Little Hope

CHAPTER 21

Sadeq's Smile

Autumn 2020

It could be the Swiss Alps. Snow-capped peaks glinting in clear blue skies, the chime of birdsong, and a handsome young man, sitting on a balcony in a mocha-coloured turtleneck, lifting a white cup from its matching saucer. As he sips he reads messages on his mobile phone with a contented smile. A serene holiday escape – at the Inter-Continental Kabul, topped off with a voice-over: 'The Inter-Continental is soothing for your mind . . .'

The face of the hotel's new publicity video, posted on Instagram, Facebook and YouTube, was twenty-two-year-old Sadeq, its acting front-desk manager. The Inter-Con was rebranding in time for Afghanistan's new, and cautiously optimistic, spirit. All of a sudden there was talk of peace. The Taliban had signed an historic deal in February with their American arch-enemies; now there was even mention of face-to-face talks with Afghans. And peace brought opportunity. 'If peace is coming, renovation is a must,' Sadeq's boss, the general manager Fazel Malik Niazi, kept telling him. 'The Inter-Continental is the place for peace-makers and foreigners to stay.'

It was all part of the manager's plan for a revamp. Things

were slowly starting to look up. Guests had begun checking in, diners showing up and conferences being booked. The Inter-Continental was hoping to reclaim its status as the finest hotel in Kabul, a mantle that had slipped after the last suicide bombing. But first it needed money – a lot of it – from the government to finish the hotel's rebuild and refresh. Every week, sometimes twice a week, the general manager came back up the hill from the presidential palace or the Finance Ministry looking dejected. 'Empty hands!' he kept lamenting, throwing his own hands in the air. Sadeq listened to his woes. All they gave his boss – his hotel – were lectures. 'Cut your costs! Boost your revenue!' But the manager wasn't giving up yet. Floor by floor, room by room, all the quarters incinerated in the last suicide bombing, as well as all the dull and dated spaces, were being knocked into shape.

So were the security arrangements. The number of guards around the hotel's three rings of steel had tripled. A fourth barrier was put up on the crest of the hill. A safe room had been installed in the basement. Every door of every guest room was now bulletproof. Sadeq truly believed his guests had nothing to fear from the hotel. The problem was Afghanistan. It was not bulletproof. Sadeq had to admit, if only to himself, that his guests were still a bit scared. But what else could he do? His job was to run the front desk, not the country.

The span of his own life was not much longer than the nearly two decades in which foreign forces had been in his country, vowing to make Afghanistan a better, safer place. Sadeq was part of an ambitious generation. He was studying at the American University of Afghanistan, the country's first private university, aiming for a BBA, a Bachelor of Business Administration. His dream was to one day run his own business. For now he needed work experience, as well as a job to help support his family.

With his sartorial flair and thousand-watt smile, Sadeq was

a natural fit for the Inter-Con: a poster boy for hospitality. His life philosophy fitted the bill perfectly: *a good smile, and good behaviour.* To add to his arsenal, one of his big brothers had put in a good word. He knew the man in charge at the Inter-Con. That's the way it often worked. And it did work. Last year Sadeq had climbed the hill for an interview, his first time in the hotel. 'Do you have any work experience?' the general manager had asked. Sadeq admitted that he didn't. 'Do you have a degree?' 'No,' Sadeq told him, but said he would really like to work. The manager, only thirty-four himself, but with a business degree and a successful venture in Turkey, said he would get back to Sadeq. And he did, after just two days. 'We found you a job.'

Sadeq had set to work as a receptionist. In no time at all he had figured out how the front desk worked, and how it could work better. He would stay long past his shift time, flashing his sunbeam smile at the guests, especially the difficult ones. He dressed the part, too. After only two weeks the general manager summoned him for some startling news. A different position had become vacant. 'From today you will be the acting front-desk manager,' he announced. Suddenly Sadeq was in charge of two dozen staff, including the new tennis teacher. Some of them were surprised, too, even a bit upset. Sadeq merely flashed his smile, was on his best behaviour. *If you behave well with others, no one will hate you* – that was his position. It seemed to have worked, so far.

The promotion had been his first test. Now, less than a year later, came a second one. A few weeks previously Sadeq had been snapped in an official photograph – one he made sure to save on his phone, so that he could send it to his family and friends. He was only in the third row of the picture, but he stood out at the back, thanks to the height of his trendy medium-fade haircut. At the front was the top American general, flanked by two Afghan government ministers, including the deputy defence minister and the interior minister. They were all wearing camouflage – including, in the case of the US general, a mottled green-and-brown face-mask. The American was the only one taking the precaution. Most Afghans didn't worry much about Covid-19 when death and dying were already part of life.

The officials had been visiting the hotel, and the *Loya Jirga* site just below the Inter-Con, the day before the traditional assembly was due to convene again on 7 August 2020. Its focus was that possibility of peace talks. Security was especially tight because it wasn't certain the Taliban were really interested in talking. Of course the Inter-Continental was part of the plans again. 'Big-tent democracy', people were calling it, even though the *Jirga* tent wasn't really a tent any more. It had a metal roof, cement walls with scalloped edges and Islamic calligraphy above the entrances. Its manicured grounds were studded with long rows of silky Afghan flags. This *Loya Jirga* was the seventh such gathering since the fall of the Taliban, and one of the biggest. More than 3,000 delegates were expected, including 700 women.

The women stayed at the Inter-Con, some with their children. They were Sadeq's responsibility. He was told to prepare for 400 guests for five nights. Some 600 showed up. They kept streaming through the door, dozens at a time – older women from the provinces wrapped in voluminous shawls, younger delegates in stylish scarves and tunics in electric pinks and yellows, taking selfies as they roamed the lobby. The din on the ground floor reached epic levels. All manner of carryalls, from shiny suitcases to bulging plastic bags, piled up at reception. Decibel levels kept inching higher as impossible decisions were made on how to divide guest rooms among three times as many guests. Dozens were squeezed into the Khyber Suite. Every possible space was crammed with beds and cots. Some even made their unhappiness with Sadeq known to the general manager. 'He's not speaking to us in a nice way . . .', 'I don't like the colour of my room . . .' Sadeq parked his smile and put his foot down. That approach worked wonders too.

The babel only subsided when delegates streamed out of the hotel after breakfasts of hard-boiled eggs or tomatoey, garlicky *tokhme banjanromi*. From 9 a.m. to 4 p.m., and often longer, they stayed down the hill at the *Jirga* tent – and Sadeq's duties shifted to supervising the housekeepers-turned-babysitters assigned to every floor to watch over toddlers and teenagers. As summer's inviting light started to leave for the day, the delegates traipsed back into the hotel and soon descended upon their special buffet, prepared for a special price. The hotel pulsed with the excitement and emotions of each day's realpolitik.

At the *Jirga* site the women delegates were afforded all the expected courtesies and customs. They had their own security entrance and separate seating. But, like every *Jirga* of the past two decades, when they stuck their head above the parapet to speak – usually more bluntly than the men – they were often insulted or shouted down. At the assembly the year before, when 30 per cent of the delegates were female, one woman was spectacularly belittled. 'Peace has nothing to do with you,' a male delegate yelled. 'Sit down! You should be in the kitchen, cooking.'

This year the women were even more determined to speak their minds. On the first day the prominent women's activist and MP Belquis Roshan rose from her seat and unfurled a banner: *Redeeming the savage Taliban is national treason.* A guard immediately moved in, asking her to sit down, to stay quiet. Afghan and foreign television channels broadcast it all, including the spectacle of Ms Roshan, still brandishing her banner, being pushed out of the hall by a female guard. In the tussle she tumbled to the floor, her powder-blue scarf slipping from her head as shouts ricocheted around the room. Even President Ghani intervened from the podium. 'Dear sister, I am not redeeming. It is your decision, your colleagues' decision.'

And what difficult decisions they were. Delegates were asked to discuss whether a last group of 400 hardcore Taliban prisoners should be freed: men accused of horrible attacks on embassies, busy public squares, government buildings, even the Inter-Continental. In exchange, the Taliban promised to hold talks with representatives of a government it had always scorned as 'puppets'. They were already deep in discussion with the United States over the withdrawal of their last troops. But, under this deal, the Taliban had also agreed to start peace talks with their Afghan enemies, under certain conditions. In the end the *Jirga* agreed that the convicts should walk free – as long as the government kept tabs on them, so they didn't return to the battlefield. No Afghan, in good conscience, wanted to vote against a chance for peace, however slim.

The women delegates checked out of the Inter-Con, embracing each other around the front desk, thanking the staff profusely. The general manager marvelled at Sadeq's skill. 'Well done, how did you manage this?' For Sadeq, it didn't feel like a triumph. For five days he had slept three hours a night on the sofa in his office. But he had been part of something much bigger than his own life – the dreams of Afghan women and men trying to pull their country in a different direction.

Malalai was no dreamer. Life had never given her the chance to dream big and, besides, she had enough to focus on right in front of her. Today she had to keep an eye on the buffet plates and serving pans, not to mention the diners, and her fellow waiters.

She was sharp-eyed enough for the job, that she knew. Standing smack in the centre of the Bukhara Restaurant, she kept the food counters – as well as the scattering of customers – in her sights. No one could miss her, dressed in a black tunic with a sunny yellow trim and a matching bright headscarf. Nor her eyes, fringed with light lashings of mascara and bold black eyebrows painted by God's own brush.

Boldness suited Malalai. She took her name from the Afghan heroine whose legend had been carried down the generations: the young woman who had brandished her veil like a flag, rallying demoralised Pashtun fighters during the Battle of Maiwand against the British in the Second Anglo-Afghan War at the start of the 1880s. Malalai had lost her life, but the Afghans had beaten the British.

A century later the life of another Malalai – the twenty-something Inter-Con waiter – was also a battle; one without heroic victories or defeats, just a daily struggle to get by. She had been working since around the age of twelve, after her mother died giving birth to her fourth child and her father fell ill. Not yet a teenager, Malalai had struggled to understand why God would treat her so harshly. But there was generosity as well as grief in His plan. Her sadness soon cast itself into a steely resolve.

When she was a bit older, a friend had introduced her to an American company with openings in its restaurant. She had performed so well that it soon doubled her salary. This had been Malalai's education. She had never gone to school, but she taught herself the ways of this world. She kept talking to herself, telling herself, 'You can do this.' She spoke both Pashto and Dari, as well as the Urdu of Pakistan, and had even taken a short course in English. And she understood, instinctively, the language of hospitality.

But the US company had abruptly shut down when its manager passed away. It was a cruel twist of fate that Malalai's kind American employer met the same sad end as her own mother, dying in childbirth. However, Malalai wasn't lost for long. A kind neighbour spotted an Inter-Continental Kabul ad on Facebook; it was looking to hire female employees. Armed with her CV and the sheer force of her personality, she was one of a few young women offered a job. The others turned it down: educated, they didn't want to work as waiters. So Malalai quietly made her own history as one of the Inter-Con's first female waiters. There were two women in the Bukhara Restaurant, one in the new coffee shop at the other end of the lobby and others everywhere, from the general manager's office to the laundry room. Seventeen women in all, out of more than 300 staff. None of them worked the night-shift. Afghan women shouldn't work late.

Malalai wanted to work, needed to work, loved to work. Her stolen childhood meant she had never enjoyed the simple pleasure of just hanging out with girlfriends. She was her family's only earner, supporting her ailing elderly father and her youngest sister, who was at school. Her older brother and sister had married and moved out, but her brother was jobless now after his contract with an American company also ended. So it fell to Malalai to put food on their *dastarkhwan*, even if they couldn't afford the expensive offerings she served at the Inter-Con.

Today had begun like any other day, with the sun. She had left her family's three-room mud house at first light, taking a shared taxi to the teeming city centre, then switching into another to wend westwards towards the Inter-Con. On busy days the journey could take as long as two hours. When she came through the hotel's staff entrance she changed her clothes, and her image: from her flowing pastel tunics and headscarves, with a bit of sparkle, into the sober uniform of the restaurant, with her own bright touches.

Malalai knew what she needed to do. And she knew she could do it. She moved methodically around the four marble counters that formed the buffet square, readying it to receive the day's all-you-can-eat feast. First to the small white bowls that stood beside the steel soup-warmer. Next to the stand of bigger plates, hidden beneath a cloth, that would display the day's selection of salads. Beside that, a plastic bread basket with a rolltop cover; it wouldn't be a proper Afghan meal without bread. Then on to the two counters taken up by a parade of unlit chafing dishes, awaiting the arrival of food-filled pans sending inviting wisps of smoke wafting from their open lids. And finally the dessert station, where a lonely pyramid of golden apples staked out their space, before the cakes and custards arrived from the fridges to steal the show. As Malalai circled her section, she was aware of the other waiting staff checking their own settings around the room, sometimes meeting their eyes with a half-smile. All was in order.

Around noon, the first guests arrived. Malalai knew how to be courteous and correct in her bearing. Guests treated her with respect in return. She never experienced any untoward looks, any improper incidents. On one occasion some of her male colleagues had taken issue with her service. 'You're too friendly,' they scolded her. 'Don't speak with men when you serve them.' Taken aback, she took her complaint to the general manager. He was the one who had told her they needed to provide a better service with a smile. He rebuked her male colleagues and demanded, 'What's your problem?' They complained that she wasn't properly trained. Malalai suspected it was jealousy, and resolved to lead them into the future. 'The old times are over,' she often reminded them. 'Now there are opportunities for both women and men.' It should make them happy that the women of Afghanistan were developing, too, she insisted. Malalai knew she was on the right side of history. And her measured words seemed to win the day. They even had a laugh about it; then everyone got back to work.

Malalai returned to her watch-post in the restaurant, occasionally exchanging asides with her female colleague Khatra, as they kept an eye on the last of the diners grazing the buffet table. The mid-afternoon quiet fell over the room. Shafts of light were already edging across the restaurant and out the door, filtering through the trees on the other side of the hotel. It was 3 p.m. Another shift completed.

She saw so much from her place in this restaurant. It was a measure of Afghanistan's moment. When summer's sun softened into winter's pale light, Afghans descended for conferences – including scores of twenty-somethings like her. In November it was the young journalists working for Radio and Television Afghanistan, spending a week training at the Inter-Con and chatting excitedly during their meals about technology and their times. In December there was an even bigger gathering organised by a group called the Youth Thinkers' Society – a club aiming to make Afghanistan a better place, even to change the world. More than a thousand young Afghans filled the ballroom and smaller banquet rooms, each person representing a country or a committee in a model United Nations. During their breaks they spilled into the lobby for tea and coffee, burning with a sense of purpose and resolve, surrounded by brilliant blue banners hailing their 'Peace Building' mission. Optimism was in the air. After the success of the *Jirga*, the first-ever formal face-to-face meetings between the Taliban and representatives of the Afghan government were under way in Doha; some of the Afghan negotiators and foreign diplomats engaged in the Qatar talks even came to brief them.

Malalai watched from the sidelines. She was building a new future, too, in her own small way. She knew that her life had given her no choice but to keep working. And she felt at her best when she was.

Sadeq's twenty-something colleagues teased him about his style. They were fashion-conscious, too, of course, showing up for work in their own smart Kabul attire. But it was hard to match Sadeq, in his well-cut suits, his fashionable turtlenecks. And it was hard for him to resist their joshing, particularly during quiet intervals of the day. Only demure Huma, in her ebony cloak and matching headscarf, not a single strand of hair showing, kept her professional demeanour behind the front desk. And sometimes even she couldn't resist a smile.

They teased him for his seriousness, too. But then Sadeq's work was a serious business. Day after day he worked on his grand plans. He was thinking about embedding an illuminated Inter-Continental Kabul logo in the front of the reception desk to brighten the hotel's welcome. First impressions could make a difference. He was working on computerising the guest-registration system, with a webcam to take photos and a scanner for IDs. Data would be stored more safely, and paper costs would come down. And that was only the beginning. Management was preparing special security cards so that only approved people could access the lifts. They were also dealing with the threat of Covid-19, ensuring every employee was vaccinated.

They had to clean up the service, too. Sadeq had seen some

goings-on – like that day the Afghan translator of a British businessman had slyly tried to cut a deal with him, suggesting that Sadeq palm him the difference between the hotel's regular room rate and its special discount. Sadeq had made quick work of that. 'We are the Inter-Continental,' he said curtly.

Floor by floor, a new Inter-Continental was finally emerging. By early 2021 some government money had come through. The effects were immediate. The lobby's chintz chairs and sofas made way for sleek replacements. The first guest floor was also transformed, its rooms fashioned with a caramel-coloured floor and furniture, tawny curtains and taupe armchairs on a traditional Afghan carpet. And they had all the expected modern amenities as well, from flatscreen TVs to tea and coffee stations. The refurb would soon shift to the second floor, money permitting, then to the third and fourth. On the fifth floor the Khyber Suite was open for business, refurbished in this same modern style. The darkness had been dispelled, on the surface at least.

Some of the former guests were trickling back. A journalist from the BBC who seemed to know most of the old staff kept showing up, sparking predictable suspicion from government spies lurking in the lobby. She informed them that she was writing a book about the hotel. The general manager said she was now Sadeq's responsibility. They settled into the stylish lobby chairs with Hazrat, who wouldn't stop talking about the towels from the king's time. The security chief, who had also pulled up a chair to listen in, soon got bored. He interjected to share with her their worry about the djinns – gesturing, wide-eyed, towards the gathering of shadows beyond the windows. Hazrat dismissed such talk as nonsense. But even the spook looked a bit nervous as they peered into the gloom. He admitted that some of his guards were scared too.

It wasn't what anyone wanted to hear. The vibe was

supposed to be business as usual. President Ghani's office had laid down the law to all government ministries. All official functions, meetings, conferences and room bookings had to be at the Inter-Con, not the swish Serena Hotel, now frequented by the wealthiest ministers and their special advisors.

But the biggest obstacle was that many of the foreigners who needed to attend government meetings weren't allowed to spend time at the Inter-Con. The hotel was still blacklisted. 'The Inter-Con is too dangerous,' a US embassy official told Sadeq while taking a look around. Sadeq had prepared a full report to prove otherwise. But it wasn't enough. For all that the Inter-Con had done – its bulletproof doors and safe rooms – it had to do more.

Besides, fewer foreigners were coming to Kabul these days – put off by the war and kept at home by the pandemic. Increasingly the hotel's visitors were Afghans. During the holy month of Ramadan straddling April and May, the poolside restaurant was packed. Every evening, under the shimmering canopy of fairy lights, more than 300 hungry diners broke their daily fast, foraging from a spread that stretched almost the entire length of the terrace. By mid-May, as *Eid al-Fitr* approached, nearly every room was booked. Afghan folk-music legends Sharafat Parwani and Ramin Fazli were lined up to entertain guests at a private party inside the hotel. In the city centre, in the exquisite garden of the Serena Hotel, Aryana Sayeed shimmied in a glistening gold tunic and brought the house down with her rollicking *Eid* concert.

With *Eid* came not just the end of fasting, but the end of fear, at least for three days. The Taliban and the Afghan government agreed to a temporary truce after a terrible surge in violence. It wouldn't be a pause like the year before, when young Taliban fighters got carried away, slipping into Kabul and other urban centres for the first time, buying ice cream from delighted vendors, even posing for selfies in the streets with self-assured Afghan women. It seemed to offer a tantalising glimpse of peace. But the adventurous Talibs were soon reprimanded by their commanders.

A year on, even a little lull was a gift, allowing Afghans to walk more freely in the streets, letting them imagine a lasting ceasefire, an end to attacks against Afghan security forces and civilians, an end to the raids by the government's own gunmen. Young Afghans took to social media to fight for peace with the hashtag #AfghansWantPermanentCeasefire. But peace talks were stuck in the mud of intransigence on both sides. The US president Joe Biden had announced that he was pulling out the last of his forces by 11 September, the twentieth anniversary of 9/11. It only bolstered the Taliban's belief that their victory was within reach.

Sadeq couldn't really savour the three-day break; not when he was working such long hours overseeing the hotel's high-profile events. The general manager kept putting him in charge of the biggest occasions, including lavish weddings for the children of top government officials, which often created traffic snarl-ups around the hotel. But the *Eid* holiday afforded him a bit more time at home in his family's second-floor flat in one of the 1960s Soviet-built Macroyan apartment blocks. Once the pinnacle of modern luxury, it was now pocked by war, but still coursing with life, peppered with parades of hole-in-the-wall shops and patchy playgrounds. Sadeq lived with his father and three sisters – two twenty-somethings and a teenager. There was Totti, too, Sadeq's bright-green pet parrot, which could squawk in Pashto. Totti adored Sadeq. And the family's bond was especially tight in the absence of their mother. They hadn't hugged her in more than six years. She was in the United States with

Sadeq's two older brothers, waiting for the rest of the family to join them. His sisters had put off any thoughts of marriage to avoid adding reasons to stay in Kabul. All their lives were on hold until they could get out.

In this unsettling time father and son shared a special ritual. Every night his father would sit by the window on their red-and-blue *toshak*, waiting with Totti for Sadeq to come home. When he arrived back from work, or from outings with friends, Sadeq would sit with them, his parrot on his shoulder, to share details of the day just gone and listen to his father's remembrances and reflections from times past. A former army officer, he had started his military career in President Najibullah's Soviet-backed army and had ended in President Karzai's American-trained forces. He had the scars to show for it, even if they weren't readily visible. A *mujahideen* ambush in the 1980s had wounded him in one eye as he made his way home from the north for a weekend of leave. When the civil war raged in Kabul in the 1990s, the family – like many others in Macroyan – often took refuge in the musty basement, then fled for a while to the relative safety of the northern city of Mazar-i-Sharif, before Sadeq was born in Kabul.

Sadeq loved his father as a teacher, a friend, a guide in a young Afghan man's scrambled rites of passage. He had long dreamed of studying abroad: to support his family, to make something of himself. He reasoned that an Afghan educated in America would have a better shot at life than an Afghan educated in Afghanistan. One of his big brothers was his role model. He had two master's degrees and was now a senior journalist in Washington DC. Hasib chivvied his younger brother to keep at his books to improve his score on the TOEFL English-language tests. Sadeq's first score wasn't too bad. But he had to do a lot better.

He had decided to put his study at the American University

of Afghanistan on hold to focus on his English fluency and his demanding job. Sadeq wanted to believe that his life, and the life of his country, would get better. Even his father, who had seen so much war, thought there was now a possibility, however small, that peace was coming. Sadeq held fast to that hope. In the hotel, in his cubbyhole of an office across from the front desk, he sometimes doodled in his thoughts about a different country. He imagined a time when they could proudly say to the whole world, 'We are Afghans, from a place of educated, talented people.'

CHAPTER 22

The Danger Hours

Summer 2021

The pressure on the hotel was relentless. New orders kept coming from the palace, some straight from the president's mouth. 'You have too many people! Three hundred and thirty people on the payroll is too many!' The general manager was told to prepare a new business plan for 165 employees. He baulked. Sadeq gulped. The general manager didn't want to sack so many; he believed there were better ways to improve the hotel's profitability. Nor did he want to disrespect the oldest staff who had done so much for this hotel, cared so much, considered it their home. But the government was fixated on the numbers.

So the Inter-Con team came up with their own plan, keeping 200 employees, to put the hotel on a sounder footing. The document sat on government desks for months. *All plans and no action*, Sadeq quietly fumed. *Every Afghan has plans, but no action.*

Sadeq increasingly felt the hotel needed to start again, from zero. They needed a whole new way of working – better people to achieve better performance. He figured that one young person could do the work of four old ones. It meant that a shake-up was essential. Who was needed, who wasn't? Who was working, who wasn't? Those who had been there since the beginning would be respected. For some, a severance package would be prepared. Even a bonus.

The changes had already begun. Fifty-five-year-old Mohammad Aqa, the restaurant manager, was taken off the night-shift in the restaurant, moved to the morning, just for a short time. Seventy-year-old Hazrat was reassigned from the third floor – the VIP floor – to the fourth. Sadeq realised that Hazrat knew everything; Hazrat never stopped reminding him of that. But housekeeping demanded stamina, and the strength to clean quickly. When one guest checked out, another waited to check in. Time was money. And Hazrat, he believed, now needed more time for each task.

The general manager still charged ahead with his ambitious blueprint, including his special projects. One was especially close to his heart: his *bijou*, the glass conservatory he had built in the cul-de-sac on the side of the hotel. Inside his oasis everything succeeded. Miniature pomegranates smiled from potted trees. Geraniums showed off their rich red regalia. Leathery rubber plants sprang from the copper-coloured planters that he'd brought back from Dubai. Spider plants spilled, fountain-like, from baskets hanging from the beams. There was even a potted fir tree, a memento of the signature evergreens that had survived every test the hotel had faced over the years.

His plans for 2021 included landscaping 50 per cent of the grounds, the rest the year after. The twenty gardeners on his payroll, almost all of them much older than the Inter-Con, were on the job. Dead patches of grass next to the upper parking lot were being nursed back to life. Decades ago the centrepiece of this Park-e Bala, the High Park, had been its chocolate-box band-stand bursting with music. Now it was a grey slab of cement platform. But the stone fountain had now been fixed. Soon this space would be transformed into a breakfast nook with a view over west Kabul. Hedges of wild roses in wake-up pink and red were already primed. Next would be the popular spot for lovers' photos – the walkway winding alongside this pocket park that led to the poolside terrace below. A canopy formed of almond and apricot trees, a ceiling of pink-and-white buds in spring, was now fronted by a white wooden gate shaped like a heart. War never killed love, or weddings, or Afghan hospitality.

Sadeq's own refuge was a quiet corner of the coffee shop in the furthest part of the lobby. He rarely indulged in cake. But he always drank a foamy cappuccino in the morning, and tea had more than enough kick after he had ladled in several spoonfuls of sugar. The café was one of the hotel's cosiest spaces, he thought. Its ceiling was a vivid painted patchwork of smiling Afghan faces and scenes of bucolic village life, created in a more optimistic time by an international charity. The framed black-and-white photographs on the panelled walls harked back even further, to the hotel's early years. Some customers came in for quiet conversation, or to sample the sweets in the misted glass display case – slices of vanilla loaf, or the circular cakes with smiley faces and *Love* scribbled in icing swirls.

Some nights, in the mellow light of the table lamps, an Afghan singer took up position just inside the coffee shop's engraved wooden door and struck up his best version of Elvis Presley. As the mood morphed from café to club, Sadeq would bundle up his documents and head across the hushed ground floor to the privacy of his own little office.

The high-ceilinged lobby, with its chandeliers above and marble below, had once exerted its own soothing influence on Sadeq. But increasingly his mind was not at ease. So many friends had already left for America. His brother Hasib, on the phone daily from Washington, kept trying to keep their hopes up, saying they would soon be together: 'Not long now . . . in three or four months I am sure they will give us an exact time. Then medicals. Then visas.' But these days schedules had a way of disintegrating. Some days Covid-19 shut the embassy gates. Other days it was security threats. It made his family in the United States more fearful than their loved ones still in Kabul.

Sadeq didn't dare dream about hugging his mother, didn't dare imagine sitting in a US classroom to finish his Kabul business degree. Not until his foot touched American soil. Besides, right now he had a very big job. The sounds of Elvis at the other end of the lobby fell away in the night:

'I spent a lifetime waiting for the right time.
Now that you're near, the time is here, at last.'

*

A pall of uncertainty hung over the hotel like Kabul's blanket of morning smog. The general manager was gone. The government said he was fired. But he had marched out the door saying, 'I resign!', protesting that he couldn't work with officials who kept ordering him to sack so many of his staff.

Malalai fiddled with the ends of her forest-green headscarf. She didn't ask too many questions. To her mind, the manager had been a professional boss, respectful of women, promoting female waiters like her, encouraging them to take on greater roles. He had even wanted to hire more women to bring a fresh face, a more inviting look, to the restaurant to attract more customers, to bring in more revenue, so he could convince the government that the Inter-Con had other ways to survive than by swingeing cuts to its payroll.

But there had been gossip. A video had surfaced on social media and been forwarded from one phone to the next; a clip from a fifth-floor surveillance camera said to have been leaked by a disgruntled someone in hotel security. It showed blurry images of the general manager and a deputy finance minister chatting and laughing with a popular female TV presenter and a female parliamentarian by the lift late at night. *What was this midnight rendezvous all about?* There was *gupshup*, too, about inflated contracts for meat supplies. At the behest of the boss, people whispered. The manager, and his defenders, dismissed all this as tittle-tattle.

Malalai knew nothing about it, wanted nothing to do with it. There was all too much weighing on her mind already. The new general manager, a senior finance official swiftly put in place by the president's office, had hit the ground running. Hotel staff had been summoned, one after another, to be interviewed about their job. It was a procession of panic. There had been a sharp intake of breath when the total number sacked was revealed. More than 160 people in all, almost half of the staff who had kept this hotel running. Everyone looked at everyone else with searching eyes, hesitating to ask, 'What's happening to you . . . ?' They soon found out.

Malalai was never called in for an interview. She was just told she would keep her job. She didn't know why; she didn't ask. Maybe the new general manager had seen her in the restaurant, poised and professional. Maybe he wanted to keep the youngest staff with a future ahead of them, not the oldest ones with a past behind them. The young women working in the laundry, like Laila and Zakia, were also staying. But Halina at reception had slipped away to the United States with her family. Malalai would miss her, and the way they had giggled and gossiped in the women's area around their metal staff lockers.

Mohammad Aqa, her restaurant manager, was kept on, too. So was Sadozai, in charge of banquets. But not Abida the cook, whose face she had first seen on the 'Employee of the Month' board right next to reception only a few months earlier. She had not met Abida until recently, when the BBC journalist – the one writing the book – came to the hotel and asked to take a photograph of them together. They had stood in the empty restaurant, arms linked in sisterly solidarity. Abida had been glowing in her chef's whites, and her pink headscarf, holding up her framed plaque marked *Star Performer*. She even wore her star pin on her coat.

And Hazrat, the grey-bearded man from housekeeping, who had until now been treated with such respect as *Agha Sahib*, their wise elder, had been told that his service, while superior, was no longer needed. He couldn't believe it, couldn't accept it. He kept coming back to the hotel.

Others were left hanging. No one was exactly sure what would happen to the acting front-desk manager Sadeq. The last general manager had never confirmed him in his role, even though Sadeq was, everybody knew, the one who got things done.

The employees of the Inter-Con were indignant. No one accepted their dismissal. There was talk of protests, even a legal battle. The management tried to soften the blow with promises of compensation, even dangling the possibility of a government job somewhere else. But the hotel seemed to sway on its heels, buffeted by the gale-force wind of the staff's outrage.

Another storm was gathering. The news was saturated with stories about a Taliban return – perhaps through power-sharing with the government, if the troubled talks in Doha succeeded, or maybe by battling their way into Kabul. Their fighters were inching ever closer to the capital, taking district after district through firepower, threats and persuasion. All anyone talked about was whether the Taliban had truly changed, whether they would let girls go to school, whether they would let women be educated and work. The Taliban leaders at the tables in Qatar kept insisting they were different now; so, too, would be their rule, which they deemed was only a matter of time. But there was much distrust. And dread, especially among the women.

Even if Malalai felt secure at work, for now, she didn't feel the same at home. Her neighbourhood, Kart-e Nau, where she was born and had spent all her life, had never really felt safe. There had always been robberies, kidnappings, crimes of all kinds. A few years ago she had been all too close to the main road when a bomb exploded, sending everyone scuttering for their lives. But now there were hushed warnings that sleeper cells of the Taliban and Islamic State were living in her neighbourhood, waiting for their moment to awake. Every morning when she set out for the hotel she wondered: *will I come home alive or dead?* So many were asking that question.

Sadeq called them 'the danger hours'. He kept telling the Inter-Con's staff to take great care, especially between 7.30 and 9.30 a.m.: the time when 'sticky bombs' were being slapped on vehicles during the gridlock of the morning rush hour. Judges and journalists, civil servants and scholars, activists and academics – the people who had come of age during the last two decades and were trying to shape a better future – had all been picked off in recent months. Nobody admitted to these attacks. The Afghan government blamed the Taliban. The Taliban blamed the government. So many Afghans had guns, and grudges, that anyone could exploit the sense of uncertainty. Hotel staff thought they couldn't possibly be on any black-list. Still, Malalai and everyone else on the early shift arrived at work, in uniform, well before 7.30 a.m. You just couldn't be sure these days.

The visitors were being extra-careful, too. There was only

a handful of guests these days at lunch, usually sitting at opposite ends of the restaurant, appreciating their privacy. In this uneasy stillness Malalai asked her colleagues questions. Half of her co-workers told her everything would work out OK. The others answered with a shrug and a 'Let's see what happens. It's in God's hands.' Mohammad Aqa, their manager, who rarely let his guard down, had a saying: 'We are only living to be alive, not to live.' It was everyone's lament. As they absently folded more napkins into perky fans, or glanced at their mobile phones or at the door, the waiting staff yearned for a future where life was about more than simply breathing in and out.

Sadeq felt danger's hot breath on his neck. Sometimes it was at the start of his day, sometimes even at the end. But that worry was always present.

One morning at 7.30 a.m., as he trundled through the streets in the car of his neighbour and colleague Ali, a minivan exploded in flames not far behind them. It was a magnetic 'sticky bomb' that killed three young men, including the popular former TOLO TV presenter Yama Siawash. Another day, as they headed home at 4.15 p.m., Sadeq and Ali saw that the crowded roundabout just below the hotel was engulfed in smoke. A police chief had been assassinated, the blast so strong it had flipped his vehicle upside-down.

The two friends didn't feel scared. As they wove their way through the diesel-fume-soaked scramble of luxury armoured SUVs, green police pickups and motorcycles revving and roaring, they simply wondered whose turn it would be next.

Sadeq's was a generation that tried to make light of the risks, boasting, 'We eat danger for breakfast.' But it did take its toll. When he was in high school it had been the monstrous suicide bombings that terrorised public spaces. Last year there had been the assault on Kabul University that took the lives of so many young Afghans exactly like him, on the cusp of pursuing their dreams. There had even been an attack on a maternity hospital while mothers were giving birth. Nothing was sacred any more. Now it was these targeted attacks in the crush of traffic.

Danger was dominating their lives. When customers came to the hotel, whether they were businessmen planning a mega-conference or families dreaming of a perfect wedding, they didn't only ask about the quality and quantity of *qabuli pulao*. They asked about security. 'How many guards will be at the door? How many security cameras are there? Do you think that what happened in 2011 and 2018 could happen again?'

And now the hotel was confronting a different kind of danger of its own making. Employees who had been fired set up a protest tent at the bottom of the road. On 7 August 2021 they even blocked the route up the hill, pushing against the striped blue-and-white barrier, shouting at the security guards: long-bearded men in traditional tunics like Hazrat, who had been at the hotel for so long he was like part of the furniture, but also young men in jeans who had just begun building their CVs. There were even a small number of women gathered in a knot closer to the tent – among them Abida, the former sous-chef.

Sadeq wouldn't cross their picket line that day. He felt their pain. But he knew the government would not budge. 'You can't even pay your electricity bills' was their constant refrain. The hotel still hadn't repaid the loan for the renovation and they weren't even halfway through it. Sadeq wasn't sure what would happen to him. The last general manager had hired him, had shared all his great plans; the new one wasn't telling him anything. His big brother in Washington gave his boss a call, and that seemed to help. But Sadeq no longer had the same sway, or the same spirit. And now, with so few staff, he had to work even longer hours, often staying the night.

Sometimes he cursed his life, wishing he had not been born in Afghanistan. It got in the way of everything. But he still tried to live his life as best he could. Sometimes, after work, he gave in to his friends' urging and joined them at the Nokhba-gan in Shahr-e Nau: a 'snooker wonderland' as it was billed on Facebook. A haven of smooth green tables and the comforting click of cues, it was a place for easy-going gab. His friends knew Sadeq had plans, but they didn't talk about them. No one talked about their plans any more; not when it was impossible to know what would happen in three months, one month, even that day. No one said it, but they all thought it: *If we don't leave Afghanistan, we might end up leaving the world.*

The Taliban had even brazenly posted a video they had filmed from a passing car, not far from the Nokhbagan, right in the city centre. The government dismissed such moments as propaganda. But there were other videos, too, filmed in the suburbs, to mock and taunt the security forces. These rattled residents. Sadeq didn't believe the Taliban could take over. *Impossible*, he told himself. Afghan security forces had thrown rings of steel around the capital. The embassies, including the American compound that he had visited so many times, were fortresses.

Sadeq had his own fortress, too. At the end of each day he would retreat to Macroyan to sit down with a close-knit group of friends of all ages who all lived in the blocks. They had built a little *gulkhana*, both a flower house and a meeting place, out of bamboo matting. But his father, patiently waiting for his son to come up the stairs, was finding it harder and harder to keep his peace of mind. He had a fright in the first week of August when news broke that suicide bombers had stormed the defence minister's heavily guarded villa in a neighbourhood not far from theirs; Sadeq had been close by, had seen the fire raging.

His father had been unable to reach him on his phone and was beside himself when he finally got through. His message to Sadeq was stark. 'Leave your job, you don't need to work, just stay at home now,' he implored him. 'I've seen this before . . . I've seen this all too many times before.'

Conclusion

The Year of Reckoning

Summer 2021

Mohammad Aqa saw the change as soon as he stepped out of the scuffed commuter minivan. Three armed Talib guards shadowed the first blue-and-white barrier at the bottom of the hill. The sentries from the former government's Public Protection Force, who had manned the Inter-Con's four rings of steel, had fled in panic the day before or been disarmed by the Taliban without a fight. Mohammad Aqa flashed a smile and his identity card; they inspected his details and waved him through. Dawn had just broken.

He hadn't shaved this morning. He wore his white shirt untucked and wouldn't take his black jacket and tie out of his staff locker. Memories zigzagged as he trudged up the hill, the summer's air washed in birdsong. No matter what life-changing shifts awaited him at the summit, it was the same path he had taken too many times to count. He had been here all too many times. As a young man he had watched the long-bearded *mujahideen* bulging with weapons stream into the hotel in the early 1990s. He'd seen the Taliban take over in the late 1990s with another set of even stricter rules. Through it all he had kept himself on a steady keel, just a waiter there to serve.

As he stepped into his restaurant, he found himself thrown back into the past. Long-haired Taliban fighters had taken over all the tables. Forks, knives and spoons had been pushed aside; his breakfast guests were ploughing into the food with their fingers. Nothing wrong with that. But this was the Inter-Continental. Everywhere he looked there were guns. On the tables. On the floor. Even a rifle propped against the scratched waiter's station from the king's time.

He turned on his heel and moved back into the lobby, where the chandeliers still kept up appearances and the walls kept their secrets. It too was now swarming with Taliban – baggy beige tunics, short-cut *shalwar* trousers, swirling turbans, embroidered caps. Old men with thick white beards, young men with barely a whisker. They sprawled across the sleek almond-coloured chairs and sofas, purchased just months ago by the old general manager. They chatted in clusters on the marble floor – sandalled, sneakered, barefoot – holding their guns.

Mohammad Aqa kept smiling, hand on heart, as he moved slowly down the corridor to the ballroom. All the staff knew what had happened there yesterday. The wedding that had come to a crashing halt; the poor bride not even having the time, or presence of mind, to change out of her emerald wedding dress and into her dazzling white one before the Taliban entered the city: 15 August, the day she and her fiancé had chosen long ago, had turned into the Taliban's special day, too.

Mohammad Aqa kept thinking about everything he had heard. By late afternoon it had all been over. Rumours had churned for hours that President Ghani had fled his palace by helicopter with his closest aides. As the last light slipped from

351

the day, news bulletins confirmed it. And stories swirled that a panicked tide of people was rushing to the airport to board any plane to get out. It was around this time that a few Talibs had made their way up the hill. By then, only a handful of staff were still in the hotel waiting, not knowing who was in charge, uncertain what they should do. Most had slipped out of their uniforms and into traditional attire, just in case. When the rattle of the front door sounded in the lobby, they had pretended to be guests and swiftly made their way to the lifts. Only one last employee at the front desk, lacking the new special pass for the floors, had been there to welcome the visitors. It turned out they were from his own province.

Upstairs, time crawled. The hiding staff kept weighing up their options. It was too dangerous to jump from the balcony; too dangerous, it seemed, to take the lift back down to the lobby. Hours on, daring to hope the coast was clear, they cautiously called their colleague downstairs on the walkie-talkie. 'Where are you?' they demanded. It was a Talib who answered, 'If you don't come down, we'll come up to get you.'

Six employees sheltering in one room, numbed by indecision, froze in fright. But the game was soon up. The Taliban took over the security cameras, located their room, rang its phone. They slowly returned to the ground floor, hands raised in the air to show they carried no weapons, emerging in a lobby teeming with Taliban. The questions started. But at around midnight the Taliban let the employees go home, after taking their names and addresses and their word that they would return the next day to keep the hotel ticking over. The Inter-Continental Kabul had switched to Taliban time.

Mohammad Aqa nudged open the ballroom double doors. A disaster zone, as he expected: the remains of the wedding party that had been plunged into chaos amidst rumours of the

Taliban's advance. Plates flipped upside-down on the patterned red carpet; mounds of rice and chunks of meat splattered in all directions; shiny soft-drink cans strewn across tables. Some of his co-workers were already hard at work, lifting white table-cloths spotted by red and yellow food stains. Mohammad Aqa pitched in to help. He noticed a jumble of equipment in the corner; it was the decks and mixers of the DJ. Someone seemed to have kicked in one of the mega-speakers. But the rest still sat where she had left them, as she beat a path to the door along with everyone else.

Mohammad Aqa's eyes darted around the Kandahar Ballroom as staff carted the tables and chairs out of the hall. Once it was clean and empty it would, for now, be the Inter-Continental's main restaurant. Food would be free for all. Rice flecked with a bit of meat and chunks of potato – the gift of a shrewd Afghan merchant based in Dubai who offered to feed all the fighters for their first month in power. From now on, twice a day every day, waiters would unfurl disposable shiny white sheeting – a traditional *dastarkhwan* – big enough to cover two-thirds of this vast floor.

At the front of the ballroom, the creamy-white backdrop with an elegant swag, chosen by the bride and groom for their new start, was still in place. The Taliban liked it too.

'We are all brothers,' declared the black-turbaned general manager of the Inter-Continental Kabul on their third day in charge. Smiley and softly spoken, Mullah Abdul Samad tried to send a reassuring message to the male staff assembled in a ground-floor meeting room. The women had been told to stay at home, for now. 'Continue your work, without fear,' the new boss told his team. And then added with extra emphasis, 'If anyone harms you, let me know.'

A new Taliban order was taking shape in the Inter-Con. The older staff knew the drill, turning up in *perahan o tunban*, collarless tunics and loose-fitting trousers, in keeping with their new bosses' style. Some of the younger employees showed up in their Western-style T-shirts and jeans, but some of these twenty-somethings, who had never met a Talib in their lives, were petrified. The older staff were less fazed. Many had worked with the Taliban the first time around. More than two decades on, they were more worried about their grown children, their daughters and their sons. Fathers had long been trapped in the painful webs woven by war. But their children, like the young staff, had come of age in an era of new freedoms, new opportunities. Just when they believed they were walking into a different future, they heard the footsteps of the past marching towards them again.

Their top manager hailed from the eastern province of Ghazni, in the Taliban's Pashtun tribal heartland. But he had grown up in the city of Mazar-i-Sharif, in the northern lands populated by Afghan Tajiks, Turkmens, Uzbeks and Hazaras. During the first Taliban time he had worked as a clerk, then as head of customs in the Taliban's Islamic Emirate. This time he had been tasked with running their biggest and best hotel. He didn't know anything about hotels. But he asked God to give him the power to serve their guests.

He set out his stall. There would soon be a new plan for the Inter-Continental. And soon, when there was more money, the staff would be paid their salaries. He blamed the old managers for their penury, accusing them of running away with all the hotel's cash. On top of that, all the banks were closed and no one could say when they would reopen, because of all the Western sanctions on the Taliban linked to charges of terrorism. For now, everyone would be given $100 in cash. That included the women, whose situation would become clear once Taliban leaders drew up their rules and regulations for their new Islamic Emirate of Afghanistan.

In these early days, as the Inter-Con shapeshifted again, the rules and the faces kept changing. Even the guards kept changing. Different Taliban groups came in and out of the hotel with their own security detail. Some days the premises were protected by the elite unit known as Badri 313, looking for all the world like American soldiers in captured war booty, from their smart camouflage uniforms and body armour to their guns – even the way they held their weapons. Other days it was rifle-toting Taliban in tunics and turbans staffing the checkposts.

The Inter-Continental was like a powerful magnet, pulling Talibs of all ages and backgrounds up the hill. Many were visiting Kabul for the first time, seeing this famous hotel they had heard so much about – especially after the two spectacular suicide attacks unleashed by their brother bombers. Some roared into the forecourt in dusty pickups or luxury SUVs; they pulled into the prime parking spaces reserved for VIPs beside the Judas trees, now bare of their crowns of purplish-pink blooms. Other fighters arrived on foot, weapons slung over their shoulders.

The Inter-Continental felt different, looked different. Talibs wandered through the lobby like tourists, pumped up with a new sense of privilege. 'We wouldn't have been allowed to enter this hotel in these clothes before,' some were heard to remark. In the Bukhara Restaurant they inspected the straight lines of steam tables, brimming with tempting Afghan fare; in the coffee shop they eyed the magnificent confections of pink and white inside the misted glass cases. When politely told that the food was not free for the taking, they wandered off, ogling the colourful scenes painted on the café ceiling and the ornate lobby chandeliers. Some started bringing their own snacks in plastic bags. Mega-watermelons were the treat of choice. Pink juice dripping from fingers, they savoured their fortune as they sat on the grass in the shade of the mulberry and apricot trees, marvelling at the greenery and the gleam of this beautiful hotel.

For some it felt like a homecoming. An older Talib who had worked in the Inter-Con the first time around showed up again, greeting old staff, taking in all the details of a hotel he hadn't seen since the late 1990s. 'In some ways it is better; in some ways it is worse,' he mused. He admired the rooms – wrecked cavities in his time that had now been repaired. But he tsked-tsked at some of the renovations. 'The historic British decoration is gone,' he lamented. 'It's an artificial, inferior new look.'

One Talib printed Islamic verses and taped them to the walls; another took them down. 'This is a hotel, not a mosque,' he insisted. One suggested traditional music should be allowed around the poolside restaurant; another categorically ruled it out. But with every day that passed, a new system was put in place that wasn't so different from the first time round. No music – in the lifts, the restaurant, the coffee shop, the lobby, the ballroom, around the pool.

There were only a few differences. Unlike the first time, when no Afghan women came to dine, this time a partition would be installed in the Bukhara Restaurant to enable them to eat, separate from the men, plus a more discreet separation around the pool. Wedding ceremonies were, of course, fine. Just not mixed, and no music. And definitely no dancing.

Amanullah had not been sure what to do. One of the old Talibs had called him: 'Where are you?' 'I am here,' Amanullah replied. 'Come to the hotel,' the Talib told him, 'I'd like to have a word with you.' It sounded like an order.

Amanullah had hung up the phone worried. *Why do the Taliban want to see me?* He waited a day before driving up the hill. It had been nearly twenty years since he had worked at the Inter-Con, rising through his decades of employment from room-service cashier to chief engineer and technical advisor. But the hotel had never left his mind, or his sights. He could clearly see the hotel's rectangular box, from his family's apartment in the faculty housing at Kabul Polytechnic University further down the hill. Sometimes he even spotted some of the old staff cycling past the university gates. They still called him *Engineer Sahib*, 'Respected Engineer', still greeted him like an old friend. Of late Amanullah had been watching the parade of jeeps and SUVs vrooming up and down the slope.

At the Polytechnic, the country's best engineering school, he was called Dr Faqiri. These days he was dean of the Construction Faculty, teaching many of the school's more than 6,500 students, both men and women. And that was how they addressed him at Bakhtar University, the private university with 3,200 students that he had co-founded and where he was now academic advisor. He had a new life; and returning to the hotel right now didn't feel so appealing.

When he entered the Inter-Con's lobby, Amanullah still felt he was walking into his own home. Which he was, in a way. It always struck him, too, that much of the Inter-Con had never changed – the colonnade of pillars, the glinting chandeliers, the elongated lobby, its elegant air. He didn't believe all the nonsense spouted by some staff about the djinns dwelling within. But there was something he couldn't quite put his finger on, a sense of the history that lived inside. So much had happened here.

Now it was full of Taliban. His worry soon vanished, though. The older Talib with whom he had worked so long ago welcomed him like family, in a traditional Afghan embrace.

'Come and work with us again!' he urged Amanullah as they settled into the lobby chairs, both of them taking up more space than they did in the 1990s. Amanullah humbly lowered his gaze, chuckling. He thanked the Talib profusely for honouring him with such a kind request. He joked about his advancing age. But the Talib kept talking, asking him for guidance about staffing, about salaries, and telling Amanullah that he'd like to recruit many of the old staff, so they could start attracting more guests, including foreigners.

Amanullah listened; he offered some advice. But then he presented his apologies. His own work now took up so much of his time. He couldn't possibly juggle both, as he had done the first time the Taliban were in charge, when he was also a young lecturer at the Polytechnic. But he had an even better idea. He could send them the second-born of his five talented sons. Twenty-five-year-old Arian had a business degree from India, spoke fluent English and was a polite and professional young man – just like his father had been. With his big smile, Arian was the perfect fit to fill their vacancy for a new marketing manager. They would need one to start building this business. It was a deal. The old Talib went back to work.

Amanullah lingered in the lobby, absorbing its ambience. Throughout these past two decades he had often come to this hotel with his wife, Shala, and his sons. In the summer they would eat at the poolside restaurant, in the winter at the Bukhara. And he had often come to buy cakes from Naser *Kolcha Paz*, the 'Cook of Cookies': Naser Ali, who had passed away from illness some years ago. But Amanullah would never forget the cake he had bought from him on 28 June 2011. He had carefully taken it down the hill in its big cardboard box with Inter-Continental branding. Soon after he arrived home and set the cake down on his kitchen counter, he heard the sound of gunfire and explosions. That was the day of the first Taliban suicide bombing. Amanullah had come to the hotel the next day to see the damage, even though it was no longer his job to fix it. When bombers struck again in 2018 he had been studying for his doctorate in India. How he had cried to see images of the Inter-Con on fire on his TV screen.

He looked around, observing the new swell of energy brought by fighters who now had to build the hotel, not bring it down. It was yet another start. Amanullah pulled himself up from his chair, admiring its sleek design as he went. He would keep an eye on his hotel. Now he would have his son's eyes inside it. And Arian was about to get married. Of course he would have his wedding in the Inter-Con's ballroom – like father, like son. And of course they would find a way to have music. It wouldn't be a wedding without it.

The Taliban were everywhere. Kart-e Nau, Malalai's neighbour-hood in the south-east of the city, had never felt safe, never been safe. But now armed men were ubiquitous: standing at check-posts, some exuding a happy-go-lucky air, others beaming looks that could kill.

Malalai hadn't stepped outside her door since they thundered into Kabul. In all her years of life she had never been face-to-face with a Talib. She had been told so many stories about their harsh rule in the 1990s – how they kept women out of work and in the home. But all this year she had been hearing on the news that the Taliban said they had changed, that this time it would be different. It toughened her spirit. On her fourth day she decided she was going to make a move.

Malalai slipped into a billowing black cloak with wide sleeves, its hem embellished with a brassy gold trim. Every day her male colleagues, even her female friends, had been calling her, telling her it was best to stay away. But she couldn't. So she had pooled her courage with that of two female co-workers to take their first steps together. She tucked her hazel-brown tresses, streaked with blonde, inside her black veil and jumped into a scuffed yellow taxi. As they drove, she took in streets that now seemed both familiar and unfamiliar. The usual sights and sounds were scattered among new ones. Fighters raced past in the back of green pickups, laughing wildly and hollering *Allahu Akbar*. Others strolled down streets, rifles strapped across their chests. Still, it felt safer somehow. The dread of dangerous bombings had gone.

She met her colleagues at the first gate. They didn't get far. Taliban guards from the elite Badri unit, sporting American-style wraparound sunglasses, gestured for them to stop, hands resting casually on their American-made guns. A message was sent up the hill by walkie-talkie to the general manager's office. A reply was quickly sent back down. 'He's busy, in a meeting.'

Malalai's colleagues buckled. But she was not for turning. The next day she took a taxi again, stopping at the bottom of the wooded slope. The guard's walkie-talkie crackled into life again. She waited silently, eyes lowered to avoid any questions from the men of war. But she stole glances at the path behind them, the first familiar blue-and-white security barrier, the second now draped with the white Taliban flag with black Islamic script. The chatter of the fighters at the top of the hill drifted down the slope. At the bottom there was just a gentle wind whispering nothings to the willows and pines, and the walkie-talkies' occasional static and squelch. After minutes that felt like hours, the new general manager appeared.

She discreetly sized him up. Gone was her boss in the dark business suit with a businesslike manner, replaced by a stout Talib with a greying beard in white traditional attire. 'Wait at home for now until the new government is formed and then we will call you,' he said quietly, but firmly. Malalai pressed him for more certainty. A lot depended on these details. 'We will need women to work at this hotel,' he reassured her, averting his gaze in line with his beliefs.

Malalai looked straight at him, her eyelashes thick with mascara and resolve. She wasn't sure whether to believe him. She had been told so many times by women older than her that, the first time around, 'for now' had become for ever. Some of her male colleagues told her everything would be OK in time. Others merely said, 'Let's see; it's in the hands of God.' But one thing was certain: she needed to work. It was the only life she knew.

Malalai tightened the veil around her face. It was so hard to be optimistic in Afghanistan. But she was heading home with a bit of hope. A clapped-out yellow taxi would take her through the busy streets to the old market in the city centre. From there, another would take her home through the new Taliban check-points. An hour-long journey to the old three-room mud house where Malalai, waiter at the Inter-Continental, would serve dinner to her ailing father and younger siblings.

Sadeq took one last selfie in his blue polo shirt on the tarmac of Kabul airport. It thrummed with the revving of hulking military transporters from armies the world over, there to fly evacuation flights out of Afghanistan. Afghans and foreigners queued in straight lines across the eerie expanse of grey, each clutching only one suitcase. Even children – exhausted, anxious, excited – seemed to sense they needed to be on their best behaviour as they stepped towards the open mouth of the waiting cargo plane, each aircraft swallowing a people denuded of all they had known.

Everything is gone, Sadeq thought. His old life, his job, his friends, the city he loved, even his beloved parrot Totti had to be left behind. And now he was about to lose his country, too. He and his family – his father and three sisters – would soon board a Polish military flight to take them away to Germany; a second carrier would then take them, at last, to America.

They had finally made it inside the airport gate at 5.30 a.m. Like thousands of Afghans, they had inched forward through the frenzied crush for a seat on a plane, for a golden ticket to another country, another life. Sadeq's family were among the luckier ones: they carried with them their asylum approvals in black and white. Others were thrusting through this agitated throng carrying nothing more than an Afghan electricity bill to confirm their identity.

The last eleven days had been a blur. Sadeq had fallen into bed, exhausted, on the third floor of the Inter-Con at 3 a.m. on the morning of 15 August, only to be wakened by the high-pitched beep of his walkie-talkie just after 11 a.m. 'Come down now and don't wear your suit and tie.' He thought his colleague was teasing. 'Don't joke on our security radios,' Sadeq reprimanded him.

It was no joke. The lift doors had clicked open to pandemonium. *Why is everyone running?* he thought. 'What's happening?' he bellowed. 'They're coming, they're coming!' came the reply. Some people were shouting that the Taliban were nearby, others that they were next to the hotel. Some insisted they were already inside. Everyone was confused, some of them terrified. Sadeq, still acting front-office manager and mindful of his responsibilities, gathered the women employees in the coffee shop and arranged transport to ensure they all reached their homes safely.

He turned his attention to the guests. Several were still

staying in this hotel. They still needed to settle their bills. One guest owed as much as 500,000 afghanis, more than $5,000. *What if they simply ran away amidst all the chaos? Who would be held responsible the next day?* Sadeq tracked them down, one by one. 'Sign here,' he instructed each of them. He took the sheets and dropped them in front of another, older manager. 'You're responsible now,' Sadeq told him.

It was past time to call his father – his go-to when times were tough. 'What should I do?' His father's reply was categorical. 'Be careful, my son. Stay in the hotel. Inside is less dangerous than outside.' His father knew the ways of war. 'The Taliban won't enter the city,' he reassured him. Sadeq always took his advice on faith.

Then his ears pricked up. A clamour rose from the banqueting office behind the front desk. Security bosses, now clad in traditional clothes, were hurling accusations that someone had been caught making an escape with a sack of cash. They even shot Sadeq an accusatory stare. Everyone in that tidy space was on edge. Some were laser-focused on securing the money to pay the last salaries, to prevent the Taliban from taking the rest. Some, Sadeq suspected, had other ideas. Accusing voices tumbled one over another.

Then Sadeq's phone rang. It was one of his best friends. 'We're in front of the hotel; we can take you home,' he informed Sadeq in an urgent voice. Sadeq paused. His neighbour Ali had not come to work today; he had known that it was better not to. Sadeq might have done the same, had it not been for his unexpected night-shift. But it meant he didn't have his usual lift home. If he was going to leave, now was his chance. 'Come out as soon as possible,' his friend warned him. 'There's a massive traffic jam.'

Sadeq glanced around the banqueting office, its posters

promoting Afghanistan's age-old beauty; its calendars marking hotel events to come. His decision was made.

'Guys, if you want to stay, stay,' he declared. 'If you want to go, go. But I'm leaving.' He shrugged out of his favourite blue-suit jacket, knowing it would mark him as a government employee. He tugged his shimmering silk tie and dumped it on a desk. Then he left everything, and everyone, behind.

Sadeq's drive dragged on. The streets were a scrimmage of car horns and bicycle bells. Many abandoned their cars, slamming doors and speeding away on foot. On a normal day the whole commute would take about an hour. Sadeq's friend Akbar, who worked for an international aid agency, was dropped off after about five hours. Sadeq and his neighbour, Omid, carried on.

After about six hours they finally fell out of their vehicle to buy soft drinks, some popcorn and crisps at their local neon-lit kiosk right next to their homes in the Macroyan apartment blocks. Sadeq wanted nothing more than just to sit with neighbours and friends, waiting for them in their *gulkhana*. He needed to unwind, to save for another day the *whys* and the *how* this could have happened.

Their hands full of snacks, the two friends sauntered into the heart of their sprawling compound. Then they saw the guns, pointing right at them. Three young men, thieves taking advantage of the disorder. His friend Omid bolted in another direction. 'Don't run, we'll shoot!' the men barked at Sadeq. He froze.

They took everything. His credit cards, his phone, his crisps and popcorn, his cans of cola. Sadeq stayed rooted to his spot, shocked into silence, staring into the darkness. His losses kept multiplying. He felt empty. *Even more is gone.* But these crooks hadn't shot him, hadn't hurt him. He calmly walked to their *gulkhana* in the parking area. Omid soon burst in, too, apologising for running; he couldn't risk losing his passport, not at this time. They sat together, Afghan neighbours cocooned inside their special greenhouse, trying to find humour, trying not to lose hope.

After an hour Sadeq climbed the stairs to his second-floor flat, where his father was, as always, waiting by the window, sitting on his *toshak*, with Totti the parrot perching impatiently too. 'Where were you?' his father demanded, relief washing over him. Sadeq fell into his arms. Totti clung to his shirt.

That was when father and son both knew, without saying, that they had to find a way out, fast. Sadeq didn't want to postpone his new life in the US a minute longer; his father couldn't bear to watch his city descend into disorder yet again. Days and nights folded into each other: a fever of anxious calls between Afghanistan and America, of calling in favours. One night they made a frightening foray to the airport to join the desperate jam of people who wanted out. They spent countless hours pushing and shoving through the tangle of people towards the last airport gate, the Abbey Gate, under the watchful eyes and swinging rifles of Taliban guards, only to return home without success. Until now.

Today, 26 August, they had at last reached the gate at daybreak, after ten hours of mayhem. They had pressed their papers into the hands of a Western soldier, lurching out of the chaos towards the nervous calm enveloping the check-in desks of foreign diplomats and doers. And now, another ten hours later, they were standing on the tarmac, waiting to board. Within touching distance of their new life.

Then they all flinched. His youngest sister shrieked. A massive explosion rocked the airfield. 'Down! Down!' the soldiers shouted. They all fell, face-down, on the hard, rough tarmac. 'No phones!' came the terse command.

Sadeq exhaled. He stole a glance at his father lying beside him, his sisters tightly holding hands. They were all together; they were all safe. The bomb had exploded on the other side of the gate – what was now the other side of their life. Sadeq stared straight ahead, letting the din wash over him. They would soon hug their loved ones in America for the first time in eight years. They would soon put all this, and much of themselves, behind.

Where are my children? Abida was screaming inside. She zapped the channels back and forth, toggling between the terrifying images on TOLOnews, Ariana TV – whoever had the latest.

At dusk the chaos at Kabul airport turned into carnage. Word was spreading that a suicide bomber had exploded his vest in the crush of panicked people close to Abbey Gate, Kabul's only escape route. Then a hail of return gunfire from American forces had shot across the packed narrow passageway. Seven of Abida's children – and all their children – were there.

The reports on the TV were horrific. Of bloodied bodies strewn across dirty ground; of bodies bobbing in the fetid drainage canal lining the passage. Of people sprinting, screaming, panicking. But Abida couldn't get through to her family. Every five minutes she called them. They didn't answer. She kept calling. Her eyes darted back and forth between her mobile phone and her TV screen. Her doctor was right: bad news was bad for her health. And this was the worst possible news.

Abida sucked in her breath. She frantically clicked her *tasbih* prayer beads. She could have been there, too. Her children had urged her to come with them. '*Madar*, it's our only chance – our best chance,' they had pleaded. They had pestered her for years to find a way out. But she could not leave, not with her high blood pressure, her diabetes, all the many ailments that would slow her down and make starting over somewhere else so hard. It sent her into spasms of regret. She should have left Kabul years ago, when there was a special aid programme to help widows start a new life in an easier country. But she said no then, not wanting to live in a strange land, with a language she did not speak, in a culture that might not welcome her, with so many young children who would need her to be strong. This time, she said no again. Anissa, her eldest unmarried daughter, would stay behind, too. She had a job as a deputy principal at a girls' primary school. They both clung to hope she would hold onto it. Anissa wasn't being paid these days. But with such uncertainty, she still went to work each day.

Abida looked down to dial the numbers yet again. She tried Raisa. And Safina. And Mariam. Nobody picked up the phone. She called her sons Najib and Hashim and Mustafa and Souleiman. Nobody answered. Heart in mouth, she kept listening to that ring, kept mumbling prayers for a voice to cut through. Panic coursed through her aching limbs.

They had dashed to the airport, like thousands of Afghans. No visas, no passports, no documents of any kind, just a desire to get out. Night after night they tried to push through the fray, all eyes on Abbey Gate, to a plane to take them to a bigger place, a better future. A Talib guard struck one of her sons on his shoulder, while another was smacked on his head, maybe with the butt of his rifle. But they still kept joining the huge tide of people unwilling and unable to give up – not yet.

There were the miracle stories of Afghans who had made it all the way to America with nothing to their name. And there were the terrible stories of Afghans who had clung to the underbelly of a US Air Force plane as it taxied down the runway, falling to their deaths on the same ground they had been trying to leave behind.

And, tonight, the worst story of all. No one could yet say how many were killed, trampled, injured, lost. Everyone had dared to believe these awful bombings had ended, now that the Taliban had swept into power. But they hadn't reckoned with the Islamic State group, striking a final blow before the last foreign forces left Afghan soil at the end of their twenty-year mission.

Abida called her children again. She could think of nothing else. It even pushed away, for a moment, the pains in her body, her pain about her own life. The fears chased one another around her head.

I won't be allowed to work, she had thought when she saw the news on 15 August that the Taliban had taken over. Yet over and over again, for the next few days, she wondered if she should go to the hotel. She almost did, several times. She discussed it, in detail, over and over with her female colleagues from the laundry section. They plucked up the courage to go together. But when the day came, they admitted defeat. They were too scared: that the Taliban might say something, do something, behave badly with them. Abida couldn't bear the thought. The first time they were in power they had told the women, 'We'll call you.' But they never did. Abida worried for herself, for her daughters; she worried for all Afghan women. Still, she had heard that some women were working now, even inside the airport terminal. It gave her a little hope.

She rang a number again, squeezing her eyes shut and pressing the phone into her ear. A voice finally cut through a racket of shouting and sirens. *Madar!* They were alive. All of them. They had been close to Abbey Gate, to the suicide bomber, but not too close.

Abida pressed her prayer beads to her chest, overwhelmed

by relief and joy. Her prayers had been answered. Her children couldn't be taken from her like this; not after she had fought so long, so hard, for them. This long night was over. It was time to take her medicine to calm her nerves. Tomorrow she would keep fighting – for her children and grandchildren, and for Abida, the Inter-Continental cook.

A newly promoted hotel official stepped across the threshold out of the Inter-Con's makeshift mosque. He pushed his bare feet into the thick leather sandals waiting just outside this repurposed room, next to his cubbyhole office recently vacated by Sadeq.

There was something about this twenty-four-year-old. It was there in his bearing, his steely look. He wore his authority and his *perahan o tunban* with style: embroidered cuffs; a neat line of buttons along one shoulder; wide trousers swirling above his ankles. Some days he was bedecked in a towering pale silk turban. Other days a perky embroidered cap. And he drew admiring looks from other young Talibs, who kept stopping him in his stride.

'This building was not built for Muslims,' he grumbled, when approached by a BBC journalist who said she was writing a book about the hotel. He had already been thinking about its history. 'The British didn't build a place for ablutions to cleanse before prayer,' he continued. There was only a prayer room in the basement. There was also the mosque that the Taliban had built around the back of the hotel, the first time they were in power. And now there was this new carpeted space in the first room right next to the front door, packed at every prayer time.

'This building was just built for the rich,' the young Talib went on. A new banner now hung above the entrance at the bottom of the hill: *Inter-Continental for Everyone*. He had, he added with a cocked eyebrow, also found the old photographs of bikinis by the swimming pool.

Suddenly the most British details in this hotel were some of the Afghan families staying there. In a strange twist, UK charities trying to help civil-society activists to escape had booked rooms for them to stay at the Inter-Con until there was a flight to fly them out. A few Afghan women wearing long patterned shawls occasionally skittered past, their children skipping and shrieking as they tumbled out the door to play. That deposit of some $30,000 had given them, and others, beds, and had helped Inter-Con staff keep this hotel humming. Bookings by a Western embassy had made a difference, too.

The young Talib's commander had first called him here on the second day of their victory. It was the day after he had walked out of his prison cell in the infamous Directorate 40 of the NDS intelligence agency. He had been thrown into jail just ten days before Kabul fell, after being caught in the act, about to draw his loaded pistol. Until then everyone had thought him merely another student at Kabul University's medical school, studying hospital management. In fact he had also been a Taliban sharp-shooter, an assassin tasked with targeting their enemies – corrupt Afghan officials, American lackeys, infidels. Not even his commander knew all the details.

When he was imprisoned, he resigned himself to his fate, believing he would spend the next decade behind bars. The regime had tried to break him with torture; he had focused on strengthening his mind, his body, his knowledge of the holy Quran. His incarceration was his destiny. God knew best. And in the end, he was only inside for two weeks.

Now, a month on, his calling had shifted. He had been newly promoted to a management role. He would acquire new skills, improve his English, get married, finish his degree. Some of the Inter-Con staff already called him Doctor.

But he had yet to fully emerge from the shadows. Like many Talibs of his ilk, he still used different telephone numbers, different names. It was hard to shake off these old habits, ingrained instincts. He had joined the Taliban at the age of seventeen to fight against the Americans and other foreign armies who, he said, had invaded in the name of democracy and freedom, to turn Afghans away from the path of Allah and the Quran. Killing was bad, he knew. But they had been angry.

His new mission was to help turn the Inter-Continental Kabul into a proper international hotel. 'It is a national guest house with a special value,' he explained to LyseDoucet. 'It presents a view of Afghanistan to foreigners who come from abroad.' And now that some of the older Talibs, who had different ideas, had left for other jobs, he could help shape the hotel's direction.

Ten young men were now working under him, some of them the twenty-somethings from the old staff, some of them newly recruited young Talibs. Two sides of a long war were thrown together in the Inter-Con, again. They eyed each other across the chandeliered lobby. On one side were the Inter-Con staff in their uniforms of black trousers and embroidered waistcoats. The other side included the *Fedayeen* in traditional attire, the young Talibs chosen for their highest calling – to strap explosives to their bodies to make the ultimate sacrifice, to be rewarded with entry into a paradise filled with beautiful *houris*, virgins, and rivers of milk and honey.

Sometimes these fighters played their own music – the only music allowed. The sound blared from mobile phones and blasted through the lobby's sound system. It was the Taliban's *taranas*, the rhythmic a cappella chants condemning foreign enemies and invaders, extolling the virtues of *jihad*:

> *Oh Afghan, the British are present in your country.*
> *They are your yesterday's enemies whom your ancestors*
>   *defeated, and then they ran away.*
> *Today, they are the rulers who dominate your soil.*

For others, the chanting was chilling. It distressed staff who had lived through the hotel's horrific attacks. There was even talk that a special celebration would soon be held in the ballroom to honour the families of suicide bombers and offer them gifts of condolence.

Sometimes the tensions triggered wars of words. 'Why would you blow yourself up?' young Inter-Con staff occasionally asked, incredulous, accusing the most zealous fighters of being brainwashed. 'It's our religion,' they shot back. 'You were a servant of foreigners in this place where the Americans and other enemies were plotting attacks against us.' Hotel workers pushed back against charges that the Inter-Continental had been a den of drinking and dancing, iniquities and infidels.

'I wish I had been chosen for the mission to attack this hotel,' mused one twenty-five-year-old Talib who sat down with the foreign journalist to drink tea in the coffee shop. He explained that he hadn't achieved the highest level of preparation. But he said growing up under American bombing raids on his village had cemented his convictions. The details of the hotel's dead – Inter-Con staff, Afghan wedding guests, foreign-aid workers, Spanish, Ukrainian and Venezuelan pilots, and more – didn't figure in Taliban accounts. If they did, they saw them as agents of their enemies.

But threaded through these fraught encounters were also rare moments of recognition. Young Kabulis sometimes acknowledged the harshness of life in frontline villages. Curious Talibs asked about opportunities for education. Both sides had only heard the worst of each other.

A few times a day they squeezed together inside the new prayer room in the lobby or gathered in the slightly bigger mosque at the back. At entranceways, brown sandals with wide straps, and the white high-topped sneakers beloved of young Talibs, were dropped alongside leather lace-ups from Kabul shops. Two worlds came together shoulder-to-shoulder in observance of a shared faith. In these moments there was only the murmur of prayer.

Hazrat wandered along the third-floor hall, the VIP floor – his floor. He didn't work here any more. But it would always be his floor.

He had come to the hotel again to urge Taliban managers to give him back his job. It had worked for some of the others. Abdul Qudus, the moustachioed waiter from Wardak province next door – the same province as many of the new Taliban managers – had been rehired after being fired from a hotel that he had been part of from its very first day. Engineer Amanullah, now known as Dr Faqiri, had been asked to return, but ultimately sent his son in his stead. There were even suggestions that some of the women could be brought back to do the body searches in the security cabins.

Hazrat hadn't had the same luck. Some of the older Talibs had greeted him warmly, remembering him from the first time they ran this hotel. But they gave him little more. Still, he was free to wander at will, with his air of owning this place.

The door to Room 319 was open, and it was empty. Hazrat slipped inside and looked straight ahead. The hole in the window was still there. The glass was still shattered, fine sharp lines shooting in all directions, like a spider's web. He couldn't remember which war, which day, had wounded this window-pane. If he looked through it from inside the room, it killed the view. But he went out on the narrow slice of balcony, putting the ugly scar behind him.

His eyes swept across the vista: the rolling carpet of tall pines cradling the hotel, the withered vineyards that had once produced the most luscious wine grapes and, beyond, Kabul's higgledy-piggledy cityscape of flat-roofed villas and half-built skyscrapers, their empty windows like eyes staring back at him. In the distance loomed the bare brown hill where a giant tricolour, the biggest flag in all of Afghanistan, had once snapped in the wind. The Taliban had pulled it down, saying they would make their own mega-flag to put in its place. Then, on the horizon, the ever-constant Hindu Kush wearing its white cape. Beneath the balcony, sparrows were swooping and singing.

Hazrat sighed. He would never tire of this view. Not even now, at the age of seventy. He stepped back inside, drawing the thick green curtains, hiding the cracked glass and taking in every corner of Room 319. His was no ordinary glance. The discerning eye of a half-century of cleaning rooms, supervising the rooms, at the Inter-Continental Kabul. Twin bed covers, in a green as deep as the pines, pulled in straight lines. He gave them a sharp tug. There, a teeny bit straighter.

He peeked into the bathroom, a veritable museum piece made up in an outdated beige palette. It still had one of those bulky plastic hairdryers with a nozzle like a mini vacuum cleaner. White hand-towels, embossed with the letter K, still hung on the rails, the gold script of the Inter-Continental Kabul trimming their edges. They weren't so fluffy now; their golden threads were faded. Hazrat could still remember how they had felt, soft and plush, in the king's time, when his guests were treated like kings and queens too.

He pulled the brown door of bulletproof steel behind him. Looking up and down the corridor, he stole a moment to sit once more in a straight-backed chair outside the housekeeper's nook. He ran his gnarled hands across his thin black trousers to smooth the creases. He was a bit stooped now, his scraggly beard and full head of hair flecked with grey. And he moved a bit more slowly than in his youth, no longer the muscled young man who boxed and lifted weights in a Kabul gym. He tried his best to be a good Muslim; he had even stopped enjoying an occasional drink, as he had done in his twenties in Shahr-e Nau. But if Afghanistan had still been a kingdom, if it had not lurched from one war to the next, he was certain he would now hold a very senior position.

Sitting in his old floor supervisor's chair, Hazrat could see every room. Every door down the dark corridor conjured up a different guest – one of his special guests. It was as if they had never checked out, every door opening into a different time.

From Room 327 comes the goateed Prince Ali – calling out to everyone, room boy to supervisor, in his deep, booming voice. '*Biyaan*, come here, let's meet.'

In 302 it's Mina, the entrepreneur with sparkling eyes and a big smile. She too called him *Agha Sahib*, 'honourable master'. Her father, Ambassador Rahim, in 303, was always smiling, too, when the Taliban were toppled the first time.

From 331 comes Mrs Leila, the British-Iranian lady who was in charge of the hotel nearly two decades ago. And 320 is the room of the Ariana Afghan Airlines boss, staying with his wife and two children.

From 312 comes Soraya *jaan*, dear Soraya, still in the room where she died when suicide bombers pumped bullets into her wardrobe.

At the very end of the hall, the door opens on the kind woman who stayed there the first time the Taliban were in charge, her children bringing life to the corridor.

And then all the journalists who came and went, in every time. They would hand out big tips and their fancy cookies. He had good memories of them.

All these faces who had come, full of hope for a new Afghanistan.

Hazrat stared into the middle distance, his eyes fixed on motes of dust eddying in the late-afternoon light. So many years of war had pulled so much life from his floor. And from him. He had given his everything to this hotel. Ninety-five per cent of his friends were now living in other countries. Of the 5 per cent who had stayed, most were dead. Maybe 1 per cent were still alive, including him.

He had survived. And his beloved Inter-Continental had survived too.

He thought of one of his favourite Afghan proverbs: 'Wheat grows from wheat; barley grows from barley.' The quality of the seed determines the quality of the harvest.

Hazrat had not given up on his hotel. He still harboured hope that it had not given up on him. His Inter-Continental Kabul training had never left him. Whoever was running it would always have to work hard, stand the place on its feet, do things professionally. But he still believed, with all his being, that the Inter-Continental could one day be the finest hotel in Kabul again.

Epilogue

I am told that much is as I remember it.

The new Taliban sign still shouts above the first gate – 'Intercontinental for Everyone'. The red geraniums still spill from painted pots along the kerb. The greenery soars, luxuriously, in midsummer.

Try as I might, I haven't been able to return to Kabul since my last trip two years ago. Visas are more difficult now. WhatsApp messages, photos and phone calls help bring me back to the hotel. But it's not the same as being there.

The short drive to the top of its gently sloping hill rolls through three blue-and-white barriers shadowed by Taliban guards in traditional tunics, guns slung over their shoulders. Anyone who passes through this obstacle course of barriers and bollards must hand over weapons – if they have any. Bodies are patted down.

There are female body searchers, too. Bright-eyed Malalai, now in her late twenties, is one of them. It's such a relief to hear this. No longer permitted to be a waiter in a Taliban-run hotel, she is at least working again. With her brother still jobless and her father ill, she remains her family's only earner. Her persistence paid off. Months after the Taliban told her to stay at home, she was still asking to come back. Finally, they called her in. So many women were told to leave their government jobs, including at this hotel. But security duties, as well as work in hospitals and factories – where women are separated from men – are still allowed.

On the crest of the slope, crowned by the parade of fruit trees now stripped of their pink and white froth, a guard shoves the black steel gate open and shut. The Inter-Con's famous façade rises, like any hotel's, as if nothing of consequence has ever happened. But it's a memory palace for so many who walk through its doors.

It's been nearly four years since the Taliban seized Kabul and took charge of this landmark hotel for a second time. I hear that behind the walnut wood-panelled front desk, under the shiny-faced clocks of Dubai, London, New York and Kabul, striving twenty-somethings – Talibs and non-Talibs – are still working together, doing the same jobs. There are only men now to offer an Inter-Continental welcome. The early tension between those who had come of age with Western-inspired aspirations and those whose lives were consumed by the fight against America's military might is said to have eased, at least on the surface. The pressing need to make ends meet, to do what needs doing, took priority. But, in those quiet moments where only time moves, young men stare in different directions, still lost in different dreams.

Many of the staff have slipped away. A young Talib with a pale silk turban has taken over front-desk duties from Sadeq, with his blue silk ties. Sadeq is now building a different life in the United States. His family is finally together, the only exception his beloved green parrot, which he was forced to leave behind; a bereft Totti, left in a friend's care, soon flew away, inconsolable. Upon arriving in America, Sadeq had first taken on odd jobs, including work on construction sites, before enrolling in business courses at a community college. A few years on, at the age of twenty-six, he has made one of his dreams come true: Sadeq opened his own café with a cousin. The young Talib who replaced him in Kabul is a dreamer, too, convinced that the hotel's future can be even brighter now that Islamic principles, and peace, prevail.

Mohammad Aqa has just left, after thirty-four years, apparently unable to carry on in his Inter-Con which no longer feels like his Inter-Con. He'd had to hang up his black waiter's jacket when the Taliban took over, and had been wearing his white shirt untucked with his black trousers. He grew a thick black beard streaked with grey. I try to imagine the Bukhara restaurant without his calm authority, his correct waiter's bearing. My abiding memory is sitting together at a table; he always insisted on serving a slice of luscious cake, its dollops of caramel perfectly matching the gold Inter-Continental insignia on the plate. Mohammad Aqa has a proverb for every situation. When I heard his news, I remembered one of them: 'If a gardener gives his garden to a carpenter, the garden will be the same colour as winter.' In other words, let the skilled do their jobs. Now he is at home with his three talented daughters, so eager to learn but unable to study under Taliban rules; their brother still goes to the university.

Engineer Amanullah – now known as Dr Faqiri – is still keeping busy as a dean of engineering at the Polytechnic University at the bottom of the hill, although he misses his female students. His son Arian, the ebullient marketing manager, is gone from the hotel too. He used to bounce through the lobby with the same can-do spirit and cheery optimism of his father. Many in the hotel were sad to see him go: powered by sheer force of personality, he was said to have achieved the hotel's best results in years. The government holds almost all its conferences at the Inter-Con. There's a wedding or two a month, without music, and with men and women kept separate.

And hard-working Sadozai is still there, still in charge of banqueting, still worried about aches in his knees, and his beloved wife's failing health. He's still riding his bicycle back and forth to work, one of the solid souls who keeps this hotel going.

The hotel promotes the Inter-Continental Kabul on its social-media platforms as the 'only national and historical hotel in the country'. They advertise a place that is both 'luxurious and relaxed', where chandeliers bathe the lobby in soft light, where successful meetings are hosted, where splendid buffets or tables of teapots and frosted cakes beckon. The government now has another landmark hotel on its books, although it hasn't reopened yet. The luxury Serena Hotel in the city centre – formerly the Kabul Hotel, rebuilt and run for nearly two decades by the Aga Khan Fund for Economic Development, and attacked twice by Taliban suicide bombers – is now the Kabul Grand Hotel.

The Inter-Con rooms are fuller than they used to be, though still far from capacity. Russia just became the first country to recognise Taliban rule, although a growing number of nations are engaging with Taliban leaders, some looking to do deals. Hotel guests include Russians invited by the Taliban Defence Ministry to revamp old helicopters and other military hardware; Chinese officials interested in opportunities ranging from gold mining to pine-nut processing; and visitors from far points of the globe, ranging from Malaysia to Brazil.

Doing business in Kabul is a different world. At the front desk, guests check in and out with big bags of bills. Credit cards don't work; international sanctions linked to terrorism charges are still cutting Afghanistan off from the global financial system. Taliban leaders keep telling the world to lift them. Staff lament, like many before them, that they need more government funds to renovate. In one of the first-floor offices, a photograph of the hotel from long ago reminds them of the glory days gone by. The details of women relaxing around the pool in bikinis have been erased with white paint.

Women are still allowed at the Inter-Con's poolside restaurant. There's a subtle partition allowing families to eat there. The bulky partition screen in the Bukhara Restaurant has also been taken down. Families, including women and girls, now dine discreetly in the furthest corners of the restaurant. It's a rare treat. The Taliban have also banned them from most public spaces, including parks and gyms. Even many Talibs don't like the harshness of all these new rules. Playing chess has just been suspended until Islamic clerics consider whether it's a form of gambling. The boards in the coffee shop are just decorations now. But I'm told the clay buddha set in the stunning frieze still takes pride of place in the Bamiyan Brasserie at the other end of the lobby. The Taliban have not smashed it this time.

Most of the female faces of the Inter-Con are gone. Abida the chef was never called back to her hotel. Her days are now spent between her home and her children's homes, her doctor and her pharmacy. She frets about her aches and pains, her children and grandchildren. It has been sorrow upon sorrow, year after year. First it was the loss of her cherished Inter-Con kitchen. Then of her oldest son Najib. He had come to her house with three sweet children and a terrible cold. She sent him packing to the doctor, who gave him an injection. But his blood pressure shot up; the next day he was dead. Then it was her youngest daughter Mariam: sad for years that she never found work as a journalist, sick for years with tumours in her ovaries, always ill, visiting too many doctors with too much different advice. Mariam's body finally gave in. But Abida hasn't given up on holding the rest of her children – and their children – close. It has been her life's work.

The guns of war are quiet now, but grief still stalks all their lives. Engineer Amanullah has also lost a loved one. His eldest son Rohullah, only thirty years old, big brother to Arian, died suddenly from a heart attack in May, shattering a close-knit family. But faith and love hold them together.

The hotel lost one of its dearest too. Waiter Qudus, with his cheeky grin and quick wit, the teenage tailor who walked through the door on the very first day in September 1969, who somehow managed to get his job back after the government sacked half the staff in 2021, had kept cycling back and forth to work. A few months ago, an accident on his beloved bicycle ended his life. Qudus, with whom I had shared many moments of laughter, had declined to play a bigger part in this book, worried there could be consequences for sharing his stories. But he embodied the unique character of this hotel, the life-force of its most loyal staff.

So too does Hazrat, who now mostly spends time at home. His third floor – the VIP floor – still carries on, without him. I can still visualise the scuffed chair outside the housekeeper's cubbyhole, the throne of the *Agha Sahib* who knew everything there was to know about the Inter-Con. Sometimes I even try to do as he did and go back in time to the corridor on the first floor, to the ever-so-plain green and brown Room 132, where I sat waiting for telephone calls to come through, writing madly at my wooden desk, wondering – and sometimes worrying – about what the next day would bring. The world of this hotel, the world outside its walls, has turned inside out so many times since I first came here.

Hazrat's part in this story has ended. His hotel never called him back, either. Most of his children are now in Germany, urging him and his dear wife Laila to join them. Hazrat keeps his quiet dignity, his strong sense of self. But his memories of the hotel that gave so much meaning to his life keep fading. They are fading for everyone.

All the staff who had been part of the Inter-Continental

Kabul from its very first years have now left the hill. There is no one remaining inside who can remember what it was like to be trained by the real Inter-Continental chain. No one left who can recall what it was like to live and work in its rooms and restaurants in the king's time, before the long war checked in and never left. No one left who was among the first to glide across its marble floor, to marvel at its chandeliers, to dare to believe that their own future could be so bright. But the hotel remembers. Its balconies are like eyes watching over the city, its glass and stone pocked with bullet holes, its spaces so full of stories. High on its roof, the K of a most beautiful blue is still kicking.

July 2025

Notes and Sources

I have relied on superb reporting over many years by many of the world's finest journalists. There are too many to name, but they include the AP's widely admired Kathy Gannon and her esteemed Afghan colleague Amir Shah, another dear friend whom I first worked with in 1988. The sharp insights and superb writing of John Burns of *The New York Times* were also invaluable.

I THE GOLDEN YEARS

With thanks for their kindness and their gift of impressive memory of life in Kabul in the 1960s and 70s, including at the Inter-Con: Sir Nicholas Barrington, Mary Lou Bigelow, Peers Carter, Susan Carter, Geoff Cowling, Christopher Edwards, Massoud Etemadi, Fatima Gailani, Benazir Ghausi, Thomas Gouttierre, Soraya Hakim, Sir David Hannay, Ameerah Haq, Jeffrey James, Mary James, Paul Johnson, Ian Kidd, Richard King, Gale King, Helena Malikyar, Mike Malinowski, Pierre Martinet, Saad Mohseni, Noorullah, Valerie Nowroz, Zalmai Rassoul, Helen Saberi, Abdullah Seraj, Hamed Seraj, Mahbooba Seraj, Fauzia Sharifi, Edward Trippe, Elizabeth Winter.

Books

These memoirs were gold dust and were drawn on, in detail:

Nasiri, Afzal, *Forced to Flee: A Tale of Two Afghan Refugees*, Page Publishing, Inc., US, 2023

Seraj, Prince Ali, *The Lost Kingdom: Memoir of An Afghan Prince*, Post Hill Press, Brentwood, Tennessee, 2017

These were colourful and authoritative references:

Ansary, Tamim, *Games Without Rules: The Often-Interrupted History of Afghanistan*, PublicAffairs, New York, 2012

Bonyhady, Tim, *Two Afternoons in the Kabul Stadium*, Text Publishing, Melbourne, 2021

Dupree, Louis, *Afghanistan*, Princeton University Press, Princeton, New Jersey, 1980

Dupree, Nancy Hatch, *An Historical Guide to Kabul*, Afghan Tourist Organ-ization, Kabul, 1972

Dupree, Nancy Hatch, *An Historical Guide to Afghanistan*, Afghan Tourist Association, Kabul, 1977

Hosseini, Khalid, *The Kite Runner*, Bloomsbury Publishing, London, 2003

Newby, Eric, *A Short Walk in the Hindu Kush*, Picador, London, 1981

Nowroz, Valerie Ann, *An Extraordinary Country, My Life in Afghanistan 1959–1978*, Book Printing UK, Peterborough, 2018

Song lyrics

The lyrics in this chapter have been reproduced from the following song: p. 4, 'Leili-Jan' by Ahmad Zahir (lyrics by Ahmad Zahir).

II THE RED YEARS

So many great journalists and former Kabul residents, old friends and new ones, found time to recall historic times and irresistible anecdotes. I wish I could have included more of John Burns, Steve Coll, Elay Ershad, Robert Evans, Robert Fox, Ameerah Haq, Tom Heneghan, Arthur and Susan Holcombe, Arthur Kent, Michael Malinowski, Shah Muhammad Rais, William Reeve, Robert Reid, Barry Schlacter, Walid Sharif, Mark Urban, Zia Zahaq, Faziullah Zaki.

Books

These books brought many stories and insights:

Ansary, Tamim, *Games Without Rules: The Often-Interrupted History of Afghanistan*, PublicAffairs, New York, 2012

Bocharov, Gennady, *Russian Roulette*, Hamish Hamilton, London, 1990

Coll, Steve, *Ghost Wars*, Penguin Press, New York, 2004

Braithwaite, Rodric, *Afgantsy*, Profile Books, London, 2012

Fisk, Robert, *The Great War for Civilisation*, Harper Perennial, London, 2006

Hewitt, Gavin, *A Soul on Ice*, Pan Books, London, 2005

Goodwin, Jan, *Caught in the Crossfire*, Macdonald & Co. Ltd, London, 1987

Goodwin, Jan, *Price of Honour*, Little, Brown and Company, London, 1994

Kent, Arthur, *Murder in Room 117*, Skywriter Communications, Inc., 2021

III THE DARK YEARS

I enjoyed conversations or email exchanges with Steve Coll, Tony Davis, John Jennings, Peter Jouvenal, Janan Mosazai, Robert Nickelsberg, Suzy Price, Shah Muhammad Rais, Amir Shah, Yasir Qanooni, Yunus Qanooni, William Reeve, Mark Urban.

Books

Banayee, Maiwand, *Delusions of Paradise*, Icon Books, London, 2025

Bowersox, Gary, *The Gem Hunter*, Geovision Inc., Honolulu, Hawaii, 2004

Coll, Steve, *Ghost Wars*, Penguin Press, New York, 2004

Corwin, Phillip, *Doomed in Afghanistan*, Rutgers University Press, New Brunswick, New Jersey, 1992

Gall, Sandy, *Afghan Napoleon*, Haus Publishing Ltd, London, 2021

Gannon, Kathy, *I is for Infidel: From Holy War to Holy Terror in Afghanistan*, PublicAffairs, New York, 2006

Sands, Chris with Fazelminallah Qazizai, *Night Letters*, Hurst & Company, London, 2019

Tomsen, Peter, *The Wars of Afghanistan*, PublicAffairs, New York, 2011

IV THE WHITE YEARS

Mohammad Garmsiri, Shah Muhammad Rais and Shoaib Sharifi provided stories and insights.

Not many journalists reached Kabul in these years. The writing of Hannah Bloch, John Burns, Kathy Gannon, Luke Harding and Amir Shah was invaluable, among others.

Books

These books contain stories and details which I have included in this section:

Banayee, Maiwand, *Delusions of Paradise*, Icon Books, London, 2025

Constable, Pamela, *Fragments of Grace*, Potomac Books Inc., Washington, DC, 2005

Corwin, Phillip, *Doomed in Afghanistan*, Rutgers University Press, New Brunswick, New Jersey, 1992

Fisk, Robert, *Robert Fisk on Afghanistan*, Independent Print Ltd, London, 2016

Johnson, Denis, *Seek: Reports from the Edges of America and Beyond*, Methuen Publishing Ltd, York, 2002

Gannon, Kathy, *I is for Infidel: From Holy War to Holy Terror in Afghanistan*, PublicAffairs, New York, 2006

Rashid, Ahmed, *Taliban*, Yale University Press, New Haven, Connecticut, 2001

Simpson, John, *News from No Man's Land*, Macmillan, London, 2002

Steele, Jonathan, *Ghosts of Afghanistan*, Portobello Books, London, 2011

V THE YEARS OF LIGHT AND DARK

Many individuals were generous with their time and knowledge, including Hamidullah Abdullahi, Nawab Ahmadzai, Shukria Barakzai, Farid Hekmat, Zabiullah Karimullah, Grant Kippen, Fazel Malik Niazi, Dominic Medley, Saad Mohseni, Khalid Payenda, Ahmed Rashid, Laila Salari-Mercier, Akbar Sarwari, Michael Semple, Khalid Wardak.

Books

Clammer, Paul, *Afghanistan*, Lonely Planet Publications Ltd, London, 2007

Mohseni, Saad, *Radio Free Afghanistan*, William Collins, London, 2007

North, Andrew, *War & Peace & War*, Ithaka, London, 2024

Saberi, Helen, *Noshe Djan: Afghan Food and Cookery*, Prospect Books, London, 2000

Seierstad, Asne, *The Bookseller of Kabul*, Little, Brown, London, 2003

Film

Afghan Star, directed by Havana Marking, Zeitgeist Films, 2009

Song lyrics

The lyrics in this section have been reproduced from the following songs: p. 280, Safdar Tawakoli; p. 302, 'Afghan Boy' by Aryana Sayeed (lyrics by Aryana Sayeed and Bakhtar Khorasani), 2011.

VI THE YEAR OF A LITTLE HOPE

On government plans for the hotel in 2020 and 2021, many provided information, including Hamidullah Abdellahi, Farid Hekmat, Zabiullah Karimullah, Fazel Malik Niazi, Khalid Payenda and Khalid Wardak. DJ Nabila spoke to me about hotel weddings. Hasib Alokozai was kindly supportive.

The Taliban who took charge in the hotel also agreed to share their ideas, including Mohammad Garmsiri, Abdul Samad and others who preferred to remain anonymous. Arian Faqiri also arranged a tour around the hotel and provided updates on the hotel's new offerings. Swiss journalist Andreas Babst wrote an intriguing article about the hotel, published in many places including the UK, in the *Guardian*, on 12 October 2023.

Song lyrics

The lyrics on p. 342 have been reproduced from 'It's Now or Never' by Elvis Presley (lyrics by Aaron Schroeder and Wally Gold), 1960.

Newspaper and online articles

A selection of illuminating articles on the Inter-Continental Kabul over the years:

Babst, Andreas, 'Inside the Taliban's Luxury Hotel', *Guardian*, 12 October 2023

Baker, Luke, 'Iconic hotel survives Afghanistan's bitter history', Reuters, 21 May 2008

Curtis, Adam, 'Kabul: City Number One – Part 5', BBC archives, 13 November 2009

Curtis, Adam, 'Kabul: City Number One – Part 6', BBC archives, 4 December 2009

Evans, Robert and Heneghan, Tom, 'Battered Kabul hotel long a haven and watchpost', Reuters, 29 June 2011

Farmer, Ben, ' "Welcome to Kabul": Taliban take over golden-era British-built hotel', *Telegraph*, 19 September 2021

Gutsch, Jochen-Martin and Grabka, Thomas, *'Wo die Suiten Stahltüren haben'* ('Where the suites have steel doors'), *Der Spiegel*, 11 January 2019

Jacinto, Leela, 'Welcome to Kabul's Intercontinental Hotel', France 24, 25 August 2009

May, Barry, 'Toiling in the Afghan Vineyard', The Baron (no date given)

Vinocur, John, 'Inside an "Interconti", Haven from the Storm', *New York Times*, 3 February 1980

I hope I have not forgotten anyone or any source. If so, do let me know and I will correct with an apology.

Photographic Acknowledgements

Every effort has been made to contact all copyright holders. The publishers will be pleased to amend in future printings any errors or omissions brought to their attention. The images come from the following sources:

The Inter-Continental in Kabul skyline, Lesley Scoular, with thanks to Dominic Medley; Hotel Inter-Continental on a post-card, public domain; Plaque commemorating Inter-Continental grand opening, ZUMA Press, Inc./Alamy Stock Photo; The Bamiyan Brasserie, Roland and Sabrina Michaud/akg-images; The Nuristan Cocktail Lounge, Hotel Inter-Continental Kabul; The Pamir Supper Club, Hotel Inter-Continental Kabul; Ariana Afghan Airlines advert, Ariana Afghan Airlines; The Esquire Set, public domain; AfghanTour advert, Afghan Tourist Organization; *Chadris* and miniskirts, Laurence Brun/Gamma-Rapho via Getty Images; Lyse Doucet and Amanullah, author's personal photo; Soldier with flute, author's personal photo; Amanullah's sketch, author's personal photo, with thanks to Amanullah; Soviet invasion of Kabul, François Lochon/Gamma-Rapho via Getty Images; A letter from the British Embassy, author's personal photo; Lyse Doucet and President Najibullah, author's personal photo, with thanks to John Renner; Boris Gromov and son on Friendship Bridge, Associated Press/Alamy Stock Photo; The *mujahideen* ride into Kabul, Patrick Robert/Sygma via Getty Images; Tracer-fire in Kabul sky, Patrick Robert/Sygma via Getty Images; Abdul Rashid Dostum and Gulbuddin Hekmatyar's forces, Robert Nickelsberg/Getty

Images; Mohammad and waiters, with thanks to Mohammad; Lyse Doucet and Haqqani *mujahideen*, author's personal photo; The Taliban arrive in Kabul, Associated Press/Alamy Stock Photo; Amanullah's portrait during the nineties, with thanks to Amanullah; Inside the Inter-Con kitchen, Rauli Virtanen; A balloon vendor in Kabul, Phil Goodwin/Getty Images; King Zahir Shah and Hamid Karzai at the 2002 *Loya Jirga*, ZUMA Press, Inc./Alamy Stock Photo; Police officers watch the *Loya Jirga*, Behrouz Mehri/AFP via Getty Images; A wedding at the Inter-Continental, Jean Chung/Chicago Tribune/Tribune News Service via Getty Images; Abida's identity card, with thanks to Abida; A hotel BBQ, Robert Nickelsberg/Alamy Stock Photo; The Inter-Con during the 2018 suicide bombing, Rahmat Gul/Associated Press/Alamy Stock Photo; The Inter-Con during the 2011 suicide bombing, Massoud Hossaini/AFP via Getty Images; Soldiers guard the Inter-Con during the 2011 attack, Pedro Ugarte/AFP via Getty Images; The family of a victim of the 2018 attack, Wakil Kohsar/AFP via Getty Images; Aryana Sayeed at the Inter-Con, Associated Press/Alamy Stock Photo; A hotel chef praying, Robert Nickelsberg/Getty Images; Qudus' portrait, Thomas Grabka/LAIF, Camera Press London; The Taliban in hotel lobby, Rauli Virtanen; The front desk of Inter-Con on Taliban time, Elise Blanchard; An employee prepares an empty Kandahar ballroom, Elise Blanchard; Hazrat's portrait, Paula Bronstein; Amanullah's portrait, Paula Bronstein; Mohammad Aqa's portrait, Paula Bronstein; Abida's portrait, Paula Bronstein; Sadeq's portrait, Paula Bronstein; Malalai's portrait, Paula Bronstein; The 'Intercontinental for Everyone' welcome sign, Elise Blanchard; Hazrat standing in a broken window, Paula Bronstein.

Acknowledgements

This book would not have been possible without the dedication and talent of a dear Afghan friend of twenty-five years and BBC colleague, Mahfouz Zubaide. He was present, in person or on the phone, during the many conversations with hotel staff over the past several years. Not only did he help translate from Dari and Pashto, but he wisely interpreted all the many emotions and experiences of Afghans living through nearly a half-century of war. In many ways, this is Mahfouz's book too.

This book also belongs to my brilliant editor Rowan Borchers, Publishing Director at Hutchinson Heinemann. From start to finish, he believed in this story and skilfully reshaped my drafts to sharpen and strengthen the storytelling. He was also infinitely patient, never protesting, year after year, as yet another major news story pulled me away from my writing desk.

My great agent, Claire Paterson Conrad of Janklow & Nesbit UK, never gave up on me either. After emailing me for years about writing a book, she kept a sharp eye on its passage, from advising on the best publisher to helping select the best cover to take it into print.

My gratitude is great to the Afghans who kept this hotel running, who trusted me with their stories, and agreed to meet or to speak again and again. I am most indebted to Hazrat, Amanullah, Mohammad Aqa, Abida, Sadeq and Malalai, as well as Valerie, Sadozai, Hashmat, Sharif and Qudus. Their impressive recall of details, and evocative anecdotes, brought this hotel to life. I am thankful to many of their families too. Shah Mohammad Rais, who ran the bookshop, Noorullah and Afzal, who worked in the Inter-Con in its early years, and Arian, who helped keep it going of late, also made a difference. They all made this story such a pleasure to discover even if their stories were sometimes difficult to hear.

General managers and directors over the years shared their memories, including Hamidullah Abdellahi, Pierre Martinet, Leila, Akbar Sarwari, Fazel Malik Niazi, Mohammad Garmsiri, Abdul Samad.

Edward Trippe helped me to understand his father Juan Trippe's vision for the Inter-Continental's global reach. Christopher Edwards assisted with the hotel's history.

Another old Afghan friend and colleague, Shoaib Sharifi, who was often my guide to Afghanistan in the decades after 2001, gave me confidence that this landmark hotel was a fitting prism. Jamshid Roshangar, whom I met in the wake of the tragic attack on Kabul University in 2020, was always at the ready to quickly translate news reports, songs and conversations, even to drop by barber shops in Kabul to check on men's hairstyles. Journalist Fazelminallah Qazizai, whose impressive book is mentioned in the Notes section, kindly agreed to read an early draft of the book to check for any errors in understanding or facts.

I am also so grateful to the many Afghan journalists and friends who helped translate conversations and documents from Dari and Pashto, and shared many moments with me during the research and writing of this book. Tenacious Afghan journalist Fatima Faizi, forced like so many to leave her country after the Taliban return, scoured Dari and Pashto sources for hotel stories.

Over the years, I also worked with Zuhal Ahad, Obaid Haideri, Zarghuna Kargar, Esmat Khosar, Hamayoun Khosar, Qais Malik, Habib Sharifi, Shoaib Sharifi, Mohammad Shoaib and Ahmed Fawad Zhwak.

So many Afghans and non-Afghans helped make this book happen. I hope I have included all their names here or in the Notes section. I will mention them in the arc of the hotel's history. I am particularly grateful to Tom Gouttierre, one of the world's most authoritative and affectionate observers of Afghanistan. His enthusiasm about the impact of the Inter-Continental Kabul in its early years inspired me to keep going. So too did an Afghan who had worked there at its start and was able to reimagine its physical space and its place in Afghan lives. Our first phone calls lasted hours. But cherished memories were soon threaded with more painful reminiscences of war, so they later declined to be included in this book.

One of my first Afghan friends, Soraya Hakim, whom I met in Kabul in 1989, was also invaluable in suggesting people to contact. Helena Malikyar generously provided wonderful accounts about her father's businesses and the life and times of 1970s Kabul. And Fatima Gailani recalled in vivid colours the hotel's very first day, and many days after. So too did the inimitable Mahbouba Seraj. And Hamed Seraj too.

Janan Mosazai and Elay Ershad shared fascinating childhood memories of growing up next door to the hotel. If I had written a different book, they would have been my main characters.

Canadian journalist and old friend Arthur Kent, who had just finished his riveting book on the murder of Ambassador Dubs in the Hotel Kabul when I was starting mine, also eagerly offered contacts and joined me in calls from Calgary to reminisce about the 1980s and 1990s when we both went in and out of Afghanistan.

Russian journalist Petr Koslov, forced to leave his own country in the media crackdown after Moscow's full-scale invasion of Ukraine, pored through Russian sources for any accounts of the hotel.

In writing this book, I also made many new friends. The ebullient Peers Carter, along with his wife Susan, shared memories of his father Ambassador Carter and perused his diaries for hotel mentions. I am especially grateful to Geoff Cowling, who brought me into their circle of former British diplomats posted in Kabul in the early 1970s who still remember it as their favourite assignment. I would have loved to include more of their own stories, including Geoff's rescue of British hippies and his remarkable adventures with his late wife Irene. Their little club includes former ambassador Jeffrey James and his wife Mary, whom I had met years ago in Tehran, and another old friend, Helen Saberi, who provided detailed accounts of embassy life, including the office of Ambassador Carter. Helen also pointed me to books and contacts. And I moved her own much-loved book on Afghan cooking, *Noshe Djan*, from my kitchen to my desk. Our mutual friend Elizabeth Winter happily revisited her memories of travelling to Kabul in that bygone time.

Through this book, I also met via email and telephone some of the finest journalists of the day who reported on Afghanistan through its many historic decades. Their names are also included in the notes. American journalist Bob Reid's experience during the Soviet invasion of 1979, and his extraordinary memory of so many details, made it into the book, along with tales from Tom Heneghan and Bob Evans and insights from Barry Schlachter. So did the lovely details from Ameerah Haq. Friends and fellow travellers Steve Coll, Tony Davis, John Jennings, Peter Jouvenal, David Loyn, Robert Nickelsberg, Suzy Price, William Reeve, Amir Shah, Shoaib Sharifi, Mark Urban and Zia Zahak provided memories from the 1990s, including stunning photographs. Dominic Medley kindly kept looking through his archives for material, including photographs, to share from the 2000s. His own Kabul magazine, *Afghan Scene*, which entertained and informed many expatriates and Afghans during that heady time, was a great source of information. Shukria Barakzai, Hannah Bloch, Ahmed Rashid, Michael Semple, Grant Kippen and Norine MacDonald added their assistance and tales.

The great photojournalist Paula Bronstein worked with me in Kabul in July 2021, capturing the essence of the hotel's staff with her fine eye just weeks before the Taliban took over. The intrepid Kabul-based French journalist Elise Blanchard kindly trawled through her hundreds of photographs of the hotel's Taliban days.

Our Afghan tribe stretches far and wide, and brought expertise and assistance born of long and much-loved connections to this country. Kate Clark, Jolyon Leslie and Mark Mallalieu helped identify birds and birdsong. Anthony Fitzherbert, who planted many seeds in Afghanistan, was my Mr Trees. Zarghuna Kargar checked wedding details and more. I learned much about music from the masters John Baily and Veronica Doubleday.

In London, Lindsey Hilsum and Jane Wellesley, who finished writing their own books long before I did, were a constant source of encouragement – and hilarity. Canadian author Louise Penny, busy with writing her major best-selling books, still found time to encourage a debut author. Authors and journalists Barbara Demick, Mellissa Fung and Kim Ghattas shared gems of advice. So too did the clear-eyed Razia Iqbal and the adventurous Emma Sky. Kim's WhatsApp check-ins always lifted my spirits. My neighbour, the anthropologist Dawn Starin, whose own writing stays with me, was always ready to offer chai or a walk.

Anna Maria Tremonti in Toronto, and Deb Whitmont in Sydney, declared my book a success even before I wrote it. Another close friend, filmmaker and author Shelley Saywell, arranged access to her archive when we filmed at the Inter-Con in 1993 and amplified the chorus of sisterly support.

Katharine Westcott and Elizabeth Winter were early readers. Katharine, a much-respected BBC editor, first spoke to me years ago about the value of finding a place, a literary conceit, to tell a wider story. She then took her sharp pen to some sentences and words in the last draft. Elizabeth read with the expert eyes of someone who first visited Kabul in the 1970s and has spent decades since, along with Robert and Tasha, ensuring the aid community in Britain does not forget Afghanistan. Fellow Canadians Kathy Gannon, Mark MacKinnon, Graeme Smith and Sally Armstrong, who have all written authoritative books, kindly offered generous endorsements. Kathy's unflinching book *I is for Infidel* was an inspiration throughout.

I am grateful to Zahra Joya, Peter Frankopan, Philippe Sands, Elif Shafak, Mishal Husain, Michael Palin, Kamila Shamsie and Kabul fellow traveller Rory Stewart for taking the time to read the book and offer generous blurbs.

The final version of this book is a work of many trained eyes at Penguin. Mandy Greenfield first tackled the copy-editing, seemingly unfazed that I was still writing as she was preparing it for publication. Sarah Hulbert was a patient and probing managing editor, Jonathan Wadman was the Sherlock Holmes of fact-checking everything from disco hits to the speed of warplanes, and Alex Bell meticulously created the index. I marvelled at the diligence and dedication of this great team. Matilda Oduntan happily exhausted every avenue for photos and spent weeks preparing plates. Penguin's impressive design team explored multiple possible covers. We were delighted by the final bold version Dan Simpkins crafted, which gave pride of place to the eponymous 'K'. Ania Gordon pitched in early, and creatively, on the marketing campaign, while Emily Harvey and Kirsten Greenwood ensured it took pride of place in all the right bookshops. Najma Finlay was, from our first meeting, the best kind of publicist any author could ever wish for. Through these years, I was always aware of the presence behind the scenes of Venetia Butterfield, who had just risen to Managing Director at Cornerstone when they acquired this book. Her warm smile and wise counsel was a constant – even as I kept missing my deadlines.

ACKNOWLEDGEMENTS

The National Archives in Kew, the British Library, Rachel Beattie and team at the Media Commons Archives at the University of Toronto and the *Kabul Times* archives at the University of Arizona provided important material.

My close-knit family never doubted I would eventually reach the finish line. My sisters Andrea and Paula were early readers and expertly caught errors and omissions. Andrea's scholarly bookwriting advice made a huge difference – from using the Scrivener writing app to organise my files, a second computer screen to ease the assembly of ideas, and the Pomodoro writing method to keep me focused. Other family members, including my dear brothers, kept cheering me on. My mother, at home on the east coast of Canada, never questioned why I would disappear for hours in the basement whenever I was able to visit. But it was certainly noted in constant conversations with her sister, my beloved aunt and godmother Grace.

I somehow managed to snatch hours early in the morning, late at night, on weekends, or on visits home, to finish this book. It took much longer than expected because the endeavour turned out to be much more demanding than expected, and the world turned in unexpected ways which kept me busy in my real job as a BBC correspondent. I am very grateful to so many impressive BBC editors and colleagues who, over so many years, have made my reporting in Afghanistan, and beyond, possible.

I kept thinking I must do more research, should do more writing. In the end, I had to hand it over to the caring hands of the team at Hutchinson Heinemann, who have now given it to you, the readers. It is you who will judge whether I have been able to convey even a small measure of the greatness of a people who have suffered all too long and far too much from the brutal vagaries of war and world politics but still keep their remarkable sense of humour, hospitality and self.

399

Index